will bringe my lyfe

... I am so muche bou[n]d

... with commendoth ye ... are

so many and so greate home ... as I

... I doo therfore according to

... bount toward ... ye ma[jes]tie ...

... harte, and that know he he ...

... intend to offend ye ... ma[jes]tie ... many

... of his ... by necessitie of

I shall therunto be ...

god shall never be ... upon me

... I shall very well

... benefitted, for is so don ...

... god, and I my self ... to end best

... tormoth ... ministers of ...

Adulatores ... we for the ...

... god, we ... of necessitie

... that ... will be ...

... ma[jes]tie ... to ... make ...

ARCHBISHOP GRINDAL
1519–1583

by the same author

THE ELIZABETHAN PURITAN MOVEMENT

ARCHBISHOP GRINDAL
1519–1583

*The Struggle
for a Reformed Church*

PATRICK COLLINSON

*Professor of History,
University of Kent at Canterbury*

JONATHAN CAPE
THIRTY BEDFORD SQUARE LONDON

First published 1979
Copyright © 1979 by Patrick Collinson

Jonathan Cape Ltd, 30 Bedford Square, London WC1

British Library Cataloguing in Publication Data
Collinson, Patrick
Archbishop Grindal, 1519–1583.
1. Grindal, Edmund   2. Church of England –
Bishops – Biography
I. Title
283′092′4   BX5199.G/

ISBN 0–224–01703–9

Printed in Great Britain by Jolly & Barber Ltd, Rugby

*To the Master and Fellows
of Pembroke College Cambridge
this biography of a former Master
by a scholar of the foundation
is respectfully dedicated*

CONTENTS

ILLUSTRATIONS

Plates

Figures

Endpapers

PREFACE

HAD there not been compelling reasons of sentiment for the dedication of this book to Archbishop Grindal's college and mine I should have made it an opportunity to commemorate two fellow historians of the Elizabethan Church, my near contemporaries, both cut off prematurely and on the brink of major achievements: Gareth Owen and James Cargill Thompson. Gareth Owen's contribution to this biography was to provide an oppositional element. At the time of his death he was engaged on a definitive study of John Aylmer, bishop of London from 1576 until 1590. It will be evident from my own work that I find Aylmer an unattractive figure, although I agree with Grindal that 'the bishop of London is always to be pitied.' But such was Dr Owen's admiration for Aylmer's undoubted administrative talents that he took a conventionally poor view of Grindal's competence as a bishop. He once told me that Grindal would have made an excellent curate of St Giles Cripplegate. I think that his judgment in this respect was faulty, but he forced me to examine my own bland assumptions. Chapter 9, on Grindal's handling of the original puritan crisis in the London of the 1560s, owes much to Gareth's important study of the Elizabethan London clergy. The major work which James Cargill Thompson had on the stocks concerned Martin Luther and his politics. But he was also learned on many aspects of the post-Reformation English Church and very interested in Grindal's first biographer, John Strype. Not long before his death he asked me whether I was sure that Sears Jayne in *Library Catalogues of the English Renaissance* was correct in reporting that the books which Grindal bequeathed to the Queen's College Oxford were no longer to be found on the shelves of the college library. An enquiry was made which met with a helpful response from Miss Helen Powell, the Assistant Librarian. The result was the discovery not only of a large portion of Grindal's library but of precious and revealing annotations to works by St Ambrose and Martin Bucer which tend to confirm what I had already suspected about his intellectual and moral formation. This experience may explain why it is easier to bring a work of this kind

11

to fruition in England than in Australia where Grindal, if not his biographer, spent some fallow years between 1969 and 1976.

From James Cargill Thompson one's mind moves naturally to Clifford Dugmore, his predecessor in the chair of Ecclesiastical History in the University of London and my colleague at King's College from 1961 to 1969. It was Professor Dugmore who first suggested that I should write Grindal's biography and signed me up for a volume in the series of which he was General Editor, 'Leaders of Religion'. I owe him an apology since in the event a life as virginal as Grindal's, from the point of view of the biographer, refused to fit the somewhat slender format of that series. I am grateful to Charles Black, whose house published the 'Leaders of Religion', for releasing myself and Grindal from our contractual obligations, and to Graham Greene of Jonathan Cape for interest shown at a time when the undertaking might have been laid aside altogether, and which has been sustained through subsequent negotiations. The very last favour I received from my old teacher Sir John Neale was encouragement in my own conviction that it would be a tragedy if a modern biography of a figure of Grindal's importance should not be published. I have once again received the most expert guidance in editorial matters from my publishers and specifically from Deborah Shepherd.

Several colleagues and friends have been kind enough to read parts of this study and to make helpful comments and criticisms. Cecile Zinberg, an authority on Strype, took a look at the Introduction. Mr John Todd of St Bees read the first chapter with the eye of an expert local historian and antiquary. Professor Gordon Rupp advised me on the theological judgments ventured in Chapters 2 and 4, and corrected some details. Dr Bill Sheils of the Borthwick Institute of Historical Research of the University of York offered helpful comments on the York chapters, and helped me to get the footnote references to materials in his care into the correct and current forms. Professor A. G. Dickens read the same chapters and pronounced his *nihil obstat*. Dr Willie Lamont of the University of Sussex read Chapter 13 and commented on the ideological implications of Grindal's famous letter to Queen Elizabeth. And my colleague Dr Peter Roberts brought his intimate knowledge of mid-Elizabethan courtly politics to a reading of Chapter 14. Finally Professor Joel Hurstfield read the entire typescript and made many helpful suggestions.

The footnotes contain references to no less than eighteen unpublished theses, in addition to my own doctoral thesis, which have some relevance for the study of Grindal. Of these sixteen have been consulted: the Cambridge theses by G. L. Blackman, V. C.

Greer, N. L. Jones and P. Lake; the Durham thesis by Jane E. A. Dawson; the Oxford theses by J. F. Davis, I. P. Ellis and N. R. N. Tyacke; and the London theses by J. I. Daeley, P. J. Laven, E. L. C. Mullins, M. Rosemary O'Day, H. G. Owen, W. J. Sheils, Susan Storer and F. X. Walker. The majority of these dissertations have been cited in connection with matters of detail but I gladly confess the formative influence on my own thinking of ideas and arguments in two recent Cambridge doctoral theses: Dr Norman Jones's 'Faith by Statute: the Politics of Religion in the Parliament of 1559', 1977, and Dr Peter Lake's 'Laurence Chaderton and the Cambridge Moderate Puritan Tradition, 1570–1604', 1978. My conversations with Norman Jones and Peter Lake have proved very helpful. My debt to Dr Gareth Owen's London thesis, 'The London Parish Clergy in the Reign of Elizabeth I', 1957, has already been acknowledged. I owe no less to the M.A. thesis by Mr E. L. C. Mullins which covers somewhat earlier ground, 'The Effect of the Marian and Elizabethan Religious Settlements upon the Clergy of London, 1553–1564'. As for more intangible influences, it is now well over a quarter of a century since I first discussed the technicalities of Elizabethan ecclesiastical affairs with Mr Mullins and we still talk about such matters from time to time. More recently I have learned much from the younger scholars who meet in a biennial Colloquium for Local Reformation Studies, and whose company I shared in Reading in 1974, in London in 1976, and in York in 1978, listening to papers for the most part still unpublished.

I must thank the librarians and custodians of archives for permission and facilities to consult and cite manuscripts in the following locations: Bodleian Library, Borthwick Institute of the University of York, British Library, Cambridge University Library, Cathedral Archives and Library Canterbury, Corporation of London Record Office, Corpus Christi College Cambridge, Dr Williams's Library, Gonville and Caius College Cambridge, Greater London Record Office, Guildhall Library London, Inner Temple Library, Lambeth Palace Library, Northamptonshire Record Office, Public Records Office and York Minster Library. Dr Bill Sheils of the Borthwick, Miss Anne Oakley of the Cathedral Archives and Library Canterbury, Mr Geoffrey Bill of Lambeth Palace Library and Miss Helen Powell of the Library of the Queen's College Oxford rendered assistance far beyond the ordinary line of duty. It is partly owing to Geoffrey Bill's pertinacity in pursuing and bidding in sale rooms for the Laud–Selden–Fairhurst MSS. (so-called), now in his safe keeping at Lambeth, that a full account of Grindal's troubles can now be written.

For their assistance in locating and supplying illustrations, and for permission to reproduce them, I thank the following: for plate 1, Mr John Todd and St Bees Parish Church; for plate 2, Mr W. S. Hutton, President of Pembroke College Cambridge, and W. Eaden Lilley; for plates 3 and 8, the National Portrait Gallery London; for plate 4, the Mary Evans Picture Library; for plate 5, His Grace the Lord Archbishop of Canterbury, copyright reserved to the Church Commissioners for England; for plate 6, Peter Newark's Historical Picture Service; for plate 7, the Dean of Canterbury and Mrs de Waal; for plate 9, Mr A. O. Meakin, Chief Librarian of the Central Library Croydon; for plate 10, Dr Bill Sheils, reproduced by kind permission of His Grace the Lord Archbishop of York and the Church Commissioners, copyright reserved to the Church Commissioners; for figure 1, the Provost, Fellows and Scholars of the Queen's College in the University of Oxford; for figure 2 and the endpapers, the British Library; for figure 4, His Grace the Lord Archbishop of Canterbury and the Trustees of Lambeth Palace Library; figure 3, transcript of Crown-copyright records in the Public Record Office (SP. 12/40/1), appears by permission of the Controller of H.M. Stationery Office.

All but finally I am in duty bound to thank the University of Sydney which in 1974 granted me a period of study leave, much of which was spent in research for this biography.

But the last thanks must go to the many friends, students and colleagues who have been constrained to suffer my strange enthusiasm for an Elizabethan archbishop who was perhaps a rather dull man, and to discuss his career both informally and in seminars and after lectures given in Brighton, Canterbury, London, Manchester, Melbourne, Oxford, Sydney and York. It is time for me to drop the subject, or at least to let it rest between these covers.

Spelling, punctuation and capitalization have been modernized in all quotations, but not in the titles of early printed books. Dates are given in New Style.

Keynes College,
University of Kent at Canterbury
1979   P.C.

INTRODUCTION

THIS biography of the second Elizabethan archbishop of Canterbury, the first to have been published since the early eighteenth century, was originally intended for a series known as 'Leaders of Religion'. The accolade of leader would have surprised some historians of the past, for whom the primacy of Edmund Grindal was not so much a significant chapter in the annals of the English Church as a curiosity, inviting investigation only in order to explain how such an incongruous appointment could ever have been made. Far from discovering in Grindal any quality of leadership, Creighton found him a weak man, 'infirm of purpose'. According to W. H. Frere, like Creighton himself a bishop, the trouble was a 'natural incapacity for government', a phrase echoed by W. P. M. Kennedy as 'a constitutional incapacity for administration', Grindal's 'outstanding weakness'. But in the view of these authors Grindal's administrative incompetence was evidently not so much 'constitutional' as incidental to a culpable sympathy for an alien puritanism which in itself disqualified him from responsible leadership of a church committed to the Elizabethan *via media*. In Sir Sidney Lee's phrase, Grindal 'feebly temporised with dissent'. H. M. Gwatkin attributed the elevation of such an unsuitable archbishop to 'some passing turn of policy', while a modern writer has called it 'a mistake'.[1]

Evidently Queen Elizabeth herself came to the early conclusion that a mistake had been made with Grindal. Within a year of his appointment, at Christmas 1575, the archbishop incurred her profound displeasure and slipped into a kind of limbo where he rested for the remaining six years of his life. It is consequently scarcely surprising that his primacy should have been marked, in Frere's words, by 'ineffectiveness'. Grindal was neither the first nor the last primate of all England to outlive the conditions which favoured his promotion, but none was overtaken by so immediate and irrevocable a disaster.

The circumstances are familiar, but not lacking in elements of obscurity. The queen had been provoked by complaints concerning the public expositions of the Bible known as 'exercises of prophesying', an increasingly popular institution of the Elizabethan Church which many bishops were prepared to endorse. Grindal was summoned into the royal presence and commanded to convey to his suffragans an order for the 'utter suppression' of all such 'learned exercises and conferences' and, less specifically, for the 'abridging' of the number of preachers in the Church. Denied any opportunity for verbal expostulation, the archbishop made his response in a lengthy epistle which gained notoriety as his 'book to the queen'. In this letter Grindal refused to assent to the suppression of the prophesyings and declined to transmit a mandate for the purpose. More than that, he called in question the governing principles as well as the style of the queen's ecclesiastical government, pleaded with her to avoid a peremptory and dictatorial conduct of religious affairs, defined the limits of his own obedience and reminded Elizabeth of where she stood as a mortal being in the sight of God: 'a particular piece of characteristically puritan crankiness', if we would agree with Bishop Frere, but for John Strype, his first biographer, the signature of a truly apostolic bishop.[2]

The grave offence of the letter was compounded by subsequent refusals to surrender any of the ground which it had defended, or to make a formal submission before the Council in the requisite terms. But for grave legal objections to such a procedure and the discreet machinations of powerful friends, the queen would have insisted on Grindal's deprivation. Instead, the archbishop was sequestered and deprived of some personal liberty. This was done with considerable informality, so that to establish the precise nature and degree of Grindal's incapacity through the next six years would demand, and might well defeat, a keen mind for constitutional niceties. Yet the suspension *ab officio* was never entirely lifted, and only the archbishop's death in July 1583 forestalled the resignation which had commended itself as the only decent way of escape from a scandalous impasse.

From the seventeenth century onwards, as the latent tensions in the English Church and in society led to revolution, civil war and a legacy of religious and political bitterness, Grindal's celebrated protest and his consequent disgrace cast a long shadow which obscured his reputation and excluded an informed and detached appraisal of his qualities. Grindal had been deeply respected by his contemporaries, not only for moderation and pastoral excellence but for learning, judgment, and even that very capacity for resolute government which later observers found wanting. Nothing could be more impressive than the sustained solidarity in his defence of courtiers, privy councillors and bishops. Grindal's troubles differed from those of Archbishop Abbot or of Archbishop Wake in later generations in that almost nobody sought to take advantage of them. For his immediate posterity he was 'a right famous and worthy prelate', affectionately made the victim of a pun in Holinshed's obituary notice as the 'Grindall' who 'ground himself even to his grave by mortification' and hard study; 'this good man' whose learning and virtue would be rewarded by 'the good name which he hath left behind him as a monument perpetual'. 'This bishop', wrote Sir John Hayward, the annalist of Elizabeth's early years, 'was a man famous, whilst he lived, for his deep judgment, both in learning and affairs of the world; famous, also, both for his industry and gift in preaching; but chiefly he was famous for his magnanimous courage, in that it was no less easy to divert the sun from his proper course than to pervert him to indirect actions.'[3] If these testimonials seem conventional, the unique profile of a career which took Grindal from the bishopric of London through York to Canterbury speaks for itself.

A generation later, the figure of Grindal had become two-dimensional, more of a symbol than flesh and blood. For puritans smarting under the ecclesiastical régime of Archbishop Laud he provided a standard of moderation and protestant integrity by which to judge the extravagance of a resurgent prelacy. And when moderation was blown away, in 1641, Grindal remained almost exempt from the general onslaught on his order. Even for Milton, who rejected the suggestion that Truth to make its way must 'bring a ticket from Cranmer, Latimer and Ridley', and who dismissed the Elizabethan bishops as Laodiceans, neither hot nor cold, Grindal was 'the best of them'; while the pamphleteer William Prynne, in an exhaustive attack on the whole race of bishops which marked his emergence as a radical, honoured this one bishop as 'a grave and pious man', in contrast to his denunciation of the other Elizabethan archbishops of Canterbury, the 'over pontifical and princely' Parker, and Whitgift, that 'stately pontifical bishop'. With the departure of the dissenters from the established Church, in the years beyond 1662, nonconformist annalists carried the stereotype with them, so that for Daniel Neal Grindal was to be 'the good old archbishop', 'of a mild and moderate temper, easy of access and affable even in his highest exaltation'; in short, 'upon the whole ... one of the best of Queen Elizabeth's bishops'.[4]

Compromised by friends of this complexion Grindal came under fire from the opposite side of the widening schism in religious and political life. Even the charitable Thomas Fuller, who found Grindal in some respects admirable, thought it apt to dub him 'our English Eli'. Like the high priest of old he died blind and brokenhearted and he tolerated the 'factious disturbers' of the Church as Eli had indulged his wicked sons.[5] And so the otherwise forgotten archbishop became a posthumous victim of the inflamed politics of post-revolutionary England.

It was on 5 November 1709 that Grindal was rudely dragged from the grave by the high flyer Dr Henry Sacheverell in a notorious political sermon, designed to provoke an ailing whig administration to suicidal counter-measures, and published as *The perils of false brethren, both in Church and State*. Among Sacheverell's targets were Archbishop Tenison and other leading whig divines, 'men of character and stations', who had proved 'false brethren' by their betrayal of the Church in maintaining the Act of Toleration of 1689 and Liberty of Conscience. But the doctor chose to veil his real intentions by directing the attack against 'that false son of the Church, Bishop Grindall', 'a perfidious prelate' by whom Queen Elizabeth had been deluded into granting a toleration for the 'Genevian Discipline', from which ensued 'the first plantation of dissenters'. 'The application is plain and home', as Bishop Wake observed in his speech at Sacheverell's impeachment. For Grindal read Tenison and his episcopal colleagues. For Elizabeth read Anne. 'And if this be not plainly to speak out what he would have done with the Act of Indulgence, I must despair of ever being able to know any man's meaning by his expressions.'[6] The whigs accepted Sacheverell's devious weapons, and among other more ponderous retorts to his seditious sermon took steps to defend the reputation of an archbishop who had been dead for 125 years. In consequence Grindal was alternately lauded and lampooned in an exchange of sixpenny pamphlets, including *Strange News from the Dead*, a letter supposedly written by the archbishop himself from the security of the Elysian Fields, in which his vindicators were assured of the warm congratulations of John Calvin 'and the representative ghosts of seven pious presbyters of the present age'.[7]

Among these curious ephemera was a tract written by the vicar of the Essex parish of Low Leyton, the Reverend John Strype; a pure encomium for 'this holy prelate', 'this apostolical bishop', and also a puff for the full-scale *History of the Life and Acts of Edmund Grindal* which was published hard on the heels of the Sacheverell trial, in June 1710. Strype described himself as 'no party man ... a good Catholic Christian ... a sincere son of the Church of England'. His *Life of Grindal* is an implicit apology for the 'moderation' so suspect to the tories of his own time, 'the good temper and spirit of the true Church of England'. Like all his works, it is not so much a biography as a valuable collection of materials for a biography,

which a hostile reviewer (perhaps Sacheverell himself) had some
cause to call 'a compendious trifle', written by 'our modern
appendix-monger'.[8]

As a business proposition the publication of Strype's com-
pilations was not without its hazards and the enterprise was made
viable only by the loyal efforts of fellow-antiquaries who scoured
the country for advance subscriptions. At this time support was
building up for Strype's projected life of Archbishop Parker but
there was no immediate prospect of Grindal seeing the light of day,
although it was three years since the author had written of the book
as 'ready finished, lying by me'. The Sacheverell affair transformed these prospects and hastened the publication of the *Life of
Grindal* under the immediate patronage of the managers of the
impeachment and with a dedication addressed to Tenison. Even
in these extraordinary circumstances Strype's publisher feared
that the book would produce 'bustle and noise' rather than 'an
encouraging recompense'. But when the lavish folio volume appeared it was, as Strype himself reports, 'mightily bought up', and
the 306 subscribers included eight bishops, as well as prominent
members of both houses of Parliament. A year later Strype was
rewarded with Archbishop Tenison's patronage. The vindictive
William Cole was to write that 'Mr Strype ought to bless the
memory of Dr Sacheverell who fairly got him this sinecure from
the zealous Tenison.' Many of Strype's old supporters, church and
king men in the parishes and universities, felt as Cole was to write,
and withdrew their support, if only temporarily. It remained to
Ralph Thoresby of Leeds, with true antiquarian disinterest, to
reassure his friend that the 'hasting' of his life of Grindal was 'the
best effect that Dr Sacheverell's heat has produced'.[9]

Since Strype's day Grindal has aroused little interest outside
those limited ecclesiastical circles for whom he continued to be a
controversial figure. No new biographers have been attracted,
apart from Dean Hook, who was bound to include him in the *Lives
of the Archbishops of Canterbury*. There was also Richard Hone,
vicar of Halesowen, who in 1843 found room for Grindal in his
series of 'Lives of Eminent Christians', a work of hagiography in
which Grindal becomes a mirror-image of the earnest evangelical,
notable for 'the steadiness of his *desire to promote vital godliness in
the land*'.[10] In the absence of a critical biography,[11] an image of
Grindal persists which is polemical in its conception and perversely at variance with the truth. A man known to his own age for
consistency is represented as weak and indecisive. A bishop whom
Alexander Nowell, dean of St Paul's, characterized as 'of the
greatest wisdom and ability to govern' is dismissed as adminis-

tratively incompetent. A reformer who deeply deplored the divisive consequences of puritanism is thought to have been complacent about puritan schism, indeed a puritan himself. There can be few figures in our history who have suffered so total a misrepresentation.

Either to admire or to despise Grindal as an archbishop who was soft on puritanism and less than loyal to Anglicanism is to fall into anachronism and to exercise judgment in the terms of a dichotomy which in Grindal's lifetime had yet to establish itself. Nor is it sound to place the emphasis, as the defensive Strype does, on Grindal's irreproachable and, as we might say, central Anglicanism, for this is to minimize the real differences which stood between his churchmanship and that of his predecessor, Matthew Parker, or of his successor, John Whitgift. The Anglicanism of Grindal was without a direct succession, either in the established Church or outside it, and it is only to be understood through reconstituting the circumstances of the years to which it belonged. His life deserves attention, not simply because it has never been 'done', nor even on the grounds that a man of integrity and some greatness has been sadly misused, but because Grindal was an exemplary figure of the English Reformation in what was arguably its most creative phase.

Grindal may be taken to represent those early Elizabethan bishops who came to maturity in the hopeful reign of Edward VI and were, so to speak, 'finished' by the experience of continental exile in the ensuing Marian reaction. First in the English universities and later in the Swiss and South German centres of reform, they came into close and appreciative contact with the seminal minds of reformed protestantism: with Martin Bucer, Peter Martyr and John Calvin himself. The consequence was that they brought to the administration of their English dioceses a conception of the Church and a standard of pastoral care which were authentically protestant and a corrective to the doctrine, so strongly entrenched in England, of the *jus reformandi* of the godly christian prince. The ideal was not easily applicable to the only partially reformed institutions of the Church of England, or to the strictly limited powers and attributes of the episcopate under Queen Elizabeth. But with Grindal the pastoral aspirations of the Reformation constantly obtruded, to the extent that his episcopal career seems to demonstrate the most determined attempt made in the sixteenth century to marry Reformation on the South German and Swiss model to the traditional structures and institutions of *Ecclesia Anglicana*.

In this there was promise not only of a reform which would

extend far beyond the minimal adherence and passive conformity of society in the royal settlement of religion, but also of harnessing the spontaneous and potentially explosive energies of the English protestant (or puritan) movement in the bringing about of such a reform. What kind of Church this manner of episcopal leadership, given its head, would have created, and whether it could have been saved from the fragmentation of the protestant tradition in the schism of Anglicanism and puritanism, church and chapel, is for the reader to judge, taking account of the treacherous political shoals around which the action was fought, and to which Grindal himself fell victim. It is a question which this book will explore but which it cannot hope to close.

PART ONE

FIRST
THINGS

I

THAT LITTLE ANGLE

THE village of St Bees on the Cumbrian coast can lay claim
to a curious distinction. For seven years of the reign of Elizabeth I this obscure community in what a Tudor official described
as 'an outward and extreme part of the realm' furnished the
Church of England with both of her archbishops: Edmund Grindal of Canterbury and Edwin Sandys of York. As Sandys recalled,
the two had lived 'familiarly' and 'as brothers' from an early age
and were only separated between Sandys's thirteenth and eighteenth years. Sandys kept one pace behind the companion of his
youth, succeeding him first as bishop of London and then as
archbishop of York.

According to the dates most often proposed, Grindal was born
in 1519 or 1520. The inscription on his funerary monument in
Croydon parish church declares that he was aged sixty-three at the
time of his death in 1583. Sandys is thought to have been his senior
by three or four years. But as in many modern non-European
societies, people were often uncertain of their age and before 1538
births were not registered. In 1588 Tobie Matthew, later bishop of
Durham and archbishop of York, thought that Grindal had died at
the age of sixty-six, and added: 'If Archbishop Sandys be now by
his own account but sixty-six and by his own brother's reckoning
but seventy at the most, his age was little or nothing above forty
when [in 1559] he was bestowed at Worcester.'[1] According to these
computations, Grindal was born in 1517 and Sandys either in the
same year or in 1521. These also happen to have been the two
acknowledged birthdays of the Protestant Reformation: Martin
Luther posted the Ninety-Five Theses in 1517 and stood before
the Imperial Diet at Worms in 1521.

To the satisfaction of Strype, both archbishops were 'sprung
from St Bees', but the statement cannot pass without comment.
For one thing the parish of St Bees was historically far more
extensive that the township of that name, embracing much of the
region known as Copeland, including the country to the south as
far as Egremont, to the north what is now Whitehaven, and to the
east the Ennerdale and Eskdale fells. Sandys was not born in

Copeland but at Graythwaite Hall, on the shores of Windermere, where the name of Sandys has persisted until our own time. At nearby Hawkshead he later erected a monument to his parents in the parish church, an extraordinary work of ostentation and mannered antiquarianism, and in the same village he founded the grammar school which William Wordsworth would attend, two centuries later. Yet in 1563 the heralds knew his family as 'of St Bees in the county of Cumberland', and the parish registers of St Bees are found to be full of his kindred. The senior stock lived at Rottington Hall, a manor to the north of the village which included within its boundaries the massive 'bergh' of St Bees Head, the nesting-place of a famous race of peregrine falcons which the family was entitled to take, by grant of the abbots of St Mary's York, the mother house of St Bees Priory. That Sandys was brought up at Rottington is very likely in view of his boyhood friendship with Grindal.

The Grindals were also numerous in the district in the sixteenth century, although their inferior social status makes the tracing of their connections an uncertain business. Evidently the archbishop was not the first of his family to be attracted to learning and a clerical career. William Grindal, Roger Ascham's pupil who preceded Ascham as Princess Elizabeth's tutor, was no doubt a relative, and a certain James Grindal was both curate of St Bees as early as 1539 and later a prebendary of St Paul's in his kinsman's time as bishop of London. When this man died in 1574 he was succeeded at St Bees by a curate whose mother was a Grindal. As for the archbishop himself, it was assumed in the seventeenth century that he was a native of 'St Bees town'. But when the Leeds antiquary Ralph Thoresby found himself in these parts in 1694 he was assured by one William Gilpin, agent to the lord of the manor of St Bees, that the birthplace was a farm a mile to the south of Hensingham, a hamlet three or four miles to the north-east and now a suburb of Whitehaven. Thoresby passed this information on to Strype and it has rarely been questioned since.[2] Indeed the tradition is still kept alive in Hensingham that this was Grindal's native heath, specifically Overend Farm within the township. It has been thought significant that the initials 'W.G.' and 'W.R.G.' appear on a slab in the wall of this house, and that in 1559 a William Grindal, son of William Grindal, was baptized at St Bees.[3] Another farm, Chapel House, is sometimes claimed as the birthplace.[4]

Nevertheless the local antiquarian William Jackson found sufficient evidence to convince him of the truth of the older tradition that the archbishop's family home was in the village of St Bees itself. The parish registers of the 1550s and 1560s contain many references to Robert Grindal: or rather, as it would appear, to two Robert Grindals, since Anna, daughter of Robert Grindal, was baptized on 11 September 1551 and Helena, also daughter of Robert Grindal, on 25 March 1552. It is certain that one of these Roberts was the archbishop's brother who, as we shall see, died in 1568, a month after his wife, and who styled himself in his will as 'of St Bees'. The other was presumably the 'Robert Grindal of Hensingham', the first of the name to be so distinguished in the registers, who was buried in 1587. This Robert Grindal was included among the original governors of the archbishop's grammar school at its foundation in 1583 but declined to serve. He left a widow who remarried and a son and heir, 'John Grindal of Hensingham'. (To complicate matters, the registers earlier record the baptisms and burials of two John Grindals, each the son of Robert Grindal, one baptized in 1550 and the other in 1560, the first buried in 1550, the second in 1564.) From these details it seems likely that the archbishop and his elder brother Robert were not 'of Hensingham', but cousins of the Hensingham Grindals.[5]

St Bees today retains the proportions of the smaller towns of Tudor England, with houses backing on to pastures and three farms accommodated in the main street. The most substantial buildings are still the reconstructed remains of the great priory church, dedicated in the dim and distant past to the mysterious cult of St Begha, and, facing it across the road, Archbishop Grindal's Grammar School, each a distinctive monument to its own cultural epoch. Away from the industrial belt to the north, the biographer of Grindal who goes in search of his origins may suppose that he has understood them, as he surveys the pastoral landscape. Today this is a country of substantial, stone-built farms, faintly reminiscent of some Alpine valley, with the cattle kept in the byre until late in the spring and the hay stored in lofts above. The farms interconnect by tracks running between hedges and, to the south, drystone walls, making up a patchwork of 'closes' and 'garths'. The environment seems to resemble the native Toggenburg of the great Swiss reformer, Huldreich Zwingli, and the imaginative historian may be tempted to dwell upon the strength of character bred in such surroundings.

Yet the immemorial appearance of this countryside is an illusion. In the sixteenth century most of the coastal plain lay in open fields: the 'infield', given over to regular arable farming and at St Bees manured with seaweed from the shore, and the more occasionally cultivated 'outfield'. Oats and barley, with 'bere' or 'bigg', a poorer, hardy variety of barley, were the standard grains,

grown for bread, brewing and stock feed. The grazing of cattle and
sheep over the extensive 'wastes' which lay beyond the arable
limits was the mainstay of existence. In the summer the livestock
migrated to upland pastures in the fells, part of the community
going with the animals, as in the Alps today. Some of the 'store'
cattle and sheep, fattened on additional fodder, found their way to
the markets of the West Riding of Yorkshire and even to Smithfield. The economy was further diversified by quarrying and fish-
ing, and by the coal which was already extracted within the bounds
of the parish. (In 1597 two St Bees men were buried who had been
'slain in a coalpit'.)[6] Yet commercial traffic with the outside world
was on a small scale. For almost all classes of the community a bare
living standard was precariously maintained. And in the bad years
local resources were insufficient to prevent the catastrophe of
famine.

The Cumbrian farmers of the period, traditionally known as
'statesmen', enjoyed the customary tenure of their land called
tenant-right, which was often tantamount to a freehold, but which
offered no ultimate security at a time of mounting economic pressures. Their farmsteads incorporated byre, barn and dwelling-
house within a single modest structure, furnished with the barest
of necessities. As with the patriarchs, the outward symbols of
prosperity were heads of livestock rather than domestic embellishments and comforts. Even gentlemen lived as yeomen might live in
the midlands or the south, inhabiting houses which comprised
little more than a hall, parlour and single bedchamber. The 'great
rebuilding' which transformed the conditions of domestic life over
much of England in the course of the sixteenth century hardly
affected the north-western counties before the reign of Charles II.
It was only then that a vernacular stone architecture began to
replace the older constructions of clay and wood built on stone
footings. As for the cottages of the poorer labouring classes, these
were little more than shanties which could be erected in three or
four hours, their contents worth a few shillings. Three out of every
four Cumberland farmers rented less than an acre of land, and only
one in twenty was fortunate enough to work the statutory four
acres. Although the potato was not present to lend its deceptive
security, the economy and society must have resembled
nineteenth-century Ireland more than twentieth-century Lake-
land. The isolation of the region, on which the county historian
could still comment more than two centuries later,[7] must have been
considerable, the harshness of existence in what Grindal called
'my lawless country' extreme, by any scale of values familiar to
modern Europeans. Kinship, clanship and mutual fidelity im-

parted much resilience to the fabric of society. But as the sixteenth century advanced, and more especially after the climacteric of the Northern Rebellion of 1569, the realization grew that these were diminishing values, not easily adaptable to a changing world.[8]

The future archbishop had ample experience of these hard conditions. Edwin Sandys was the son of a gentleman and a justice of the peace, a veteran of Henry VIII's wars who was represented on his tomb in medieval armour, a lion at his feet. As a bishop Sandys was given to boasting of the excellence of his pedigree and was devoted to the social advancement of his sons. But Grindal's father was a poor tenant farmer. In 1570 the family inheritance, including a house which the father and his eldest son Robert had built at their own charges, was worth less than a pound a year in rent.

As a lifelong bachelor, Grindal adhered to the traditional values of his native society in looking after the interests of his kindred, who included connections by marriage among the Woodhalls, another numerous St Bees family. His brother Robert's son and one of his sister Elizabeth Woodhall's sons were both christened Edmund. Both were doubtless godsons. All the surviving children from these two families were remembered in their uncle's will. Grindal was particularly solicitous of the interests of his nephew William Woodhall. As bishop of London he set him up with a lease of 'certain grounds pertaining to a prebend in Paul's', and as archbishop of York found him further leases in Yorkshire. Finally, at the time of his death, he appointed Woodhall a governor of his newly founded grammar school at St Bees and bestowed on him many tangible remembrances, including a favourite horse and sundry items of bed linen, and forgave him various debts. An unmarried niece, Isabelle Woodhall, was another recipient of a York lease, at a time when she was described as living in St Martin le Grand, London. The Woodhalls had evidently risen modestly in the world in the shadow of their distinguished relative, William being described as 'William Woodhall of Walden, Essex, gentleman'. The husband of another niece, a certain Mr Wilson, was one of the archbishop's chaplains at the time of his death, the father of John Wilson, an early minister of Boston, Massachusetts. Having acquired the rectory of St Bees, Grindal appointed relations to the curacy. And he found room in his household at Lambeth for 'my servant William Grindal', yet another kinsman.[9]

There is no need to assume that in the closely-knit society of West Cumberland the Grindals were estranged from the local gentry. On the contrary they had freely intermarried with them.[10] But as bishop of London Grindal would inform Cecil with marked bitterness of the problems of 'that little angle' of Copeland in the county of Cumberland where he was born, 'the ignorantest part in religion, and most oppressed of covetous landlords, of any one part of this realm'. His report finds an echo in the draft of a parliamentary bill of 1571 which represented the tenantry of Cumberland and Westmorland as threatened by the loss of their ancient tenant-rights and oppressed by excessive entry fines.[11]

At St Bees the lands of the dissolved priory passed in 1553 into the hands of the distinguished diplomatist, Sir Thomas Challoner. Seven years later Challoner, or his local agent, followed current practice in attempting to replace the estates of inheritance of ninety of his tenants (who included Grindal's brother) with fifty-year leases, granted against the payment of enhanced fines. The innovation was at first resisted by the statesmen and eventually accepted only after some of the accustomed services had been relinquished, and on condition that the new leases should not infringe traditional tenant-right. It was Grindal, by now bishop of London, who found the ready money to purchase the lease of the family farm. Contrary to what might be expected, he was on good terms with this arriviste landlord, and it has even been suggested that it was through their acquaintance at the court of Edward VI that Challoner settled at St Bees.[12] Certainly Grindal was able to make further and substantial provision for his family by the purchase from Challoner of the impropriated tithes of the parish. When Challoner was sent on an embassy to Spain, in 1563, Grindal wrote to congratulate him on the appointment, to thank him 'for your favours towards my poor friends in my country', and to renew a request for six or seven hundred loads of St Bees stone for the repair of St Paul's, after the recent fire.[13] Whether or not this 'old begging suit' was successful, Challoner's son would later contribute one-and-a-half acres of land and forty loads of coal from his mine at St Bees towards Grindal's foundation of a free grammar school for the town.

If all had gone smoothly for the Grindals this would have been about the sum of our knowledge of the archbishop's family circumstances. But in 1568 and 1569 they were victims of a multiple calamity. Grindal's brother Robert, his brother's wife and Edmund, their only son, aged six, all died within the space of five weeks, and at the time of harvest. Presumably the cause was an epidemic, perhaps of plague which is known to have come into the Borders from Scotland at that time. The second of four surviving daughters, Anne, was made sole executrix of her father's will, with the provision that she should be directed in all things by her uncle. Yet within six months, and in defiance of the bishop's wishes,

Anne Grindal married William Dacre of Acton near Carlisle, a member of a famous northern family. A dispensation had been obtained from the archbishop of Canterbury's Court of Faculties for the marriage to take place without the calling of banns.[14]

In the following winter of 1569–70 Dacre became involved with his cousin Leonard Dacre in that aspect of the disorders of the time known as Dacre's Raid. This episode was no more than the carrying into armed insurgency of a private quarrel with the Howards for the possession of the Dacre baronies and other estates. But like the rising of the earls of Westmorland and Northumberland three months earlier, the Dacre Raid was sustained on the agrarian grievances of the tenantry. After their defeat at Naworth in the most considerable engagement of the Northern Rebellion, the Dacres fled over the Border and eventually to Flanders, where Leonard was to die in poverty three years later. With the threat of attainder hanging over the leases and tithes in which Grindal's remaining nieces all had an interest, the bishop wrote to Cecil to beg the first option of buying them back, either from Sir Thomas Challoner's executors, who included Cecil, or from the Crown. Five days later a royal proclamation offered a free pardon to all persons who had attended or assisted Leonard Dacre, although it excluded Leonard himself and his brothers. But it was not until late December 1570, after his translation to York, that Grindal was successful in purchasing, for a fine of £40, the Crown's interest in 'all leases and chattels' which were said to be in the hands of the Crown by reason of William Dacre's indictment for treason and by his flight, outlawry and attainder. As for William Dacre himself, he was pardoned after his cousin's death and in 1574 returned to live quietly at St Bees, where six children were born within the next eight years. Grindal was eventually so far reconciled to his niece's husband as to appoint him a governor of his grammar school. But misfortune was to pursue the affairs of this family to the end. Before the grant of Letters Patent for the foundation of the school Dacre died, in April 1583. A fortnight later a posthumous daughter was born, only to be buried within a matter of days. Three years later Anne Grindal remarried and took the little estate with her. In the end it became a drop in the ocean of the great holdings of the Lowthers, successors to the Challoners and the creators of modern Whitehaven.[15]

These details of family history illuminate the formation of Grindal's mind on matters of religious and social policy. As an Elizabethan bishop he regarded poverty, the oppression of landlords, ignorance, irreligion, disobedience and lawlessness as related symptoms of a general disease in the body politic, for which the only remedy was preaching and education. What, he would ask the queen in his famous letter, had bred the troubles of 1569?

> Was it not papistry, and ignorance of God's word through want of often preaching? And in the time of that rebellion, were not all men, of all states, that made profession of the gospel most ready to offer their lives for your defence?

As archbishop of Canterbury no amount of personal embarrassment or political pressure could alter his conviction that the ordinary ministry of the Church should be a preaching ministry. The same response to the needs of society was implied in his last public action, the foundation of the grammar school in his native country. And when the leases of the St Bees tenants expired in 1610, those statesmen whose rents formed part of the endowment of the school alleged that in purchasing their tenements it was Grindal's intention to give them, 'his countrymen, amongst whom he was born', some security against eviction or hard dealing, 'thereby doing the tenants as much good as by founding the school, conferring thus a double and equal benefit on both school and tenants'.[16] Grindal's views on such matters were conventional, drawn from the common stock of the 'commonwealth's men' of mid-Tudor England, by the end of the century virtually 'a national conviction'.[17] But Grindal had better cause than most holders of high office to be so convinced. There are many indications in his correspondence of instinctive sympathy for the plight of the poor. For example, as archbishop of York he made representations on behalf of the 'poor inhabitants' of one Yorkshire village, whose dependence on a piece of 'thorny ground' for hedging materials and firewood was threatened by enclosure.[18]

Grindal was only one of as many as fifteen bishops of north-western origin whose benefactions, from the late fifteenth to the seventeenth centuries, gave priority to the educational advancement of their native communities. In the neighbouring county of Lancashire we find what the historian of English philanthropy in this period has called an 'almost fanatical preoccupation ... with the founding of schools', 'a Lancastrian obsession regarding the virtue of education', based on the conviction that poverty, ignorance and want of opportunity could be best cured by making the coming generations literate and self-sufficient. There was a correspondingly low interest in the direct alleviation of poverty.[19] In Lancashire the purposeful direction of such charity was a force contributing to the extensive social and cultural changes which were preparative of the vast developments of the industrial age. It cannot be claimed that the character of Cumbrian society was transformed by the efforts of Archbishop Grindal and other like-minded benefactors. As late as 1895 a Royal Commission on Agriculture found that the statesmen of the region were generally impecunious, and inefficient as farmers; while a modern sociological study of Cumberland village life describes a persistently insular culture and relates the very low level of religious practice, no recent phenomenon, to a long-standing tradition of clerical absenteeism and neglect.[20]

To a modern eye, and to a mind capable, as Grindal's was not, of comprehending 'society' and its mechanisms, it will appear that his diagnosis of the ills of his native country was less than profound. Surely the backwardness of the economy, rather than ignorance, was basic to its problems. Even irreligion had economic roots, for the poverty of the region was reflected in the dilapidated finances of the sprawling Cumberland parishes, and in the inadequacy of the dependent chapelries into which they were divided. That Grindal's mind was incapable of a radical or even rational analysis of existing social arrangements is suggested by his willingness to provide for his own family with the impropriated tithes of his native parish. But poverty was not the only obstacle to change. There were also problems of mentality and communication, and of a culture profoundly unfriendly to novel and exotic influences. At the end of the eighteenth century the county historian would record of the inhabitants of one West Cumberland village (the simplicity of whose life he tended otherwise to idolize) that their speech consisted 'much of antiquated words and phrases', and that their opinions were too frequently governed by superstition.[21] When an Elizabethan bishop of Carlisle had complained of the woeful ignorance of 'the poorer sort' in his diocese he found 'the chief spring' in the insufficiency of clergy who were not only unlearned but 'unable to read English truly and distinctly'.[22] Yet a parson who was articulate in the civil speech of the south would at once put himself beyond communication with his people. It is worth recalling that regeneration beyond anything dreamed of by Grindal came about in rural Wales in the eighteenth century, largely through a breakthrough in the communication of religious ideas in the vernacular. But to Grindal the robust culture of the northern fells was so much ignorance, lawlessness and barbarity.

This alienation he owed to his own schooling. Northerners who regarded education as the most effective of social and moral escalators were paying tribute to their own beginnings. Grindal's friend Alexander Nowell, the dean of St Paul's, a Lancastrian, together with his affluent brother Robert, took steps to refound on the basis of secure endowments the school at Middleton 'where we were brought up in our youth'.[23] By opening the path to advancement in the south (a path taken by both the Nowells as well as by Grindal and Sandys) the northern schools drained away the native talent of the region which never returned to refresh its place of origin.

We do not know where Grindal went to school, although Jackson assumed that it must have been in St Bees itself. We know from John Foxe that the Marian martyr John Bland who was burned at Canterbury in 1555 had been Sandys's schoolmaster.[24] Then he was presumably Grindal's schoolmaster as well, and perhaps the cause of his conversion to protestantism, although it is odd that Foxe, who was closer to Grindal than to Sandys, does not mention him in the same connection. Bland was a native of Sedbergh who is sometimes reported to have taught in a school maintained by the great abbey of Furness. But this is not documented and it is equally possible that Bland's employment was at St Bees: unless the absence of any reference to a previous school in Grindal's endowment of his grammar school implies that there were no local educational facilities of which he could have taken advantage in his youth.[25] In that event we must picture him travelling down the coast and across the sands of the Duddon to school in Furness; or in the opposite direction, to Carlisle.

In place of documented fact, all that survives of Grindal's boyhood are two edifying little stories. He is said to have preserved his father from certain death by snatching him back from an old rotten bridge moments before it collapsed into a flooded beck. On another occasion, when the young Edmund was walking in the fields, an arrow fell and, striking close to the heart, would have killed him if it had not lodged in a book (according to one version a copy of Terence or Plautus) which the studious youth was carrying in his breast.[26] This tale is told by Conrad Hubert of Strasbourg, a close personal friend, who may well have had it at first hand. Although there is no reason to doubt their authenticity it is fair to say that no life lived in a spirit of piety in the sixteenth century seems to have been bereft of such instructive and reassuring 'providences'.

Note. After this chapter was written an undated letter was discovered (PRO, S.P. 12/129/20) written by James Grindal clerk, presumably the curate of St Bees. From the letter it can be inferred that James Grindal was Sir Thomas Challoner's agent and wrote during his master's absence overseas. It contains much information about the economy of St Bees, including coal-mining and salt production, rents and tithes. It was carried to Challoner's associates in London by Robert Grindal.

2

THE GLORY OF
PEMBROKE HALL

THE contribution of Cambridge University to the English Reformation is a matter of such familiar knowledge that even to state the case is to labour it. There is no need in these pages to trace yet again the annals of those who made a 'Little Germany' of the White Horse Inn, of the translators, the twenty-five Cambridge martyrs and the ninety Marian exiles from Cambridge who almost monopolize the history of the early protestant tradition in this country. But the strength and distinctive quality of that tradition in one of the smaller colleges, Pembroke Hall, is not as notorious as it deserves to be. It was no secret later in the sixteenth century, when Gabriel Harvey recalled 'those singular men' of an earlier generation, 'Bishop Ridley, Bishop Grindal, Mr Bradford' and others, whom he called 'the late ornaments of Cambridge and the glory of Pembroke Hall'. This was to echo the congratulations of the college sent to Grindal on his advancement to the archbishopric of Canterbury, an event 'ad sempiternam Pembrochianam gloriam'. At that time, or so Harvey claimed, it had passed 'for a good consequent, he is a Pembroke Hall man, *ergo*, a good scholar.' And a century later Bishop Matthew Wren's biographer would extol the college which had bred not only Grindal and Wren but John Whitgift and Lancelot Andrewes as 'that fruitful soil of bishops'.[1]

Grindal joined this distinguished little society at some point in the later 1530s, after an earlier removal to Christ's from Magdalene (or Buckingham College as it was then still known), where he had first entered the university. As Strype plausibly suggests, these migrations indicate an impoverished student in search of 'some encouragement and exhibition'. We know nothing of Grindal's life as a student, or subsequently as a scholar, but we are told how some equally penniless undergraduates acquired some erudition in the Classics, the Fathers and Scripture of the kind which he would later command. Thomas Lever speaks of the 'poor, godly, diligent students' who toiled throughout an eighteen-hour day which began at four in the morning. They were in chapel from five until six, and at lectures or private study from six until ten. For dinner, eaten at ten, a penny piece of beef might be shared amongst four, 'having a few porage made of the broth of the same beef, with salt and oatmeal and nothing else'. They would then study or teach until five, when they would eat a poor supper. 'Immediately after the which they go either to reasoning in problems or unto some other study until it be nine or ten of the clock.' The long day was then over, but with no heating in their chambers the students were 'fain to walk or run up and down half an hour to get a heat on their feet when they go to bed'. Highly coloured this account may be, but it is consistent with what Holinshed's *Chronicle* recorded of Grindal after his death: that he was 'so studious that his book was his bride and his study his bridechamber, whereupon he spent both his eyesight, his strength and his health'. In this way qualities of mind were acquired and exercised which were solid rather than meteoric, reliable rather than brilliant.[2]

The strengths and the limitations of such an intellect are reflected in the large collection of books which Grindal would bestow on the Queen's College Oxford at the end of his life, many of which are still there.[3] This was not the entirety of his library, excluding as it did books in Greek and German which he is known to have possessed,[4] as well as the ephemeral and polemical works which he must have owned in some profusion. But we may regard the bequest as a fair sample of the more learned works which he had acquired in the course of his career and which he considered to be of abiding value. If so, then Grindal was well read in the Fathers: Athanasius, Basil, Ambrose, Gregory of Nazianzus and many others. He was familiar with much modern theology and especially with the great systematic 'Common Places' and biblical commentaries of Musculus, Peter Martyr, Brentz and Bullinger. He had a representative collection of modern scholarly editions of the Bible, or of portions of the Bible. He was also a collector of chronicles, which suggests a serious interest in the events of the recent past, and of his own time. But if this collection of some one hundred authors is representative, Grindal had few eclectic interests, and little abiding interest in literature for its own sake, in the sense of classical 'good letters': a narrow, applied and practical mind.

In 1538 Grindal proceeded Bachelor of Arts and was admitted to a college fellowship. In 1540 he took his Master's degree and became junior treasurer. Four years later he received a title to be made deacon by John Bird, bishop of the newly constituted diocese of Chester, which included Grindal's native St Bees at its most remote frontier. No record seems to have survived of the date and other circumstances of his ordination to the priesthood. In 1549 he proceeded to the Bachelor's degree in Divinity, and in the same year he became president (or vice-master) of the college and primarily responsible for its affairs in the permanent absence of the master, Bishop Ridley. According to Bishop Wren he was by this time called upon to assist the vice-chancellor 'in judiciis', which suggests that the talent for practicality and the instinctive sense of legality which marked his episcopal career (and which posterity has so perversely overlooked) had already been noticed. There is evidence in Archbishop Parker's papers in Corpus Christi College of his involvement in the financial affairs of the university. But although Dean Hook gathered from Wren's statement that Grindal must at some point have studied law, such an episode cannot be reconciled with the known chronology of his career. As a bishop and a commissioner for causes ecclesiastical he was careful to take professional advice from the trained civilians on his staff.[5]

Grindal was to remain deeply attached to his college and much involved in its affairs. He retained the presidency throughout Edward's reign and in 1559, after the deprivation of the Marian master, the college offered to elect him as its head, in spite of his nomination to a bishopric. Apparently the fellows preferred the patronage of an absentee with court influence to the care of a resident master, and eventually they had their way. But it was not an arrangement to which Grindal was easily reconciled and he relinquished the mastership within three years. This was far from marking the end of his friendship, or of those good offices for which the fellows had angled. In the choice of the next three masters, Matthew Hutton, John Whitgift and John Young (two future archbishops and a bishop!), his seems to have been the decisive voice, and he proved a generous benefactor at his death.

Although he served as senior proctor in 1548–9, and as Lady Margaret preacher in 1550, Grindal did not proceed immediately to a higher degree and never held high university office. The progress of Edwin Sandys's career makes an instructive contrast. While Grindal was president of Pembroke Hall, Sandys was already master of St Catherine's Hall and a Doctor of Divinity. In 1552 he was vice-chancellor, a dignity not attained by Grindal, alone among the three Elizabethan archbishops of Canterbury. By that time Sandys had secured the extraneous means of support which traditionally sustained the higher reaches of academic life: a Buckinghamshire living and prebends at both Peterborough and Carlisle. His position was secure but peripheral, and in the normal course of events it would not necessarily or immediately have led to higher things. Grindal, on the other hand, was drawn away from the university midway along the academic *cursus honorum* and brought to London, and to Court. At the end of Edward VI's reign, when aged no more than thirty-four, he was already nominated for the bishopric of London. Such rapid advancement is not to be explained without reference to patronage, and there is no doubt who Grindal's patrons were: as we shall see, he was promoted by Bishop Ridley and Sir William Cecil. But whereas the uncovering of a patron will sometimes provide sufficient explanation in itself for a career, in dealing with someone as innocent of careerism as Grindal, and with patrons of the calibre of Ridley and Cecil, it can only increase our interest in the personal qualities of the man and the circumstances in which they first attracted attention. This leads us back to Pembroke Hall and to the progress of protestant doctrine in the university.

When Grindal's association with Pembroke began, the college already had a name for biblical learning of a more or less protestant tendency. In his famous farewell exhortation, written from Oxford in 1555, Nicholas Ridley included a characterization of the college:

> Thou wast ever named since I knew thee, which is now a thirty years ago, to be studious, well learned, and a great setter-forth of Christ's gospel, and of God's true word. So I found thee, and blessed be God! so I left thee indeed.

Ridley's words, which gloss over the cautious evolution of his own opinions over three decades, seem to refer to the notable lectures on the Epistles and Gospels, delivered in the 1520s by George Stafford, a fellow of Pembroke Hall since 1513 and university reader in divinity. It was Stafford's novel exegesis rather than the specific content of his discourse which aroused interest, for he strove to master the original sense of the text and to set forth St Paul 'in his native colours'. In this respect he was no more (and no less) of an innovator and heretic than John Colet in late-fifteenth-century Oxford. Yet in a loose sense Stafford must be reckoned among the very first of Cambridge protestants, earlier than Hugh Latimer who, before his conversion by Thomas Bilney to a fervently experiential but theologically somewhat inchoate piety, 'could in no case abide in those days good Master Stafford'. Later it would be a common saying, placed on record by Thomas Becon, that 'when Master Stafford read and Master Latimer preached, then was Cambridge blessed.' Stafford died of the plague in 1529, leaving a succession in Ridley, a fellow since 1524 and already a learned scholar in 'good letters' as well as in philosophy and theology, and with experience of the great continental universities of the Sorbonne and Louvain. As yet, and even after he became master in 1540, Ridley was not known as a reformer, but he would later recall that it was in Pembroke orchard that he learned 'without book' almost all the canonical Epistles, and that there were others in the college 'that did the like'. A contemporary, John Clerk, was among the younger dons chosen to stock Cardinal Wolsey's grandiose collegiate foundation at Oxford. John Foxe has it that after a heresy charge Clerk and his companions were incarcerated in the cellars of Cardinal College where they died, succumbing either to an exclusive diet of the salt fish stored there or to 'the filthy stench thereof', which would make this Pembroke man in a sense one of the first of the protestant martyrs.[6] John Rogers, the biblical translator and true 'protomartyr' of Mary's reign, was a student at Pembroke Hall in the time of Stafford and Clerk and proceeded B.A. in 1526.

Those who were fellows of the college in Grindal's time included Latimer's nephew by marriage, Thomas Sampson, a sour puritan critic of Grindal in the days of his elevation, and one of the most arresting figures in the history of the English Reformation, John Bradford, the army paymaster and lawyer turned scholar, to whose conversion at the inns of court Sampson contributed, perhaps by taking him to hear one of his uncle's electrifying sermons. This was in 1547, when Bradford was thirty-seven years of age. In the following year he went up to Cambridge and to St Catherine's Hall, took his Master's degree by a special grace, and in 1549 transferred to a fellowship at Pembroke Hall, to the disappointment of Sandys who had hoped to retain him in St Catherine's. His 'godly companion', Thomas Horton, became a fellow at the same time, and Sampson had gained his fellowship a year earlier. Not long afterwards both Bradford and Sampson were made deacons by Ridley, with rare deference shown to that puritan scrupulosity which Sampson would later visit on the Elizabethan Church.

Another militant puritan publicist of the future and a fellow from 1530 was William Turner, Ridley's pupil, Latimer's disciple, and later physician to the duke of Somerset. Like a sixteenth-century Charles Kingsley, Turner attacked popery and 'monkery' with the aggressive common sense of a naturalist, for Turner was the founder in England of scientific botanical studies.[7] Much of the knowledge which stocked his *Herbal* was acquired empirically, in the field, and from 1540, when he retired abroad in the face of Henry VIII's reactionary policies in religion, his observations took in much of the continent, from Venice through Switzerland to the Rhone, and north to Friesland. These journeys, in which the tradition of English natural history was born, had their starting-point in the Cambridge orchard where Ridley memorized St Paul and, as Turner tells us, joined his pupil in archery and tennis. Of the herb *myrrhis* Turner wrote: 'I never saw greater plenty of it than I have seen in the hortyard of Pembroke Hall in Cambridge, where I was some time a poor fellow.' Grindal, a lifelong valetudinarian, shared Turner's interest in botany, or at least in its practical application. He would later introduce to his gardens at Fulham the first specimens seen in England of tamarisk, a plant esteemed by physicians and common around Strasbourg and elsewhere in Germany.[8] In his description of English fishes communicated to the great Zürich naturalist Conrad Gesner and subsequently included in Gesner's *Historia animalium*, Turner noted that in Cumberland the little boys caught a small fish called a 'grundlin' under the stones on the sea-shore.[9] It is hard to resist the thought that Turner owed this information on the fish now known as a sea scorpion (and in Scotland as a 'snotchie') to that native of the Cumbrian coast, Edmund Grindal. Many of this generation of Pembroke men were northerners. Ridley, the third successive Northumbrian master, was a native of Tynedale, wilder country even than Grindal's Copeland. Turner too came from Northumberland and Bradford, who was born in the parish of Manchester, was to return to the north in the reign of Edward VI to preach extensively in Lancashire and Cheshire.

Needless to say, Pembroke Hall, a little company of less than fifty scholars and students all told, was not united in religion in the thirteen years of Grindal's residence. That it remained a divided house in 1559 appears from the letters of the fellows to Grindal inviting him to accept the mastership which were warm in their commendation of the late master, John Young, the leading conservative in the university and regius professor under Mary. Nor is it always possible to say where individuals stood with respect to controversial theological issues, particularly in the period of fluctuation and confusion in doctrine as officially sanctioned, in the later years of Henry VIII.

Up to 1535 the protestant cause depended upon wholly private initiatives. But in that year Bishop Fisher was replaced as chancellor by Thomas Cromwell, who as vice-gerent also exercised the visitatorial powers now vested in the Crown. Through Cromwell the university received a body of royal injunctions which J. Bass Mullinger described as 'the line that in university history divides the medieval from the modern age'. That was an extravagant judgment, but there can be no doubt that the injunctions of 1535 were more than half a sanction for the adoption of protestant doctrine. Degrees and lectures in canon law were abolished. Stafford's method of expounding the Bible 'according to the true sense' was officially endorsed and the scholastic commentaries, including Peter Lombard, the standard theological text of past ages, swept away. Daily lectures in Greek as well as Latin were instituted in every college, and undergraduates were encouraged in private Bible-reading. It would take more than this to convert the university, and when the Strasbourg reformer Martin Bucer arrived fourteen years later it seemed to him that a majority of its senior members were either 'most bitter papists' or 'profligate epicureans', an expression which presumably categorized 'neutrals' like Andrew Perne of Peterhouse, later as proverbial as the vicar of Bray for his many prompt responses to the winds of change.

Nevertheless, by 1547 the fundamental protestant assertion on the matter of man's standing before God was becoming distinctly less controversial. In Thomas Cranmer's 'Homily of Salvation', official doctrine within a year of Henry VIII's death, Luther's affirmation received one of its classic English expressions. The grace of God has no room for human justice, 'that is to say, the justice of our works, as to be merits of deserving our justification'. Consequently St Paul declares nothing necessary for justification but only 'a true and lively faith', which in itself is not a human achievement but a divine gift. Faith is far from excluding repentence, hope, love and fear, 'but it excludeth them from the office of justifying'. Good works are to be done 'afterwards' and 'necessarily', but not 'to this intent, to be made good by doing them'. Or as Richard Hooker would state the case forty years later: 'Christ hath merited righteousness for as many as are found in him. In him God findeth us, if we be faithful; for by faith we are incorporated into him.' In John Davenant's neat formula, good works are 'not the cause of our justification, but the appendage'. This, it can be assumed, was at the heart of Grindal's theology and the mainspring of his religious experience, as early as his opinions became significant. It is also clear from explicit pronouncements and implicit attitudes that he fully accepted the logical consequences of salvation by unmerited grace in the doctrines of election and predestination which, if by no means peculiar to John Calvin, became so indelibly associated with Geneva as to be tantamount to 'Calvinism' and its identifying feature. But these were convictions which came to Grindal in maturity. Unlike several of his contemporaries he was ordained under the old dispensation and in Elizabeth's reign he would express public regret for having said mass.[10]

By the time Grindal became president of his college, in 1549, the focal point of dissension was not so much the article of justification as the sacrament of the altar, and especially the question of the real presence, although to the theologically competent the connection between these two poles of controversy was sufficiently clear. It is true that in Cambridge in 1550 Martin Bucer's opponents chose to challenge him on the doctrine of salvation. But more indicative of the times were the elaborate disputations on the eucharist in which Grindal took part, both in Cambridge and later in London. On the occasion of the royal visitation of the university in June 1549 the subject for debate was: 'Whether transubstantiation could be proved by plain and manifest words of Scripture?' and 'Whether it might be collected and confirmed by the consent of Fathers for a thousand years after Christ?' In London two years later the subject for two days of private conference was: 'What the true and genuine sense of those words of Christ was: "This is my body"; and whether they were to be understood in the letter, or in the figure?'[11] This was indeed the sixty-four thousand dollar question of the age.

The eucharist in the sixteenth century served a function analogous to that of christology in the early Church. It was in relation to this doctrine that a man's 'religion' was defined, and on that basis that the major alignments within protestantism occurred. 'But perhaps ye think', wrote the Italian reformer, Peter Martyr, probably the most learned protestant writer on the subject, 'that the controversy about the eucharist is a certain small dissent: which is not so, seeing in it there is strife about the principal points of religion.'[12] Followers of Luther, Zwingli, Bucer, Martyr and Calvin all rejected the traditional doctrines of transubstantiation and the propitiatory sacrifice of the mass, but otherwise suffered from mutual incomprehension and suspicion of their respective intentions. As for the English reformers, the alignment of their eucharistic opinions and doctrines in relation to the major schools of continental thought involves problems of notorious delicacy which remain controversial.[13]

Taking the crudest view of the matter, there were only two positions with respect to the real presence: either to hold it, or to reject it. Luther understood the words 'Hoc est corpus meum' to mean what they said, so that if a single line were to be drawn it would find the Lutherans on one side with the Roman Church and those who adopted the Zwinglian doctrine on the other, with the South German reformer Bucer and later Calvin striving with limited success to straddle the divide. When Cranmer at his trial corrected Dr Thomas Martin and insisted that he had held in turn not three but two contrary doctrines of the sacrament, he may have had this basic distinction in mind. We know that no later than 1538 he had abandoned what he called 'the *opinion* of the transubstantiation', which implies that for him it was less than a doctrine, and it was perhaps only when he relinquished faith in the real presence itself that he was conscious of changing his 'religion'. This alteration can only be located in the period between 1546 and 1548, when by Cranmer's own testimony, reinforced and even dated by Sir John Cheke, Ridley 'drew him from his opinion', after Ridley had been prompted to review his position by reading a modern edition of the ninth-century treatise by Ratramn of Corbie, *De corpore et sanguine domini*. Cranmer's position before 1546 owed something to the theological method of Luther in that, like Luther, he took care to affirm the real presence in scriptural terms, and to eschew philosophical explanations. In this unspecific sense the late Henrician doctrinal formularies had affinities to Lutheranism.

The intellectual *renversement* which occurred for Ridley and Cranmer was not unconnected with the change of régime which followed the death of the old king, and involved a new appraisal both of continental theology and of the ancient christian texts which by common consent provided an authoritative commentary upon Scripture. The continental debate was now to invade England, with the arrival of some of the leading contenders, Bucer, Martyr and the Pole John à Lasco, to name only the most learned and articulate, but not including any ranking Lutheran theologian. The question of how far Cranmer can be said to have been converted at this juncture to the views of the Swiss theologians and to have impressed that doctrine on the English Prayer Book, in the recension of 1552, has often been awkwardly put. For the problem to be placed in perspective it has to be understood that the negative assertion of a 'real absence' of the body of Christ from the eucharist, which some Anglican apologists of the nineteenth century supposed to be of the essence of 'Zwinglianism', which is inadequate as an account of Zwingli's own sacramental outlook, in no way corresponds to what reformed theologians were saying by the mid-sixteenth century. Indeed it fails to do justice to the considerable resources of Zwingli's own sacramental theology. Differences of emphasis persisted and, as between Bucer on one side and some of the 'Zürichers' on the other, could still be made to seem fundamental. But by 1549, the year of the *Consensus Tigurinus* uniting the Swiss churches, there were encouraging signs of a convergence on what has been identified as 'the true gravitational centre of the Reformation',[14] what Dr Peter Brooks, following Cranmer himself, has chosen to call the 'true presence' doctrine.

When Christ said, 'This is my body,' he did so 'in a figurative speech', and to speak of eating his body and drinking his blood was to use the language of symbolism, signifying the exercise of a true faith. Far from being locally confined to the sacrament, such feeding upon Christ was possible at any time. But by feeding corporally on the sacramental bread, 'spiritual feeding is increased.' At the communion, eating occurs at two levels: 'The earthly is eaten with our mouths and carnally feedeth our bodies; the heavenly is eaten with our inward man and spiritually feedeth the same.' Consequently, 'Almighty God worketh effectually with his sacraments', kindling faith by the power of the Holy Spirit, although it could neither be said that Christ was in the sacrament in the sense of a real and bodily presence, nor that grace was conferred by virtue of the sacrament. The bodily presence of Christ in Heaven, at God's right hand, no more precluded his power to sustain his people as they participated in the sacrament than the distance of the sun could prevent the warmth of its rays from penetrating our bodies. But the emphasis was less on asserting the presence of Christ on the altar or in the action than on rising to the heavenly places by faith, there to contemplate and feed upon him. As Paul had advised the Colossians, seek those things that are above, not things which are on the earth. Although Cranmer, unlike so many of his English co-religionists, remained distant and unfriendly towards Zürich, his understanding of these matters cannot be easily distinguished from the mature Swiss doctrine, represented, for example, by Peter Martyr in his later years.

Grindal's account of the conversion of his own mind on this question, although brief, provides evidence as precise as any that we have for the crucial theological reorientation which occurred for so many, and in a sense for the whole Church as a public body, with the reign of Edward VI. Writing in February 1567 to the leading pastor of Zürich and Zwingli's son-in-law, Heinrich Bullinger, whom he had never met, Grindal acknowledged that it was Bullinger's early tract *De origine erroris* (a work rich in patristic citations) which about twenty years before had led him to embrace a true opinion concerning the Lord's supper, whereas before that time he was given to the Lutheran opinion.[15] This letter had the happy effect of prompting the author to send a copy of the latest edition of this work, published in Zürich in 1568. The book survives, inscribed by Grindal: 'Ex dono authoris, 1568. Edm. London'.[16] Grindal's indebtedness to Zürich provides a gloss on his recorded utterances concerning the eucharist. The most substantial of these was the only work of controversial divinity to which he ever publicly committed himself, 'A fruitful dialogue between Custom and Verity declaring these words of Christ, "This is my Body"', written shortly after his return from exile in 1559 and included by John Foxe in his *Acts and Monuments*.[17]

Since Grindal was concerned on this and other occasions to demolish the Roman doctrine it is not easy to assess the positive side of what was for him, after about 1547, the 'True opinion'. But one observes a marked emphasis on the local presence of Christ's body in heaven, 'wherefore they are far deceived which, leaving Heaven, will grope for Christ's body upon the earth'; a clear explanation of the difference between bodily and spiritual feeding, 'for as ye receive sustenance for your body by your bodily mouth, so the food of your soul must be received by faith, which is the mouth of the soul'; and the insistence that to receive the body of Christ 'with the instrument of faith appointed thereunto' meant not to pluck Christ down from Heaven 'and put him in your faith, as in a visible place', but with faith to 'rise and spring up to him, and, leaving this world, dwell above in heaven'. Such 'heavenly' language matches the twenty-ninth of the Forty-Two Articles of Religion of 1552, and if this was Grindal's consistent position from 1547 it places him to the left of centre in the sophisticated niceties of the eucharistic debate. At the time when Archbishop Parker followed the lead of Bishop Guest in moderating the wording of this article as it appeared in the revised Thirty-Nine Articles of 1562, Grindal is reported to have represented in his sermons the Zwinglian wing of the episcopate.[18]

But Grindal brought no rancour into theological debate, not even in respect of this most divisive of topics which engaged his liveliest interest. In 1561 he would have occasion to write to the Lutheran magistrates of Frankfurt and to comment on the differences between those of their religion and other protestants. Would that the matter had rested where it had been left at the Colloquy of Marburg in 1529 when it had been agreed that each side should cultivate peace until the Lord should reveal otherwise to each! Two years later he would entertain under his roof a distinguished German Lutheran, express the keenest pleasure in his company, and spend the evening in good-natured discussion of their theological differences: 'We were contented one to hear another's reasons, and each to suffer the other to abound in his own sense.' But Grindal remained a firmly committed adherent of one side. In 1565, as a much harassed and overworked bishop, he studied a book written against the Lutheran Brentz by Theodore Beza of Geneva as soon as it appeared and wrote to congratulate the author.[19]

We have dwelt on this matter at some length, with the purpose of defining Grindal's 'religion' according to the principal shibboleth of the time. But since no one will pretend that Grindal was a theologian of any stature, or that he had original arguments to offer in the eucharistic debate, it was the manner rather than the matter of his contribution which was significant for his reputation and his career. As a disputant Grindal showed himself to be schooled in the Fathers, although many of the places which he cited were already well-worn weapons in the controversies of the time, and were handled in a manner which was more polemical than scholarly, in any modern sense. His method of argumentation was donnish and conservative, even in the 'fruitful dialogue' which was presumably intended for popular consumption. But his performance in debate was frugal of words and entirely lacking in the dialectical conventions of verbal violence. This quality of reserve is very familiar to a modern student of Grindal's correspondence, but it may well have been in disputation that it was first noticed by his future patrons, together with his erudition and transparent sincerity. Of all the intellectual and moral attributes these were the most admired by the generation in which the Reformation came to its maturity: reserve, self-restraint, even a certain reticence (except in the pulpit!) — the marks of a 'grave and reverend divine'.

The Cambridge disputation of June 1549 was an 'extraordinary act', laid on for the benefit of the king's visitors, and these included those young government servants and intellectual pace-setters of the Cambridge of their day, Sir Thomas Smith and Sir John Cheke, as well as Bishop Ridley, whose formal determination concluded the three-day 'exercise'. Ridley must already have known Grindal intimately, but his decision to employ him in the diocese of London may have been influenced by what he saw of his potentialities on this occasion. The private conferences on the eucharist held in London two years later once more served to expose Grindal to the appraisal of men who counted. The first of these was held in the house of William Cecil, and Cecil was to become both a close friend and the principal source of all Grindal's high preferments.[20]

3

BUCER AND RIDLEY:
THE EDWARDIAN STANDARD

THE brief reign of Edward VI is the Jekyll and Hyde of English history. Through one set of eyes we are shown a commendable if shaky experiment in what may be called without irony protestant government. Through other eyes we see only bad government. The Protector Somerset is for Professor Jordan 'one of the true architects of the modern world'. Professor Elton finds him 'disastrously incompetent in politics ... the creator of nothing that endured, the architect only of his own ruin.'[1] Modern studies will not allow us to resolve the contradictions of the age by casting 'the good duke' as the beneficent Jekyll, the duke of Northumberland as the malevolent Hyde. While Somerset's image has suffered damage, a case has been made for Northumberland as less monstrous, more competent and less dictatorial than the traditional stereotype.[2] 'He understood the requirements of the successful governor' and headed 'a genuine reform administration, the first since Cromwell's fall and the first to follow up the initiatives started by Cromwell'.[3] We have been reminded that it was in the infrastructure of this government that some of the most accomplished and disinterested public servants of the century served their apprenticeships: William Cecil, Thomas Smith, Nicholas Bacon, Walter Mildmay — and Matthew Parker and Edmund Grindal, all Edwardians before they were Elizabethans.[4]

As our appreciation of its affairs gains in depth and complexity it becomes all the more necessary to recognize that moral verdicts on this reign are to be made, if at all, at the two extremes, not in the middle. The unusual political circumstances offered to intellectuals and idealists elusive opportunities to influence the quality of government in the direction of protestant paternalism; but simultaneously provided for self-interested politicians solid encouragement to make a mockery of the notions of reformation and commonwealth by their pillage of church property. 'I pray you,' ran a pamphlet of 1548, 'who in these days are such oppressors, such graziers, such shepherds, such enhancers of rents, such takers of incomes, as are those which profess the Gospel?'[5] 'Economic individualism' coexisted with a constructive concern for the well-

47

being of society which transcended the more casual charitable
impulse of the past, and both were in some measure the product
of the protestant ethic. Or so it appeared to R. H. Tawney, who
placed the contradiction at the heart of his famous lectures on
Religion and the Rise of Capitalism.[6]

It is sometimes said that the English Prayer Book was Edward
VI's only enduring monument. But liturgical reform displayed
only one facet of an Edwardian interest in the renovation of the
commonwealth which embraced such matters as law reform, the
public relief of poverty and disease, and the more adequate provision of schools. The modern observer may even risk the semi-
anachronism of crediting Edward's Council with an enlightened
immigration policy. In some fields the groundwork was laid for
more famous Elizabethan achievements. In others, the Edwardian
promise remained unfulfilled, for the mystique of the Elizabethan
Age conceals the barren conservatism of government under the last
of the Tudors.[7]

'My lord,' Thomas Sampson would tell Lord Burghley in mid-
Elizabethan times, 'this matter of reforming the state of the
government of the Church was in hand in the days of King Edward.' For Sampson it was self-evident that 'all states and sorts of
persons in England are now more corrupt than they were then,'
while Bishop Richard Cox, once the young king's tutor and almoner, looked back on the reign of Edward as an age of gold, beside
which the Marian years were an age of iron, Elizabeth's an age of
brass.[8] If there were wicked men in high places their wickedness
was apparent and, like the evil of some Old Testament characters,
an incentive to prophecy. For as long as the greatest preachers of
the century, Latimer, Hooper, Lever and Knox, denounced social
and political sins as well as spiritual and moral decay it was possible
to believe that the mere force of utterance might yet amend the
commonwealth. What we know as Elizabethan puritanism represents the carrying on of this prophetic tradition in the face of a
government not so much hostile as indifferent to its values, evasive
and hence more frustrating.

Grindal was one who looked back to the reign of Edward with
approval and nostalgia. As bishop of London he would rebuke a
group of schismatics for behaviour which condemned 'the whole
state of the Church reformed in King Edward's days, which was
well reformed according to the word of God', and which slighted
the memory of the many good men who had shed their blood for
it.[9] Martyrdom made all the difference. Those who had survived
could only compare themselves with the ashes of Cranmer and
Ridley to their own shame. As an Elizabethan bishop Grindal was

not so much progressive as retrospective. Bliss had it been in that dawn to be alive.

I Bucer

Among the reformers of Edwardian England there was one voice so insistent and compelling that its owner might dispute with Latimer the right to be called the conscience of the age, although he was a foreigner who spoke no English and lived for less than two years in the country, much of that time in academic seclusion. This was Martin Bucer, the reformer of Strasbourg, honoured by his friend and colleague Peter Martyr Vermigli as 'the most excellent divine of our age'.[10] 'This profound and famous clerk', as he was called by an English visitor to Strasbourg, was brought over by Cranmer in 1549 and set up in Cambridge in the regius chair of divinity. His colleague Paul Fagius, the noted Hebraist, accompanied him, but according to the master of St John's, James Pilkington, Fagius 'never read, he never disputed, he never preached, he never taught', before his premature demise.[11]

It was far otherwise with Bucer who lost no time in diagnosing and exposing the inadequacies of a reformation imposed by edict on a largely indifferent and uninstructed nation. 'It is fallow ground here, such as the devastation of Antichrist is wont to leave.' There was too little preaching and no ecclesiastical discipline worthy of the name. According to Thomas Horton, a fellow of Pembroke Hall and the friend of Bradford, the German professor cried 'incessantly' in lectures and sermons against the perennial failings of academic life, 'even *ad nauseam*'. Students of Bucer's writings will take the point. No protestant reformer was more prolix. But the ceaseless and sometimes turgid flow of words was charged with a moral as well as an intellectual urgency which profoundly impressed those who shared Bucer's company and came under his personal spell. Even a brief encounter was not likely to be forgotten. On a visit to Oxford in the summer of 1550 Bucer preached a sermon in Christ Church which one of his hearers was able to give some account of more than twenty years later. There is no reason to doubt that the celebrated lectures on Ephesians, delivered in Cambridge in the same year, had a more than passing effect on their hearers, who must have included Grindal, especially where the text allowed scope for exposition of the proper functions and behaviour of ministers of the Gospel.

But like Peter Martyr, who held the corresponding chair at Oxford,[12] Bucer found the university at large resistant to his

doctrine. In Strasbourg the reformers had countered the reluctance of the magistrates to provide for the effective pastoral care
of church members by the formation of select christian societies
whose members were willing to submit themselves to a voluntary
religious discipline over and above those standards which the state
was willing to enforce. Now in Cambridge he reassembled the
model household which had been an object of admiration in
Strasbourg, and it was no doubt in this environment that he met
with those whom Sampson later identified as his 'familiars': Grindal, Parker, Sandys, Bradford 'and such like'. James Pilkington,
later to become the most puritanical of all Elizabethan bishops,
similarly speaks of his 'familiarity and acquaintance' with Bucer.[13]
Many of these friends were Pembroke men, so it is appropriate that
one of the two manuscript copies of Bucer's great book *De regno
Christi* which was prepared under the author's personal super-
vision now reposes in Pembroke Library.[14] Nicholas Carr, fellow
of the college and a distinguished professor of Greek, was to write a
moving account of Bucer's last days and deathbed speeches,[15]
although after reverting to catholicism under Mary he would later
give testimony at Bucer's posthumous trial for heresy. Bradford,
Sampson, Horton and Grindal can perhaps be called disciples.
According to Foxe it was by Bucer's persuasion that Bradford
submitted to ordination and became a preacher. 'Right familiar
and dear unto him', as Sampson puts it, Bradford went with the
master on his summer jaunt to Oxford, comforted him in his final
illness, studied his writings in prison, and in the 'Farewell to
Cambridge' cried: 'Remember the readings and preachings of
God's prophet and true preacher, Martin Bucer!'

Grindal's name is absent from the list of seventy-seven Englishmen whose Latin and Greek verses and epigrams adorned
Bucer's memorial volume.[16] Intimacy did not come easily to him
and neither his character nor his education bore much trace of the
'humanism' which nourished a certain effusive style of friendship
and found expression in polished literary exercises of this kind.
But it is significant that when Bucer's position in the university
seemed to be threatened he made Grindal his intermediary in
reporting the circumstances to Ridley, addressing him as 'doc-
tissime et carissime Grindalle'.[17] At the reformer's funeral Grindal
as a pall-bearer was less prominent than Matthew Parker, who
preached the sermon, and whom Bucer had appointed as one of his
executors. But Bucer addressed Parker as 'clarissimus', not 'ca-
rissimus'. Their relationship was one of esteemed colleagues and it
does not seem to have been theologically grounded. The Marian
years, which Parker spent in England, loosened even sentimental

ties with continental protestantism. As archbishop of Canterbury
it was the antiquity of the British Church, not the contemporary
example of sister churches, which inspired him.[18] But Grindal
spent Mary's reign in Bucer's own city of Strasbourg, where he
came to know the reformer's faithful secretary, Conrad Hubert.
On his return he would make it his business to despatch to Hubert
such of Bucer's literary remains as had survived in England, many
of them in Parker's possession. He would also 'cause to be carefully
drawn up' an account of the macabre ceremonies of February
1557, when the bones of Bucer and Fagius were exhumed, chained
in Cambridge market place, and burned, after a formal process for
heresy: but not before yet another ceremony in Great St Mary's
had reinstated whatever was left of Bucer's mortal remains and
reconsecrated his memory.[19] Although the hard-pressed Elizabethan bishop was content to leave the German editor to decipher
Bucer's ferociously difficult handwriting, it was appropriate that
when the great tome called *Scripta Anglicana* at last appeared from
a Basle press in 1577 the whole collection was dedicated to Grindal. By then he personified the memory of Bucer in England, and it
was in the Church of England, more than in Lutheran Strasbourg,
that religious policy promised to continue along some of the lines
which Bucer had laid down.

'As Master Bucer used to say' was a phrase which readily fell
from Grindal's pen, and in correspondence with Hubert he speaks
of 'the memory of our common instructor'. When Strasbourg
diverged from his doctrine in the direction of a more orthodox
Lutheranism Grindal expressed surprise and distress. 'But do you,
most learned Conrad, persevere in defending the fame of Bucer
and in maintaining the truth.'[20] Grindal's own perseverance can be
demonstrated in detail, for there are many Bucerian touches in his
administrative conduct. Indeed, the application of Bucer's distinctive teachings is reflected in his episcopal activity as a whole.

If Bucer deserves to be remembered at all it is as the reformer
who drew upon the common resources of early protestant teaching
to lay the foundations for a reformed political and social policy, a
protestant polity, inspired by a distinctive vision of the christian
society as community, the most perfect of all communities, knit
together in love and common obedience to the kingship of Christ.
God had predestined and chosen every member and had given to
each his part in the consolidation of the whole body.[21] Whatever
their callings, men should live not for themselves but for others:
such was the very title of one of Bucer's earliest publications.
Among other vocations those of minister of the Church and magistrate were of particular importance in achieving the integration of

the entire Church and commonwealth. Somewhere near the centre of these convictions stood Bucer's high evaluation of the sacraments, of the Lord's supper and of baptism, to which he joined a reformed rite of confirmation. Worship was more than a mystical and 'spiritual' contemplation of truths felt to be remote. The body of Christ was to be received in real and faithful participation in his body.

Bucer's ecclesiology consisted of much more than a collection of theological principles. These were practical measures by which he had guided the reformation of one great city and had advised on the conduct of church affairs in many others, including Cologne, the Rome of Germany. To his contemporaries he appeared less as a theologian, in the modern sense of an academic specialist, than as a type of the godly and 'primitive' bishop. In 1543 Peter Martyr had written from Bucer's house to his friends in Lucca, where he himself had exercised a kind of episcopal leadership: 'Behold, well-beloved brethren, in our age, bishops upon the earth, or rather in the Church of Christ, which be truly holy. This is the office of a pastor, this is that bishop-like dignity described by Paul in the Epistles unto Timothy and Titus. It delighteth me much to read this kind of description in those epistles, but it pleaseth me a great deal more to see with the eyes the patterns themselves.'[22]

In Strasbourg, as *de facto* bishop, Bucer worked out, practically and painfully, and over a period of twenty-five years, the civic model of a disciplined and socially responsible christian community: only to see events (the victory of the emperor over the protestant princes) wipe out an achievement already blunted by contrary political pressures within the city itself. While Calvin's Geneva superseded Strasbourg as a model 'school of Christ', Bucer turned his experience to account in a work of applied theology called *De regno Christi*, 'The Kingdom of Christ', more of a compilation than a book and written as a New Year's gift for Edward VI. This has been called his final word, summing up all his life work for the advancement of the Reformation.[23] Although other sixteenth-century writers found more elegant ways of describing christian society as it ought to be, Bucer's badly flawed masterpiece has not deserved the almost total neglect which it has suffered in its country of origin.

Bucer's theology has been called 'typically urban' – even 'bourgeois'. It was impressed with the civic humanism of South-West Germany and it stressed those aspects of the christian life which were most commensurate with the *societas christiana* of the city state.[24] We have been asked to believe that it was, at least to an extent, a theology sociologically conditioned and distinguished from Lutheranism not only dogmatically but by the strong ties which linked it with the civic notion of *publica utilitas*. That the English reformers looked increasingly for guidance to the cities of 'High Germany' and Switzerland, and decreasingly to Lutheranism and the princely territories which supported it, may tell us something about the affinity which existed between protestantism and the more socially advanced and progressive sections of English society. But most of England in the mid-sixteenth century was anything but advanced, if social and cultural comparisons are to be made with the German imperial and Swiss cities. So there remains some incongruity in the spectacle of Tudor bishops modelling their conduct on the example of the great Central European *entrepôts*.

Certainly Grindal, who came from the wilds of Cumberland and had received an old-fashioned education, belonged to a different world of thought and experience. He was not and could not be another Martin Bucer and it may not even be appropriate to call him a Bucerian. Nevertheless his pastoral understanding and activity seem to have had Bucer for their conscious model.

The pastoral ministry was for Bucer a matter of extreme importance, a theme to which his preaching and writings constantly returned, but one which he handled pragmatically rather than as a purely dogmatic topic. Bishops and other ministers of the Church should be effective in teaching and discipline, free from secular distractions. Bishops should conduct annual visitations and their government should be conducted not autocratically but with the assistance and counsel of fellow ministers. Superintendents ought to be appointed under episcopal authority to take care of small and manageable groups of parishes, and the pastors themselves should be men capable of exercising the ministry of the word and fit to safeguard the integrity of the sacraments. This was how Bucer adapted what he read in the documents of early Christianity to the conditions of the Church in a German city and its dependent countryside and to the Christian empire. In England there are echoes of these principles in the code of reformed church law drawn up in 1552, *Reformatio legum ecclesiasticarum*. But as in Edward's reign, so later under Elizabeth: no attempt was sanctioned from on high to bring ecclesiastical organization and government into line with the new theological premisses, or even with rational practicality. The implementation of Bucer's pastoral vision required administrative and financial reconstruction beyond anything which was politically feasible in Tudor England. But in so far as it was possible to apply Bucer's doctrine and example to the traditional system of diocesan government it will appear that Grindal made the attempt. In particular we shall see that he made what allowance he could for the participation of those ministers who in England were deemed 'inferior clergy', and that while not reluctant to enforce his episcopal authority he was incapable of lordly and arrogant behaviour towards those he regarded as brethren.[25]

As we should expect of a reformer who was thoroughly at home in a civic environment, and whose sense of the *corpus christianum* embraced Church and State in equal and strictly reciprocal proportions, Bucer's insistence on the necessity of church discipline did not exclude a positive evaluation of christian magistracy. Rather he trod a judicious middle way between Erastianism of the English type and the clerical theocracy which was to reappear in the subsequent evolution of the Calvinist churches. Ministers must submit to lawful magistrates, but conversely the earthly kingdom with all its members must defer to the overriding rule of Christ. As Sampson later explained to Burghley: 'He that concludes that to have the Church governed by meet pastors and ministers taketh away the authority of christian magistrates is by Bucer sufficiently confuted.'[26] That Grindal's understanding of this vexed question resembled that of Bucer appears in almost every line of his celebrated letter to the queen.

The greatest of all the problems confronting Grindal's biographer is to place him in the right relation to Elizabethan puritanism, and here too Martin Bucer provides the key. Much of his teaching was an anticipation of what would later be called puritanism: the prominence in his theology of the doctrine of election, his exalted conception of the ministry, his sense of reformation as an ongoing process of ceaseless edification, his concern with abuses, the high moral tone of his utterances. In all of these respects Grindal, too, was a puritan. Yet Bucer was markedly unsympathetic to those characteristics of puritanism which attracted the pejorative adjective 'precise'. The mark of a 'precisian' was an extreme scrupulosity with respect to ceremonial vestiges of catholicism, as well as to the inherited structures and institutions of ecclesiastical government. In the eyes of non-puritans such scruples amounted to a narrow and 'Jewish' legalism. Just as Bucer did not equate reformation with the mere destruction of the past, so he could not regard it as the part of a truly godly conscience to set such store by external symbols which were of themselves *adiaphora*, things indifferent. If the superstitious veneration of such things could impede the evangelical ministry, so might the errors of a conscience excessively preoccupied with its own rectitude. The pastoral motive was paramount.

The first damaging case of puritan scruples within the reformed English Church arose in 1550, when the acknowledged leader of the protestant ultras of the time, John Hooper, was appointed bishop of Gloucester, but declined to undergo consecration unless he might be excused the use of the vestments specified in the Ordinal. The exchanges which followed between the man whom some believed to be 'the future Zwingli of England' and Grindal's master, Bishop Ridley, covered ground disputed between the royal government of the Church and the christian conscience, bound by scripture. On the resolution of these matters the ultimate destination of the English Reformation depended.[27] Several reformed theologians of international repute offered advice, Bucer included. Bucer was not prepared to support a pastor whose principles had landed him in the Fleet Prison rather than in the neglected diocese where his talents were so much needed. He held no brief for ceremonial vestments and hoped to see them abolished, but they were not high in the order of *delenda*. What offended were not so much 'the marks and signs' as 'the nerves and joints of Antichristianism'. Bucer was never a one-sided controversialist, and in the renewed agitation over vestments in the early Elizabethan Church[28] each side could and did quote from his writings to its own advantage. But to put the matter into the perspective in which Bucer saw it, it is sufficient to turn to his letter to Hooper: 'This controversy afflicts me exceedingly, since it places such an impediment in the way of the ministry of yourself and others.'[29]

We shall find that Grindal's scale of priorities matched that of Bucer exactly. Where there were valid pastoral reasons for non-conformity, and for the toleration of it, he was indulgent. But where a rigid puritan scrupulosity seemed to threaten both the progress of the Gospel and the unity of the Church the puritans had no more resolute opponent. This may explain what might otherwise appear strange: that this 'puritan' bishop sometimes had harsher things to say about puritanism than his less sympathetic colleagues whose only concern was to secure an outward, administrative obedience and conformity.

Having said all this we have not exhausted the influential elements in Bucer's practical theology. The comments on the English scene of this most public-spirited of reformers were not confined to the religious sphere in any restrictive sense, and no concession was made to a governing class which, as he complained, 'would reduce the whole of the sacred ministry into a narrow compass, and who are altogether unconcerned about the restoration of church discipline'. *De regno Christi* has been interpreted by some as a protestant *Utopia*, for it displays a concern with such diverse matters of public policy as marriage and divorce (a disproportionate 33 out of 76 chapters), enclosures, poor relief and law reform, as well as more strictly ecclesiastical matters. To Professor Rupp it appears significant that Bucer, like another reformer whom no one could accuse of narrowness, Thomas Muntzer, had studied Plato's *Republic*.[30] No doubt, like other more recent prophets of a socially orientated Christianity, Bucer suffered from a lack of local and technical knowledge of the great range of topics which came within his scope, and what Canon Smyth called his 'mine of curious suggestions' has not attracted much attention from social historians. But no amount of donnish conceit could blunt the edge of this principle, which R.H. Tawney himself was glad to employ as a motto: 'Neither the Church of Christ, nor a christian commonwealth, ought to tolerate such as prefer private gain to the public weal, or seek it to the hurt of their neighbours.'

Among the books which Grindal bequeathed to the Queen's College Oxford was his own copy of the first edition of *De regno Christi*, published in Basle in 1557 and perhaps acquired in the later years of his Strasbourg exile. Grindal rarely annotated his books and it is significant that he made extensive use of his pen in studying one and only one chapter of Bucer's testament: the twelfth chapter of the second book on the restoration in their primitive fullness of the ministries of the Church. In particular the passages which concern the functions of a bishop are underlined and their sense tersely noted in the margin in Grindal's distinctive hand: 'Episcopi debent uti consilio presbyterorum' ('bishops should make use of the counsel of other ministers'), and again, 'Presbyteri consultores episcopi'; and 'Visitatio est inspectio doctrinae, disciplinae'. The paragraph is prominently marked in which Bucer lists those places in the Roman Civil Law and in the Fathers which were most relevant to episcopal conduct: 'Loci legendi de munere episcopale'. There can be little doubt that these notes were made in 1559, as Grindal prepared to enter into the role defined for him by his preceptor, Bucer, and standing behind Bucer, the ancient Fathers of the Christian Church.

II Ridley

IN the early months of 1550 Bucer enjoyed a period of strenuous activity between bouts of illness. It must have been very shortly after this that Grindal left Cambridge, and he was certainly in London by August of that year, a month or two before a young student called John Whitgift matriculated at Pembroke Hall and secured as his tutor Bucer's bosom friend, John Bradford. Grindal went to London at Ridley's appointment, but in a sense at Bucer's command, for if anything had been said *ad nauseam* in recent months it was that the universities, properly developed as seminaries, held the key to reformation, and that scholars whose studies were complete should give place to others and devote their talents to the active service of the Church. Not that Grindal severed his connections with Cambridge. He remained president of Pembroke and involved in the management of university affairs.[31]

In 1545 Henry Brinklow had complained: 'What a plague is this, that in no man's time alive was ever any christian bishop reigning over the city of London, but every one worse than other.'[32] Five years later, too late for Brinklow to see it, London had its first protestant bishop in Nicholas Ridley, who was installed in April 1550. Ridley's approach to the reform of his diocese was vigorous and decisive. His primary visitation, in which he was personally active, was concerned with suppression of lingering traces of the mass in the ceremonies and gestures with which some of the clergy celebrated the 1549 service, and with the destruction of altars. But, like Bucer, Ridley did not expect reformation to come from the suppression of the old religion alone but from the proper deployment of reliable and learned preachers. He now brought into his diocese three of his own collegians chosen, not, as a cynic might suppose, for old time's sake, but for their fitness 'both with life and learning to set forth God's word in London and in the whole diocese of the same'. The three were probably selected as much for their dependability as for their zeal, if, as seems likely, their appointment was in part a response to the unauthorized, charismatic leadership already exercised in London by the most radical of the leading reformers, John Hooper.

Ridley's general staff, if we may so describe it, was headed by Grindal, 'a man known to be both of virtue, honesty, discretion, wisdom and learning'. The other members were Bradford, 'a man by whom (as I am assuredly informed) God hath and doth work wonders, in setting forth of his word', and John Rogers, who lost little time in launching a vigorous campaign of preaching and writing against both papists and 'anabaptist' sectaries in Essex. In July 1551 Ridley wrote that he had appointed these preachers 'to be with me', but fourteen months later he reported that they were 'men known to be so necessary to be abroad in the commonwealth that I can keep none of them with me in my house'.[33] Although Ridley was a most monarchical bishop, supreme and often authoritarian in the conduct of his diocese, he was not distant in his relations with these three. With Bradford it was 'dear brother' and 'well beloved in Christ', with Grindal 'dearly beloved brother Grindal'. When Grindal evaded the Marian persecution Ridley would be content 'to make up the trinity out of Paul's church' to suffer the flames with Rogers and Bradford, so placing himself on a level with his lieutenants.[34]

William Turner, in a communication to John Foxe, later accorded Grindal the precious and significant title of Ridley's 'fidus Achates'. The classical reference, to the companion of Aeneas, implies an inseparable and intimate friend rather than a subordinate. There is only room for one Achates in a man's life. But with Ridley, as perhaps with others, Grindal seems to have aroused more warmth and demonstrative affection than he was able to give in return. To abandon a correct and formal mode of address, even to his dearest friends, was more than he could manage. In the only one of his letters to Ridley which survives, written from Frankfurt to the Bocardo prison in Oxford, it was 'Sir', and the communication of public news, necessary business and spiritual encouragement in phrases of depressing conventionality. Ridley's frustration is apparent in the reply to 'dearly beloved brother Grindal', 'o charissime in Christo frater et dilectissime Grindalle':

> I ensure you that it warmed my heart to hear you by chance to name some, as Scory and Cox etc. Oh that it had come in your mind to have said somewhat also of Cheke, of Turner, of Lever, of Sampson, of Chambers ...

The letter ended on a note of singular poignancy. Ridley apologized for his prolixity, 'for after this I believe you will never again be troubled, my dearest brother, with letters of mine'.[35] Letters from as far away as the sixteenth century are often impenetrable or deceptive as sources for our understanding of human character. If we could cross the divide of the centuries and hear for ourselves Grindal's economical, northern speech we might hope to pick up the fine shades of a relationship frozen for us in the classical model of Aeneas and Achates.

We return to the happier days of Edward. At first, Ridley's 'trinity' had no other support than their patron was able to provide. But the bishop of London was entitled to collate to all the dignities within his cathedral church with the exception of the deanery.[36] The prebends of the thirty major canons were most unequally valued, all but six being worth less than £20 a year, while the remainder were handsome livings, comparable with at least the middle range of parochial benefices.[37] The customs of the chapter, based upon the financial interests of the residentiaries themselves, discouraged the residence of more than three or four 'stagiaries' at a time. Consequently the revenues of St Paul's could be made to finance the reform of the diocese. In 1550 the dean, William May, was a staunch protestant but the canons were a legacy of Ridley's conservative predecessors, including figures from the remote past like the historian Polydore Vergil, resolute papists such as Gilbert Bourne and other chaplains and relatives of the recently displaced bishop, Edmund Bonner. According to Ridley, 'they could never brook me well, nor could I never delight in them'.[38] As luck would have it, three of the better prebends fell vacant in 1551, the devastating epidemic of sweating sickness of that summer perhaps assisting, and with them the precentorship, worth £46. In August of that year the 'trinity' was installed, together with the fourth of Ridley's Pembroke chaplains, Edmund West, a man never linked with the other three and who would recant under Mary and die, according to Miles Coverdale, 'for sorrow'.[39] But before these appointments were consummated Grindal gained an instructive glimpse of the other face of Edwardian England.

Ridley was not alone in having an eye on the rich pickings at St Paul's. There were others who saw the prebend of Kentish Town, worth more than £34 in the king's books, as a suitable living for the clerk of the Privy Council, and these included the clerk himself, the learned, Italianate and by no means insignificant William Thomas.[40] In June 1550 the Council had granted Thomas what was called the king's interest in the prebend, in effect a reversion of the office, placed at the disposal of the Council by the incumbent, William Layton. Ridley might condemn this as 'an ungodly enterprise' but such manoeuvres were commonplace and it may be that a bishop's right of collation to the wealthier livings in his gift was no more than nominal. Ridley resisted, but the Council gave him a rough ride and extracted a promise not to bestow the prebend without due notification. As soon as Layton was dead there came an order not to collate, while Thomas, for some reason despairing of his own success, obtained a letter informing the bishop that the king's majesty had reserved it for some secular use connected with the royal household. Ridley reacted forcefully. As he told Sir John Cheke in a passionate letter: 'I would with all mine heart give it unto Mr Grindal, and so I should have him continually with me, and in my diocese, to preach.' The outcome was a rare victory for the integrity of the Church and its possessions. The precentorship now fell vacant, and Ridley succeeded in promoting Grindal to this even more desirable dignity. This left the prebend of Kentish Town for Bradford and two other prebends, St Pancras, worth £28. 16s., and Mora, worth almost £20, for Rogers and West. All four were admitted to the chapter on the same day, 24 August 1551, a St Bartholomew's Day which deserves to be remembered as a minor landmark in the history of the English Reformation. But at the time any rejoicing on Grindal's part must have been held in check by alarm at the 'extreme plague of sudden death' which had visited London in July. So severe was the outbreak of sweating sickness that according to the Venetian ambassador all ordinary business ceased: 'nothing attended to but the preservation of life'.[41]

With the return of normality Rogers preached the divinity lecture in the cathedral and Bradford preached almost everywhere. No trace of Grindal's movements over the next eighteen months has survived, but Ridley's letters suggest that he served as a preacher in many parts of the diocese. His rhetorical talents were not those of a Bradford, and Ridley may have had in mind his rather different qualities when, in the *Piteous lamentation*, he spoke of Latimer, Lever, Bradford and Knox as preachers whose tongues were sharp, and then mentioned other 'very godly men and well learned, that went about by the wholesome plasters of God's word, howbeit after a more soft manner of handling the matter'.[42]

Be that as it may, in mid-December 1551 Grindal was one of six preachers appointed 'chaplains ordinary' to the king, as part of a scheme to increase the official patronage of itinerant preaching, one of the most distinctive of Edwardian experiments. As the young monarch himself noted, 'it was appointed' that of the six, two were to remain at any one time in attendance, while the other four were to be 'always absent in preaching' in annual circuits, beginning with the hard soil of Wales and Lancashire. At first the list included Grindal and Bradford, with William Bill, John Harley, a certain Mr Eastcourt and Andrew Perne, but the names of Bradford and Eastcourt were later omitted. Each of these chaplains received an annuity of £40, and a further £40 was found for John Knox, at this time preacher at Newcastle upon Tyne. In June 1552 Grindal was licensed to preach throughout the province, which may indicate an extension of his activities. Finally, in July, he received a further token of official favour in the grant of a prebend in Westminster Abbey.[43]

Grindal was now drawing an income of more than £100 a year, one of a small group of divines close to the centre of power, available for employment in special capacities, and likely candidates for higher promotion. That he had any part in the preparation of the Second Edwardian Prayer Book of 1552, which theologically and liturgically marked the high-water mark of the officially inspired Reformation in England, is unlikely, and certainly unrecorded. Nor was he one of the committee which drafted the abortive code of reformed canon law, *Reformatio legum ecclesiasticarum*, in the spring of 1552. But in October with Harley, Bill, Perne, Knox and Robert Horne, dean of Durham, he was required to review a draft of the Forty-Two Articles of Religion, the newly definitive statement of Anglican doctrine.[44] In November 1552 Ridley wrote to Sir John Gates and William Cecil anticipating Grindal's appointment to a bishopric and seeking to ensure the right of nomination to the precentorship of St Paul's which in the event would be vacated.[45]

The circumstances in which Grindal's name was first linked with a bishopric brings us close to the heart of the paradox of the Edwardian Reformation. The dominance in government of John Dudley, earl of Warwick and now duke of Northumberland, had proved favourable to the more 'forward' protestants so far as concerned 'religion', if not in respect of 'discipline'. In expectation of what he might accomplish, Hooper had called Northumberland 'a most holy and fearless instrument of the word of God', while to another of the 'Anglo-Zürichers' he appeared to be one of 'the two most shining lights of the Church of England'.[46] But at the time of his fall the duke admitted that his protestantism had been no more than a pose. No wholly satisfactory explanation for this improbable alliance has ever been offered, although the complex motivation of its political aspects has recently been clarified.[47] There are parallels with a problem of Elizabethan history, concerning the understanding between Northumberland's son, the earl of Leicester, and the puritans.[48] Something in the complex personalities of father and son has so far escaped our complete understanding. To say, as Professor Jordan does, that Northumberland knew that 'the thrust of sentiment was now in the direction of evangelical protestantism' imposes an unacceptable determinism on the course of history. To suggest that he had no choice but to follow the lead of his royal master strains credibility. No doubt Northumberland's ecclesiastical interests were focused on ecclesiastical property, but it is not clear that he depended upon the radical protestant party to make the wealth of the Church available. On the side of the forward protestants it has often been thought that they were content to be putty in the lord president's hands, so long as he favoured their theology and secured their preferment. But such an analysis hardly fits the events of 1552–3.

By the last year of Edward's reign some of the most celebrated and outspoken of the preachers had come to doubt the sincerity of Northumberland's profession and to suspect his designs for the Church, so confirming an opinion which Bucer, for all his ignorance of English, had formed two years earlier.[49] It was not solely with the benefit of hindsight or to clear themselves of Northumberland's treason against Mary that the victims of the political disaster of 1553 denounced the régime which had failed them. Ridley, Cranmer, Knox, Anthony Gilby, Thomas Wood and Sampson all testify with some precision to an estrangement between courtiers and preachers, and point to the sermons preached at Court in the Lent of 1553. Ridley, who spoke of the governing class in general as 'never persuaded in their hearts, but from the teeth forward', remembered that Latimer, Lever, Bradford and Knox were 'men of all other' that 'these magistrates could never abide', and if Wood is to be believed even the greatly favoured Bishop Hooper may be added to his list. Gilby appealed to the Lenten preachers themselves to confirm a similar testimony, and referred to a threat made by Northumberland to John Harley 'that the liberty of the preachers' tongues would cause the Council and nobility to rise up against them, for they could not suffer so to be entreated'. Knox, who spoke in 1554 of 'that wretched (alas!) and miserable Northumberland' gave details of the sermons preached by Grindal, Lever, Bradford and Haddon, and of his own last sermon before the Court, which dwelt on the examples of Achitophel, Shebna and Judas:

> Almost there was none that occupied the place but he did prophesy and plainly speak the plagues that are begun and assuredly shall end. Master Grindal plainly spake the death of the king's majesty [foretold it], complaining of his household servants and officers, who neither ashamed nor feared to rail against God's true word and against the preachers of the same.

Yet for all his obstinate prophetic integrity Knox — 'the poor soul', as Northumberland wrote indulgently — continued in good odour up to the death of Edward VI, and Harley remained Northumberland's chaplain.[50]

The contradictions in this love-hate relationship with the preachers came to the surface in Northumberland's revolutionary plans for the bishopric of Durham, a matter which involved Grindal's future. The duke had steadily increased his stake in the north-eastern counties, after sizing up the potentialities of the area during his Scottish campaigns. He was lord warden of the Marches and lord lieutenant of Northumberland, Cumberland, Newcastle and Berwick, while his dukedom was suitably sustained by extensive grants of land formerly held by the Percys. His attention was now drawn to the great see of Durham, which was unlike any other

English bishopric both in the palatine authority vested in the bishop and in its wealth, which by the sixteenth century was already greatly increased by the exploitation of coal. In October 1552, after a long and relentless pursuit, Northumberland engineered the deprivation of that old-fashioned prelate Cuthbert Tunstall, and so cleared the way for an audacious scheme of rationalization which he outlined to Cecil on 28 October.[51]

The bishopric of Durham was to be dissolved, along with the county palatine, and two new sees created. The dean of Durham was to become bishop of one, with a thousand marks added to his living and continued possession of the deanery. The chancellor of the diocese was to lose his living to the dean, and to be compensated with the emoluments of the vice-chancellor. The bishop of Durham's suffragan was to be removed and his living to be augmented by a hundred marks to 'serve to the erection of a bishop within Newcastle'. By an Act of Parliament of March 1553, which put into execution a more sober and equable measure than Northumberland's original scheme, the new see of Durham was provided with 2,000 marks and Newcastle with 1,000. The Crown was to benefit by appropriating the temporalities of the see, including the bishop's castles at Durham and Bishop Auckland and £2,000 a year of the best land in the north of England. This reorganization, although enacted, had not been completed when the death of the king placed everything in abeyance. But to return to the devices of Northumberland, this 'masterly and almost instinctive conspirator':[52] the bishop's coalmines at Gateshead and Wickham were to be annexed to the town of Newcastle, so securing the collusion of the richest merchants in the north. The embarrassing presence of John Knox in Newcastle was to be removed by making him bishop of Rochester, where he would usefully serve as 'a whetstone to sharpen the archbishop of Canterbury, whereof he hath need'. The dean of Durham who was to be offered the new and denuded bishopric was Robert Horne, one of the 'sharp' preachers of the time who had been dean for less than a year and whom the duke seems to have regarded as his creature. And the man singled out for the new diocese of Newcastle was none other than Edmund Grindal. This is the most likely construction to be placed upon a letter of 18 November in which Ridley reported 'the constant rumour which is now spread about in London that Mr Grindal is or shall be named to be a bishop in the north parts'.[53]

Northumberland had thought of everything: except the likely reaction to his schemings of the very men whom he had selected for promotion. Their opposition had not been anticipated, for in all its ambivalence his ecclesiastical policy matched at some points the principles of the preachers themselves, who professed to dislike episcopal grandeur and who found their model in the bourgeois way of life affected by Bucer and Peter Martyr. The financial nexus between stipendiary bishops and the secular authorities would have corresponded to Bucer's concept of a relationship of mutual confidence between ministers and magistrates, whereas sacrosanct endowments suggested a state of pontifical independence which it was not easy to reconcile with the thinking of the reformers. Yet on this occasion both Knox and Horne courted official displeasure in spurning the approaches made to them. The formidable Knox proved 'neither grateful nor pleasable' in his rejection of Rochester, and Horne not only refused the bishopric of Durham on Northumberland's terms but virtually called his patron a dissembler in religion. For several weeks the duke's correspondence is full of a menacing anger at such a display of 'hypocrisy' and 'ingratitude', and of something else: a kind of superstitious terror of Knox.[54] Evidently Cranmer and Ridley were no longer alone in protesting against the spoliation of church goods. Whether Grindal, too, chose to be 'one of these new obstinate doctors' is not known, but it is very probable, and his name does not occur again in connection with a northern bishopric. By January Northumberland was hoping that Durham might rather be given to 'a stout honest man that knoweth his duty to God and to his sovereign lord, than to one of these new obstinate doctors without humanity or honest conditions.' Just so: solid Henrician churchmen (like Tunstall himself) ought to have served his turn, which makes it hard to understand why he continued to hunt with the obstinate doctors.

For several months to come Northumberland continued to complain of the neglect of the vacant sees, which included Hereford, Rochester and Bangor, as well as Durham and Newcastle. With a man so impenetrably devious these protests may even have been sincere. But resistance to dishonourable and simoniacal conditions of appointment may have been the real obstacle, and this situation perhaps underlies the vehement tone of the Lenten sermons at Court. Harley was named for Hereford in October, 'admitted' by the Council in December, but not consecrated until May 1553.[55] Yet when the Council looked at the remaining vacancies in early June the same cards were shuffled, which suggests that Northumberland was either unwilling or for some reason unable to break the ties which bound him to the godly party, ties which the young king was responsible for keeping intact if we can believe Jordan's interpretation of the last year of Edward's reign.[56] By the distribution now contemplated, Ridley was to be translated to Durham and Grindal was to replace him as bishop of London.[57]

Ridley's expectation of a remove to his native country and his pleasure at the prospect have never been a secret. But hitherto historians have presumed to correct the Elizabethan writer, Thomas Rogers, a well-informed cleric with court connections, who wrote in 1607 that 'in King Edward's days (had the prince lived a while longer) [Grindal] had been promoted unto the bishopric of London, upon the translation of Bishop Ridley unto Durham; for these things had the state then in purpose.' The same circumstance was referred to in 1588 by the future Archbishop Tobie Matthew as a matter of familiar knowledge: 'How old was [Archbishop Grindal] when at the death of precious King Edward he was elect of London?' The matter is clinched by a state paper of 11 June 1553, a terse memorial of one of the last items which Edward VI's Council transacted: 'The declaration of the king's majesty's pleasure to the new bishops: Grindal, London; Bill, Newcastle; Meyricke, Bangor; Whitehead, Rochester.'[58] If Edward had lived a little longer Grindal would have been bishop of London not in 1559 but in 1553. Probably he would have remained at his post, and if he had suffered the fate of Ridley someone else would have become bishop in 1559 and there would have been little occasion for the writing of this book.

Enough of might-have-beens. On 6 July the death of the fifteen-year-old king brought to an abrupt end an epoch which was a unique amalgam of reform and corruption. The effect of the six years which now interrupted Grindal's career was to hallow the memory of the past with the deaths of Ridley, Rogers, Bradford and the rest, and to bring Grindal and his fellow-exiles into immediate contact with what the puritans would later call 'the best reformed churches overseas'. Both the Marian persecution and the Marian exile would transform the character and prospects of the English Reformation, and both would impress themselves deeply on Grindal's episcopate when at last he took it up under Elizabeth.

Flagitat itacp à S. M. T. falus populorum tuorum, ut legem con
dat, quę uetet, templa Altiſsimi ullis reſerari actionib. alijs, quàm
ad quos ſunt à Domino conſecrata: ſolis ſcilicet diuinarum Scri
pturarum recitationibus & explicationibus, ſacramentorum diſ
ſpenſationibus, precibus, & gratiarum actionibus, diſciplinǽcp
Eccleſiaſticæ exercitio.   Qua lege caueri & illud oportet, ne cui
liceat alijs, quàm his ipſis actionibus, in templo uacare. Ita efficiet

Pſalm.29.   S. M. T. ut impleatur illud Pſalmi: In templo eius omnes prædica
Pſalm.48.   bunt maieſtatem eius. Item & illud: Cogitamus & expectamus, ô
Pſalm.5.   Deus, bonitatem tuam in medio templi tui. Et illud: At ego fre
tus multa bonitate tua, ingrediar domum tuam, adorabo ad teñ
plum ſanctum tuum, in timore tuo.

Lex quarta, de ſolida omnis Eccleſiaſtici miniſterij reſtitutione.

CAPVT XII.

Quarta lex, de
plena omnium
miniſteriorum
eccleſiaſticorũ
reſtitutione.
Epheſ.4.
1.Cor.3.

Orrò, cum ita Domino uiſum ſit, ut eius religio per i
doneos adminiſtros & plantetur, & rigetur aſsiduè:
atcp det ipſe ideo eccleſiis, quibus regnum ſuum reſti
tuere planè dignatur, præter Apoſtolos & Euangeli
ſtas, etiam paſtores & doctores, qui in qualibet eccleſia myſteria
Dei omnia perpetuò miniſterio diſpéſent, qua de re ſuperius nõ
nihil diximus: erit S. M. T. totis quocp uiribus incubendum, ut ec
cleſiis ubicp per regnum ſuum S. miniſteria iuxta inſtitutum Spi
ritus ſancti ſolidè reſtituantur, quamprimùm id fieri poterit.

Paſtoralis mu
neris reforma
tio ſummè dif
ficilis, credenti
autem omnia
poſsibilia.

Marc.9.
Matth.11.
Inter presbyte
ros, qui & Epi
ſcopi eccleſia
rum à Spiritu
ſancto uocan
tur, unus ſemp
eccleſiarum ſu
premam curã
geſsit, ſicut cõ
ſul reipub. in
ter Senatores.
Act.20.
Phil.2.
Tit.1.

Negocium quidē hoc ſummæ erit difficultatis: ut paſsim, proh
dolor, obtinuit propè infinita uocati cleri, in omnibus gradibus
& ordinibus peruerſitas: utcp Antichriſtus arcem ſuam & prædã
ſtrenuè tuetur, ómneḿcp regno CHRISTI aditum, quantum ua
let, præcludit. At quia horum miniſteriorum reſtitutio non tam
difficilis, quàm ad ſalutem electorum Dei eſt neceſſaria, cogitan
dum S. M. T. erit, ſicut Deo omnipotenti, ita etiam credenti, om
nia eſſe poſsibilia, imò facilia, ſi pius & conſtans adhibeatur co
natus, ac labor aſsiduus.   Iam ex perpetua eccleſiarum obſerua
tione, ab ipſis iam Apoſtolis, uidemus, uiſum & hoc eſſe Spiritui
ſancto, ut inter presbyteros, quib. eccleſiarum procuratio potiſ
ſimum eſt cõmiſſa, unus eccleſiarum, & totius ſacri miniſterij cu
ram gerat ſingularē: eácp cura & ſolicitudine cunctis præeat alijs.
qua de cauſa Epiſcopi nomen, huiuſmodi ſummis eccleſiarum cu
ratorib. eſt peculiariter attributũ: tametſi hi, ſine reliquorũ preſ
byterorũ conſilio nihil ſtatuere debeãt: qui & ipſi, propter hãc cõ
munè eccleſiarũ adminiſtrationē epiſcopi in Scripturis uocãtur.

De re

Figure 1 Grindal's annotation of the chapter relating to the function of a bishop in
Martin Bucer's *De regno Christi* (Basle, 1557). Grindal's copy of the work is
preserved in the Library of the Queen's College, Oxford. See page 56.

4

A GERMANICAL NATURE

A MISUNDERSTANDING between Archbishop Matthew Parker
and Bishop Edwin Sandys in Elizabethan days was to find
Sandys pleading with his metropolitan that he should not 'utterly
condemn all Germanical natures'. 'For Germany hath brought
forth as good natures as England hath.'[1] The Germanical natures
were the property of those English protestants — some eight
hundred all told — who, unlike Parker, had chosen to spend the
years of the Marian reaction in exile, overseas. Their experience
had been brought to bear on the Elizabethan religious settlement,
with formative consequences for the Church of England and
ultimately for English civilization. As Sandys implied, some of
the subsequent friction in the Elizabethan Church reflected the
difference in the environments to which its leading officers had
been exposed in the years of opposition.

While no one disputes the important consequences of the
Marian Exile differences still occur in the interpretation of the
event itself. In protestant historiography it was a near-miraculous
deliverance from adversity, John Strype assuring his readers that it
was 'by the good providence of God' (and by no other acknowledged means) that the exiles 'made their flight into foreign countries from these storms at home'. But for the modern historian of
their migration the movement was neither hasty, nor improvised,
nor to any conspicuous extent a response to persecution. Far from
impeding the movement out of the country, the Marian authorities
encouraged what Miss C. H. Garrett, not without the use of a
creative and somewhat anachronistic imagination, calls 'one of the
most astute manoeuvres that has ever carried a defeated political
party to ultimate power'.[2] Miss Garrett was right to insist that the
exile was a retreat undertaken with the next advance already in
mind. But the exiles did not participate in our historical perspectives, and it would be wrong to assume that national sentiment
and political calculation took priority above religion and conscience in their motivations.

To turn to the writings of those directly involved is to find the
matter handled more in terms of present conscience than of future

opportunity: and specifically to find that the prime reason for emigration was to avoid the necessity of celebrating, or even attending, mass. Bishop Ridley's casuistical essay on 'how the true Christian ought to behave himself in the time of trial',[3] written in prison, considers the options open to 'the man of God' who is still a free agent. If he stays at home he may have to choose between life and conscience, and although 'to die in Christ's cause is an high honour', not all men are called to be martyrs. Rather than incite those with no such vocation 'of their own swing to start up into the stage', Ridley warns them to 'fly from the plague', to avoid 'the infection of the Antichristian doctrine'. This was calculated advice, based on the supposition (which events would almost disprove) that when faced with the alternatives of death or compromise the majority will not choose death. But it rests on the premiss that to remove the conscience beyond the range of intolerable pressures was an act requiring no special justification. There was authority for such pragmatism in the writings of the Fathers. In a letter from Germany Grindal quoted Cyprian to Ridley. The exile was one who had departed because he would not deny his faith: 'confiteretur utique si fuisset et ipse detentus.' But if he had been detained he too would have confessed it.[4]

This was to place the question of flight in time of trouble in the context of personal integrity, the safety of a man's own soul. But for the minister of Christ there was also a pastoral problem, concerning his responsibility for the souls of others. How could he avoid the censure of the tenth chapter of St John's Gospel which extols the good shepherd who gives his life for the sheep and castigates the hireling as one who flies when the wolf approaches? This question was considered by that 'courteous, gentle ... affable man' William Alley, soon to be bishop of Exeter, himself no exile but one who had passed Mary's reign in quiet retirement as a physician in the north of England.[5] Resolution was found in the writings of Augustine, Athanasius and other patristic writers. If the presence of the pastor was absolutely necessary for the survival of the flock then he must not flee 'but ought with danger of life to govern, keep and deliver his sheep committed to his charge from the peril of spiritual death ... For it is a noble thing to suffer death for the commodity of a public weal.' But if the life of a prelate or pastor was in danger then it might be right for him to preserve it. (As Sandys put it, 'if our lives be particularly sought we may lawfully flee.') 'And it may happen that a greater commodity may follow if he fly from them than if he had remained with them.' In a situation where there was but one pastor he should remain and suffer. But if there were many, some should stay and others flee.

'And if they contend who shall tarry and who shall fly, they may, calling for grace of the Holy Ghost, decide the matter by lots.' All this was said in the published version of sermons delivered in St Paul's, early in 1560, no doubt in Grindal's presence.[6]

It appears that the sort of calculation spoken of by Alley, if not the actual casting of lots, had determined Grindal's own withdrawal to Germany, leaving behind his closest colleagues, Rogers and Bradford, and his master, Ridley. These three were all to burn. Ridley's comment was: 'Grindal is gone (the Lord, I doubt not, hath and knoweth wherein he will bestow him)...' It was surely not by chance that the survival of one, and this particular one, of Ridley's lieutenants had been secured, leaving the bishop himself, as he said, to 'make up the trinity out of Paul's church to suffer for Christ'. Ridley's Achates, already named before Edward's death to succeed him, was consigned to the future, 'to light and set up again the lantern of his word in England'. If Rogers and Bradford had most to give by their courageous and inspiring deaths, Grindal was to survive and, eventually, to succeed and to lead.[7]

But by 1555, after the failure of Wyatt's rebellion, it was not possible to envisage a future which would include a new protestant settlement within four years. At Strasbourg Sandys and John Ponet, lately bishop of Winchester, applied for citizenship, and there and elsewhere exiles with the means to do so bought houses and prepared for an indefinite sojourn. As for Grindal's assessment of the future prospect, it can be judged from the fact that at some point in his five years overseas he 'laboured hard' to learn German, with such good effect that twenty years later he retained an adequate reading knowledge of the language, although by then 'the habit of conversing in it' had been lost.[8] (By comparison his understanding of French was sketchy.)[9] According to Conrad Hubert of Strasbourg these German studies arose out of despair of the future and a consequent desire to find employment in the German Church: 'ut vox tua etiam in Germanicis Ecclesilis audiri potuisset.'[10] Was it the example of that other expatriate, Hubert's master Martin Bucer, which encouraged Grindal to make some effort to break out of the restrictions of a refugee existence? Or was it simple economic necessity? All that can be said with confidence is that no Englishman of this generation identified himself so closely with German protestantism. It is significant that the only circumstance of Grindal's exile recorded by Foxe is that he 'went into the country to learn the Dutch tongue'.[11] Later he would instruct Secretary Cecil himself on the personalities and the geography of German politics. Among his contemporaries, Grindal's was the 'Germanical nature' *par excellence*.

As bishop of London Grindal would employ a German secretary in order, as he told Hubert, that he should not 'entirely forget your language'. This was Diethelm Blaurer, son of a distinguished reformed pastor, and Blaurer was to share the bishop's household with a servant from Cologne who spoke little or no English. On one occasion Grindal would be asked by Cecil to entertain the agent of the duke of Württemberg, and what for any of his colleagues would have been a tedious chore proved a delightful and nostalgic experience. 'I could have been contented to have had his company longer, I like it so well. He was a student in the civil law at Strasbourg when I was there, but we were not then acquainted.' The evening was passed in warm but amicable theological disagreement over the Lutheran doctrine of the Lord's Supper, an argument which Grindal must have rehearsed a hundred times before, for the years of exile had coincided with a renewal of the 'supper strife' in South Germany.[12]

Grindal's experience of German theological polemics left him with the rare gift (for an Englishman) of being able to measure Luther against the Lutherans, so that he could write of 'that opinion on the sacramental question which they *attribute* to Luther'.[13] On returning to England he was to send for the German works of Luther and three years later he would remark that those Lutherans who were opposed to the doctrine of predestination should read their own master *On the bondage of the will*. 'For what else do Bucer, Calvin and Martyr teach that Luther has not maintained in that treatise?' Luther had deserved well of the Church but his standing would have been higher still if his followers had not contrived to make him a god, and to expose those parts of his writing which most deserved to be decently concealed. The sentiment echoes similar remarks of Calvin's, and testifies less to the originality of Grindal's criticism than to his participation in attitudes which were typical of the South German reformed churches at the time.[14]

It would not be the best choice of words to suggest that Grindal as a bishop retained a sentimental affection for the scenes of his exile. Wistful sentiment is not lacking in John Jewel's Elizabethan correspondence with Zürich, but Grindal's letters to his old friends convey a more practical regard and the sense of tangible debts to be repaid. The magistrates of Frankfurt were told: 'England owes it to Strasbourg, Zürich, Basle, Worms, but above all to your renowned republic, that she has so many bishops and other ministers of God's word who at this day are preaching the pure doctrines of the Gospel.'[15] After the visit of the duke of Württemburg's agent, Grindal reminded Cecil that the duke had at one time given three or four hundred crowns for the support of the English at Strasbourg (the gift is recorded in the city archives), besides what he had bestowed on the congregation at Frankfurt. Grindal suggested that the queen should indicate that she had heard of this munificence, 'that it may appear his liberality is not altogether buried in oblivion'.[16] As for Strasbourg itself, Conrad Hubert was assured that the returned émigrés not only prayed for the peace of his city but were 'prepared to show every manifestation of gratitude in our turn, if we can any way be of use to it'.[17]

These promises were no empty epistolary form. In early Elizabethan days Grindal continued to inform himself on German affairs, and for a bishop he played an unusually positive role in the development of English policy towards that part of Europe. From 1562 he was an active participant in diplomatic contacts with the county of East Friesland and its little port of Emden, an area of interest to English political and commercial circles as a source and embarking post for mercenary troops and as a possible alternative to Antwerp as an outlet for cloth exports; while for protestants it was a noted mother church and an important centre of English protestant activity in Mary's reign. Grindal's role was that of an intermediary between Cecil and Jan Utenhove, the lay leader of the foreign protestant community in London and an agent for the ruler of East Friesland, the countess Anna, known to Englishmen as 'the lady of Emden', and her sons. In his correspondence Grindal was knowledgeable about the political and commercial possibilities of Emden and eager to procure an English pension for one of the Friesland counts, 'a goodly young gentleman' who was another of his acquaintances in Strasbourg.[18]

We have been forced to turn to Grindal's Elizabethan correspondence for illustrations of his 'Germanical' involvements by the relative dearth of evidence for his movements during the exile itself. The date and circumstances of his departure from England are unrecorded. Unlike his friend Sandys and his master Ridley he does not seem to have been politically compromised by the events surrounding Mary's accession and he was not involved in the riotous scenes at Paul's Cross in August 1553 when his colleagues Bradford and Rogers rescued Bonner's chaplain Gilbert Bourne from protestant violence, only to suffer arrest themselves for their pains. Foxe's account of Sandys's journey to the continent in May 1554 seems to imply that, as we should expect, Grindal was a member of the same company, together with Richard Cox, the future bishop of Ely, and Thomas Sampson, lately dean of Chichester, who was to become the puritan conscience of early Elizabethan England.[19] It is no doubt significant that Grindal formally resigned the precentorship of St Paul's by 28 April and his Westminster prebend on 10 May 1554, although why this latter resignation should have been registered at Landbeach, between Cambridge and Ely, is not clear.[20]

The ultimate destination of this distinguished party seems to have been the great Rhineland city of Strasbourg, where Grindal was to be found no later than the month of August 1554. Thereafter there are traces of his presence in Strasbourg from every one of the succeeding four years of exile. For one period of twelve months, from May 1555 to May 1556, his whereabouts are unrecorded, and it may be to this period that we should assign his language studies, which according to Hubert took place at Wasselheim, where he lodged with the pastor, Jakob Heldelin.[21] We know from Grindal himself that he also spent some time at Speyer, where he stayed with a local Scottish resident called Leach, and we hear of a trip to Baden in 1556. But an ambition to visit Basle and Zürich remained unfulfilled, and the death of Mary was to find Grindal still resident in Strasbourg.[22]

One of the attractions of Strasbourg must have been that this was Bucer's city, still impregnated with his memory. Another was Peter Martyr, who had returned to his old post of divinity lecturer in the cathedral: in effect a university chair, for the cathedral lectures furnished Strasbourg with the basis of a university course to crown the excellent schools which were the most typical achievement of the city's reformed administrators.[23] The English exiles attended Martyr's lectures on Aristotle's Ethics, as well as his readings on the book of Judges. Some of them, including Jewel, Sandys and Christopher Goodman, composed his household, living in what the Elizabethan biographer of Jewel called 'hoc literatissimo collegio'. It was a projection of the circle which Martyr had gathered in Oxford, but as a Cambridge man Grindal would have enjoyed no earlier opportunity to sit at the feet of this famous theologian whom he described to Ridley as 'a very notable father'. Martyr would later address Grindal as 'my most dear friend in England'.[24]

When increasing Lutheran intolerance drove this 'apostle of the English nation' (as Foxe called him) to a more congenial climate at Zürich, Sandys and Jewel followed. They were scholars, with a limited experience of affairs outside the university, and in moving to Zürich, which lay off the main routes of European traffic, they joined a colony of students, many of whom had been glad to retire from more active commitments. Martyr's presence made Zürich a source of almost final authority on matters of doctrine, conscience and church order. It was Martyr to whom the English at Frankfurt resorted with a question about the legitimacy of having their children baptized according to the Lutheran rite. And when Thomas Bentham as pastor of the protestant congregation in London had urgent questions to refer to Thomas Lever at Aarau he assumed that the answers depended upon Lever finding 'leisure at any time to walk to Zürich' to obtain the counsel of 'Mr Martyr'.[25] But Strasbourg continued to be favoured by those exiles who had been prominent in Edward's reign as public figures. Its English residents included Sir John Cheke, Sir Richard Morison, Sir Anthony Cooke, and Sir Thomas Wroth, in whose arms the young king had died, as well as Bishop Ponet of Winchester and Richard Cox.

As a major centre of communications, Strasbourg provided a suitable base from which this rump of the Edwardian establishment could exercise such co-ordinating leadership as the English *diaspora* might be willing to accept. It also provided excellent facilities for maintaining contact with friends in England, and for receiving those letters and other literary remains of the victims of the Marian persecution which were to be deployed by John Foxe and his fellow martyrologists. Strasbourg, in short, was engaged in practical measures for the vindication and perpetuation of the Edwardian achievement. That Grindal shared in this engagement was shown within a few months of his arrival overseas by his intervention in the celebrated 'Troubles of Frankfurt'.

There was nothing remarkable in the revival at Frankfurt-am-Main of the disputes over ceremonies which had already complicated the progress of the English Reformation. Exaggerated and ingrown feuds are a normal consequence of that paradoxical combination of liberty and restriction which conditions the life of the refugee. At Basle too, as we learn from John Bale's caustic pen, 'our brethren of the purity' were to quarrel with those whose affections were still tied to the Prayer Book, defaming the English communion office as if it 'bore the face of a popish mass', with 'other fierce despisings and cursed speakings'.[26] But at Frankfurt Prayer Book matters, and those underlying considerations of freedom and authority which were never absent from the Reformation debate about ceremonies, were subordinate to the root issue. This was an essentially political contest for the right to consolidate the English Reformation in exile and to determine its destiny. The 'troubles' consequently had a more than local significance, and it was with a sound instinct that a group of radical puritans with its roots in these quarrels first preserved and later, in 1574, published the documentary annals by which they are known to us.[27]

Under the Tudor dispensation the unity of the Church and the uniformity of its worship were defended by strong legal sanctions. Could coherence be maintained in the totally different, voluntary conditions of the exile? In Strasbourg it was supposed that the integrity of the protestant church depended upon continued respect for the Edwardian settlement, and for its residual legatees, the survivors of the Edwardian establishment in exile. Yet Strasbourg had no jurisdiction over any other English colony, and it was at Frankfurt-am-Main that political conditions appeared most to favour the erection of a wholly autonomous English congregation, something not yet achieved either at Strasbourg or at Emden. The first Englishmen to settle at Frankfurt were nonentities, in the sense that they had held no high offices in government, the Church, or the universities. Even the leading personality, William Whittingham, though a learned cosmopolitan of some social standing, had no public reputation, having spent the whole of Edward's reign overseas, largely in French-speaking reformed circles. In the summer of 1554 this undistinguished colony proceeded to adopt a form of worship which made a radical adjustment of the 1552 services to the practice of what English puritans would later refer to as 'the best reformed churches overseas'. The omissions included the responses, the Litany, the surplice, and 'sundry things' of a 'superstitious and superfluous character' in the administration of the sacraments; the additions a new form of confession and the singing of metrical psalms. These innovations were far from inflammatory in themselves. The Frankfurt magistrates were not inclined to allow the English to depart very far from the practice of the French congregation led by Valerand Poullain which enjoyed the use of the same building. And not even the more conservative of the exiles were so attached to ceremonies as to hazard the very existence of the congregation on account of things which of themselves were 'indifferent'. They later insisted to Calvin on their willingness to forgo private baptism, confirmation, saints' days, kneeling at the communion, the surplice and the cross, 'not as being impure and papistical' but as things indifferent, *adiaphora*.

But it is clear that among Whittingham's party resistance to 'the dregs of superstitious ceremonies' was differently motivated and based on rigid principles which severely narrowed the range of *adiaphora*. It is also probable that these early puritans intended to provide a model for any future protestant settlement in England itself. Whatever the source of their liturgical practice, the sense of strategical opportunism in which they were seldom lacking smacks of Geneva, where Whittingham had already lived as a student.

Frankfurt, no less than Strasbourg, was a European crossroads, a place from which to command. In August 1554 Whittingham's group seized the initiative with an attempt to gather the whole dispersion under its own standard of unity. The exiles at Strasbourg, Zürich, Wesel, Emden and Duisburg were told that it was the duty of every true brother, 'as pigeons which flee by flocks into their dove-house' (Isaiah 60.viii), to join together in 'one faith, one ministration, one tongue and one consent to serve God in his Church'. The suggestion was that God had already founded a providential dovehouse at Frankfurt. The English at Zürich were careful not to reject this peremptory summons out of hand, but they pleaded the priority of their studies and made the use of the 1552 Book a condition of their adherence. The 'learned men of Strasbourg' proved sufficiently disingenuous to find in the Frankfurt manifesto a request to send one or two seniors to take charge, and their minds turned to three ex-bishops, Ponet, Scory and Bale, and to the former dean of Westminster, Richard Cox. It was Grindal who wrote to John Scory at Emden, 'persuading him to be superintendent of this church of Frankfurt'. But so far from requiring oversight the Frankfurt congregation had already framed a constitution (or 'form of discipline') from which all considerations of rank, learning or ecclesiastical dignity were excluded, and which placed the government of the church in the hands of two or three elected ministers of equal standing, 'as is accustomed in the best reformed churches'. Their response to Strasbourg was to proceed to the immediate election of three ministers, one of whom, John Knox, accepted their calling and in November moved to Frankfurt from Geneva.

Strasbourg had been dealt a direct challenge. After the financial agent of the exile, Richard Chambers, had visited the scene, Grindal accompanied Chambers on a formal visitation, bearing a letter in which Strasbourg appealed for a measure of conformity to the Prayer Book, as the necessary basis of unity, and as a gesture of confidence in its authors, some of whom were facing martyrdom in England. A church meeting was summoned at which Grindal enquired into the extent of the autonomy enjoyed by the congregation and explained that the purpose of his mission was to establish 'the effect and substance' of the Edwardian Book, and not necessarily such ceremonies as were incompatible with local conditions. He was soon to inform Ridley that the Frankfurt magistracy had 'gently' required the omission of such details as the surplice and kneeling, 'not as things unlawful but to their people offensive'. In a reply which was critical of Knox ('Alas! that our brother Knox could not bear with our book of common prayer!'), Ridley found these conditions reasonable:

Where ye say ye were by your magistrates required gently to omit such things in your book as might offend their people, not as things unlawful, but to their people offensive, and so ye have done, as to the having of surplice and kneeling; truly in that I cannot judge but that both ye and the magistrates have done right well; for I suppose in things indifferent and not commanded or forbidden by God's word and wherein the customs of divers countries be diverse the man of God that hath knowledge will [not] stick to forbear the custom of his own country, being there where the people therewith will be offended; and surely, if I might have done so much with our magistrates I would have required Mr à Lasco to have done no less when he was with us.

It was presumably Ridley's condemnation of Knox and the damaging implications of continuing protestant disunity which led to the suppression of this passage by both Miles Coverdale and John Foxe in their editions of Ridley's letter in the 1560s. It was left to the puritans to give full coverage to the 'Troubles of Frankfurt' when they published the documents, in 1574.[28] But the position with respect to *adiaphora* which Grindal adopted and Ridley endorsed was almost normative among the English exiles. At Wesel the congregation ruled 'touching common prayer' that it was better 'with judgment' to retain as much of the English Book 'as now most fitly standeth with this time, place and persons' than 'through any singularity or disease of mind' to utterly reject its forms.[29] But Knox and Whittingham implied a radical difference of view when they invited Grindal to define what he meant by the 'substance' of the Prayer Book. When the visitors protested that they had no authority to negotiate and withdrew to Strasbourg they took with them a letter in which Frankfurt tartly warned that 'to appoint a journey for the establishment of ceremonies should be more to your charges than any general profit'.

Strasbourg now dissociated itself with dignity from a situation which it felt powerless to alter and the Frankfurt church was abandoned to indulge both eclecticism and passion in the search for an acceptable liturgy. Already in Edward's reign precocious Calvinist publicists had taken pains to inform England of a purer form of worship than Cranmer's liturgy. In 1550 Thomas Huycke (later to serve as Grindal's chancellor in the diocese of London) had printed in London the earliest English text of *The forme of prayers* of Geneva, while in 1551 Valerand Poullain had published, also in London, the liturgy used by his French congregation in Strasbourg.[30] A proposal by one of the Frankfurt factions to use Huycke's edition of the Geneva liturgy at first seemed precipitate even to Knox, although he was later a member of the committee which commended the Geneva Book to the congregation. The desire of the contrary party to enjoy the 'Book of England' was countered by sending a prejudiced account of its contents to Calvin, whose cautious censures cannot have entirely pleased either side. 'In the end', as we read in the *Troubles at Frankfurt*, 'another way was taken.' Following a suggestion first made by Thomas Lever, who from December 1554 shared the pastorate with Knox, a 'liturgy of compromise' was devised, with elements drawn partly from 1552, partly from other sources. This was adopted in February 1555 in a mood of general reconciliation.

Up to this point Strasbourg had played fair. But with the spring of 1555 the opponents of Frankfurt radicalism adopted the tactics of direct, counter-revolutionary action. Someone, presumably Richard Cox, had come to understand that the way to prevail was not to bluster with the faint echoes of episcopal authority but to adhere to the Frankfurt church and to exploit the democratic constitution by which its affairs were regulated. Arriving from Strasbourg and not, as the account in the *Troubles at Frankfurt* may seem to imply, straight from England, a party led by Cox joined the congregation at worship and created a disturbance by conducting themselves liturgically 'as they had done in England', answering the minister with the responses of the Litany. That their intervention was not resisted by Lever suggests collusion and a design on the part of Lever's faction to wreck the February compromise. Knox was provoked to preach a sermon which roundly censured the Prayer Book as containing 'things superstitious, impure, unclean and unperfect', and which struck at other abuses of the Edwardian Church. This was intended as a personal attack on Cox as a pillar of the late Henrician and Edwardian establishment, and a noted pluralist. But the Knoxians could scarcely exclude the Coxians and all that they represented from the true protestant Church of England, and they could not prevent their accession to the Frankfurt congregation without making nonsense of the appeal for unity which had been addressed to the exiles in other centres. Cox's stratagem was to exploit the contradiction which their appeal contained. Once admitted to a voice in the affairs of the congregation, which was done by Knox's own 'entreaty', the newcomers created a majority against the radicals which promptly removed Knox from the pastorate. The intrigues and counter-intrigues which followed led to the expulsion of Knox from Frankfurt, the setting aside of the democratic orders by which the church had hitherto been governed and, finally, the secession of the defeated radicals in response to an invitation from

Calvin to form a new congregation in Geneva. Each side blamed the other for the schism, which ended the attempt to gather a single and uniform English Church in exile. Even such an extremist as Christopher Goodman was to express regret and 'great uneasiness' over this outcome, although for him the strong line taken by the Knoxians was justified by the establishment of an English congregation at Geneva in which unity was enjoyed without any surrender of principle.[31]

After the exile was over, Grindal would remark dispassionately to Bullinger of Zürich that 'the English, I allow, were somewhat troublesome in Germany'.[32] Had he himself been an active party to the Coxian coup at Frankfurt? One is tempted to identify his views with those of John Foxe, who was to write in Elizabethan days: 'If there cannot be an end of our disputing and contending one against another, yet let there be a moderation in our affections.' Although no neutral in the Frankfurt troubles, Foxe could see faults on both sides and told Peter Martyr: 'As for me, so far as I can I shall always be a promoter of concord.'[33] Grindal is not named in the *Troubles at Frankfurt* or by Knox as an active opponent of the Knoxians. Yet he seems to have sent Ridley a critical account of Knox's notorious sermon, and with Sandys he was present in Frankfurt in the spring of 1555, when he wrote to Ridley that the church was 'well quieted by the prudence of Master Cox'. He signed the letter to Calvin which reported the success of the Coxians and put a favourable construction on their motives.[34] (But other signatories included two such puritans of the future as Thomas Lever and Thomas Sampson!) Foxe on the other hand joined the secession of 'the oppressed church', although he chose to settle in Basle rather than at Geneva. Refugee politics, it must be remembered, are as full of exaggerations as they are volatile. Within two years the rump of the Frankfurt congregation was flung into a second 'stir and strife' in which neither the personalities nor the issues were those of 1554–5. As late as July 1558 Thomas Sampson reported to Peter Martyr that the English at Frankfurt were 'in a perpetual motion, more perverse than useful'.[35]

In the summer of 1557, or it may have been 1558, John Jewel extended an olive branch to Whittingham and Goodman and other brethren in Geneva, seeking to blot out of recollection 'that most unhappy circumstance of the Frankfurt contention'.[36] But Jewel wrote from Zürich, not Frankfurt. The author of the *Troubles at Frankfurt* went too far when he wrote that by the end of the exile 'the old grudges' were 'clean forgotten'. At that time the English in Geneva revived the tactics of the radical left by circulating the other colonies with a new call for solidarity. The coolness of the Frankfurt reply shows that nothing had been forgotten. Yet it remains true, as William Haller has insisted, that the ample documentation of the Frankfurt affair has earned from historians a disproportionate interest in what was but one aspect of the exile, to the neglect of the major purpose to which all the exiles, regardless of their differences, were devoted. This was the advancement of the general protestant cause to which their friends in England were testifying with their lives.[37]

Detached as they were from the struggle, the only weapon at the disposal of the exiles was the printing press, but in the sixteenth century few instruments of war were more potent. Wherever a group of exiles had access to a press, money and matter to print, a flow of polemical literature resulted, directed towards England and Scotland.[38] At Emden, for example, the press of Egidius van der Erve produced at least sixteen items (heavily disguised under false colophons), a miscellaneous collection which included translations from Zwingli and Bullinger, works by Ridley and Cranmer, and bitter pamphlets from the pens of Knox and William Turner.[39] A minority with developed political, or, more properly, prophetical instincts — Ponet, Knox, Goodman and Gilby — contributed to the literature of the exile tracts which advanced notions of popular resistance to tyranny, with the direct aim of overturning the English and Scottish governments. These writings, published in Geneva, were so subversive as to be counter-productive, at least in England.

At the same time another group of exiles was occupied in what looks like a more sober and scholarly exercise. This was the preservation and publication of the letters, disputations and treatises which together contained the last confessional statements of the more celebrated and learned of the victims of the persecution: their final testament. But combined with emotive accounts of their sufferings, these writings would form the basis of an English martyrology, propaganda with more power to change the course of history than anything in the inflammatory tracts of Knox and Goodman. An Elizabethan preacher was to tell his hearers that after the death of the fifteenth-century Czech leader John Žižka his skin had been flayed to make a drum to call the militant Bohemian Hussites to battle.[40] With a similar instinct John Foxe was to create from the ashes of the Marian martyrs the great tome called *Acts and Monuments of the Church* or, popularly, 'The Book of Martyrs'. No book except the Bible itself has had more influence on the protestant consciousness which the English people were to develop of themselves, of their past and present place in the divine scheme of things, and of the contrary, inimical role of the Roman Antichrist. In as much as this famous book began its course, as Foxe himself tells us, 'in the far parts of Germany', it must be reckoned the most important of all the fruits of the exile.[41]

Ultimately, the identification of the Book of Martyrs with its author was complete. It owed its form to the grand historical perspectives, apocalyptical in their conception, which were supplied partly by that most erudite of protestant publicists, John Bale, partly by the fertile brain of Foxe himself. Its bulk, steadily increasing through successive editions, derived from the relentless industry with which Foxe sought out his materials. But originally the literary vindication of the English confessors was a co-operative undertaking, with ramifications both in England and on the continent. The managers included the most prolific of English protestant authors, Thomas Becon, and Miles Coverdale, who would later edit the *Letters of the Martyrs*. We read of those 'labouring in this business', of a proposed 'division of labour', and of various documents 'in the possession of our friends'. All these phrases are Grindal's, and they occur in a series of letters to Foxe, preserved in the Foxe papers, which indicate that in so far as the enterprise had a single manager he was Grindal, and that Foxe's role was at first no more than that of a technically gifted subordinate.[42]

Grindal at Strasbourg and Foxe at Basle complemented each other in a loose partnership. Strasbourg lent itself to the amassing of the 'acts' of the martyrs and the other documents which passed to the continent from the Marian prisons without undue difficulty. Grindal possessed excellent contacts among 'our friends' in England, as well as along the main routes of continental traffic, and had besides an instinct and care for the preservation of any written thing which might conceivably prove of value to which Foxe paid graceful tribute, and which would later be devoted to the rescue of Bucer's English writings. As early as May 1555 he had acquired Ridley's Oxford disputation and two of Ridley's treatises. Later there came to hand Cranmer's 'Defence' against Gardiner, an eye-witness account of the burning of the archbishop, John Philpot's examination, Bradford's letters, and many of the other pieces which now fill out the Parker Society volumes of the 'Fathers of the Reformed English Church'. But Strasbourg was not a centre of the book trade, and moreover it proved difficult to persuade the local Lutheran printers to handle writings by English divines which touched on the eucharistic question. Basle, on the other hand, provided incomparable facilities for book production and lay within striking distance of Christopher Froschauer's

famous press at Zürich. Foxe himself, like many another alienated
intellectual of his time, made a poor living from proof correction and
practically inhabited the printing house of Osorinus at Basle.

But Foxe had more to offer than his proximity to a good printer.
He had arrived in Germany not only with the germ of his great
work already planted in his mind but with the manuscript of the
first part of his History ready for the press. *Commentarii rerum in
ecclesia gestarum ... liber primus*, which traced the thin red line of
reformation from Wyclif through the fifteenth century, was published at Strasbourg in 1554. Grindal lacked the imaginative and
constructive gifts of a maker of books. Left to his own resources,
the writings which he had amassed would probably have been
offered to the world as separate items, lacking the cumulative effect
which Foxe was to give them. Nevertheless it is in Grindal's letters
that we find the first reference to 'the history of the martyrs', and
we cannot exclude the possibility that the conception was partly
his. As early as the summer of 1556 Grindal hoped to have the
History ready for almost simultaneous publication in English and
Latin. Foxe was to oversee the translation and printing of the Latin
edition, while the English version was to be a collective enterprise.
'For so it was arranged, that by a division of labour certain persons
should manage this business.'

Be that as it may, what subsequently happened serves to demonstrate the relative ineffectiveness of a committee when matched
against the *idée fixe* of a dedicated individual. A year later little
progress had been made at Strasbourg. The documents were
arriving 'slowly and grudgingly', while the editors were distracted
from their task by 'travels and engagements'. They were left with
'a somewhat rude quantity of matter', of which some did not
'altogether despair' that it might yet be turned into a work of
history. Strasbourg had now to decide whether to cut its losses and
turn the material over to Foxe wholly. In order to avoid this
painful decision, Grindal suggested that Foxe should proceed with
the publication of his second volume, which would bring the story
up to the death of Henry VIII, while he and his friends would
press forward with a separate history of the Marian persecution.
That Grindal was actively engaged in his side of the undertaking is
shown by a printed leaf among Foxe's papers:[43] *A declaracion of the
reverent father in God Thomas Cranmer Archbishop of Cāterbury,
cōdempnyng the untrue and slaunderous reports off some which have
reported that he should set up the masse at Canterbury at the first
coming off the quene to her raygne*. This is dated 1557. It bears in
Grindal's hand the note: 'Joyne in thys letter hoc signo A.' But by
the end of 1557 it would appear that any attempt to publish an

English martyrology apart from Foxe had been abandoned, although Grindal still professed to direct the undertaking, advising Foxe on the principles of translation which he should employ and on aspects of theological obscurity or delicacy.

Matters had reached this point when the news of Mary's death arrived in the centres of continental exile. Grindal at once wrote to Foxe to suggest that in the altered circumstances the History of the Martyrs should be suspended until he could be supplied with 'more certain and more copious intelligence' from England. But Foxe disregarded this advice and in August 1559 he was to produce from a Basle press a substantial folio, *Rerum in ecclesia gestarum*, of which some five hundred pages were devoted to recent events. This was in effect the first edition of *Acts and Monuments*, to which the more copious intelligence which Grindal had hoped for would later be added. This display of characteristic independence was not the end of the association between Grindal and Foxe, nor even of their friendship. When Grindal captured Foxe for the ministry (although it was as a literary freelance that he continued to live) the event was given special prominence in his register of ordinations. For the remainder of his life he continued to be visited from time to time with examples of Foxe's familiar but elegant Latin epistles.[44]

Acts and Monuments itself tells how the report of Elizabeth's accession was received in Zürich. Sandys was seated at dinner with Peter Martyr when the news arrived. Martyr was joyful but Sandys was despondent, especially at hearing that he was 'sent for by his friends at Strasbourg', for 'it smote into his heart that he should be called to misery.' No such anecdote could have been attached to Grindal. Throughout the years in the wilderness he had never lost touch with public commitments, and now he hurried to get back into full harness, 'compelled', as he wrote to Foxe, 'by the urgency of my friends to set out for England'. Sandys met up with him in Strasbourg and on 21 December the two old companions set out homeward together. The Rhine was frozen and they had a tedious journey by land which brought them to London on the very day that Elizabeth was crowned, 15 January 1559.[45] Grindal's baggage was burdened with a small library of works of continental theology, evidence that his exile had not been a time of abject poverty. They included Bucer's *De regno Christi* in the Basle edition of 1557, the Bible in Sebastian Castellio's version and the first of the seven large folio volumes of the *Commentaries* of Wolfgang Musculus, these two last both published in Basle in 1556.[46] And of course, if we are to believe Thomas Fuller, his baggage train also included the first specimens of the tamarisk bush to be imported into England.[47] No doubt he was glad to be home.

PART TWO

LONDON

5

IN THE WINGS:
THE ELIZABETHAN SETTLEMENT

T HE Elizabethan statutes of supremacy and uniformity, which embodied the fundamental elements of the new religious settlement, implied, in substance if not in every detail, a return to the 'state of religion' which had prevailed at the time of Edward VI's death. This was equally the significance of the first episcopal appointments of the reign, which entrusted the implementation of the settlement to men whom Cranmer and Ridley would have recognized as their legitimate successors. In the person of Matthew Parker the Cranmerian tradition of a scholarly and moderate protestantism returned to Lambeth, while in London Bishop Bonner was for a second time ejected, to give way to Ridley's Achates, Grindal.

This much, the end result, is certain. But little else concerning the religious settlement is beyond dispute among historians and there was much which was not clearly understood at the time that it was made. Even the fact that the settlement represented an effective terminus to the bewildering succession of religious changes, a definitive settlement, was not comprehended and could not be conceded by extremists on either side. Sir Nicholas Bacon, as lord keeper, implied as much when he warned M.P.s as they dispersed from the 1559 Parliament against the subversion of the settlement both by 'those that be too slow, ... those that will not follow', and 'those that be too swift, ... that go before the laws, or beyond the laws'.[1] These, the puritans of future years, would conclude that matters had gone 'but halfly forward and more than halfly backward'[2] and they would never cease to urge the completion of what in their eyes was an arrested, if not aborted, reformation. 'We in England are so far off from having a church rightly reformed, according to the prescript of God's word, that as yet we are scarce come to the outward face of the same.'[3] Grindal himself, at the height of the first major controversy with puritan non conformists in 1566, would concede that he and other bishops had been defeated and disappointed by the 1559 legislation. 'We who are now bishops, on our first return, and before we entered on our ministry, contended long and earnestly for the removal of those things that have occasioned the present dispute.' But they were 'unable to prevail'.[4]

As this implies, the terms of the religious settlement had been hotly disputed. Sandys wrote when it was all over of 'these tossings and griefs, alterations and mutations'. When Sir Nicholas Bacon wrote to Parker in May 1559 to renew the contacts which were soon to translate him to Canterbury he explained the cause of his long silence: 'I could by no mean understand to what end the matter mentioned in those letters would certainly grow unto'. Yet Bacon as lord keeper was an inner member of the government. On 20 March John Jewel had reported to Peter Martyr that the queen favoured the cause of the reformers and was 'following up her purpose', but 'somewhat more slowly than we could wish. And though the beginnings have hitherto seemed somewhat unfavourable, there is nevertheless reason to hope that all will be well at last.' Five weeks earlier, Sir Anthony Cooke, a member of the House of Commons, and a key member so far as these transactions were concerned, had informed Martyr that 'we are moving far too slowly.' Like Jewel, he represented the queen (as in prudence he was perhaps bound to do) as well-intentioned, but hinted darkly at certain 'Sanballats and Tobiases' who, as in the days of Nehemiah, were obstructing the rebuilding of Jerusalem. Jewel was more direct: 'The bishops are a great hindrance to us.'[5]

Who were the movers and who the impeders in and around the parliament house in the early months of 1559 will never be known for certain, since the slender documentation of this parliament is not of a kind to speak for itself. Before 1950 most historians supposed that the settlement as it eventuated was more or less what the queen and her advisers — 'the government' — had intended, concentrating their attention on the means by which a predetermined policy was implemented and opposition to it overcome. The anonymous state paper known as 'The Device for Alteration of Religion' predated the convening of parliament but provided what appeared to be an accurate blueprint of what subsequently transpired.

In an article which proposed the relegation of the 'Device' to the category of 'rejected addresses', Sir John Neale overthrew the familiar interpretation of these obscure events with a radical new hypothesis.[6] Elizabeth's propensity was to avoid precipitate action. She was religiously conservative and she possessed a keen sense of the political dangers of the time. Consequently she was resolved to reassert the royal supremacy over all ecclesiastical causes and affairs but not to proceed to an immediate alteration in 'religion', that is, to a protestant prayer book and an act of uniformity enforcing its use. The demand for a change in religion in this sense came from a radical protestant element in the House of Commons, led by returned exiles within the House and encouraged by their clerical friends, whom Neale imagined clustering outside its doors. When the scope of the supremacy bill was broadened by a Commons committee to embrace the matter of protestant worship this was contrary to government policy, and when the Lords restored the bill to something like its original form they acted in response to the wishes of the Court. As Easter approached and preparations were made to dissolve parliament, an act enabling the queen to claim ecclesiastical supremacy and, almost incidentally, permitting the protestant practice of communion in both kinds was the full extent of the ecclesiastical settlement so far achieved. But the show of force by protestants in the Commons was one of the factors persuading Elizabeth to alter her original intention and to continue parliament beyond Easter. It was in these later sessions that not only the Acts of Supremacy and Uniformity but most of the legislation of this parliament reached the statute book.

But once again Neale doubted whether the Act of Uniformity and the Prayer Book to which it refers represented royal policy. Elizabeth may well have favoured something more conservative than the second Edwardian Prayer Book: 1549, perhaps, with its superficial affinities to a Lutheranism which was both diplomatically advantageous and to her own taste. But the inclination of the returned exiles and their sympathizers was to go beyond 1552 and to adopt something closer to the model of the best reformed churches overseas. Neale detected a compromise between these widely divergent aspirations in the Act of Uniformity as we know it, which enforced the 1552 Prayer Book, modified in a conservative direction in some significant particulars, and which in one of its provisions revived the ornaments of the Church, including the ecclesiastical vestments, associated with the earlier Edwardian liturgy, and indeed with the mass itself. Hence the disappointment of the puritans, and indeed of Grindal and his friends. And hence too the determination of a queen who had been blown off course to stick to the terms of the compromise with which, characteristically, she converted defeat into a kind of victory. Through this startling reconstruction of events Neale redefined the terms of much of Elizabethan religious and political history.

But it was no more than a possible reconstruction and it is a pity that so many writers, including the authors of textbooks, have hardened hypothesis into fact. Recently the problem of the 1559 parliament has been reopened in a study which revives older interpretations, rehabilitates the 'Device', and trusts the writers of the 'Zürich Letters' when they reported that the queen was cautiously committed to their side, and identifies as the major obstacle to the success of the protestant settlement the Marian bishops and their allies in the House of Lords.[7] Much remains and will always be obscure, and debatable. We do not know and may never know whether the views and intentions of the 'government' in these matters were those of the queen simply, or primarily, or were substantially formed by Cecil and his brother-in-law Bacon and other courtiers and newly appointed councillors; or, if they are to be regarded as representing the queen's own mind, how far that mind was responsive and susceptible to protestant opinion, as it was marshalled and orchestrated in her vicinity in these crucial months. We know that the making of the settlement was accompanied by preaching at Court which the returned exiles almost monopolized. We do not know what determined the choice of preachers. We know that these same preachers were about to become bishops. We do not know how they were selected for appointment. But when the queen's favourite, Robert Dudley, later asked a correspondent to consider 'all the bishops that can be supposed that I have commended to that dignity since my credit any way served',[8] the implication was that the 'commending' was at least as instrumental as the royal hand which signed the *congé d'élire*. 'My lord, I am yours to the uttermost of that little that I may do,' Sandys told Dudley in 1560.[9]

Fortunately our task is not to solve these conundrums but to suggest what Grindal's part may have been in the making of the religious settlement. The 'Device for Alteration of Religion' named him as one of seven divines 'apt' to confer with Sir Thomas Smith and to prepare the 'plat or book' which would contain the substance of the 'alteration': that is to say, to revise the Prayer Book.[10] If we assume, as historians once did, that this committee, consisting otherwise of Bill, Parker, May, Cox, Whitehead and Pilkington, did the work proposed for it, then Grindal must be regarded as an architect of the settlement. Admittedly since the Prayer Book as enacted was the second Edwardian Book amended in only three places the 'Prayer Book Committee' seems to have found little enough to do, and it may be reasonable to wonder, with Professor Neale, whether such a committee ever met.

But there is no reason to doubt that Grindal was one of a very small group of divines, most of them returned exiles, whose position in relation to the new régime was privileged, and even influential. In Strasbourg it had been reported that the return of these men was 'very acceptable to the queen', who had 'openly declared her satisfaction'.[11] If Cox, who preached at the opening of the parliament, was the sometime tutor and mentor both of the new queen and of her dead brother,[12] Grindal could count on his good standing with the new secretary, Cecil. He soon took his turn as a court preacher.[13] And when in March the government staged the disputation with the papists in Westminster Abbey which opened the way to the altered strategy of the second parliamentary session, Grindal was one of the protestant spokesmen, along with Scory, Cox, Whitehead, Horne, Aylmer, Sandys, Jewel and Guest, with the exception of the last all exiles.[14]

But within the terms of Neale's scenario Grindal must be cast as a figure of the opposition as much as a government man: one of the lobby of émigré divines persuading their friends in the House of Commons to outmanoeuvre the intentions of a less than friendly administration. Although Neale's critics have been justified in their complaint that there is little evidence for the activities of such a lobby,[15] Grindal's reports of his own activities in the early months of 1559 suggest an outsider, almost an agitator, rather than a tame court divine. On 23 May 1559 he assured Hubert of Strasbourg that 'we were indeed urgent from the very first that a general reformation should take place. But the parliament long delayed the matter ...' And to Bullinger seven years later he explained that he and other future bishops had laboured for the removal of the ceremonies to which the puritans were objecting: but in vain.[16]

The truth is that Grindal and his friends were ambiguously placed in 1559, an ambiguity which for Grindal at least would persist at least until 1576, when as archbishop he would write his fateful letter to the queen. They were both insiders and outsiders. As insiders they were about to be elected to bishoprics and must have already anticipated their promotion. As outsiders their correspondence betrays great insecurity, even a trace of the near-paranoia expressed by the reformed churches generally at this point in their evolution on the subject of 'worldly policy' and its machinations. From Zürich Rodolph Gualter had warned the queen herself against those who might induce her to accept an 'unhappy compound' of popery and the gospel, a religion of 'a mixed, uncertain and doubtful character', while the duchess of Suffolk, still on her European travels, betrayed to her old friend Cecil the same fear that England might yet succumb to a religious 'compound', perhaps in the form of Lutheranism. A hint from Bishop Grindal that all was not as it should be in the newly settled Church would be enough to bring from Calvin a pointed warning: 'It may be as well that the queen should know that you will have nothing to do with whatever smells of the temporal arm, since the authority required for spiritual functions is properly conferred by

God alone.'[17] This was the Calvin who had written, in his Commentary on the prophet Amos:

> For this evil has ever been dominant in princes — to wish to change religion according to their will and fancy, and at the same time for their own advantage, ... as they are not for the most part guided by the Spirit of God, but impelled by their own ambition.[18]

The edge of Calvin's pen was turned not so much towards the princes themselves as against those who were, so to speak, parasites of princes' natural ambitions. The enemy was not Henry VIII but those who gave King Henry supreme power in all things and blasphemously extolled him as Head of the Church: above all Stephen Gardiner, who 'surpasses all devils in that kingdom'.[19] With the same spirit Grindal's colleague James Pilkington denounced the 'desperate Judases' of the age: 'The proud papist at this day ... doth not hinder the building of God's Church and preferring of his Gospel so much as these faint-hearted protestants, white-livered hypocrites, double dissemblers and servers of time.'[20]

The insecurity of the returned exiles consisted in part in the fear that instead of themselves the government would promote time-servers, the innumerable vicars of Bray on whom, indeed, the continuity of ecclesiastical life depended. Grindal would later explain that it was to prevent the Church falling into the hands of apostates, Lutherans and 'semi-papists' that he and others had overcome their scruples in accepting high office.[21] Those with wives had an additional cause for concern. The first Elizabethan parliament had done nothing to legitimize their married status. As Sandys complained to Parker: 'The Queen's Majesty will wink at it but not stablish it by law, which is nothing else but to bastard our children.'[22] And all the exiles were prey to nagging anxiety as long as they were left in poverty: which was their condition for months, if not years. Jewel told Zürich that they were strangers in their own country. Property sequestered by the Marian government had not been restored, so that according to John Parkhurst they were 'poorer than Irus himself'. Parker had been deprived of all his preferments under Mary and when he was offered the archbishopric he had £30 in the world. How would that pay for the furnishing of a great household?[23] It was not that the government and parliament had somehow overlooked these bread-and-butter matters in the excitement of making a new religious settlement. On the contrary, the 1559 parliament spent more time on questions of ecclesiastical property than on any other issue: but it was the interests and claims of laymen which were paramount in their deliberations.[24] Sandys found that for his profession the times were given to taking, not receiving. 'In the time of our exile were we not so bare as we are now brought.'[25]

The irony was that these were the men already destined for high preferment: Grindal most surely. As Cecil's client and friend and Ridley's designated successor it was as certain that he would be bishop of London as that Bonner would be deprived, both necessary concessions to the exceptionally strong protestant sentiment of the city. The bishop of London enjoyed a unique position as the spiritual leader of a large but compact and self-possessed civic community, and it is significant that when Edwin Sandys was named to succeed Grindal in 1570 he sought to avoid translation until he was assured of what he called 'the full consent and calling of the people of London'. 'It is you, it is you, dearly beloved, that have drawn me hither,' Sandys told the audience at Paul's Cross in his first sermon as their bishop.[26] So Grindal might have said.

On Whitsunday, 14 May, the new Prayer Book came into use for the first time in most of London's parish churches. Grindal, in the first sermon preached at Paul's Cross since Easter, 'proclaimed the restoring of the book of King Edward', at which, as another returned exile reported,[27] 'the lords and people made (or at least pretended) a wonderful rejoicing.' The sermon was attended by the Privy Council with the cream of the nobility, the whole illustrious company afterwards dining with the lord mayor. There can be little doubt that the preacher was already bishop of London, not only *in petto* but morally, in the eyes of the populace.

Conspicuous by his absence from the Cross on this occasion was the bishop incumbent, Edmund Bonner, together with the entire chapter of St Paul's, and on this same Whitsunday mass was sung inside the cathedral, not fifty yards from the pulpit where Grindal stood to extol the Prayer Book. Soon afterwards the Council applied levers to prise Bonner out of his bishopric and to ease Grindal in. According to the Mantuan observer, Il Schifanoya, Bonner was requested 'earnestly with loving exhortation' to resign in favour of 'one Master Grindal', after he had resisted the persuasion of the Council to suppress mass in the cathedral. This account suggests that the dean and chapter had already received some kind of formal instruction to elect Grindal in his place. When Bonner stood his ground he was deprived, on 30 May, together with the dean, Henry Cole. Since the Prayer Book was not legally enforceable until St John the Baptist's Day, 24 June, the true cause of their deprivation is likely to have been refusal of the oath of supremacy, perhaps coupled, as with the remainder of the London clergy, with a

demand to acknowledge the legitimacy of the Prayer Book. Significantly it was on 23 May that letters patent empowered a committee of the Privy Council to tender the oath to ecclesiastical
persons and lay officers under the Crown. Later it was by the
authority of Grindal and other ecclesiastical commissioners that
Bonner was confined to the Marshalsea Prison.[28] When he died in
that same prison, ten years later, his successor allowed him Christian burial, although Bonner had remained excommunicate for
many years, and arranged for the funeral to take place at night, to
avoid not only the 'flocking of papists' but also the 'inconvenience'
of protestant counter-demonstrations. Grindal's laconic reporting
of the death of 'Dr Bonner' was in character, and in contrast to
Foxe's spirited description of 'the stinking death of Edmund Bonner, commonly named the bloody bishop of London'.[29]

With a similar restraint Grindal wrote to his friend Conrad
Hubert on 14 July 1559 with news that 'many of our friends ... are
now marked out for bishops', but without mentioning his own
selection, although the *congé d'élire* had been signed on 22 June,
one of the first six episcopal appointments of the reign.[30]

Grindal was now bishop elect, but the road to full assumption of
the office of a bishop was an elaborate obstacle race. In August
Peter Martyr addressed Richard Cox as 'domine ... dei gratia
episcopo', but in a subsequent letter had to apologize for the
embarrassment caused by jumping the gun, reverting to 'clarissimo
viro'.[31] Before the formalities of consecration and installation and
enthronization could be completed there had to be royal confirmation of the election, and these stages were not expedited until
late December. It was then necessary to recover the temporalities
of the see out of the hands of the Crown, and to compound for the
payment of first fruits. Only after all this would Grindal be in a
position to explore and exploit his inheritance, and to discover to
what extent his predecessor might have mortgaged his future by
granting long leases at low rents, and by depriving him of his
patronage through grants of patents and reversions to office: a
solemn moment of truth for any incoming Tudor bishop. To
achieve the unimpeded enjoyment of a benefice worth many hundreds of pounds a year was never easy, least of all under Queen
Elizabeth's government, and the procedure was calculated to sap
any pretensions to spiritual independence.

In 1559 the matter was further complicated by the passage of a
new statute which threatened a major spoliation of episcopal income. Under this act, the Crown could take advantage of the
vacancy of a see to effect a compulsory exchange of bishops' lands
for spiritual revenues within the same diocese, in the form of the

tithes of impropriate rectories, formerly associated with the mon-
asteries and other religious foundations and now in the hands of
the Crown, together with the taxes on parochial income known as
tenths. No sooner was the first batch of new bishops named than
steps were taken to implement these measures, and to investigate 'a
like exchange with the rest of the bishoprics that be richly endowed'. In the case of London, Letters Patent of 13 December
ordered the surrender of fourteen manors in eight counties estimated to be worth annually the sum of £491. 16s. 5½d. When the
temporalities of the see were at last restored, on 21 March 1560, it
was with the express exclusion of these lands. On subsequent
survey the specified manors were alleged to be worth no more than
£388. 5s. 4½d., and only in February 1562 were grants made of
rectories, rents and pensions to a value nominally equivalent to this
lower figure.[32]

The enforced exchanges of 1559 appear to stand in the tradition
of a politically motivated aggression against the bishoprics which
originated in the 1530s.[33] Under Henry VIII and Edward VI such
sees as Canterbury, York, Lincoln, Exeter, Norwich and Bath and
Wells lost many, and in the case of Bath and Wells most, of their
ancient possessions; while the Edwardian bishop of Winchester,
John Ponet, had been constrained to surrender his exceptionally
rich temporalities in exchange for an annual stipend of 2,000
marks. Much of parliament's time in 1559 was occupied with the
disputed status of these lands, arising from their restitution to the
bishops under Mary and the revived claims of the sundry lay
patentees to whom they had been granted under Edward.

The newly enacted exchanges represented a bad bargain for the
protestant bishops.[34] Not that they spelt financial disaster. It has
been shown, for example, that the seventeenth-century archbishops of York enjoyed an income almost equal to the value of
the see in the 1530s, much of it derived from impropriate rectories,
and that the income of the bishops of Ely remained 'remarkably
constant'. So did the revenue of the bishops of London, leaving
aside the inflationary factor. The effect of the 1559 act was not to
impoverish the bishops but to prevent them from becoming richer.
The social prestige and political influence associated with traditional manorial lands were not easily replaced. Tithes were a
depreciating asset where they were already commuted for money
payments, troublesome to collect where still payable in kind, often
subject to leases and pensions, and as royal grants not freely
negotiable. Above all, assets in this form threw into conflict the
financial interests of the bishops with responsibilities which they
above others might be expected not to neglect. The impropriator

of a parish church was required to maintain the fabric of the chancel, to keep the parsonage house in repair, and to provide a fit ministry for the parish, morally the first charge upon the tithe income. With what reads like legislative cynicism the 1559 act describes parsonages as 'most apt' to be in the governance and at the disposal of the clergy. Admittedly the exchanges promised to enlarge the ecclesiastical patronage of the bishops, an important consideration. But only at cost to their consciences could the bishops exploit to their financial advantage the terms of this new deal. And for any churchman who cared to analyse the economic problems of the Church which underlay its poor pastoral performance it must have been open to question whether there ought to be any impropriations at all, let alone whether they could be appropriately applied to support the dignity of a bishop.

The bishops of the reformed Church of England were not to persist in agonies of conscience over this issue. But in 1559 the atmosphere was exceptionally sensitive. Richard Cox even drafted a statement in which he and his colleagues declared themselves 'persuaded in conscience that the parishes ought to enjoy [these revenues] in such sort and for such end as they were godly appointed at the beginning'. Concern about the proposed exchanges nourished suspicion concerning the sincerity of the queen's intentions with regard to religion. It coincided with an ecclesiastical crisis over the cross in the queen's chapel, a small but ominous symbol of a religion 'of a mixed and doubtful character'. In the autumn of 1559 some of the still unconsecrated and penniless bishops were offering resistance both to the exchange of lands and to the practice of the queen's chapel, which threatened an interpretation of the 1559 settlement so conservative as to be all but unacceptable. Their campaign was not entirely unsuccessful. The demands of the Crown were reduced. In October it was intended that the see of London should lose all but £150 of the £1,000 derived from its manors. But in the event only two-fifths of the lands were taken. None of the five bishops initially affected by the act escaped more lightly than Grindal, perhaps a token of his good standing with Cecil.

The posture adopted by these bishops who were almost prepared to resign before the mitres touched their heads suggests contradictory impulses, the confused mood of men who were about to exchange the luxury of irresponsible poverty for the cares of office and of financial management. As private individuals they could afford to doubt whether bishops should enjoy any freehold possessions at all, rather than an honest 'maintenance'. As late as 1576 a bishop could publicly state the opinion that lordships, manors and tithes were a hindrance to scholars and preachers and that it would be better to pay them salaries and free them from temporal cares.[35] The men of 1559 were both authors and prisoners of an exaggerated propaganda which for twenty-five years had drawn a vivid and unreal contrast between the devotion and simplicity of the apostolic bishops and the corruption of the false and worldly prelates. 'The bishops are in future to have no palaces, estates or country seats,' wrote John Parkhurst with satisfaction, which did not prevent him from censuring the 'ambition' of some of his friends who were marked out for preferment. 'Let others have their bishoprics.' 'This burden I have positively determined to shake off,' echoed his erstwhile pupil, John Jewel.[36] Yet these attitudes, which may have owed as much to a reading of Horace as to any experience of the real world, did not prevent Parkhurst from accepting Norwich, or Jewel Salisbury. Once in office the new bishops were faced with facts remote from literary and polemical clichés. Thomas Bentham of Coventry and Lichfield would find himself without ready cash and without credit to borrow, worried above all about the market price of salt fish and cheap cloth.[37] In some dioceses there were massive arrears in the first-fruits and tenths owed by the clergy to the crown, for which the bishops were personally accountable as soon as they were installed.[38] The cost of preferment was not absent from the minds of the bishops when they made their concerted resistance to the enforced loss of their lands, and spoke of 'consideration of our chargeable expectation, and for the burden of necessary furniture of our houses'. But they hastened to add that their concern was 'not in respect of any private worldly advancement or temporal gain'.[39] Evidently the émigré bishops were torn between double standards, poised on the horns of a dilemma as old as the presence of the Christian Church in the world of temporal possession and power. A wealthy church and wealthy churchmen were hard to square with the protestant ethic. Yet a poor church would be a despised church, lacking influence. The enforced exchanges were not accompanied by any redefinition or reduction of the dignity and onerous responsibilities of the bishops.

The biographer of Grindal finds comparatively little to say about matters of worldly survival and worldly advancement, not only because Grindal was unworldly and innocent of careerism but because he was a bachelor, free of many of the considerations which perplexed his boyhood friend Sandys, father of seven sons and two daughters. Yet it is at this point that we have to contend with a tradition which represents Grindal as the most diffident of the new bishops, the one most inclined to shrink from the inevitable compromises of office into a scrupulous and self-preserving *nolo episcopari*. The roots of the tradition are to be found in some letters addressed to Peter Martyr by a correspondent threatened with elevation to a bishopric and written in a tone which Martyr found distasteful. 'I deposit, my father, with all simplicity, with yourself alone, the secrets of my heart, and I entreat you, for Christ's sake, to keep my secret to yourself, and return me an answer as soon as possible, as to what you think I ought to do in this case.' Although such outpourings could not have been more foreign to his nature, this correspondence by a grave lapse of judgment was attributed by Strype to Grindal, and it became the keystone of a totally false construction of his character. Their true author was not Grindal but his old college friend Thomas Sampson, and to Sampson they were correctly assigned by the nineteenth-century editor of the volumes known as the *Zurich Letters*.[40]

We know from Grindal's later correspondence with Zürich that his thinking in 1559 turned on the consequences which would follow if he and others of his party refused episcopal office. The Church would be abandoned to the leadership of 'semi-papists', Lutherans and mere time-servers.[41] Reading his copy of Bucer's *De regno Christi* on the restitution of the true Christian ministry Grindal took particular note of Bucer's opinion that it was better for the Church to have no pastors at all than to be served by 'wolves, thieves, robbers, or at least hirelings'. The passage is marked and summarized in the margin and it was perhaps at this critical moment in his life that this was done.[42] When all doubts had been resolved Grindal wrote to tell Peter Martyr of his firm resolve to undertake episcopal appointment on the grounds that the greater evil would be to allow the Church to fall into the wrong hands. Martyr received the news of his decision with enthusiastic approval. 'As to your decision not to forsake the Church nor refuse the positions offered, I strongly approve it. For if you who by the grace of God are especially instructed in religion and are pillars of that Church in such a dearth of ministers withdraw your hands and arms from the task, by whom will the work proceed? ... What you say afterwards concerning external matters that they did not seem to you sufficiently contentious for you to refuse a calling, you seem to me to speak piously and correctly.'[43]

Peter Martyr's encouragement was easily given by a distant and to that extent irresponsible observer. The Swiss commentators on the English scene were sufficiently pragmatic to urge on their co-religionists compromises which they themselves might well have found unacceptable. They remained ignorant, and perhaps wilfully ignorant, of English political conditions, insensitive to the true relationship which existed under the Tudors between ministers of the Gospel and the civil power. The ultimate wisdom of Grindal's acceptance of office, as conversely of the renunciation of some of his friends, could not be proven in 1559. Even the puritan extremist John Field would later censure David Whitehead, one of those who made the great refusal, as 'a man that would have all well first, and then he would labour that all should be well'.[44] Where did the responsible exercise of conscience end and mere scruples begin?

In November 1559 this question was nicely posed when a small silver crucifix and candles reappeared in the queen's chapel. This may have been intended as no more than a diplomatic gesture in support of the negotiations for a royal marriage then in desultory progress. But Sandys was one of the bishops who feared a general reaction, in the form of the restoration to the churches of the images of Christ on the cross, with Mary and John, which had so recently been removed and destroyed. Could the old images be tolerated? Did they possess the quality of indifference which would make them a legitimate subject for a royal edict? Even Archbishop Parker was unhappy and Cox drafted a letter to the queen offering reasons 'why I dare not minister in your grace's chapel, the lights and cross remaining'. But it was one thing to judge such ornaments inexpedient and another to take a stand in resistance to them as actually unlawful. Jewel, Sandys, and, almost certainly, Grindal were prepared to take such a stand. Jewel thought that the queen would have to choose between crosses and the bishops whom she had just appointed and Sandys later reported that he was 'very near being deposed' because of his vehemence in the matter.[45]

Among the Parker MSS. at Corpus Christi College Cambridge there is an unsigned and undated document consisting of a letter to the queen, prefacing a treatise headed 'Reasons Against Images in Churches'. Towards the end of a catalogue of scriptural citations and 'proofs out of the Fathers, Councils and Histories' comes a bold affirmation:

Having thus declared unto your Highness a few causes of many, which do move our consciences in this matter, we beseech your Highness most humbly not to strain us any further; but to consider that God's word doth threaten a terrible judgment unto us if we, being pastors and ministers in his Church, should assent to the thing which in our learning and conscience we are persuaded doth tend to the confirmation of error, superstition, and idolatry, and finally to the ruin of the souls committed to our charge, for the which we must give an accompt to the Prince of pastors at the last day. We pray your Majesty also not to be offended with this our plainness and liberty, which all good and Christian princes have ever taken in good part at the hands of godly bishops.

Elizabeth was reminded of the examples of the emperors Theodosius and Valentinian II who had accepted the admonition of St Ambrose, and she was invited to refer 'these and such-like controversies of religion' to a synod of bishops and other learned men, as Constantine and other christian emperors had done. There are obvious resemblances between this document and the famous letter which Grindal addressed to the queen in December 1576,[46] both in the kind of church–queen relations which it envisages and in the appeal to the example of St Ambrose in his dealings with the christian emperors of his day. According to Foxe, who printed 'Reasons Against Images' in the 1583 edition of *Acts and Monuments*, the treatise was Edwardian in origin, and had been drawn up by Bishop Ridley 'in the name, as it seemeth, of the whole clergy' for presentation to King Edward VI. But there are difficulties in believing this and the strong possibility remains that Grindal was the compiler of a document which reads like a dry run for his later manifesto. A copy of the letter preserved (but without the treatise) among the Laud–Selden–Fairhurst papers recently restored to Lambeth Palace Library is dated in Grindal's hand '5 Feb 1559(/60)'.[47]

Nor can we be confident that the queen ever saw 'Reasons Against Images'. Even if she did she was unlikely to consent to refer the question to a synodical free-for-all. But in early February 1560 the Privy Council arranged the next best thing: a formal disputation between Parker and Cox on one side and Jewel and Grindal on the other, before a lay tribunal. Jewel, who is our only source for the staging of this debate, expected a dire outcome, warning Martyr: 'I shall not again write to you as a bishop.' But he was wrong and Sandys was soon telling his Swiss friends that God had delivered his Church 'from stumbling-blocks of this kind', leaving only the popish vestments in dispute, which he hoped would not remain for very long.[48] Since the cross and candlesticks remained undisturbed in the queen's chapel for years to come, Sandys must have meant that Elizabeth was no longer insistent on the replacement of roods and the rood statuary in parish churches. If this is indeed what the queen had wanted then it had been a narrow squeak, for the credit of the newly appointed bishops could hardly have survived such a public rebuke to their reformist convictions. And we know that some of them, Grindal no doubt included, considered the matter to be non-negotiable.

A battle had been won but not the war. When Grindal became archbishop of Canterbury sixteen years later, further evidence of the queen's deep lack of sympathy for cherished principles of reformed religion provided fresh incentive to exercise 'plainness and liberty' in speech and writing. Should resistance be offered, or was it safe in conscience as well as prudent to avoid a confrontation? On that occasion Grindal chose to stand his ground, with disastrous consequences.

Yet even in his disgrace Grindal is not likely to have regretted the decision of 1559. All but the most disenchanted critic of Elizabeth's religious policies would have been forced to admit that under her aegis and in her name, within the structure of the Elizabethan settlement, reform had proceeded, and that nothing had so much assisted its progress as the promotion of notable protestant leaders. By a sure instinct the Accession Day of Elizabeth came to be called the Birthday of the Gospel.[49] Since the omnicompetence of the Supreme Governor was necessarily a constitutional fiction, the holder of high office enjoyed many opportunities to lead the Church in directions which the queen had not intended. In the long run it was in the power of these subjects to determine not only the immediate destiny of the Church of England but the quality of English civilization, which by the seventeenth century was profoundly protestant in character: a world which Elizabeth, with her old-fashioned catholic oaths,[50] never knew. It was above all necessary to be in office, to enjoy, within whatever limitations, this capacity.

The royal visitation which was mounted in the summer of 1559 to set the Church in order and to impose the terms of the settlement, including the oath of supremacy, provided an early example of the extent to which the effective control of ecclesiastical policy lay with its agents. The Injunctions prepared for the visitation dealt generally with 'the suppression of superstition' and ordered specifically the removal and destruction of a variety of 'things superstitious', including shrines, candlesticks, pictures and 'all other monuments of feigned miracles, pilgrimages, idolatry and superstition, so that there remain no memory of the same in walls, glasses, windows or elsewhere'. Yet they directed, in effect, that the practice of the Church should stop short of the more thoroughly reformed models. There was no relaxation of the ornaments rubric arising from the Act of Uniformity, which appeared to require the use of the eucharistic vestments, while the outdoor apparel of the clergy was to conform to the traditional pattern, including the clerical square cap abhorred by the reformers. Inventories were to be made of 'vestments, copes and other ornaments', as of plate and liturgical books, implying the preservation of such articles for some undeclared but probably pecuniary purpose. There was no specific order for the removal of altars, and no reference to rood-lofts, crosses and the images of Mary and John which were normally erected on the rood-loft.[51]

Few protestants with experience of the Swiss and South German churches could regard stone altars as matters of indifference. Rather they were all too solid affirmations of the popish doctrine of the mass. The matter was of sufficient gravity for some of the clergy to place on record 'Certain reasons to be offered to the queen's majesty's consideration why it is not convenient that the communion should be ministered at an altar'. After marshalling appropriate precedents from Scripture and church history the memorandum listed a number of pragmatic and circumstantial arguments. Altars were said to be inconsistent with the practice both of the Edwardian Church and the continental protestant churches, the eccentric case of Lutheran Saxony alone excepted. Moreover they were incompatible with the Book of Common Prayer, already enacted, which had been thought sufficient mandate 'in a great number of places' for their removal.

> It may also please your Majesty to join hereunto the judgment of the learned and godly martyrs of this realm who of late have given their lives for testimony of the truth: as of Dr Cranmer, archbishop of Canterbury, ... and also of Dr Ridley, bishop of London, who travailed specially in this matter of altars and put certain reasons of his doings in print which remain to this day; of Mr Latimer, Mr Hooper, Mr Bradford and all the rest, who to the end did stand in defence of that book. So that by re-edifying of altars we shall also seem to join with the adversaries that burned those good men, in condemning some part of their doctrine.

This document bears a distinct family resemblance to Grindal's letter to the queen of 1576 and to the letter and treatise 'Reasons Against Images' of February 1560. So it is with no surprise that we find a copy endorsed and annotated in Grindal's hand.[52] It may have been as a response to this *démarche* that the queen sanctioned the addition of an injunction which recognized the *fait accompli* of the removal of altars 'in many and sundry parts of the realm', provided an orderly procedure for future removals and made appropriate directions for the ordering of holy tables in the place of altars. But Grindal and other sometime exiles can hardly have been pleased with the order with which this was joined, requiring that the common bread used in the communion in Edwardian days and assumed in the 1559 revision of the Prayer Book be replaced with a modified form of wafer bread, 'for the more reverence to be given to these holy mysteries'.

Flimsy though our knowledge of the visitation is (only certain proceedings in the northern province and in the dioceses of London, Norwich and Ely are documented)[53] events in London suggest that the zeal of the visitors exceeded the terms of the Injunctions, to the extent of effecting an almost irreversible alteration in the physical setting of Anglican devotion. In their meeting in St Paul's, for example, the visitors seem not only to have ordered the purging of the cathedral of images, idols and altars, and the substitution of decent tables for altars, but to have enjoined that none of the cathedral clergy should use the tonsure or wear amices or copes, but 'to use only a surplice in the service time'.[54] The intrusion of the cross in the queen's chapel soon after she returned to Court after the summer's progress may have been a retort to such generous interpretations of the queen's orders. Subsequent efforts by the bishops to devise a common policy on ceremonial matters reflect the recognition that the royal visitation had made some aspects of the religious settlement according to the queen's interpretation of it all but unworkable; while orders taken by the Ecclesiastical Commission in October 1561 reveal much variety of practice, 'much strife and contention' about aspects of the ecclesiastical fabric not specified in the Injunctions.[55]

London's chroniclers recorded the more spectacular acts of officially inspired iconoclasm which accompanied the activities of the visitors appointed for the dioceses of London, Norwich and Ely.[56] The visitors included Robert Horne, the future bishop of Winchester, and Thomas Huycke, a civil lawyer and Genevan exile who was about to be appointed Grindal's vicar general. 12 August 1559 saw the removal from St Paul's of altars, roods and rood-lofts, with the Mary and John. The first day of St Bartholomew's Fair, 24 August, was chosen to ensure the maximum audience for two great fires lit in Cheapside and fed with roods and images, the people observing 'with great wonder'. 'The time after Bartholomew-tide', wrote Machyn, they burned 'all the roods and Maries and Johns and many other of the church goods, both copes, crosses, censors, altar-cloths, rood-cloths, bells, banners, books and banner-stays, wainscot, with much more gear'. As an undertaker Machyn knew the value of such 'gear'. Jewel wrote after his own labours in the western dioceses of the harvest, or rather 'wilderness' of superstition which the Marian years had left for the gathering.[57] Unauthorized acts of iconoclasm were regarded in the sixteenth century as particularly violent symbols of insubordination. The bonfires of Cheapside were a demonstration that a revolution had been launched from above. Bishop Frere called them 'a mild revenge ... for the grislier burnings of Mary's reign'.[58]

Although Strype named Grindal as one of the visitors for the northern province this was a mistake. It was Sandys, not Grindal, who was sent north. Grindal's place was already at the centre. The letters patent directing the visitation of the northern province (as presumably for other divisions) spoke of a procedure for referring cases to 'commissariis nostris Londini residentibus et ad ecclesias-ticarum rerum reformationem designatis'.[59] When the visitors had finished with the capital in late August and had proceeded to Hertfordshire and Essex and on into East Anglia they left behind the permanent Ecclesiastical Commission which had been set up on 19 July, and which included, besides its function as a court of reference, comprehensive powers of ecclesiastical correction as a court of first instance and a special charge to enquire into matters of public order within the city of London and ten miles' compass. Parker, 'nominated bishop of Canterbury', and Grindal, 'nomi-nated bishop of London', were named first in the Commission and were part of the inner quorum.[60] According to the chronicler Wriothesley, the orders of 12 August relating to St Paul's were made not by the visitors but by Grindal and Dr May, the new dean, 'and other of the commissioners'.[61] On 20 October an oversight in the original letters patent was remedied when the Commissioners were empowered to administer the oath of supremacy. A letter from Cecil implies that the Commissioners, rather than the visitors, would be expected to handle with appropriate delicacy any refusals of the oath by public figures of some consequence.[62]

Thereafter the business which came into the hands of Grindal and his fellow commissioners in London was of greater importance than the functions of the itinerating visitors, who for the duration of the visitation assumed responsibility for all the normal, hum-drum procedures of ecclesiastical administration. This included the proving of wills and the prosecution of cases of adultery and breach of promise, while a major portion of the visitors' time was spent on business arising immediately from the religious settle-ment if often relatively uncontentious: for example, the hearing of pleas from married clergy for the restitution of the benefices of which they had been deprived under Mary.[63] In contrast to the experience of his recent companions of the exile, Grindal's attention was concentrated on more momentous and politically sensitive business.

Nor was this a passing episode of the months before Grindal assumed his episcopal functions. As we know from the extant act books of the corresponding body in the northern province, the Commissioners for Causes Ecclesiastical approximated from the earliest years of the reign to a court, resembling in its procedures other ecclesiastical courts, but far outstripping them in its powers, an immediate arm of the royal supremacy.[64] From such fragmentary records of its activities as survive it is clear that it was before the Ecclesiastical Commission, meeting in London, rather than in the ordinary ecclesiastical courts, that matters of major consequence received attention: above all, matters concerning the Old Religion. In 1561 a number of prominent catholics imprisoned in the Fleet, including Bishop Scot of Chester, Dr Cole, the late dean of St Paul's, and Dr Harpsfield, late archdeacon of London, were there by order of the Commissioners, headed by Grindal, who were keeping more than fifty other leading divines and scholars of the old faith under close surveillance.[65] In 1566 Grindal was named as the fit person to control the entry of slanderous and seditious books into the port of London, in his capacity as a commissioner.[66] In 1568 the Commissioners expressed surprise when the vice-chancellor of Cambridge University questioned their authority to intervene in its affairs, 'having in fresh memory our continual proceedings in this Commission, since the first time of it; and that we have from time to time called as occasion served out of both the universities'. Those summoned had always made their humble appearance, and by authority of the Commissioners more than forty 'stubborn papists and hard adversaries of God's truth' had been removed from the two universities.[67] In the same year the Commissioners ordered a raid on the Portuguese Embassy to detect English recusants attending mass on the premises. When the ambassador asked who had signed the letters ordering this intervention he was told: 'the bishop of London and others that were in commission for such matters.' It was considered scandalous that the ambassador had declared that 'he cared not for the bishop of London his hand if the queen's hand were not at it.'[68]

When the Ecclesiastical Commissioners concerned themselves with such small beer as a case of conjugal rights, it was because the woman in question was kept from her husband by her mistress, the Lady Ratcliff, a prominent lady of the Court. This case occupied the Commissioners on numerous occasions between December 1560 and March 1562, not to mention two embarrassingly personal confrontations between the bishop and the lady at Grindal's own house and at Court.[69] The more portentous business of Lady Catherine Grey's clandestine marriage to the earl of Hertford, as well as the tragi-comedy of her unfortunate sister Mary's incongruous match with Sergeant Porter, were other *causes célèbres* where the facts and attendant circumstances were established by Grindal and his fellow Commissioners.[70]

In the absence of the bulk of the records of the Ecclesiastical Commissioners the historian of the Elizabethan Church is deprived of many of the headline stories and may even decide that his task is rendered impossible. For the biographer of Grindal this hiatus may seriously distort his judgment. It seems likely that in the 1560s it was as an ecclesiastical commissioner that this lawyer-like, judicious bishop was principally engaged in church government. If these activities were to be placed on record in their completeness it is inconceivable that he could ever have won his posthumous reputation for mild incompetence. July 1559, when Grindal may have assembled for the first time with his fellow commissioners, or November, when the unfinished business of the royal visitation began to come in, not the month of December when he was made bishop, marks the beginning of Grindal's public service in the Elizabethan Church. It is a service largely obliterated by the almost total loss of the documents which must have once recorded it.

But in the Public Record Office and in the Cecil papers among the Lansdowne Manuscripts in the British Library there is suggestive evidence of Grindal's commanding role in early Elizabethan ecclesiastical government: a total of ninety-eight letters

Figure 2 A 'familiar' letter from Grindal to Cecil, 15 October 1563. The first page reads, 'Salutem in Christo servatore. As I am gladde to heare that yor disease dimminisheth, so I am sorie it hangeth on youe so longe. Yt is sayd yor payne is in yor backe. I wille be bolde to communicate unto you my coniecture off the cawse theroff and off the meanes to avoyde the lyke hereafter, nott by anie arte off physicke, but apon some experience of myne owne bodye in the lyke case. When I came firste frome beyonde seas, I felte great heate in my backe and feared the stone. I cutte my dublettes, my peticotes in the backe, I wente ungyrte, I coulde nott abyde to sytte by a quission [cushion] etc. In continuance I strived so to coole my backe that I felle into the contrarie, so that a smalle colde taken by that parte, by goynge syngle and specially by rydynge single, to this daye casteth me into a stitche which begynneth under the poynte of one shuldre or bothe, and sodeynly claspeth on the smalle off my backe, and ther remayneth XV or XX dayes. I doo remember one morninge a yeare and more agone, ye shewed me yor dublettes cutte, and voydett in the backe, and that ye feared the stoone. I am surely perswadett that by resystinge heate (which mighte come then by some accident) ye have cooled yor backe to moche, rydden and goone syngle, and so have browghte those partes to great imbecillitie.' The British Library, MS. Lansd. 6, no. 77, fol. 1.

Sal. in Christ Seruãpe. As I am gladde to heare y
yo[ur] disease diminisheth, so I am sorie it hangeth
on yo[ur] s[o] longe. It is sayd y[t] payne is in
yo[ur] backe. I wille be boilde to hemiurate vnto yo
my semiltence of ye raw[e] thereof, & of the
meanes to avoyde the like hereaftee, nott by
anie arte of Physirke, but apon some experience
of mynne owne bodie in y[e] lyke case. Whe[n] I
came first from beyonde sea, I felt great
heate in my backe & heard y[e] spone, I rubbe
my subilitie, my periodes in the backe, I was
hungryrte, I coulde nott abyde to sytte by a
quisshoy &c. So settimance I stirred to
roote my backe, & y[t] I sitte into y[e] contrarie,
so y[t] a smalie colde takt to y[e] parte, by
coynge synepe, & sperialle by rycynge
singe of this daye raseth me vnto a stitching
w[hich] begynneth vnder the poynte of one hatche
or bothe, & odermy rasyeth on sore matte
of my backe, & ther remayneth xv. or xx.
dayes. I doo remember one morninge
a yeare and more agone, we shewed me
yo[ur] subiltter matter, & voideth in the backe,
& y[t] y[e] feared y[e] spone. I am surely
perswadett y[t] by relyssinge heate (w[hich] mighte
hame theis by some accident) ye haue
cooled yo[ur] backe to moche, ryddny and groone
synepe, & so haue broughte those parkes to
greate imberishitie.

written to Cecil, sixty-eight of them in his ten years as bishop of London. They are what the sixteenth century knew as 'familiar letters', tossed off in the bishop's own hand, without deference or literary affectation, and usually concerned with a single item of urgent, public business. Written as man to man, they suggest that in the 1560s Grindal was Cecil's ecclesiastical counterpart. He was also a friend, often exchanging solicitude and advice about matters of health and, when the grapes ripened at Fulham, sending a bunch of the first fruits to his patron.[71]

On 21 December 1559 Grindal was consecrated bishop by Archbishop Parker in the chapel at Lambeth, on the same occasion as his old companion Sandys, together with Cox and Meyrick, nominated for Bangor. (Parker's own consecration, a subject on which much controversial ink has been spilt, had been consummated only four days earlier, in the same place.) Two days later he was at last installed and enthroned in St Paul's Cathedral. A minor canon intoned the Te Deum 'in lingua materna, viz. anglicana', and the choir and organs joined in. The cantor then intoned: 'O Lord, save thy servant our bishop,' the choir responding: 'And send him help from thy holy place.' But Grindal was not present to hear these encouraging words. According to custom both he and the archbishop were represented on this occasion by proxies.[72]

6

THIS CUMBROUS CHARGE

THIS office 'requireth a perfect man, to teach, govern and guide this learned and wise people: this great and large diocese doth wish for one furnished as Samuel, or rather as Solomon, with all graces and gifts of learning, policy, wisdom and knowledge of things belonging both to God and men.' So, with a judicious mixture of hyperbole and flattery, pronounced Grindal's successor, Edwin Sandys, as he occupied the pulpit at Paul's Cross 'at his first coming to the bishopric of London'.[1]

London itself was daunting. A population of perhaps 50,000 at Henry VIII's accession had already nearly doubled in size and by Shakespeare's time would be on the way to doubling again.[2] This was not the product of natural increase for the city was mercilessly consumptive of its own. In 1562, when more than 17,000 persons died of the plague alone, the city fathers made repeated orders to prevent the landlords of property in 'alleys and back lanes' immediately re-letting houses and shops vacated by death to newcomers from the country who were scrambling over the dead, as it were, to find accommodation. Multiple occupancy was established as a way of life.[3] London was already wreathed in smog, burning 'sea coal' from Newcastle in such quantity that the fabric of St Paul's Cathedral was soon to be threatened by its corrosive effects, 'especially in moist weather'.[4] The city, in the shape of the varied and overlapping forms and institutions of its government — civic authorities, liveried companies, parish vestries, church courts — confronted overcrowding and the threat to public order with an old-fashioned confidence in civic values and in the sterling qualities of the economically independent householder, placing a heavy burden on those traditional guarantors of the social fabric. The measure of its success is reflected in the title of a recent study of the government of Elizabethan London: *The Politics of Stability*. 'If stability is a virtue, Elizabeth London must be proclaimed a paragon.'[5]

Yet Sandys was reminded of that city which Christ, casting his eye towards it, 'bewailed the lamentable estate thereof, and that with tears'. 'This cumbrous charge hath made many a good and godly man to withdraw himself, to shrink back, utterly to refuse the like place and calling.'[6] As was said of a later bishop of London: 'Quis enim curae tantae molem sponse subeat?' Who would willingly undertake such a burden?[7] It was Grindal's view, after his promotion to higher things, that 'the bishop of London is always to be pitied.'[8]

An Elizabethan bishop was not primarily an agent of social welfare. London as a melting pot provided no more than the challenging setting within which its father in God perceived the specific functions of his 'cumbrous charge'. (Grindal's comment on the problem of over-population was remote and bookish: Aristotle disallowed it, 'like as he doth the other contrary extremity'.)[9] But as diocesan of one of the largest and most populous sees in England the bishop was stretched almost beyond endurance by the scale and complexity of his ecclesiastical and political functions. Besides the archdeaconry of London itself the see consisted of four rural archdeaconries, Essex, Colchester, Middlesex and St Albans, embracing Essex, Middlesex and part of Hertfordshire. In the city 92 out of a total of 111 parishes came under episcopal jurisdiction (most of the remainder being peculiars of the dean and chapter of St Paul's or of the archbishop of Canterbury), and in the country 480. The archdeaconries of Essex, Colchester and Middlesex were subdivided into rural deaneries, 'but thereof hath been no deans within the memory of man'. Besides the five archdeacons the bishop was supported by two commissaries in Essex 'whose jurisdictions', it was said in 1563, 'in some points are above the archdeacons' and in some points equal with theirs'.[10]

Beyond his diocesan function, the bishop of London was charged with the spiritual government of Englishmen overseas, the chaplains and their congregations of merchants, government agents and soldiers. Conversely, Grindal and his successors were also responsible for oversight of the churches of protestant 'strangers' in London: French, Dutch, Italian and Spanish. Moreover the bishop of London occupied a position of special responsibility and sensitivity in the hierarchy. In all matters concerning the implementation of ecclesiastical policy the London churches were supposed to be the model. Their pulpits were sounding-boards for government policy: or for private and sectional discontent. The loudest sounding-board of all, the pulpit at Paul's Cross, was the bishop's care, in more than one sense. Week by week he had to find the preacher, never an easy task. (In Edward's time Bishop Ridley had charged the future Archbishop Parker to take his turn 'as ye will answer for the contrary ... to Almighty God, at your own peril'. And John Foxe would write to Grindal: 'Why do you want to crucify me at Paul's Cross?')[11] Politically, the bishop of London was under the immediate eye of the Court. Ecclesiastically, he was the right arm of the archbishop of Canterbury, as dean of the province the normal channel for transmitting archiepiscopal mandates and letters to the other bishops. The metropolitan was often himself acting on higher orders so that the bishop of London formed the third link in a chain of command which ran down from the Supreme Governor, or Privy Council, the constant recipient of demands for action, or information; recipient too of numerous more trivial commissions, such as briefs for public collections for the relief of the victims of personal calamity, or of townships destroyed by fire.[12] Over and above all this Grindal was a most active member, almost the quorum in himself, of the Ecclesiastical Commission. Nor should we forget that he was the manager, in effect, of a major landed estate, with great houses in London and at Fulham and Hadham, and a revenue of a little over £1,000 a year, equivalent to the income of some of the wealthier secular landlords.

If the biographer of a bishop of London were to be supplied with adequate information for all of these sectors of activity he might find his task as daunting as that of the public life of the bishop himself. As things are, his problems are greatly simplified. An earlier historian thought that 'puritan zeal plus the Great Fire effectually wiped out the story of the diocese of London.'[13] This, happily, is nonsense, but the story of the diocese is not the same thing as the story of its bishops. The archives which survive are voluminous, but they record the least personal, most institutionalized aspects of the episcopal office. The documentation for any episcopate of the later sixteenth century is likely to include, with varying completeness, some of the records of visitation, and the act books of the bishop's own consistory court and of the archdeacons' courts, recording matters requiring reform and detected through the process of visitation or at other times by the churchwardens, together with much other business brought before the courts by parties. There will also be the depositions of witnesses, testimony as generous in circumstantial detail as that of Shakespeare's Mistress Quickly. These are windows, if not into men's souls, at least into sixteenth-century society, its tensions and moral values. But leafing through the act books and noting any number of sexual crimes and misdemeanours, disputes over tithe, contested wills, breaches of promise and breaches of the peace, the ecclesiastical historian will find little to supply the history of the Church in a more momentous sense, and for the purposes of ecclesiastical biography, still less. The bulk of this business was in the hands of the bishop's officers, the chancellor (in London combining the distinct offices of vicar-general and official principal) and his subordinates; while the archdeacons, those 'eyes' of the bishop, themselves deputed the conduct of their courts to their own officials and other professional lawyers and administrators. (One recalls the old rhyme about fleas: and so *ad infinitum*.) Apart from sometimes disturbing the tenure of these offices, the passing of one bishop and the advent of another might have little perceptible influence on day-to-day administration. The records will reflect dimly, if at all, the degree of concern and energy which a particular bishop may have brought to his pastoral oversight.

The bishop might and often did involve himself directly in visitation, appearing personally in his cathedral and in the various deaneries and other centres of the diocese. But the questions asked and the injunctions delivered on such occasions were as likely to reflect what other bishops had ordered or enquired as any informed concern with the particular state of the diocese, while a bishop would normally leave to others the prosecution of the disciplinary cases initiated by his visitation. The ordination of clergy and their institution to benefices (or 'collation' where the bishop was patron as well as ordinary) were also matters where the bishop intervened directly in the care of his diocese. It was through the making and placing of clergy that he could hope most reasonably to influence the quality of religious life, for, as with all administrative systems of an essentially medieval character, the power of patronage was paramount. Yet in this area, too, the freedom of a bishop was circumscribed. To a great extent he was obliged to ordain, and to institute in livings, the men who appeared before him, products of a system in which he himself was caught up and over which he exercised little control. Nevertheless we shall come across Grindal not only on the fairway but in the rough of these often mechanical procedures, obtruding his person to an unusual extent, evidently searching for the tangible reality of pastoral care in the unpromising thickets of traditional ecclesiastical practice.

Only accidentally have more telling records survived of the matters which concerned a bishop most properly, and which allowed for little delegation. For only two Elizabethan bishops are there substantial collections of correspondence, enabling us to inspect what passed across the desk from day to day. In one of these we can observe Thomas Bentham of Coventry and Lichfield in the early months of his episcopate, struggling to gain a financial and political toehold in an alien environment; in the other, John Parkhurst of Norwich, ten years on, deep in the toils of his own benevolent ineptitude in administration.[14] There is no prospect of

finding the materials for such a frank portrait of Grindal as bishop
of London. From the Jacobean period there survives the remarkable diary of a famous and long-lived archbishop of York, Tobie
Matthew.[15] Matthew was a popular as well as courtly preacher,
and his diary takes the form of a record of almost 2,000 sermons
preached up and down the north of England during a preaching
career of forty-one years. We learn how this indefatigable prelate
struggled against snow and flood and the frailties of his own
constitution ('wonderful great distillations of rheum'), journeying
by coach or on horseback through the length of his vast and
scattered diocese. We also catch sight of him, frequently, confirming children: as many as 500 on a single occasion. But for Grindal's
biographer this is a painful reminder that we do not know whether
as a bishop he was a regular preacher, and that far from there being
any record of the circumstances in which he confirmed children it
is an open question whether the rite of confirmation was in regular
use in the early Elizabethan Church.

Curiously, we are better informed about Grindal's minor responsibility, although by no means of minor interest to him: his
role as superintendent of the 'stranger churches', which is the
subject of the next chapter. As diocesan he appears dramatically
only in certain extraordinary episodes, to which the two following
chapters are devoted. The remainder of this chapter examines his
approach to the initial challenge of his diocese; and first, to his
attack on the problem of manpower.

To analyse the record of Grindal's early ordinations is to be
struck by an ambiguity which lies at the heart of an understanding
of the mandate of this or any other leader of a reformed Church,
such as the English Church now aspired to be. The ambiguity was
present in the Church itself, which was at one and the same time an
inherited institution, embracing the entire population, and requiring to be staffed with clergy qualified to perform a routinized role
and traditional functions; and the Church as protestants understood it in the light of biblical, and especially Pauline symbolism,
composed of 'lively stones' and constantly in the process of building or 'edification' through the preaching and reception of the
gospel — more a movement than an organization. In making
ministers, Grindal was pursuing two not entirely consistent objectives: staffing and maintaining the ongoing institution; and sending out the evangelists and pastors capable of erecting within his
diocese a godly, reformed, instructed Church such as hardly existed except as an ideal. Inevitably the administrative, routinized
aspect of his ordaining function took a kind of precedence.
Parishes could not be left unserved. Candidates for orders with a

valid title and the minimal qualifications (or even, at a time when manpower was scarce, without them) could not be turned away. Patrons could not be disappointed without legal repercussions.[16] But at the same time Grindal could and did use his own powers of patronage, both his capacity to confer orders and his right to appoint to many offices and benefices, to advance well-qualified men who understood their ministry in the creative, dynamic terms of the Reformation.

At the end of 1559 Grindal's diocese, in common with the Church of England as a whole, faced a gross deficiency of clergy. This was due in part to the deprivation of those who had refused the oath of supremacy. In the London diocese all five archdeacons were deprived, eleven prebendal stalls were empty, most of them through deprivation, and twenty of the ninety-one city churches under the bishop's jurisdiction were vacant as a result of the royal visitation.[17] Other vacancies may have arisen from the recent devastating epidemic of influenza.[18] In some vacant London churches there were emergency arrangements, with ministers doubling up. Partly the problem was due to a decline in recruitment in a period of uncertainty about the ecclesiastical future, and of a pervasive anticlericalism which by now was coming home to roost. 'The general contempt of the ministry', wrote William Harrison, himself an Essex parson, had led 'the greatest part of the more excellent wits' to enter other professions and occupations, 'utterly giving over the study of the scriptures, for fear lest they should in time not get their bread by the same'.[19]

In 1559 there was a sudden flood of recruits to take advantage of a labour market so short of supply, but their quality was dubious.[20] Within a year Grindal had ordained no fewer than 221, and in the following year seventy-three more, not all with titles to serve in his own diocese. These included in January 1560, at the peak, forty ordained to the diaconate and seven to the priesthood on one occasion, and on another thirty-seven to the diaconate and thirty to the priesthood, including twenty-six made deacons in the previous session. These 294 were only some fifty less than the total number whom Grindal would ordain in the remaining eight years of his episcopate. Although a start was made with ordinands appropriately qualified in age and academic standing, the bottom of the barrel may soon have been reached. A high proportion of the ordinands of 1560 were non-graduates, and 126, or more than half, were over the age of thirty, no less than twelve of them more than fifty years of age. They were not spared examination of their fitness, but the examinations seem to have been conducted by the archdeacon of London single-handed, and always in a single day.

Within a few months Archbishop Parker wrote to Grindal re-marking that hitherto, 'occasioned by the great want of ministers', both he and Grindal had admitted to the ministry 'sundry artificers and others, not traded and brought up in learning, and, as it happened in a multitude, some that were of base occupations'.[21] ('Lay hands suddenly on no man,' St Paul had warned Timothy.) In the future Grindal was to be more circumspect. It is one of the many blows that he has suffered at the hands of posterity that this often-quoted letter has been read as a personal rebuke from the metropolitan for a particular fault of this one bishop's slack admin-istration. Strype was stung to the unprecedented course of print-ing Grindal's ordination lists in full up to the date of the letter, giving prominence wherever possible to university experience and charitably explaining away its absence in other cases.[22] But Parker blamed himself as much as Grindal, and the letter stands in Grindal's Register only because, as dean of the province, it was his function to advertise all the other bishops of the matter, 'so that you and they may stay from collating such orders to so unmeet persons, unto such time as in a convocation we may meet together, and have further conference thereof'. In Parker's own diocese there were 233 ordinations in the first eight months of his archi-episcopate, as against less than fifty in the following fifteen years, and 150 of these were ordained on a single day. The quality of many, perhaps most, cannot have been other than mediocre, at best.[23]

It is well known that for a time Parker sought a solution to this crisis by reviving the office of 'lector' or reader to serve in the less desirable livings. In the first two years of the reign he appointed more than seventy such readers, although he later thought better of this stopgap device.[24] In one of their meetings at Lambeth, probably held in the first half of 1560, eleven bishops, Grindal included, put their names to a collection of injunctions to which all admitted to be readers were to subscribe, undertaking to read the service plainly and audibly but not to presume to preach or to administer the sacraments.[25] In London diocese thirty-nine readers were listed in Grindal's primary visitation, almost all of them in Essex, and all but a few were manning parishes single-handed.[26] Grindal was not pleased with such unsatisfactory rem-edies. Some years later he had occasion to correspond about church policy with the Scottish regent, the earl of Murray. The key, as he saw it, was to secure the Church's wealth for the support of the reformed ministry. In so far as England had diverted resources to 'private gain' while putting up with 'readers instead of teachers' it was not an example to follow.[27]

Many of Grindal's ordinands could not have been justified in more favourable circumstances. Nevertheless, scrutiny of the names suggests that far from ordaining blindly 'as it happened in a multitude' Grindal kept a weather eye for the needs of a reformed church, and clung to a defensible policy, even in the midst of the mass ordinations of 1560. One striking feature of the lists is a sprinkling of newly returned exiles. Although positive identification is not always possible, they seem to have been as many as twenty-one, or 10 per cent of the total.[28] Some of these were well qualified academically, including the martyrologist, John Foxe, whose name was written large in the Register, simply as 'Mr Fox'. Another familiar name was that of Thomas Horton, the Pembroke student who had been so deeply impressed with Bucer's incessant preaching and who was now back from Frankfurt. But other exiles had more unconventional qualifications. They included three or four members of the community of mostly proletarian exiles who had gathered under the patronage of the duchess of Suffolk at Wesel and had eventually settled at the obscure Swiss city of Aarau, where they had enjoyed the ministry of Miles Coverdale and, for a time, Thomas Lever.[29] On 25 April 1560 the thirty deacons ordained included two weavers from this group, no ordinary 'artisans'. William Betts, aged thirty-six, a Suffolk man from Hadleigh, must have been a survivor of the famous Rowland Taylor's Edwardian flock, while Thomas Upcher hailed from Bocking in Essex, a district notorious for its forceful and unorthodox vernacular protestantism. Upcher ('whom', Grindal wrote, 'I like right well') was soon placed in a parish in or around Colchester with a radical protestant tradition. A year later Grindal collated him to the rectory of Fordham, in the same district.[30] Was this a case of the poacher turned gamekeeper?

On the same day that Betts and Upcher were ordained Grindal conferred priest's orders on another Suffolk man, Walter Richardson of Saxmundham, who may have been a weaver and ex-member of Knox's Geneva congregation. A week later he was laying hands on Robert Pownall, one of the Aarau ministers, and within a month he wrote of a certain Essex living: 'I would gladly bestow it on Mr Powndell, but both I think it too little for him, and also his friends in London are about another purpose for him here.'[31] So Grindal was recruiting men known and valued, not so much for their academic learning as for their reputation in those intimate protestant circles which had so recently formed a sectarian minority group. Some of his recruits, it may well be, had proved themselves in the heroic ranks of those who had preserved a protestant church in Marian London itself, such as John Gough, at thirty-eight one of the older men and of no university. Gough seems to have been the son of an early protestant propagandist and printer of the same name. He was presented in the same year to the rectory of St Peter Cornhill, became one of the leaders of militant nonconformity, and was deprived of his living seven years later.[32]

We have already quoted from a letter which reveals Grindal as actively involved, not only in ordaining ardent protestants but in placing them. 'Fordham is well provided for ... I lack one for Tolshunt Darcy. I promised it to one and he now refuseth it ... I trust we shall do well enough for your archdeaconry.'[33] These parishes were at the farthest limits of the diocese, where the new archdeacon was John Pulleyn, in succession to a trimming Marian churchman, John Standish, who having subscribed was nevertheless deprived, being held to have 'satisfied not in other things'. Pulleyn had ministered to the secret protestant congregations of the Marian years, when his 'most common abiding' had been at Colchester, the 'city upon a hill' which was a place of refuge and inspiration for gospellers from many parts of the country. After various missions to the continent and a spell at Geneva, where he had some part in the Geneva Bible, he was again preaching around Colchester early in the new reign, irregularly. In April 1559 the Privy Council had ordered his arrest.[34] His appointment as archdeacon formalized the natural leadership which he had exerted among the godly of this precociously protestant region. But whether his elevation transformed him into a responsible administrator of the established Church may be doubted. In 1561 thirteen of the fifteen livings in the deanery of Colchester were vacant, and two years later the position was substantially unchanged. In Colchester itself in 1563, where some of the churches were admittedly too poorly endowed to support an incumbent (vacant 'per exilitatem' is the phrase of the formal certificate), there were only two clergy listed, while in the archdeaconry as a whole thirty-one parishes were unserved out of 156, including the important cloth town and protestant centre of Dedham, without a vicar for at least two years.[35] In Marian days the Colchester 'professors' had conducted their secret meetings in the inns of the town.[36] Were they still persisting in these sectarian habits? One wonders how far Grindal had succeeded in his evident desire to integrate the godly protestant community of north-east Essex with the established, parochial Church.

All but one of the remaining archdeaconries were also filled with returned exiles, in every case with Frankfurt men, which makes the choice of Pulleyn for radical Colchester all the more pointed.[37]

During the vacancy of the see John Mullins became archdeacon of London, an office he would hold for the next thirty-two years. One of Grindal's first acts was to collate to the archdeaconry of Middlesex his great friend Alexander Nowell. Two days later he appointed yet another prominent Frankfurter, Thomas Cole, to the archdeaconry of Essex. And when Nowell became dean of St Paul's, later in 1560, Grindal replaced him with Thomas Watts, whose house at Frankfurt Mullins had shared, and whom Grindal had recently ordained. In appointing to other offices and in filling the vacant prebends exiles and other known reformers were similarly favoured. The chancellorship, the senior administrative post in the diocese, went to the Genevan, Thomas Huycke. Thomas Donnett, another Frankfurt man, became one of Grindal's commissaries. The prebendal appointments included John Pilkington, the new bishop of Durham's younger brother; Thomas Penny, like William Turner a radical protestant naturalist and associate of Conrad Gesner who would later be deprived for nonconformity; Humphrey Alcockson a fellow exile at Strasbourg; the Scot James Calfhill, one of Grindal's chaplains, who succeeded William Alley after his preferment to the bishopric of Exeter; and Jean Veron, a noted preacher, writer and translator of French origin who had spent the recent past in the Tower and now re-emerged into prominence in the London pulpits, the most famous preacher of funeral sermons of his day.[38] Mullins, Nowell, Watts, Cole and Pulleyn were all sustained with prebends in addition to their major offices, not without pecuniary adjustments of a kind almost traditional in the affairs of St Paul's, and which Grindal had cause to remember from Edwardian days. Watts was obliged to lease his rich prebend of Tottenham Court for ninety-nine years at a fixed rent of £46 to a syndicate of officers of the royal household. The purpose of the transaction seems to have been to secure the timber and firewood from Highgate Wood for the use of the Court.[39]

The chapter, now more than partially reformed, was itself a valuable seat of patronage, holding twenty-one city livings in its gift. In 1563 it bestowed the rectory of St Peter-le-Poer on another printer-preacher, Robert Crowley, soon to be a leading agitator among London nonconformists, and in the same year Crowley was added to the chapter itself. When Veron died, also in 1563, Grindal collated Crowley to one of his London livings, while the other passed to Percival Wilburn, a major name in the radical puritan movement of the future. He collated to the living of St Christopher-le-Stock another Londoner, John Philpot, whom he had ordained in 1560, and who would be the companion in arms of Crowley and Gough. To the richest living in the city he appointed

Bucer's Cambridge disciple Thomas Horton, and, when Horton died of the plague in 1563, the living was given to that grand old man of the English Reformation, Bishop Miles Coverdale.

The more conservative type of churchman, even the crypto-papist, was by no means swept away by the new régime. John Standish, whom Pulleyn had replaced as archdeacon of Colchester, continued to enjoy his prebend until 1570. So did one Elisha Ambrose, who dated from 1537. And the new canons included Gabriel Goodman, soon to be dean of Westminster, a root of that anti-Calvinist stock which would run through Archbishops Richard Bancroft and Richard Neile to Laud, blossoming in the high Anglicanism of a future age. Among the lesser functionaries of St Paul's, in the ranks of the minor canons and vicars choral, reform had not penetrated far. The organist and (as we should say) choirmaster, Sebastian Westcott, was a known catholic, whose excellent court connections enabled him to temporize as a way of life, but without 'doing anything schismatical', as a catholic source tells us.[40] Westcott steadfastly refused to communicate with the Church of England and in 1563 stood excommunicate, having, as Grindal said, 'in doings ... excommunicated himself'.[41] Grindal resisted court intervention on Westcott's behalf and evidently intended to remove him from a post which placed in his suspect hands the education of the choristers. Yet sixteen years later 'Master Sebastian' was still secure, still taking 'the children of Pauls' by boat to Westminster to perform their plays at Court. At the end of 1560 no less than thirty-six London livings remained in the hands of their Marian incumbents,[42] while in rural areas the proportion must have been higher. Between these superficially converted mass priests and those who had emerged from exile or from hiding there could be no love lost. The truculent nonconformity in matters of apparel on which the hotter London ministers were later to take their stand expressed their refusal to be 'clothed like [the pope's] chaplains, that burned the blessed Bible and our faithful fathers and dear brethren in our eyes'.[43]

Grindal was second to none, fiercely loyal as he was to the memory of Ridley and of other martyred 'fathers', in his inability to forget and forgive the past. When he learned that the Cambridge turncoat, Dr Perne, was to preach before the queen on the occasion of her visit to the university he begged that no public honour be paid to him, 'his apostasy being so notorious', since to countenance him would comfort 'all dissemblers and neutrals and discourage the zealous and sincere'.[44] Although the conformity and passivity of the majority of clergy (and people) mercifully disguised the fact, rival religious communities coexisted in early

Elizabethan London, and in the country. In one Kentish parish there was sharp division between those who sang psalms and those who would not sing, between some who pressed for the removal of the rood-loft and other monuments of superstition and the 'enemies of God' who dragged their feet in seeing to these things. The vicar himself was in the enemy camp, refusing to read from the Bible, saying the service in the old manner, a blind leader of the blind. The protestants in the parish, presenting these matters to the archdeacon, ended their complaint: 'The Lord move you by some means to rid him from us.'[45] There can be no doubt that Grindal was sympathetically related to only one of these factions. In these early years there was little to impede the progressive protestantization of his diocese.

In the London churches the physical process of reformation was thorough and radical. Most altars and rood-lofts were speedily removed, one parish recording the proceeds from the sale of the timber 'that was of the rood-loft which we were commanded by my lord of London and other of the queen's visitors to take it down'. The iconoclastic process had gone so far that in September 1560 a royal proclamation sought to restrain the widespread spoiling and breaking of tombs and other monuments of antiquity. During the 1560s the sale or conversion of such church goods as vestments and chalices continued, and in some churches the organs were removed. As the London chronicler Machyn reports, metrical psalm-singing was now all the rage. After a Paul's Cross sermon preached by Veron in March 1560 'they sang all, old and young, a psalm in metre, the tune of Geneva ways', according to Bishop Jewel 6,000 persons joining in. At the various sessions of Grindal's primary visitation in the following year a psalm was always 'in Anglicano sermone per congregacionem decantabatur'. Several parish account books record the purchase of 'Geneva books', 'psalm books of Geneva tome of the greatest', in advance even of the new Prayer Book.[46]

Such giant strides towards a more perfectly reformed Church outran what was required by statute and injunctions and were offensive to the great residual body of conservative sentiment. Orders taken by the Ecclesiastical Commission in October 1561 were designed to avoid the 'strife and contention' which had arisen over alterations to the fabric of churches, and to stabilize the position. Rood-lofts where they still remained were to be converted into 'comely' but religiously neutral partitions between nave and chancel. Where chancel steps remained, or the tombs of noble and worshipful persons, they were not to be disturbed, but where the steps had already been removed the area was to be 'decently paved'. Fonts were to stay where they were and the clergy were not to indulge in the novelty of baptizing in basins.[47] Already in 1560 Grindal had cause to complain of those who 'intend to make my diocese a place of liberty for every man to break the common orders at his own pleasure'.[48] But the disorders which troubled Grindal and the other commissioners were not a simple matter of indiscipline. They arose from the provocations and counter-provocations of two mutually hostile factions, in effect of two religions and two churches.

Yet it would be false to represent Grindal as narrowly devoted to the advancement of a faction and less than diligent in the execution of his ordinary pastoral and administrative functions. A register of an unusual kind surviving from these years proves the contrary.[49] Called a 'Vicar General Book' this document records the hearing of a great many disciplinary cases outside the regular sessions of the consistory court, some by the vicar general, Huycke, but many by Grindal in person, sitting judicially in his house beside St Paul's or in his country manors at Fulham or Hadham. Late in 1561, for example, he acted in this personal, judicial capacity on five occasions: on 6, 11, 12 and 17 November and on 12 December. It looks as if he preferred to deal with erring and recalcitrant clergy himself, with some of the directness of evangelical discipline. On one occasion he admonished the rector of St Mary Milk Street to conform to the Prayer Book. On another he disciplined a London minister for christening a child from another parish, and on another a curate was dismissed for scandalous conduct and debarred from ministering in the diocese. An Essex minister was suspended and excommunicated for making a violent assault on a fellow cleric. On three occasions Grindal is to be found personally examining clergymen applying for institution to livings and finding them ignorant and unfit. When the London diarist Henry Machyn defamed the French preacher Jean Veron it was the bishop himself who summoned Machyn before him on more than one occasion and who imposed the public penance at Paul's Cross of which the victim has left a resentful account.[50]

The record of Grindal's first visitation of his diocese, in 1561, equally displays him as an earnest and indefatigable pastor, if somewhat cramped by the conventions of an over-formalized procedure.[51] A bishop was canonically bound to visit his diocese in the first year of his translation and subsequently at triennial intervals. Grindal's primary visitation was delayed until April 1561 in obedience to the archbishop's general inhibition imposed in May 1560, which was no doubt prompted by fear of the complaints which might be voiced if the fees associated with a visitation (and often cynically assumed to be the *raison d'être* of the exercise) should be levied again, so soon after the royal visitation of the preceding summer.[52] Grindal therefore held his first visitation at the earliest opportunity. He dissolved it in November 1562 and held subsequent visitations in due season, in 1565 and 1568. All records of these last two visitations have perished but from 1561 the call-book survives, detailing the various sessions held and the appearance or non-appearance of the clergy and churchwardens, but not the matters detected.

On 17 April 1561 Grindal commenced the visitation of his cathedral church. After mutual salutations in the great chamber of his palace, abutting on the north-west corner of the church, the bishop, in full episcopal habit, took his place with the other clergy in the choir. The bishop preached and a psalm was sung, in English. The causes of the visitation were then declared and a schedule of those present read, the bishop declaring those absent contumacious. After dinner he returned to sit judicially. The dignitaries, canons and other officers of the cathedral bound to present themselves on this occasion were, in order of precedence: the dean, archdeacons, treasurer, chancellor and precentor; thirty canons or prebendaries (although seven prebends were held by the dignitaries already listed and three were vacant); the subdean and fourteen minor canons; six vicars choral and nine choristers; four vergers and two bellringers ('pulsatores campanarum'); and the sacristan. Sixty-five persons in all should have appeared. In fact, on this first day, three of the archdeacons (Watts, Cole and Pulleyn) and the precentor were 'impeditus' and represented by proxy, and of the remaining canons, only two were present. Most of the minor canons, vicars choral and choristers attended, but Sebastian Westcott, the master of the choristers, was absent, as he would be from every one of the remaining sessions of the visitation of the cathedral. There were no less than eight of these, on 29 May, 2 July and 2 December, and on 9 April, 22 June, 5 October and 16 November of the following year, some of them conducted on Grindal's behalf by the chancellor. At every one of these sessions the absentee rate was high. Sometimes proxies were appointed, or apologies sent, as when the aged Elisha Ambrose pleaded 'debilem languidem et senectute confectum ut coram domino in visitatione sua absque summo periculo corporis compere nullo modo poterit.' But often no reason for absence was forthcoming, and the declaration of the absentees contumacious, 'reservata poena', appears to have been little more than a formal gesture.

As we shall see in a later chapter,[53] quite apart from the natural disaster which struck the cathedral in the midst of this visitation, the disorders associated with St Paul's were notorious and endemic, the prospects for converting it into a power-house of evangelical religion and instruction not bright. At the second session the cathedral statutes were exhibited, together with a scrappy and inadequate inventory of the goods of the church, which was found to be 'imperfectam et non authenticam'. At a later session the sacristan would be suspended for misappropriation of some of the sacred objects and being absent was declared contumacious into the bargain. Two of the vergers were dismissed and reinstated only after appearing before the bishop to be admonished to conduct themselves properly and decently.[54] At another session attention was paid to the rights and responsibilities of married minor canons. In December, when the chancellor was in the chair, the heart of the matter was reached with solemn admonitions to the entire community that they should attend the divinity lecture read in St Paul's, that they should be present and should communicate at the forthcoming Christmas services, and that the vergers should be diligent in maintaining good order in the cathedral in the time of divine service. (A royal proclamation had recently addressed itself to the problem of disorder in St Paul's and other churches.)[55] In October 1562 Grindal appeared in person to transmit a body of injunctions designed to place his cathedral on a platform of sound reform. An order of sermons at Paul's Cross imposed on the leading dignitaries and prebendaries the duty of preaching in their turns at a month's warning from the bishop, or to find a substitute, or to pay a fine into an educational charity. A similar order introduced a roster for sermons inside the cathedral on festival days throughout the year, the minor canons, vicars choral and choristers being admonished to attend on all such occasions. Other orders provided for regular celebrations of the communion and for collections for the poor to be taken up at all cathedral services. The treasures and other goods of the church were henceforth to be kept in secure custody and the inventory checked annually by the dean. The dignitaries and prebendaries were not in future to make leases of their prebends for more than twenty-one years. It is these last orders, at the most practical and down-to-earth level, which are extensively corrected and annotated in Grindal's own hand.

It is unlikely that the formal record contains all that was done. Grindal later reported that it was at this visitation that Sebastian Westcott had been accused of abstaining from the communion, and that both he and the dean and other members of the chapter had reasoned with him on many occasions during the months of the visitation. Three weeks after the visitation ended, Westcott was again before the bishop and solemnly enjoined to receive communion in St Paul's at Christmas. His excommunication followed seven months later.[56] Perhaps it will not be unjust to take Westcott's continued and untroubled enjoyment of his influential office as symbolic of the limited effectiveness of this protracted visitation.

By contrast, the visitation of the diocese was compressed into little more than a month, immediately following the opening session in St Paul's. There were sessions in London between 21 and 24 April, and then at South Weald, Chelmsford, Maldon, Colchester, Dunmow and Stortford, which was reached on 9 May. The final sessions, for Middlesex, were held in St Clement's Dane on 20 and 21 May. Grindal was present on most of these occasions and preached at Chelmsford and Colchester. The procedure was always the same. The bishop was given an honoured place in the church, a sermon was preached and a psalm sung. The causes of the visitation were declared and the clergy were summoned to appear before the bishop or his chancellor after dinner to hear his 'beneplacitum' or 'voluntatem'. Unless Grindal was more distant from his clergy than some seventeenth-century bishops, which is unlikely, dinner was the occasion for fellowship and perhaps discussion of some appropriate topic. Finally the incumbents and wardens of the parishes exhibited their bills, containing the matters of presentment which would occupy Dr Huycke and the staff of the consistory court in the coming months.

It has been suggested[57] that this visitation commanded less respect and was markedly less effective than others conducted by some of Grindal's successors, in years of greater ecclesiastical stability and enhanced administrative efficiency. In London itself, of the 102 parishes cited only seventy-six were represented, a mere 75 per cent, whereas 93 per cent of the London parishes were represented at one of Bishop Bancroft's visitations, thirty-seven years later, and only three were then absent without excuse. In 1561 only forty-five London parishes returned their bills of presentment by the due date. In 1598 virtually all the parishes were on time. Although it is hard to arrive at exact figures, the remainder of the diocese appears to present a healthier picture: some seventy-one clergy, or roughly 15 per cent, were absent, and some seventy-seven bills, or 16 per cent, were not returned. (The absentees were in due course excommunicated.)[58] But as we have already noted, in the deanery of Colchester and to a lesser extent in other parts of that archdeaconry the visitation disclosed a scene of deplorable neglect and deprivation, which remained unaltered two years later.

The utility of the whole cumbersome operation is open to grave doubt. To Grindal it must have appeared remote indeed from the direct, personal, decisive discipline spoken of in the documents of primitive Christianity and rediscovered in the reformed churches. He had good reason to know the difference. For only two days after presiding over the opening formalities of his primary visitation in St Paul's he sat judicially, but without the same ceremony and presumably without his episcopal rochet and mitre, in the church of the Austin Friars, in the midst of the congregation of Dutch-speaking protestants which had the use of the building. This was the sequel to certain events of the preceding month when he had confirmed a solemn sentence of excommunication against a member and minister of that church in circumstances radically different from the legalistic forms of his own courts spiritual.

This was the other half of Grindal's double life, in which he kept more colourful and in some respects more distinguished, if troublesome, company. From the point of view of the Church of England, and even for the English church historian, this was a sideshow. But for Grindal himself this little world may have been more absorbing, if no less frustrating, than his more proper sphere of episcopal government. Here was an open window on the international world of the Reformation, through which he dealt with the major centres and the great names, John Calvin included. The issues with which he grappled in this arena were those of genuine theological magnitude, classical christian heresies, the great question of orthodoxy versus free opinion, issues rarely encountered among the dusty lumber of the Church of England. It was the English Church, by comparison, which was the backwater, the congregations of the Dutch in Austin Friars and the French in Threadneedle Street the main stream. 'Only they,' writes a modern historian of early Elizabethan culture, 'relieve the general barrenness of the sixties.'[59] To their affairs, in so far as they concerned Edmund Grindal as their superintendent, we now turn.

7

CALVINISM WITH
A HUMAN FACE

Early Elizabethan London was a metropolis of the international protestant world: not so much a city set on a hill, a second Geneva, as a crossroads, another Strasbourg or Frankfurt, especially for protestant refugees. Other foreigners were in London for more mundane reasons. There were French and Flemings in large numbers, and smaller clusters of Italians and Spaniards. Towards the end of the first Elizabethan decade upwards of four thousand 'strangers' inhabited the city and its adjoining liberties, by far the greatest number of Dutch origin. Rather more than half made up the membership of the French and Dutch-speaking churches, with a substantial minority adhering to the English parish churches or 'of no church'.[1] Those who chose to submit to the discipline of their own national churches had the means to worship in their native language and according to the reformed manner, and something besides, which religious organizations have so often offered to migrants: a measure of social identity and representation. There were other communities, and other congregations, in provincial towns such as Norwich, Colchester, Canterbury and Sandwich. Such were the beginnings of that distinctive and enduring contribution to our history summed up in the word 'Huguenot'.

But for the time being these were strangers, spiritually and even actively indentified with events across the Channel and the North Sea, where the consolidation of French and Dutch protestantism within the structures of Calvinism coincided and interacted with cataclysmic political and popular movements. This was the time in many parts of Europe, from Poland westwards, when a struggle was joined between the disciplined, jealously orthodox faith and polity demanded by such stern times and alternative visions of what it meant to be a christian man. Some of the resistance to ascendant Calvinism was only the eclecticism of those who had learned their theology from Erasmus or Melanchthon and would not grant Geneva monopoly rights. Others displayed the pertinacity of the born heresiarch and 'fanatic', others still an appealing spirit of true liberality, which the Spaniard Antonio del Corro expressed when he wrote: 'What is he of any judgment at all who will not fear to forsake the tyranny of the papistry to enter into another, almost of like condition?'[2] For many years to come such liberal sentiments would find expression in political resistance to the oligarchical and clerical organization of the churches which took Geneva as their model.

For the mannered Anglican historian R. W. Dixon, the expression of these tensions in the London stranger churches spoke only of the 'intestine commotions' of troublesome folk which required the attention of the authorities and 'may perhaps, in some interval of languor, merit that of the reader'.[3] But from a more cosmopolitan point of view it may appear that the contest between these strongly opposed tendencies was the true crisis of protestantism, the moment of transition from protest, protean and still in some measure free, to the seamless orthodoxy of a settled institution.

At the centre of this turbulent scene, distracted by contrary pressures, sometimes maladroit, but indispensable as a kind of fulcrum, was Bishop Grindal: invaluable as a patron too. With his own sense of the indebtedness of a stranger still fresh, Grindal was sympathetic. In the case of a poor Frenchman cast into prison on a flimsy pretext he achieved a rare display of public anger and promised to deal severely with the party responsible. Like some liberally-minded Home Office official of the 1970s he sanctioned the use of Paul's Cross to scotch the malicious rumour that there were as many as 40,000 foreign migrants in London. Not that his outlook was 'liberal' in any modern sense. He could advise Cecil that London was 'marvellously abused' by strangers, and that many of the Dutch were 'evil-livers, drunkards, schismatics'. The good should be separated from the bad by a census of communicants. 'They that are not of that number are not truly religious,' and for their sort Grindal held no brief.[4]

Grindal's interest in the strangers, which went far beyond the line of duty, was that of a co-religionist. Although it would be anachronistic to call him a Calvinist, Grindal's theology was not in conflict with Geneva. He enjoyed and reciprocated the confidence not only of Calvin (who died in 1564) but of Calvin's successor as virtual bishop of Geneva and counsellor of the churches which looked to Geneva for guidance, Theodore Beza, a Calvinist in a sense that Calvin himself never was. In a letter written to Beza not long after Calvin's death Grindal praised his activity in defence of pure doctrine and sealed his approval with a gift of five gold angels.[5] In the affairs of the stranger churches he was content to be used as the instrument of a rigorous discipline which strove to bring the more eclectic of the protestant refugees into line, on occasion ratifying the ultimate spiritual sentence of excommunication with a personal and pastoral severity which contrasts with the more formal and remote procedures of his own episcopal courts.

Yet it appears from the handling of a series of disturbances in the stranger churches that Grindal was spiritually and intellectually estranged from mature Calvinism as we find it personified in Beza and the many lesser Bezas rising to positions of commanding leadership, especially in the French churches. There was a difference of mentality between those who lived and breathed in an atmosphere of continuing doctrinal refinement, and whose theological organ was hypersensitive, and a bishop who while not ignorant of doctrine was content to rest on what he had learned and to apply it practically, in life and in pastoral administration. There was also a temperamental difference. Grindal's inclination was always to hope for the best of mankind, not to suspect the worst. He had no taste for witch-hunts, no capacity for dirty tricks. And in relation to Beza there was a kind of generation gap. Not a difference in age: although Beza would outlive Grindal by a quarter of a century they were born in the same year and had met in Strasbourg as contemporaries,[6] each on the verge of seniority in their respective churches. But Grindal's charitable and even pragmatic spirit perpetuated the influence of Bucer and contrasts with the marked intolerance which Beza brought to bear on the affairs of the churches, together with a neo-scholastic theological method. It is fair to add that Grindal as a leader of a church established and peacefully enjoying the gospel was not engaged, as Beza was and the French in general were, in continual definition and defence of the truth, in circumstances where the support of the christian magistrate was not available, and often with respect to particular cases.

Grindal's responsibility for the stranger churches was not properly episcopal but was exercised as their superintendent. When the churches were first constituted, in Edward's reign, the generous charter which made available the great church of the Austin Friars (and later St Anthony's Chapel, Threadneedle Street) set up a partially autonomous corporation, a 'corpus corporatum et politicum', empowered to elect its own officers, determine its own forms of worship and exercise its own peculiar discipline. 'We have nothing to do with the bishops,' exulted the original leaders. Admittedly the charter spoke of a superintendent, a vaguely episcopal office which also symbolized the authority of the crown of England. But the first superintendent was himself a stranger, the

Polish nobleman John à Lasco (Jan Laski), a prince of the old Church turned reformer, an aristocrat of the republic of letters and a friend of Erasmus.[7]

Laski was a constructive if radical ecclesiastical statesman, and the Edwardian constitution of the stranger churches balanced the office of superintendent with a stiff measure of congregational democracy. This marked a primitive stage in the evolution of the reformed church polity, first applied to Emden and now more fully worked out in Edwardian London. However, when the stranger churches resumed their interrupted existence under Elizabeth their status was altered, and the office of superintendent vested in the bishop of the diocese *ex officio*. The new deal was a curb on freedom, requiring that no religious forms be used 'contrary to our law'. No doubt Queen Elizabeth intended that the superintendent-bishop should not only keep the peace but should reduce the fractious strangers to an orderly conformity to the English Church. But the thinking of the reformed had moved beyond Laski's early devices to more sophisticated schemes of synodical government and there was every reason for Calvinists to resent the office of superintendent as an anachronism and a political imposition, restricting the proper freedom of presbyteries and synods. Later the institution would lapse, leaving the strangers to deal directly with a government and with bishops who were not always friendly.

It is all the more notable that Grindal should have chosen to exert his powers within the economy of the churches, not as an alien intruder into their affairs. Ordinarily, each congregation was governed by its own ministers and elders, comprising the consistory, with deacons to look after the money, and a federal *coetus* to represent the various national consistories. (In addition, from 1581, the French-speaking churches in various parts of the south and east of England were confederated in annual *colloques*.) Grindal maintained a fraternal rather than political connection with these officers and bodies, and normally intervened only when asked to do so, and then with that heroic and self-effacing patience which was the mark of the man and a rarity in his age. Baron de Schickler, the historian of the 'églises du réfuge', calls his appointment 'singulièrement heureux'. 'As superintendent it was protection he sought to exercise more than surveillance or control.'[8] In this respect quite unlike his old master, Bishop Ridley, Grindal found nothing to embarrass him in the separate existence of churches so different in their forms of worship and church order, defying by their very existence the cherished Tudor ideal of uniformity. Admittedly there had been cause for Ridley to suspect a body which was outside his jurisdiction and rejoiced in its immunity. But Ridley's hostility was principally occasioned by the transparent hope of the more radical of English protestants, the proto-puritans, that the stranger churches would prove to be model churches, their practice normative for the Church of England itself.[9] John Hooper, the 'Anglo-Züricher' who before he became a bishop was a rival to Ridley in his own diocese, was intimate with Laski and with the leading figures in the Dutch community, Maarten Micron, the first Dutch pastor in London, and Jan Utenhove. Both Utenhove and Micron boarded with the Hoopers when they first arrived and it was Micron who called his host 'the future Zwingli of England'.[10]

With the disappearance of Laski from the English scene and his death in Poland in 1560 the mantle was now to fall upon Utenhove, a native of Ghent and member of an erudite family of the minor Flemish nobility (he styled himself 'patritius Gadavensis') closely connected with Erasmus.[11] Utenhove had shared in Laski's last journey to the Polish court and now he returned to London the original charter and negotiated with the government for the restoration of the strangers' privileges. With some justice tradition revered him as second in line of the superintendents, intervening between Laski and Grindal, although never recognized as such by authority. In these circumstances Grindal might have seemed an intruder. But in spite of some grumbles in the ranks,[12] Grindal as superintendent remained on good terms with the Dutch elder, acknowledging his moral ascendancy in all matters of church discipline. And when Utenhove had bigger fish to fry, a scheme for closer political and commercial ties between England and Emden, Grindal was deeply committed to the enterprise and served as the go-between in the dealings of Utenhove with Cecil.[13]

In Elizabethan London the stranger churches were once again considered excellent models by those desiring 'further reformation', above all in their enjoyment of congregational self-government, now to be modelled more closely than in Laski's time on the modish example of Geneva.[14] But far from fearing their infectious attractions, Grindal instructed the parish clergy of London not to admit to communion foreigners who had withdrawn from the discipline of their own churches: 'a remarkable act of the bishop', as the clerk of the French consistory noted in his minutes.[15] At the outset, in 1560, he was conscious not so much of the danger as of the opportunity posed by the presence of more radically reformed churches in the heart of London itself. There was, after all, another model much less to his taste: the queen's chapel with its lights and crucifix.[16] It is clear from the correspondence between Grindal and Calvin over the supply of a French pastor that the bishop related this appointment to the state of 'our churches' — 'not so settled as all good men wished and at first hoped.'[17]

The French congregation was ambitious that 'a Viret, a Théodore de Bèze, a Macar or a Pierre de Collonges' might be spared, naming the ranking Geneva pastors. In the event Calvin sent them des Gallars, sieur de Saules, who stood third or fourth in the informal Genevan hierarchy, a pastor with the aristocratic and juristic background which French protestantism found so invaluable, and a true Calvinist who could say of the disputes inside the London congregation: 'Je trouve cecy plus dangereux que les persecutions.'[18] Des Gallars had served as moderator in Geneva in Calvin's absence and, not long before his arrival in London, as envoy to the first national synod of the French reformed churches, carrying to Paris the blueprint for the constitution which that assembly duly adopted.

The communications which passed between des Gallars, Grindal and Calvin provide an edifying spectacle of mutual admiration. Calvin in writing to des Gallars rebuked those parties in the French congregation which resented Grindal's superintendency and wanted to assure them that in the bishop they had 'a faithful and sincere protector of their liberty'. Grindal was to thank Calvin and his colleagues for having spared such an excellent man. And des Gallars reported to Calvin that the bishop was always accessible and sympathetic. 'Indeed, if such a man were not presiding over our churches in no way should we be able to hold our own.'[19] By the time these words were written the alliance had been tested by fire in the first of many 'intestine commotions'.

When des Gallars reached London in June 1560 it was necessary to make good his title to the pastoral office against the rival claims of those who had come to the aid of the congregation in the early months of its revived existence, but who had received no formal call or election to the ministry.[20] These included Ebrard Erail, an Antwerp preacher who was to build up a party among those church members who had apostacized in Mary's reign, and one Jean Janvier, best described as a failed divinity student. Above all there was Pierre Alexandre, an agent in the representations made to recover the use of the Threadneedle Street church which was to be the permanent home of the congregation. Alexandre, a native of Arras, was a man of some distinction,[21] an ex-Carmelite monk, sometime chaplain to Mary of Austria in her governorship of the Netherlands, and sometime professor at Heidelberg. He was one of the foreign scholars initially attracted to England by Cranmer and

had been rewarded with a London parish and a Canterbury prebend. Four substantial Latin treatises survive, based on courses of
lectures given in Canterbury Cathedral in 1552 and 1553.[22] After
some years in Strasbourg he now returned to England to recover
his benefices.

These birds of passage were men of irrepressible individuality
and variable talents, but what they had in common and shared with
many other aspiring students and preachers whose lives were to
end in blighted obscurity was their lack of the entire confidence of
the Honourable Company of Pastors of Geneva. They were written off, not necessarily on account of doctrinal deviations but
because in character and behaviour they failed to conform to the
model of personal and pastoral excellence admired in Geneva and
drawn from sources ancient and modern, not least from Calvin
himself. They were indiscreet, above all 'ambitious'. In their
idiosyncracies they were transitional figures, representatives of the
dawn of the Reformation when it was still a revolution and an
adventure of the mind and spirit. They bore little resemblance to
the somewhat standardized product which the Geneva Academy
and the seminaries modelled on it would turn out in the future.

It was to rescue the infant church from unsound leadership that
des Gallars had been invited by what Baron Schickler called 'les
plus sérieux' of the members, a minority of those in full sympathy
with 'the discipline' and therefore, no doubt, 'the best'. But the
other party included professional men, a couple of physicians and
some of the more affluent members, laymen opposed to the neo-
clericalism of Geneva. We are confronting the tension between
aristocracy and democracy, and between the lay and clerical
principles, which pervades the early history of the reformed
churches:[23] and a very human, spirited resistance to the narrow
rigours of the discipline, which was no respecter of persons.
When the consistory of the French church investigated dancing at
a wedding and included in its admonitions the wife of an elder
who had danced a round, and even some of the elders themselves,
Geneva was indeed reproduced in London. On his arrival des
Gallars found that the majority was against him and made clear his
dislike of majorities.

When he waited on the bishop with Calvin's letter of commendation the occasion was not without embarrassment for Grindal, for Alexandre had provided him with hospitality in Strasbourg. The elders were warned to be submissive to their duly
appointed pastor but Grindal then 'added some words' about the
necessity of treating as a colleague Alexandre, who was acceptable
'to the people', and whose English benefices would enable him to

serve without charge to the congregation. This was the first of many vain attempts to reconcile des Gallars and Alexandre and their respective partisans. Des Gallars's opponents now contested the validity of his election and demanded a popular vote, which Grindal refused, insisting that a pastor could not be elected twice, that des Gallars had been called by the more substantial elements, and that to refuse him would be an insult, not least to Calvin. Nevertheless the congregation postponed his installation for a week, during which time Erail suggested that under the Edwardian charter it was necessary to obtain royal confirmation of the appointment, and that it was doubtful whether the queen would favour a pastor sent from Geneva 'by those who have gravely offended her'. Grindal brushed this aside by insisting that he stood between the strangers and the government and 'they may be sure that if any danger should arise I will face it alone'. On 24 June he came to Threadneedle Street to install des Gallars. With Alexandre as interpreter (!) he exhorted the church to follow the teaching of its pastor and to submit to ecclesiastical discipline. Des Gallars intervened to ask the bishop to allow any objections to be voiced. There was silence. And so, des Gallars reported to Calvin, 'l'affaire fut terminée'. It was not, of course.

Grindal had ordered new elections, the elders and deacons to lay down their offices 'that the church may be in peace and may grow daily to the glory of God'. Des Gallars now found it prudent to overcome his objections to democracy and in a carefully managed election conducted by Utenhove, an English merchant from Strasbourg and two other English brethren 'newly come from Geneva', he won the upper hand. The deacons, members of Ebrard's faction, were defeated, and Ebrard retired to France where he was to die violently in the first of the religious wars. Later des Gallars would consolidate this victory by the introduction of a new Form of Discipline, modelled on Geneva. This constitution[24] continued to provide for popular election to church offices, but it looked forward to a second step in the direction of aristocratic and clerical government, which would be taken in the time of des Gallars's successor.

Meanwhile Alexandre continued to enjoy support and Grindal tried to keep the peace by persuading des Gallars to admit his rival as an honorary colleague, to preach on Sunday afternoons and alternate Thursdays, but without the title of minister. Neither these terms nor the award of a small salary could pacify Alexandre, while des Gallars informed the bishop that if Alexandre were to be imposed on him he would be forced to uncover evidence from his earlier career which would tend to discredit him even in the eyes of his supporters. In December violent words were uttered in the consistory and it was perhaps at this juncture that Alexandre addressed Grindal in a formal *Apologia* to which des Gallars replied.[25] On the last day of the year Grindal entertained both sides to dinner and effected a formal reconciliation.

This was short-lived. Alexandre broke the latest terms for alternating his ministry with that of the pastor and open hostilities were resumed. In July 1561 the annual elections confirmed the elders in office and pointed towards the entrenchment of a clerical oligarchy. Alexandre alleged electoral impropriety from the pulpit and with his faction absented himself from the communion on the following Sunday. Grindal was warned of the impending ruin of the church and was persuaded to suspend Alexandre from preaching while the matter was investigated. On a Monday in early August the principal parties waited on the bishop at Fulham: the elders of the French church, des Gallars, Alexandre, and the leaders of the Dutch church. The meeting lasted from ten in the morning until six in the evening. The pettinesses of the unhappy past were raked over. Des Gallars, not for the first time, threatened to resign and won from Grindal what he no doubt expected: a vigorous and public demand that he should contemplate no such thing. At the day's end yet another reconciliation was effected, Alexandre withdrew his charges and everyone consented to forgive and forget.

Soon after this des Gallars was called across the Channel to more momentous employment at the Colloquy of Poissy, a major summit conference between the French religious parties. From the French court he sent reports to Grindal and, through the English ambassador Throckmorton, to Cecil. In France there were pressing and flattering invitations to remain, but des Gallars could not be prevented from returning to his bed of nails in London.[26] Since Alexandre had acted as locum tenens in his absence it is not surprising that he found the congregation once again in disarray, his party among the elders faltering, the form of discipline which he had established threatened. He rapidly regained control, but this time without much support from Grindal. When Alexandre refused to submit his cause to the arbitration of the consistory and was again suspended he appealed to the superintendent who received him cordially and even asked des Gallars to recommend him to the congregation as his successor. When this met with an indignant refusal, Grindal proposed to make the nomination off his own bat. But the consistory proved solid for des Gallars. Alexandre was now unwise enough to accuse the deacons of embezzlement and when they were exonerated in the ensuing enquiry des

Gallars was poised to strike. The church was told to choose between himself and Alexandre. His rival did not wait for the verdict but withdrew from London, to die a few months later. This was the end of organized resistance to 'discipline'. As if to make the point that he had fought not for his own interests but impartially, for the establishment of that discipline, des Gallars himself resigned in the summer of 1563, after a serious illness and the death of his wife and several children. As he proceeded to a new and distinguished career at Orléans he handed over an orderly congregation to Jean Cousin, a minister from Caen, a safe and sound appointment from the point of view of Geneva. Grindal's final testimonial could not have been more cordial: 'When he arrived he found his church in total confusion. He has passed it on to his successor Cousin at peace and well governed. As for me and our churches, his counsels and his wisdom have been of the utmost profit.'

But why had Grindal withheld his support at the crucial moment? Was he moved by the old debt incurred to Alexandre at Strasbourg, which he mentioned to des Gallars at this time? Or was he revealing a deep-seated uneasiness about Genevan rigour? Or simply exhaustion? The question is important but cannot be resolved. The historian can only note that most of our evidence comes from sources hostile to Alexandre: the des Gallars – Calvin correspondence, mainly.

Even des Gallars conceded that Alexandre was orthodox in doctrine, hostile to sectaries and against sin. His faults were those of wounded pride and a passionate temper. The fracas in the French church, while not without its deeper implications, was primarily a clash of personalities. The *cause célèbre* of Adriaan van Haemstede was more serious, in that it concerned doctrine, the ultimate question of the coherence of the reformed churches and their faith. If the French quarrel impinged on Grindal from time to time, the Haemstede affair was forced upon him almost daily, over many months. The details occupy scores of pages in the act book of the Dutch consistory, 140 separate entries between July 1560 and August 1561, or no less than 25 per cent of all the matters noted in the minutes.[27]

Adriaan Cornelis van Haemstede might be called the John Foxe of the Dutch Reformation if this were not to misrepresent an impulsive activist and an inveterate noncomformist.[28] In March 1559 he published the first martyrology in the Dutch language, *De geschiedenisse ende den doodt der vremer martelaren*, in circumstances which were extraordinary. At the time he was a pastor in Antwerp, where the church was well and truly 'under the cross', and living like the Scarlet Pimpernel with a price of 300 florins on his head. His book described events which had occurred within three weeks of the commencement of publication, yet it bears no trace of fugitive preparation. There was even a seven-page index of names. Haemstede may be said to have created some of his own copy. When he came to Antwerp with commendations from Emden he found the protestants maintaining a low profile, meeting in small and dispersed groups under the strict discipline of their leaders. There had been no execution for five years. Haemstede was disposed by his background (collateral descent from the counts of Holland) and his considerable learning to practise a centralized and public ministry, based on the houses of the well-to-do and with his books about him. His policy of preaching and debating in the open was contrary to church order and was held responsible for the tougher line soon taken by the authorities. In the summer of 1558 when there were many protestants in prison and some had already died Haemstede was still preaching in the centre of Antwerp. Later he went underground and it was in these circumstances, as a hunted man at odds with his own church leaders, that he gathered the materials for his book and saw it to the press. Then he left for Aix-la-Chapelle, Emden and Norden, and after encountering one cold shoulder after another arrived in London in the early summer of 1559. This was before the return of Utenhove and the arrival of the future minister of the Dutch congregation, Peter Deleen, son of a former Dutch pastor in London. Although without accreditation from Emden he plunged into preaching and other activities, one source describing him as a bookseller.[29]

Those who welcomed Haemstede would later form a party for his defence: a group of the more cultivated and liberally-minded strangers, including the merchant-historian van Meteren, and relations of the famous scholar Ortelius.[30] Within a few months this circle included the Italian Jacobus Acontius (Aconcio), one of the most notable of protestant 'libertines' and a mathematician and logician of the first rank, author of a *De methodo* from which a route is traced to Descartes.[31] Acontius's entrée to Elizabethan England was eased by his acquaintance with the Strasbourg group of Marian exiles, including Grindal, by the future earl of Leicester's liking for Italians, and by his skill as an engineer. He came from a flexible intellectual background and, as with other Italian academicians turned heretic, 'the urge to pose persistent and penetrating questions'[32] would lead him ever farther away from any of the orthodoxies. His connection with the group of Italian exiles in Switzerland known to Calvin as 'academic sceptics' (Lelio Sozini above all) favoured the enunciation of advanced liberal views.

These were crystallized by the execution of the arch-heretic Michael Servetus at Geneva and the resultant literary storm, blown up by Sebastian Castellio's *Concerning heretics, whether they are to be persecuted*. The end result was Acontius's own book *Stratagematum Satanae libri octo*, published at Basle in 1565 with a dedication to Queen Elizabeth.[33] The practical religious principle which Acontius shared with Castellio, but derived from principles of his own, was that there ought to be a reduction of religious truths to what is beyond dispute. Of these truths reason in its free interpretation of scripture is the sole judge. Beyond what was common ground there should be mutual toleration of 'truths' which were only relatively true, and no coercion to believe. Persecution on grounds of religious difference Acontius explained by means of a psychologically powerful and original analysis of human nature, pessimistic where Castellio was optimistic: these were the 'stratagems of Satan'.

The tragedy of Haemstede was that he was probably much closer than Acontius to mundane orthodoxy, and certainly far less original in this thinking. But his response to the experience of discipline, a 'human' rather than philosophical reaction, was to denounce it as persecution and to range himself with all the 'heretics' and with Christ himself, who had suffered the cruel and arrogant justice of the elders and scribes. Like Foxe he seems to have been physically offended by the fact of religious persecution and absolutely opposed to capital punishment in the name of Christ. A year after his arrival in London he put himself in the wrong with the guardians of orthodoxy, now consolidating in his own church, by his friendly overtures to certain anabaptists in the Dutch community.

There is no evidence that Haemstede was himself an anabaptist. He had excluded known sectaries from his tally of martyrs. But in words repeated a hundred times in the proceedings of the next two years he was said to have given the right hand of fellowship to members of that sect and to have offered to make representations to the civil authorities on their behalf, at a time when they were threatened with deportation under the terms of a royal proclamation.[34] In Haemstede's opinion the London anabaptists were innocent of the excesses of Munster and in error through ignorance. They were weak members of the body of Christ ('among the anabaptists as well as among the papists and other pestiferous sects weak members of Christ are found') of whom better things were to be hoped.

The anabaptists confronted the Dutch reformed with a dilemma. Under the leadership of Menno Simons they had become a peaceable and numerous denomination, with which other faiths in practice coexisted. In principle they might hold damnable heresies. In daily encounter they appeared to be simple god-fearing folk. When a conventicle of Dutch anabaptists was surprised in London in the following decade, and two of those taken actually burned in Smithfield, the matter was a scandal in the Netherlands and members of the Dutch church in London defended themselves against the charge of having betrayed the sect to the authorities. In fact, shortly before the execution the Dutch church had moved in the *coetus* for steps to be taken to procure a moderation of the sentence and that 'the simplicity of these people' should be brought to the bishop's attention. On that same occasion Foxe addressed appeals to the queen and other English notables. 'I would not countenance their errors but I would spare their lives.'[35] Yet Haemstede's complacency towards a movement which was a byword for seditious enormities was thought to endanger the reputation of the whole London Dutch community. Moreover anabaptists were known to hold opinions which were fundamentally erroneous, concerning the nature of Christ himself. Specifically, it was a tenet of the Mennonites that Christ's flesh was not derived from the Virgin Mary but was a 'celestial flesh'. One version of this near-Gnostic heresy was associated with Servetus, another had taken the Englishwoman Joan Bocher to the stake under the protestant government of Edward VI.[36] It is not apparent that Haemstede himself subscribed to this doctrine. But he adopted the formal position that the Christological question was 'circumstantial', not 'fundamental'. This was as much as to say that a dogma of this importance was among the *adiaphora*, a matter of indifference. With good reason des Gallars suggested to Calvin that Acontius was Haemstede's 'subtle and acute patron'.[37] Worse still, Haemstede's suspicious conduct aroused fears of a link with the mysterious and much dreaded spiritual fraternity known as the Family of Love. As with known familists, such as the great Antwerp printer Plantin, whose opinions were concealed in his lifetime, it is not impossible that Haemstede's inmost thoughts and beliefs were hidden from his contemporaries and remain inaccessible to us.[38]

Haemstede compounded his offence (if this was not the deepest of all his sins) by his contempt of church discipline. At an early stage he walked out of the consistory and subsequently deployed against it a polemic which identified the church's jurisdiction with 'the rulers of the Jews' and associated his own cause with that of the rejected Christ. By now he was suspended from preaching and without financial support. As early as July 1560 there was talk of referring the matter to the superintendent-bishop. The Dutch, never as confident about Grindal as the French, strove to keep the case in their own hands, but after repeated negotiations and encounters within the two congregations it was referred to Grindal in September, partly because Haemstede would recognize no one else as competent to judge him. All parties appeared before the bishop and his chancellor and archdeacon: the ministers and elders of both churches, Haemstede and some of his supporters. The upshot was that Haemstede professed his willingness to subscribe to articles concerning the Incarnation, and to renounce any doctrine inconsistent with the Belgic Confession of Faith.

And there, if the initiative had been Grindal's, the affair would have ended. But the witch-hunt was only just beginning. Utenhove and Deleen were now busy collecting evidence from Haemstede's writings and utterances in the congregational prophesying which were in conflict with his submission. In another encounter with the superintendent when all parties were again present Grindal was confronted with these 'loca pugnantia' and every effort was exerted to persuade him to issue a punitive sentence. Proceedings took a protracted course. Questions were referred to Haemstede through the chancellor, Huycke, and further testimony was delivered to Huycke against him. The bishop was lobbied by Haemstede's friends, who included the two most learned foreigners in London, van Meteren and Haemstede's 'patron' Acontius who shared van Meteren's house. In September Acontius and des Gallars were engaged in the logical and linguistic toils of an intellectual wrestling match in which the stakes could hardly have been higher: the view which each took of the fundamental nature of Christianity. And Grindal received a major manifesto from Acontius.[39] In mid-October the various documents were undergoing scrutiny among Grindal's staff while the Haemstedians, fearful that a definitive sentence would place their hero in physical jeopardy, were pressing the bishop for a public and unprejudiced debate. It was in Grindal's nature to permit endless discussion so long as any hope remained of reconciliation, but Utenhove pushed hard and successfully for a summary sentence. On 17 November Grindal appeared in person at Austin Friars before the combined congregations and after Deleen had pronounced the excommunication of Haemstede in Dutch, he confirmed the sentence and addressed the company from the pulpit.[40] Haemstede thus became (on the face of it) the noblest kind of martyr: victim not of what he himself believed but of defending the liberty to believe of others.

The matter did not rest. A disputation was planned, to be

conducted in Latin so that the learned of other nations could be involved. Either Grindal was to preside, or, as was later proposed, Bishop Pilkington of Durham, Alexander Nowell, dean of St Paul's, and the Scottish reformer John Willock. The ministers and elders were busy internationalizing the affair, despatching the documents overseas and corresponding with all the major centres of Dutch and Flemish protestantism.[41] Haemstede, on the other hand, now wished to confine further debate to the Dutch congregation where he still enjoyed a solid body of support. But in the midst of all this activity he suddenly withdrew to face an uncertain welcome at Emden. On the way his ship nearly sank, he was robbed of all his possessions (including his library) and his wife gave birth to triplets, two of whom survived. One was christened 'Charitas', a name which may just possibly clinch the association of the father with the *Domus Charitatis*, the Family of Love.

In some quarters the rough handling of Haemstede was deplored. Utenhove's own half-brother wrote a letter of rebuke from Antwerp and in London steps had to be taken to put down those who continued to demonstrate against the sentence, including Haemstede's sister who arrived to swell the opposition. Grindal was now at the centre of a secondary process against the Haemstedians, who were required on pain of sharing their leader's penalty to acknowledge the error of asserting that the Incarnation was less than fundamental and their fault in impugning the justice of the sentence imposed. Some submitted but most held out. By May 1561 there was nothing for it but to excommunicate as many as ten of Haemstede's friends, including his sister, van Meteren and Acontius. An obviously reluctant Grindal again served as executioner and later in the month he agreed to take steps to prevent those under sentence from finding a refuge in the more liberal atmosphere of some London parish churches. No wonder that one of the Haemstedians boasted in his cups of having said to Grindal's face: 'My lord, so ye had the pope's power you would be more cruel than the pope himself.'[42] Grindal himself was uneasy, as he demonstrated when some of the Haemstedians made a limited submission in which they remained critical of the way in which the case had been handled but agreed to say no more about it and to ask forgiveness for any offence given. He recommended the Dutch elders to readmit them to the congregation, 'all the more as we ourselves may have given offence by our excessive severity'. And he was ready to discuss the terms on which Haemstede's own excommunication might be lifted.

Meanwhile Haemstede had been persuaded by Acontius to return. His reappearance in July 1562 had a touch of provocation reminiscent of Servetus coming willingly to his fate in Geneva, the clerk of the congregation recording: 'Adrianus Hamstedius compt optenlick in de kercke, hoort die predicatie.'[43] On the same day a warrant was obtained for his arrest and Utenhove and his supporters began to amass a new file of evidence to persuade Grindal to act decisively. On 4 August the bishop presented Haemstede with a humiliating form of recantation which bore the names of four English 'doctors' as well as his own: Miles Coverdale, David Whitehead, Robert Crowley and John Philpot. (Three of these would themselves be branded as recalcitrant nonconformists within four years and the fourth, Whitehead, had deliberately distanced himself from the Elizabethan Church.) Predictably, Haemstede rejected it.[44] Once again Grindal came to Austin Friars to ratify a second sentence of excommunication, and this time Haemstede was summarily deported to East Friesland, where soon afterwards he died. He was thirty-seven. The second excommunication aroused a second protest from Utenhove's liberally-minded brother. 'But of this *basta*, as they say in Italy.'[45]

It was far from *basta* for the troubled Dutch congregation. In 1563 it was necessary to deal with a real heretic, a certain Justus Velsius, who had a diverse background in Bologna, Louvain and (inevitably) Strasbourg. Velsius was a stormy petrel who told Grindal that he had never joined himself to any church 'because hitherto he findeth none rightly to be called a church of Christ'. Using the congregational prophesying as a platform, he taught that in the christian sinful nature was extinguished, drowned 'like Pharaoh in the sea', and he advanced a remarkable doctrine of human perfection and deification (a christian was God in Man and Man-God) in a manifesto which he sent to the queen and Cecil as well as to Grindal. There were claims of miracles in confirmation of his doctrine and the beginnings of a sectarian following. Grindal warned Cecil that this was how the Munster holocaust had begun and had Velsius arrested. After an electrifying appearance before the Ecclesiastical Commissioners in which he threatened his judges with divine judgment, he too was deported. Velsius was a loner, in Grindal's words 'altogether fanatical', and cases such as this were easily dealt with.[46]

Matters of discipline and church order were more contentious and recalcitrant. They revived in the Dutch congregation with the arrival of a new pastor to replace Deleen who had succumbed to the same outbreak of plague which had devastated the family of des Gallars.[47] This was Godfried van Winghen, translator of the Old Testament in the Dutch Bible in common use in the sixteenth century, previously minister at Sandwich and before that at

Frankfurt, whither he had conveyed a letter from Grindal appealing to the magistrates for a fair deal for the small Dutch congregation.[48] The nominal cause of dissent was Winghen's insistence
on the participation of godparents in baptism. This conservative,
almost 'Anglican' principle was consistent with a prejudice
which he would later reveal against those radical elements in the
Netherlands whose reckless iconoclastic attacks on the churches
accompanied the beginnings of active resistance to the Spanish
government. On both issues, and on his interpretation of the
pastoral role, the new minister was opposed, especially by the
deacons, on grounds which vaguely resemble the position adopted
in the same years by the English puritans in their early disputes
with ecclesiastical authority: principally the ground of 'christian
liberty'. He was supported by the elders, and notably by Utenhove. The dispute was referred to Grindal on the advice of the
French consistory, but since it was a foregone conclusion that the
bishop would side with the minister and elders his intervention
was unwelcome to the dissidents, and even to an element in the
French church which was critical of the minister, Cousin, for
his over-familiarity with the bishop. In September 1564 Grindal
and other ecclesiastical commissioners issued a decree underwriting the authority of the minister and elders and their order
relating to baptism, and requiring a complete re-enrolment of
the congregation. At least one dissident was sent to prison for the
contemptuous words with which he greeted this sentence: 'Our
mouths are now stopped. We must send to Antwerp for a lock-
smith to open them.'[49]

In November a 'formula pacificationis' was negotiated, in which
the deacons for their part were to signify their acceptance of the
principle of godparents and their recognition of ecclesiastical authority, asking forgiveness of minister, elders and bishop; while their
opponents were to apologize to the other faction if their behaviour
had been unduly vehement and harsh. 'Homines enim sumus.'
Grindal and Cousin signed as 'mediators', together with four
English ministers, Fox, Calfhill, Philpot and Christopher Cole-
man. In conclusion Grindal issued a conciliatory statement, to be
read from the pulpit by Calfhill, announcing that the church was
reunited, that there were to be no recriminations, and that peace
was to be cemented in an administration of the Lord's Supper. The
clerk of the French consistory has left a vignette of the civilities
with which peace was signified on this occasion, as perhaps on so
many other occasions. The bishop 'touchy le main a tous' (does
this refer to shaking hands or joining hands?) and then there was a
general drinking of healths at Grindal's expense.[50]

The reader who has persisted thus far will have guessed that this pacification failed to hold. The dissidents complained that it was as dissidents that they were still treated by the seniority, and that the bishop had failed to convince them of his impartiality.[51] In the following summer Grindal tried again with a fresh 'formula'. This provided for new elections, and these in due course confirmed the ascendancy of the Winghen–Utenhove party, thanks to the intervention of a delegation from Emden. Those unwilling to adhere to the congregation under this government were now permitted to join the English parish churches, but under stringent conditions, and as individuals, not as a group. But the parishes favoured by the Dutch dissenters were those where in the spring of 1566 the ministry was seriously disturbed by the vestiarian dispute between the puritan ministers and the authorities.[52] The crisis deepened when the arrival of refugees from the troubles in the Netherlands coincided with Winghen's provocative denunciation of the iconoclasts. Eventually a schism of serious proportions took shape. Fifty or sixty church members with their families withdrew altogether from Austin Friars and proceeded to elect their own minister and elders by simple majority vote, in effect unchurching the parent body. Grindal now invoked the authority of the Ecclesiastical Commission in an uncompromising decree which revoked all earlier attempts at settlement, confirmed the original constitution of the Dutch church and identified all separatists from it as contumacious persons. Grindal could not tolerate formal schism, and this corresponds to his tough and decisive proceedings against English separatists at about this same time.

The climax came with a remarkable initiative undertaken by the Dutch consistory. Twenty-seven articles were composed, after extensive consultation with sister churches, and were sent to Geneva and other continental centres. These dealt with the topic of christian liberty and discipline which was at the heart of the dispute, and their theme was obedience and restraint. The due authority of superiors was not an infringement of christian liberty and in the sphere of 'things indifferent' (such as the procedure to be followed in baptism) it was legitimate for the civil as well as ecclesiastical authorities to determine policy. These were not things to be left to 'the judgment of the common people, or of some simple man': a conservative document, an insular historian might mistakenly say an 'Anglican' document, condemning with equal severity insubordination towards due authority in the church and unlawful resistance to secular rulers. The articles were endorsed in a letter from Cousin, totally condemning the dissidents, backed in its turn by an accompanying note from Grindal. But the other party made its own approach to Geneva, sending a delegation which had the support of the stranger community in Norwich and of the Dutch minister in that city, himself no nonentity. The Geneva pastorate was placed in a quandary. Their instinct must have been to underwrite the clerical-aristocratic principle, proscribing congregational democracy. They even found it politic actually to strengthen those articles which condemned resistance to lawful rulers, be they godly or ungodly. But they found it expedient to moderate the language of the articles and in an accompanying letter to express criticism of the intransigence of the London consistory. They must have known that the dissident group they were obliged to condemn was in sympathy with the English puritans whose resistance to popish ceremonies and worldly policy had been inspired from Geneva and had won approval there only two years earlier.[53] It could hardly have pleased Beza that Grindal had the articles published in Dutch, English and Latin, for by their terms the English puritans stood condemned no less than the Dutch dissenters.[54]

Meanwhile the tact of Geneva was no more effective than Grindal's earlier efforts in promoting peace. In 1569 the annual elections which all true Genevans deplored led to the total defeat of Winghen's supporters, and when Grindal left London a year later the dispute was still only partially resolved. This prolonged schism was particularly scandalous in that it threatened a more extensive division in the continental Dutch churches, and because an appalling example had been set by what was supposed to be a model church. Although the acts of the French consistory are missing for these years, it appears that it was as a sequel to this affair that Cousin succeeded in completing the work of des Gallars by excluding democratic elections from the constitution of his own church.[55]

None of the cases so far discussed aroused more excitement than the affairs of two learned Spaniards with which we end this account of Grindal's adventures among the strangers.[56] And none illustrates more sharply the clash of free thought at odds with dogma and 'discipline' which has been its theme: or shows up to better advantage the temperamental and intellectual differences between Grindal and the leaders of French Calvinism. At first sight the story we are about to tell looks like a classic example of smear tactics: what a modern authority on the Spanish reformers has called 'heretical packaging'.[57] Two Spaniards who were perhaps guilty only of intellectual integrity, not to say pride, were accused of gross heresy and various moral failings. They were incessantly abused and no effort was spared over many years to destroy them, or at least to nullify their supposed corrupting influence. And yet the instinct of the Calvinist inquisitors may have been sound. A Spanish protestant in the age of Philip II was the ultimate outsider, the freest of all free spirits. The cloak of Calvinist orthodoxy may have been assumed for opportunistic reasons and worn lightly. The available sanctuaries and openings for employment were Calvinist. As for Grindal, always insisting on fair play, he was as far out of his depth as any English churchman has ever been, confronted with theological infighting among foreigners.

Casiodoro de Reina and Antonio del Corro (who assumed the French name of 'Bellerive') were two of a group of Spanish evangelicals whose spiritual progress had begun as young monks with 'Erasmian' and cryptically protestant leanings in the monastery of San Isidro del Campo, outside Seville. With a younger member of the group, Cipriano de Valera, who was also resident in London in the 1560s but as an orthodox Calvinist kept out of the limelight, they were dedicated to the project of a Spanish Bible. Building on foundations laid by earlier translations of the New Testament, de Reina was to achieve the first complete translation of the Bible into Castilian, the so-called Bear Bible printed at Basle in 1569, the basis of Spanish protestant bibles ever since and only superficially revised by de Valera in the definitive edition of 1602.[58]

In 1557 de Reina fled from Spain with other members of a nascent protestant church and after brief sojourns in Geneva and Frankfurt came to London in 1559, perhaps in company with returning English exiles. He attached himself to the French church and negotiated with Grindal and Cecil for accommodation for a separate Spanish congregation. According to the ambassador, de la Quadra, who kept the Spanish heretics under surveillance, the little church first gathered in the bishop of London's house, with preaching three times a week.[59] Later they were granted the use of the church of St Mary Axe after de Reina had insisted on the need to make their meetings public and above suspicion. As pastor of this barely viable church, de Reina composed a confession of faith[60] expressive of what Calvinists called 'syncretism' (a mediating position between their own doctrine and Lutheranism) and of 'adiaphorism', the distinction between essential and non-essential doctrine. There were other more alarming traces of unsoundness, easily detected by the sensitive noses of des Gallars and other leaders of the French congregation, who were already alerted by reports of de Reina's contact with antitrinitarian circles in Geneva. In October 1560 de Reina appeared before the French consistory to make a statement in his own name and that of other Spaniards which would give the lie to reports that he shared the errors of

Servetus. Instead of clearing his reputation he gave unsatisfactory answers to questions about van Haemstede and Acontius. Evidently the French and Dutch were afraid that the Spanish congregation would provide a stalking horse and a haven for the dissident Haemstedians. Indeed, in the following year Acontius became an elder of de Reina's congregation.[61] Although the record of proceedings against de Reina in the French consistory is lost, it seems unlikely that he was left in peace after this interview.[62] But in 1563 all hopes and fears for the little Spanish church were extinguished when de Reina suddenly withdrew to Frankfurt.

There was doubtless more than one reason for his precipitate flight. The Spanish ambassador and other Spanish agents were at least indirectly responsible, since de Reina lived in constant fear of being kidnapped and brought within reach of the Inquisition. The ostensible cause concerned a charge of homosexuality, 'peccatum sodomiticum' as Grindal put it explicitly in an account of the Spanish business sent to Cecil some years later.[63] As with similar allegations in more recent history, these were murky waters, stirred up by those who had an interest in getting de Reina out of London. Yet it is clear from the manner of his departure and from attempts over many years to clear his name that something had happened to de Reina in bed, 'ainsi qu'il advient aux hommes en dormant', and that a boy was involved. But the event was without criminality or perhaps even an immoral intention.[64] Casiodorus fled from the preliminary hearings into the affair by a commission appointed by Grindal which included Cousin and Utenhove and two London ministers, Robert Crowley and James Yonge. His action may have been precipitated by the mistaken belief that sodomy was a capital offence.[65]

From this time onwards the Calvinist jungle telegraph hummed with rumours. De Reina was said to have kissed a book by Servetus and to have declared that Servetus alone understood the mystery of the Trinity. Des Gallars in Orléans told Utenhove that the news about Casiodorus had thoroughly upset him. 'May the Lord avert such plagues from his flock.' Beza was not one to be impressed with rumours and in 1565 he was prepared to recommend de Reina to the French church at Strasbourg, where Calvin himself had ministered thirty years before. But a conference with the Heidelberg theologian Olevian aroused new imputations of his doctrinal probity and moral reputation, and renewed the utterly damaging charge of 'Servetianism', the ultimate in 'heretical packaging'.[66] From a position of judicious neutrality Beza was later persuaded to set his face against de Reina. It was true, he recalled, that he had never heard the Spaniard expressly dissociate himself from Servetus. (De Reina had been heard to say that when resident in Geneva he could never pass the site of Servetus's execution without tears.)[67] Beza's ultimate verdict was: 'May God wash him clean if he has been wrongly accused, but if not sink him and drown him in his own filth before he infects others.'[68]

Grindal's part in this affair was wholly honourable. He thought well of de Reina, and indeed there was a certain theological affinity between them, derived from a common veneration of Martin Bucer. In the midst of the débâcle Grindal was instrumental in preserving the manuscripts of the Spanish Bible, and in due course the translator would dedicate to him a copy of the completed work, in gratitude. This copy of the 'Bear Bible' (so named from its engraved title-page) was among the books which were left to the Queen's College Oxford at the time of the archbishop's death, and there it still survives, with its graceful inscription recalling Grindal's action in rescuing the work 'ex hostium manibus'.[69] Many years later, when de Reina needed a complete clearance of his name in order to qualify for a post at Antwerp, he returned to London and the commission of enquiry which his flight had interrupted was reconvened, under Grindal as archbishop of Canterbury. It found in his favour on all doctrinal and moral points. But the London French church remained frigidly hostile, declining to comment on the archbishop's sentence or to issue a testimonial in de Reina's favour, or even to admit him to its fellowship.[70] Beza, after all, had pronounced the sentence that mattered, in Letter 59 of his *Epistolae*, by then in print and in international circulation.

This was but the curtain-raiser to a closely related but more vociferous heresy hunt in which the quarry was Antonio del Corro, 'dit Bellerive'. Corro came to England in 1567 on a visit which lasted until his death a quarter of a century later, and only gradually did he cease to be a controversial figure. The prolongation of the Corro affair makes it the proper climax to the themes of this chapter, continuing as it did beyond Grindal's time as bishop of London and extending beyond the little world of the stranger churches into the Church of England itself, where Corro and his theology found their ultimate habitation.

The story began on Christmas Eve 1563, when Corro wrote to his 'dear friend' Casiodoro de Reina in London. The letter concerned the plans for printing the Spanish Bible but also initiated, or perhaps continued, a theological discussion, with what Corro's accusers regarded as affirmations and Corro insisted were innocent questions, but which we may perhaps call leading questions.[71] Corro seemed to regard fundamental articles of the faith as open to discussion and expressed a desire to read writers whom no good Calvinist could wish to consult, such as the spiritualist Schwenkfeld. And he asked de Reina what he thought of Velsius and Acontius. Beza had the answer to that question. Velsius was insane and Acontius 'full of paradoxes'.[72] Corro's letter had been included in a packet directed to a member of the French congregation and endorsed (but it was not the letter to de Reina which was so endorsed) 'for matters of great importance touching the church of God'. De Reina's whereabouts by this time were unknown and the French consistory waited three months, then opened the letter, found that it contained nothing of a public nature, advised Corro that de Reina was unavailable, and filed it away. The letter was one of at least twenty-one which Corro wrote to de Reina at this time without receiving a reply.[73] It remained an embarrassment to his detractors that the root of the matter lay in a private letter which had been tampered with, albeit in good faith: 'providentially' as was said, to put a bold face on a dubious procedure.[74] We may compare the 'extraordinary miracle' and 'singular providence of God' which enabled des Gallars to discover a collection of letters in Orléans and with them to discredit Jean Morély, sieur de Villiers, the leader of an alternative French Calvinism.[75] Corro would later allege that his letters had been intercepted over a period of four years.

By the time he arrived in London with the intention of preaching in Spanish and perhaps of regrouping the Spanish congregation Corro was consequently an object of suspicion, the good standing with which he had left the Lausanne Academy and Beza's company in 1559 already damaged beyond repair. The portmanteau charge of 'Servetianism' had been mentioned in correspondence between France and Geneva and Corro had acquired the reputation of an 'ambitious' man, which may only mean that he was not, as we should say in the twentieth century, a good party man, or that he conducted himself like a Spaniard, as one report suggests. Driven from pillar to post by the violent disturbances with which some regions of France were now convulsed, he came to Antwerp in 1566 with excellent recommendations from the church of Montargis and Chatillon, south of Paris, and from Renée de France, dowager duchess of Ferrara. At Antwerp he tried to establish himself as minister of the Walloon church, but succeeded in causing multiple offence with 'a godly admonition', a notable but in the circumstances provocative essay in eirenics addressed to the local Lutheran community. Although this manifesto was ostensibly aimed at these Lutherans for making the Confession of Augsburg 'a fifth gospel or new symbol of the Creed', its latitudinarian denigration of 'confessions, catechisms, commentaries and traditions', and of those who would make 'gods or idols of our doctors', was not the sort of apologia to give Calvinists much comfort.[76]

When Corro commended himself to the French church in London all this and much more was remembered. Even the testimonial from Montargis and Chatillon was suspect 'by the excessive eulogy it contains'. Corro could only be admitted to fellowship if he would subscribe to true doctrine and publicly admit that his letters to de Reina of 1563 were 'imprudenter scriptae'. This he declined to do. Corro now 'ran to the bishop', as his enemies contemptuously put it. Grindal conferred with him in the presence of his advisers and issued a formal certificate of soundness in doctrine.[77] It was the van Haemstede case all over again. Grindal was satisfied when Corro renounced the heresies alluded to in his letters. This demonstrated his inability, or perhaps unwillingness, to tune his ear to theological undertones. He would continue to praise Corro's 'good learning' long after he had been repelled by his conduct, which is to say that Grindal did not have the mind to translate faults of character into a suspicion of intellectual deviance. He granted Corro a small pension and did what the French church had been careful not to do: handed him a copy of the notorious letter which he had written three years before.

Armed with the bishop's testimonial, Corro successfully applied for membership of the Italian congregation, where he began to preach to the Spanish-speaking members. He had no ambition, he said, to become a minister in the more prestigious French church, which brought the comment 'sour grapes' from Cousin. But now what Corro called 'an atrocious war against me by tongue and pen' intensified, orchestrated by Cousin. There was slanderous talk in Lombard Street and at public eating places, which Grindal advised the victim to ignore. But Corro could not so easily disregard a stream of letters from the French consistory to Paris, to des Gallars at Orléans, and to other churches, giving wide publicity to the affair and adding to his incrimination. This bore fruit in a sentence of the French National Synod which barred him from the ministry everywhere until he had cleared his name. As with de Reina, it appears that Cousin's fear was that Corro's ministry would provide a haven and a focus for the 'libertines' who had abandoned their own churches. True enough, the so-called Italian church was a curiously mixed society.[78]

Corro gave as good as he got. He circulated copies of Grindal's testimonial with an added endorsement which implied quite improperly that the bishop had condemned the 'malice' of his opponents. He prepared an *Apology*, no longer extant, which upset Grindal with its 'sharp invectives' and untruths. He supplied the bishop with details of an elaborate conspiracy with its roots in Paris and the machinations of a certain Balthasar Sanchez, the same man who had denounced de Reina. He wrote besides to Parker and Cecil and sent his *Apology* with many other papers to Beza. Here are some examples of his own sharp tongue and pen. Cousin and his henchmen were said to be more cruel and tyrannical than the Spanish Inquisition, worse than Turks or pagans. With clear reference to Acontius's notorious book the disintegration of the Spanish group within the Italian church was said to be 'a stratagem of Satan'. And he had this to say at his trial before the Ecclesiastical Commissioners: 'It seems that you English are making not only a civil war but an ecclesiastical war against the Spaniards: a civil war in seizing our shipping and treasure, an ecclesiastical war in my person.'[79] It was in December 1568, in the midst of the trial, that Alva's pay-ships were impounded and their cargo of bullion diverted to the queen's coffers. If this was a little too apt it was ingenious to send the French text of his Antwerp *Admonition* to Archbishop Parker with the suggestion that his daughters might care to use it in their French lessons.[80]

It was this provocative conduct rather than any suspicion of actual heresy which turned Grindal against Corro. He was also stung by a frank 'remonstrance' from the French consistory. Why have a magistrate and why have a superintendent if such a man were to be allowed to conspire against the church and to claim the bishop as his supporter? The French church prepared a dossier of charges under four heads, dealing with Corro's ambition, his calumnies, his lies and his jests, the man being 'versé en l'art de moquerie': all to the effect that here was 'un troubleur des églises reformées', but not impugning his doctrine. In response Grindal took the unusual course of referring the case to a joint commission composed of staff members of the Ecclesiastical Commission and no less than six French pastors. After a protracted hearing he pronounced sentence in March 1569. On account of his evil speaking, slander and unshakeable obstinacy, Corro was suspended from preaching, teaching and all other ecclesiastical functions.[81] Beza, not entirely happy about an affair of which the details were intercepted letters 'and other crudities', was content that judgment should rest with the bishop. But the sentence was confirmed, in effect, in a devastating letter which Beza wrote to Corro in response to his *Apology*, which would later gain notoriety in a watered-down version as no. 59 of his *Epistolae*.[82]

Once again Grindal appeared in something like the role of

Pontius Pilate, sadly confirming the sentence of the Sanhedrin
when his instinct was probably to scourge Corro and let him go.
But unlike the verdict of the Roman governor, his sentences were
acts of conscience and pastorally motivated. No sooner had he
pronounced against Corro than he was labouring for his reconciliation. That was the purpose of ecclesiastical discipline which
was in no ultimate sense punitive. Grindal was also under pressure
from Cecil and perhaps from other courtiers whom Corro had
taken care to cultivate and who had heard only his side of the story.
In August 1569 Corro undertook to admit the fault of his slanderous speeches and to live peacefully hereafter. It was not until
November that Grindal forwarded this partial retraction to
Cousin, apparently because a suspicion of plague in the French
pastor's house had interrupted communications. But he now
begged Cousin to meet Corro half-way. 'You could do nothing
that would please me more.' Corro had already sustained eight
months' suspension, and for a matter of conduct rather than of
doctrine. But the consistory was unimpressed. Corro must explicitly retract the scandalous imprudence of his 1563 letter to de
Reina, and of his Antwerp *Admonition*. In other words, he must
thoroughly purge himself theologically. This Corro could not or at
least would not do, not ever.[83]

Grindal's refusal to admit that the root of the matter was
theological, his very Anglican attitude, was the more remarkable in
that he well knew that by now a new scandal, unmistakably doctrinal, had arisen with Corro's publication at Norwich of a controversial theological statement in the form of a broadside, *Tableau
d'oeuvre de Dieu*.[84] The eloquent silence of this publication on the
subject of the Trinity and its casually incidental mention of predestination were suggestive, and a new *Apology* which followed
indicative, of Corro's digression from Calvinist dogmatics. Again
it is revealing of Grindal's correctitude, and perhaps of an essentially untheological mind, that he considered this to be a domestic
matter between Corro and the Italian church, which technically it
was, since Corro was a member of that congregation. It is also
significant that Grindal was careful to express no view of his own
on Corro's doctrine but merely noted that the *Tableau* had been
printed without the approval of Corro's own church, an offence
against church discipline, and that the church disapproved of the
doctrine.[85] Early in 1570 the Italian consistory excommunicated
Corro.[86] The long arm of Cousin, Beza's arm, had reached even
into that pleasingly varied assembly.

Corro had now burned his bridges with the stranger churches
and was looking for a future in the Church of England. As a New

Year's gift he sent copies of the Latin version of his *Tableau* to the queen and various notables. Episcopal hearings into his case continued as Grindal prepared to leave the diocese, and pressure on the bishops continued to be applied by Cousin and successive national assemblies of the French Reformed Church. In 1573 Corro made a new and much more comprehensive submission, but it is likely that by this date his motive was to impress the Anglican authorities. In consequence, Bishop Sandys did nothing to impede his appointment to a lectureship at the Temple (through Burghley's patronage). Some years later the help of the earl of Leicester established him in Oxford as a theological teacher, albeit deprived by the successful resistance of Oxford Calvinists of the doctorate which Leicester as chancellor of the university had sought to obtain for him, and which was conferred with alacrity on one of his principal French-speaking opponents.[87] In international Calvinist circles it became a commonplace that Corro was tolerated in England 'by the silence of the bishops'. In the late 1570s a prominent English politician and brother-in-law of Burghley, Sir Henry Killigrew, included regular reports of Corro's ups and downs in his correspondence with the English ambassador in the Netherlands, William Davison, who shared his deep prejudice against the man.[88] By then the dominant note in Corro's theology had become the repudiation of Calvinist predestination doctrine, so that he appears to posterity as a proto-Arminian, together with Peter Baro, another foreigner who held a divinity chair at Cambridge, a pioneer of the intellectual reaction against John Calvin.[89] When Richard Hooker's views first became known (in the same Temple Church where Corro had lectured) comparisons were at once drawn with the Spaniard.[90] Cousin had known what he was about.

We end what it would be a serious mistake to regard as a merely silly symphony with a coda. Among the Haemstedians excommunicated in 1562 was the author of *The Stratagems of Satan*, Acontius. On the face of it this was the penalty not of heresy but of rising to the defence of Haemstede who was not a heretic either but who had taken a stand for the right of others to hold peculiar and even pernicious opinions until better persuaded. (But behind the face of it it is clear that these views had the power to dissolve the very foundations of reformed christianity as the Calvinists articulated it.) In a lengthy manifesto addressed to Grindal, Acontius reminded the bishop that whereas he, Acontius, had attributed salvation to those who denied but a single article of the faith there were precedents for refusing to unchurch those who were ignorant of the faith in its entirety. Zwingli, for example, had been willing to offer posthumous baptism, as it were, to noble pagans such as

Socrates. If this was a shrewd thrust, the letter ended with a truly Parthian shot. It was remarkable that as a stranger Acontius was denied membership of the stranger churches while the English parish churches were not only willing to admit him but were required by law without any test of belief whatsoever to constrain the adherence not only of himself but of countless others who dissented radically from the truth of the Gospel.

Acontius found it more remarkable still that these inconsistent policies, one of extreme narrowness, the other of excessive latitude, were both administered in the name of the same individual: Edmund Grindal, bishop and superintendent.[91] What Acontius could not have foreseen (and within two years he was dead, not long after the publication of his *Stratagems of Satan*) was that the tolerant latitudinarianism and advanced adiaphorism of which he was a lonely advocate would have a more secure future in the Church of England than Calvinism, even the Calvinism with a human face which characterized Edmund Grindal.

8

FIRE AND PESTILENCE

GRINDAL'S decade as bishop of London was punctuated by three extraordinary calamities: in 1561 the burning and partial destruction of his cathedral church; in 1563 one of the worst outbreaks of plague in the history of the city, comparable to the terrible visitations of 1603 and 1665; and finally, in 1566, a major ecclesiastical crisis from which the name of 'puritan' and the almost continuous history of a coherent Dissent in English religious life historically derives.

Old St Paul's was the largest church in late medieval Christendom, the greatest of the English cathedrals, in bulk at least.[1] Its glory, 'the chief ornament and beauty' of the city,[2] was the central tower and steeple, taller than Salisbury, soaring to a total height of almost 500 feet. Until it was blown down in a gale in 1547 the spire surmounting the central tower of Lincoln Cathedral made that the tallest building in England. And then for fourteen years, until its own downfall in 1561, St Paul's steeple was pre-eminent. No higher monument was to be erected in London until the Post Office Tower made its appearance on the skyline of the 1960s.

The steeple of Grindal's day was no more than a century old, the achievement of restoration which had followed the fifth fire in the long history of the church, in 1444, caused, like the fire of 1561, by lightning. The fabric was surmounted by a great ball nine feet in circumference containing sacred relics,[3] on which stood a cross fifteen feet high, topped with a large weathercock, or eagle. The ball and eagle were overlaid with gilded copper, the cross with copper varnished in red. At coronations and other days of triumph the steeple would be hung with flags and banners and stuntmen would perform acrobatic feats on the top. Ordinary mortals paid a penny to climb the tower and to carve their names on the leads. At Mary's coronation the protestant gentleman pensioner Edward Underhill, sitting on horseback at the west end of Paul's, noted that the steeple was dressed over all 'like a royal ship' and prophesied 'shipwreck ere it be long'. He expected a gale of wind rather than lightning and thunderbolt. 'But such are the wonderful works of God, whose gunners will not miss the mark that he doth appoint, be it never so little.'[4]

It was on the afternoon of Wednesday 4 June 1561, the eve of the catholic feast of Corpus Christi, that Underhill's prophecy was fulfilled. In the midst of a frightful thunderstorm there was 'a marvellous great fiery lightning' and 'a most terrible hideous crack of thunder, such as seldom hath been heard', directly over the city. The tower of St Martins Ludgate was struck and the church damaged, when almost simultaneously observers on the Thames and in the fields saw lightning strike Paul's steeple, 'two or three yards beneath the cross'. Eyewitness accounts disagree over the hour the lightning struck and consequently whether the effect was immediate or delayed. But they agree that it was between four and five o'clock in the afternoon that fire broke out below the ball, the timber having ignited through the holes left in the covering of the steeple for scaffolding. Within a quarter of an hour the cross and eagle fell on to the roof of the south transept while, as the steeple burned 'downward, like as a candle consuming' as far as the battlements and bells, burning timbers ignited the remaining roofs 'all four ways', so that after an hour the steeple and most of the roof were consumed. The air was full of sparks and brands and molten lead and soon the surrounding streets 'seemed to be paved with lead'.

Crowds collected, 'expecting a general calamity of the city'. Somewhere in the throng Bishop Grindal was conferring with the lord mayor and aldermen, the lord keeper and the lord treasurer who had all been hastily summoned. An alarming proposal to shoot the steeple down with artillery was overtaken by events, as were attempts to scale the roof and attack it with axes. On the advice of Mr Winter of the Admiralty all efforts were applied to saving the bishop's palace which adjoined the church on the north side and provided a route for the blaze to reach adjoining property. The fire was stopped short of the palace by the exertions of more than five hundred people carrying water, gentlemen and sub-stantial citizens lending a hand 'as if they had been labourers'. By ten o'clock at night, when Lord Admiral Clinton arrived from the Court at Greenwich where the fire had been witnessed by the queen, the wind had died, the danger passed and the timber of the roof was burning on the stone vaulting which survived intact. Inside the church little was burned except the communion table, a fact which must have impressed susceptible minds. This official ac-count of the facts was entered in Grindal's register by the diocesan registrar and formed the basis of a report published in English within less than a week. The briefer narratives by Machyn, Stow and Hayward are mostly consistent. But this version of the event had to compete with contrary rumours: in particular that the fire was caused by the negligence of a plumber who had left a pan of hot coals in the steeple when he went to dinner. Although it was established that there had been no workmen in the cathedral for six months this tale was given a new lease of life by Heylyn in the seventeenth century and was repeated by Dugdale.[5]

According to the official version 'the true cause ... was the tempest, by God's sufferance'. These last three words were indispensable to the comprehension of such an event by the minds of the sixteenth century, more especially because the church alone was burned, 'as if it had been destined only for the ruin of that place'[6] — the reverse of the miracle of 1941. But how was God's intervention to be construed? On the one hand the ball with its catholic relics had fallen. On the other the protestant communion table had burned. Within a few days Bishop Pilkington of Durham appeared at Paul's Cross to interpret the visitation as 'a general warning for the whole realm and namely to the city of London of some greater plague to follow, if amendment of life in all states did not ensue'. (These words proved prophetic.) Pilkington was particularly concerned to correct any impression that the event was a token of divine disapproval of the recent alteration of religion. But this was precisely how it was interpreted by John Morwen, a deprived Marian prebendary of St Paul's and chaplain to Bonner who circulated a clandestine tract which purported to be *An addicion with an apologie to the causes of the brinnynge of Paules church*: 'But consider, how far now contrary the church has been used; and it is no marvel if God have sent down fire to burn part of the church as a sign of his wrath.'[7] A similar moral was drawn as far away as Italy in the correspondence of two cardinals of the Roman Church, commenting on what had happened 'in Londra, la vigilia del Corpus Domini, all'ora del vespero ... '[8] In due course Pilkington replied in a 63,000-word *Confutation of an addicion*, part of the so-called 'great controversy' between catholics and protestants of the 1560s.

If protestants and papists had not been so seriously at odds they might have agreed that there was much to distress christians, not to speak of their God, in the condition of Paul's church. Pilkington indeed was prepared to admit that 'we both do agree the church of Pauls to be abused, and therefore justly plagued'.[9] His *Confutation* is one of many sources for our knowledge of the multitudinous and teeming activities to which the vast pile of old St Paul's was dedicated, a matter of complaint for at least two hundred years before this time and for satirical and scandalized comment for a century still to come. As Bishop Earle characterized the building in the reign of Charles I: 'It is a heap of stones and men with a strange

confusion of languages, and were the steeple not sanctified nothing
liker Babel.'[10]

Christian worship and instruction, whether catholic or protestant, was an almost marginal activity in what served as a great
sheltered market place and general concourse for Londoners,
whatever their business. Bishop Pilkington summed up the principal divisions of the fabric: 'The south alley for usury and popery,
the north for simony, and the horse fair in the midst for all kind of
bargains, meetings, brawlings, murders, conspiracies, and the font
for ordinary payments of money, are so well known to all men as
the beggar knows his dish.'[11] Apart from the font for settling
debts there was the 'serving man's pillar' where servants were
hired and where Bardolph would have been engaged by Falstaff,[12]
and the 'Si Quis' door in the north nave where clergymen adver-
tised their availability for benefices and lectureships.[13] The nave
was significantly known as Paul's Walk. The positioning of doors
facing one another midway along the north and south walls of the
nave and in the two transepts turned it into a convenient thorough-
fare, a short-cut for pedestrians and porters and even horses and
mules with their loads, 'great vessels of ale or beer, great baskets
full of bread, fish, flesh and fruit, fardels of stuff and other gross
ware', as one complaint runs. It was also, notoriously, the place for
gallants to stroll and engage in social display, especially after
dinner, from three to six in the afternoon. In Shakespeare's time
walkers were advised to make no more than four perambulations,
and then on to the tobacconist and the booksellers. The throng
made a happy hunting ground for pickpockets, 'the thieves' sanc-
tuary, which rob more safely in the crowd than in a wilderness'.
According to Bishop Earle, 'The visitants are all men without
exception.' Much of the traffic was in no commodity more substantial than news. 'In the middle aisle you may hear what the
protestant says, and in the aisles what the papists whisper,' wrote
one Elizabethan.[14] Earle again: 'It is the ears' brothel and satisfies
their lust and itch.' No wonder he observed the sound of Paul's as
'a strange humming or buzz,... a kind of still roar or loud whisper.'
But the decibels rose on Sundays and holidays when the children
from the surrounding parishes played in the church 'in such manner as children use to do till dark night, and hence cometh principally that inordinate noise which many time suffereth not the
preacher to be heard in the choir'.[15] In the aftermath of the fire a
royal proclamation censured the profane abuse of churches and
churchyards, and namely the 'divers outrageous and unseemly
behaviours used within and near the cathedral church of St Paul in
London'.[16] In December a man was pilloried and lost an ear for

making an affray in Paul's churchyard.[17] But the proclamation made no lasting alteration in long-established habits. In 1598 Bishop Bancroft's visitors were assured that such disorders had been complained of at every visitation 'and yet continue in their old irregularity'.[18] In the 1630s, when the carrying of 'base things' through the church was still of concern to the High Commission, a Bedfordshire man was arrested for pissing against a pillar. It was his first visit to London and he was walking through St Paul's on his way to be married. He told the Commissioners that 'he knew it not to be a church',[19] so revealing a greater depth of ignorance than Henry Mayhew's Victorian crossing sweeper who, asked what St Paul's was, answered: 'A church, sir, as I have heard. I never was in a church.'

So much for the moral reckoning. What of the material remedy for the terrible damage inflicted on this great building? An early estimate of the likely cost of the repairs made horrifying reading. With timber scarce and expensive and lead more costly still the accountant arrived at a grand total of £17,738, not including most labour costs. His estimate included £326. 13s. 4d. for timber for the roofs, £434. 6s. 8d. for timber for the spire, £400 for boards and laths, £500 for repairs to the stonework of the spire, and the stupendous sum of £7,540 for lead for the roofs, with a further £1,500 for lead for the spire, with additional heavy charges for the casting and laying.[20] Where could this kind of money be found?

No doubt it was the general utility of Paul's for many sorts and conditions of men, and above all its civic function and value which accounts for the expedition with which both temporary and more lasting repairs were undertaken: that and the continuing storms of a summer monsoon. (In the late evening of 30 July there was lightning and thunder such as nobody could remember and 'a great rain' until midnight, so that 'everyone thought that the day of doom were come at hand.')[21] The response of the city and from the Court was especially prompt. Within six days of the fire the city had voted the sum of three thousand marks, to be collected in the form of three levies or 'fifteenths', the first to be paid immediately, the second within six months, and the third within a year. At the same time all the inhabitants of London, whether citizens, gentry or strangers, were to be exhorted to contribute their further 'aid, devotion, charity and help': these sums to be collected and accounted for before the end of June. On 16 June the mayor and aldermen were summoned to the Court at Greenwich and soon afterwards the joint initiatives of the city and the Privy Council led to the appointment of a commission for the repair of St Paul's, representative of both authorities. Judging by the frequent intervention of his distinctive hand in the various drafts of these documents, Cecil was the prime mover of urgent action.[22] The Court of Common Council also took steps to establish a kind of fire brigade to provide some protection against the danger of 'all such huge and sudden fires' as might occur in the future: a force of artificers and labourers, a supply of buckets, axes, saws, ladders and hooks, and premises in which to store this equipment. The work on St Paul's began on 1 July. By 5 July, when rain and thunder returned, all four great roofs were covered with temporary boarding: 45,000 boards were employed, at a cost of more than £90. In early September the rails around the battlements of the tower were replaced. By 1 November the choir was again in use and the lord mayor and representatives of all the crafts of London attended a great civic service. Grindal preached, apparently at length, for the company was escorted home after dark with eighty torch bearers. Within a year the nave and choir roofs were entirely rebuilt.[23]

The response of the Church to this crisis was less prompt and less effective. On 24 June Cecil worked over the draft of a royal letter to Archbishop Parker which invited an extraordinary response from the clergy of the entire province. In its original version this letter authorized the metropolitan 'by way of convocation or by other some manner of good conference with the bishops of your province and the principal members of the clergy thereof to devise upon some contribution of money to be levied and collected'. Did Cecil envisage a special meeting of the Convocation of the Province of Canterbury, held apart from Parliament? If so he at once changed his mind and altered the wording to 'by way of any manner of usual or other good conference'. In the event the response of Parker when he received the letter was to follow normal procedure in referring it to Grindal, who as dean of the province forwarded it to the remainder of the bishops. The bishops were required to confer with their clergy and collectively to 'resolve upon' the rate of contribution. But perhaps the bishops in their turn passed the matter on to their archdeacons. At the end of the line there may have been meetings to consider an appropriate response to the calamity in London. More likely the parochial clergy were taxed, by administrative order, and more likely still avoided payment. Parker had proposed that the lowest acceptable contribution might be fixed at a twentieth of the value of their livings for the clergy of the London diocese and from other dioceses a thirtieth payable by those no longer liable for their first-fruits, a fortieth by those still so burdened.[24]

At a very rough estimate this rate, literally enforced, should have yielded a sum of £1,500, perhaps £2,000. But after more than six months the whole province of Canterbury outside the diocese of London had offered no more than a 'benevolence' of £100. Two years later the Privy Council was pursuing the bishops for payment and Cox of Ely was required to explain why it was that his diocese had contributed almost nothing.[25] Anticipating a sluggish response, Parker had revised his original instructions, advising Grindal on 1 September 1561 that the clergy of London should bear a proportionately greater share of the burden, 'it being their cathedral and head church'. Beneficed clergy should pay a twentieth of their livings, those still paying their first-fruits a thirtieth and curates and stipendiaries a token of at least half a crown. In communication with his archdeacons and with the dean of St Paul's, Grindal optimistically asked them to use such persuasion that the clergy might exceed their rates by voluntary contribution, and called for the money by 30 November. By April 1562 the diocese had collected the sum of £395. 18s. 6d., which included gifts from the archdeacon of Middlesex and from the dean and chapter.[26]

But by this time the repairs had already cost a total of £2,530. 15s. 4d. In the second month of the works alone, nearly £700 had been expended on timber, stone, iron, lead and labour. With such a feeble effort by the admittedly hard-pressed clergy it was fortunate that the laity was more generous. The queen herself gave a thousand marks in gold and a thousand loads of timber from her woods, forests and parks north of the Trent. A further 481 loads of timber was obtained from thirty-nine other sources at a cost of £296. 13s. 7d. It was in Yorkshire that the nave and choir roofs were framed by two hundred workmen, costing locally more than £1,000 in labour and additional timber. The two fifteenths so far collected from the city had yielded £813. 8s. 10d., not the two thousand marks (£1,333. 6s. 8d.) anticipated, but the benevolence of the citizens had brought in a further £1,045. 7s. 2d.: a total of £1,863. 16s. from the city. With certain private gifts the sum in hand by the end of April 1562 amounted to £3,205. 11s. 2d. But expenditure already incurred came to £2,976. 13s. 7d., so that the treasurer had only £228. 17s. 7d. still available. The great roofs had yet to be completed, shipped to London and erected, and well over £2,000 would be required for lead, even if the original estimates were excessive. Further repairs were needed in the stonework of the partition between the nave and the choir and in the paving. When the transept roofs were taken into account, with the iron and glasswork and, finally, the rebuilding of the steeple, further expenditure of £6,000 was envisaged, and only another £1,000 could be looked for from the city.[27]

These figures were communicated to the Council by a new commission for the repair of St Paul's[28] which was given wide powers of enquiry and coercion. According to the annalist Sir John Hayward, public contributions, voluntary and compulsory, eventually yielded the grand total of £5,968. 16s. 1d., which almost exactly met the actual cost of reroofing the choir and nave. Of this total the city contributed £3,247. 16s. 2d., the clergy of the province £1,461. 12s. 11d., the bishop 'of his benevolence' £284. 13s. 11d., the dean and chapter £136. 13s. 4d., and the judges and officers of the courts of Common Pleas and King's Bench £52. 1s. 8d.[29] But by the summer of 1563 the works had ceased for lack of money and the transepts remained unroofed.

There is no reason to doubt that from this time forward the most active member of the commission was Bishop Grindal himself. We find him begging stone from the landlord of his native St Bees, Sir Thomas Challoner, badgering Cecil, as master of the Court of Wards, to tap the 'benevolence' of that well-endowed institution, making similar approaches to all the courts of justice, and conspiring at Court to secure the lead from the disused church of St Bartholomew.[30] In 1564 it was at his prompting that commissions were issued to the J.P.s of the counties within his diocese to 'use gentle persuasion' with the laity for contributions.[31] As late as 1567 Grindal was preoccupied with the search for scarce supplies of lead to cover the transepts and with the problem of paying for it.[32] According to Hayward it was out of his own pocket, to the tune of £720, that he eventually provided for the two cross-roofs. In fact Grindal was later able to show that the reparation of Paul's had cost him personally more than £1,100, accounting for a little over one year's income, or a tenth of the total receipts of his ten-year incumbency. Consequently he had gone into debt in his later years as bishop of London.[33] A later bishop, John Aylmer, wondered whether all this money really came from Grindal's private purse, and somewhat sourly pointed out that according to some legal opinion bishops were bound by law to spend a quarter of their incomes on repairs: as if any Elizabethan bishop had ever contemplated such a thing! This would have amounted to £2,500, not grossly in excess of the sum of about £2,000 which Grindal could show to have been spent on all aspects of property repair and maintenance during his tenure of the see.[34]

The truth was that the city was far from satisfied with Aylmer's own care for the fabric of St Paul's and in 1581 invited Grindal's intervention in the matter, as archbishop. At that time he reported that 'he did in his time as much or more than either by law or reason he was bound'. When Aylmer died the sum of £4,000 was owing for dilapidations of the church and the bishop's houses.[35] Hayward was a more objective as well as charitable witness when he suggested that almost the chief thing preserving Grindal's virtuous memory was his responsibility for the last work bestowed on St Paul's 'worthy of any account'. That was written in the reign of James I when the corrosive effect of the heavily polluted atmosphere inspired fresh talk of further restoration, but when little was done towards the performance of works then estimated to require more than £22,000. The last major repairs and embellishments of old St Paul's took place in the 1630s, at the hands of Inigo Jones and in the time of Laud, the only bishop after Grindal to apply himself with energy to the problems of the great decaying fabric. Laud's personal contribution was in fact equivalent to Grindal's (not allowing for inflation): twelve hundred pounds.[36] But as anyone knows who has ever looked at Wenceslaus Hollar's panoramic engravings, the steeple never was rebuilt. From the beginning the city had regarded the replacement of the steeple as a separate and perhaps purely secular undertaking, it being of value only as an 'ornament'.[37] The failure of a subsequent public collection for its rebuilding was satirized in the late Elizabethan play *Nobody and Somebody*: 'I'll ... build up Pauls steeple without a collection. I see now what becomes of these collections.' 'Why, Nobody receives them.'[38] After the immensely greater calamity of 1666, 1561 was forgotten, and with it Grindal's achievement as the restorer of St Paul's. No author since Hayward has remembered him particularly in this connection.

The only partially repaired cathedral was the scene of some remarkable assemblies: most notable of all in January 1563, the opening ceremonies of the Convocation which coincided with the second Elizabeth Parliament.[39] It was at this first synod of the reformed Elizabethan Church that the English Confession of Faith was reduced to the permanent and familiar form of the Thirty-Nine Articles of Religion. The synod was also the scene of a momentous struggle between progressives and conservatives over projected reforms in ceremonies and ecclesiastical discipline and, in effect, for the control of the future destiny of the Church. Although the loss of the official records of Convocation in the Great Fire of 1666 has hidden much from our eyes, it appears that this was the last occasion when anyone, the puritans included, supposed that Convocation held the key to that destiny. The failure of the various proposals for reform advanced by the progressive party in the Lower House, in one notorious instance a defeat by a single vote after the counting of proxies, suggests the nearly equal balance of forces among the senior and erudite clergy who represented the early Elizabethan Church on this occasion. Thomas Sampson, the dean of Christ Church Oxford, of whom we shall hear again, put himself in a potentially nonconformist position when, as a member of Convocation, he subscribed the Thirty-Nine Articles 'with a protestation to the words of the article touching ceremonies'.[40]

Grindal, as dean of the province, was prominently involved in both the ceremonial and the political business of Convocation. It was at St Paul's that the preliminary formalities took place, including the election of Grindal's friend and dean Alexander Nowell as prolocutor of the Lower House, unusually on the archbishop's nomination. The proceedings were then prorogued to Westminster where the bishops were otherwise engaged, in the House of Lords. It was there, in Henry VII's chapel in the Abbey, that the debates on matters of reformation proceeded. A recent historian has argued that Grindal's annotating hand on one or two of the surviving documents may indicate nothing more than a necessary administrative concern as a principal officer of the synod.[41] Yet his corrections and additions to the paper known as 'Certain Articles' suggest at least a degree of sympathetic identification with those who desired that certain rites and ceremonies 'may be reduced to edification, as nigh as may be to the godly purity and simplicity used in the primitive church'.[42] It seems equally clear that the efforts of Archbishop Parker were exerted in a somewhat contrary direction, so that 'mediocrity shall be received amongst us': the characteristic stamp of the Anglican *via media* which, in the event, this Convocation served to confirm.

A year later St Paul's witnessed a different spectacle: the funeral solemnities held in honour of the Holy Roman Emperor, Ferdinand. We are bound to take notice of the sermon preached on this state occasion since it happens to be the only sermon of Grindal's to have survived.[43] It would be unfair to judge his powers as a preacher, highly esteemed as they were in his generation, by the performance on this highly artificial occasion. The themes were commonplace: the inevitability of death, which even the greatest of princes could not escape; the exalted lineage, exploits and virtues of the deceased emperor; a protestant justification for the absence of prayers for the repose of his soul. But the sermon nevertheless provides the most complete and developed expression that we have of Grindal's mental properties: fluently erudite in the Fathers and in Church History, well informed about recent European events. As for the embarrassment of the fact that Ferdinand had lived and died a papist, that was handled with tact, charity and optimism. Let his hearers pray that God would in his

appointed time enlighten the hearts of all christian princes to see
the light of the truth and to set forth and maintain sincere religion.
But it was by no means clear that the emperor had been a hardened
or abandoned papist. Certainly he had treated the pope with no
great respect. 'But, as I have said, we will commend that matter
unto God; and whatsoever his religion was, this solemn action for
memorial of him may very well be used notwithstanding.'

Grindal's text on this occasion came from St Matthew: 'Therefore be ye also ready, for the Lord will come at the hour which ye
think not on.' His observations on the ever-present possibility of
death were informed by still vivid experience of the second great
calamity of his episcopate: the visitation of the plague in the
summer and autumn of 1563. The infection is supposed to have
been introduced into the city by soldiers returning from the ill-
fated military expedition to 'Newhaven' (Le Havre), for which
Grindal had enthusiastically prayed in a form of invocation promulgated throughout the diocese:

> Oh Lord have regard to these her subjects which be sent over the
> seas to the aid of such as be persecuted for the profession of thy
> holy name and to withstand the cruelty of those which be com-
> mon enemies as well to the truth of thy eternal word as to their
> own natural prince and countrymen and manifestly to this
> crown and realm of England.[44]

According to John Stow's analysis of the casualties week by
week, based on bills of mortality no longer extant, a total of 17,041
persons died of the plague within the city itself in the twelve
months between June 1563 and June 1564: one in five or six of the
population, which was probably a higher proportion of the total
inhabitants than the 30,578 who were victims of the next major
visitation, in the more populous city of 1603. The outbreak
reached its terrible climax in September, when in consecutive
weeks the deaths recorded were 1,454, 1,626, 1,372 and 1,828.[45]
The city was in a state of siege, under the various plague orders
imposed by the Privy Council and the Court of Common Council
and enforced by a special commission.[46]

An order of July that householders should light bonfires in the
streets on three evenings in the week to 'consume the corrupt airs'
seemed to Stow only to have precipitated the intensification of the
plague. Infected households were required to display, on pain of a
fine, a blue headless cross 'painted in a white paper', apparently
with the words 'Lord Have Mercy Upon Us'. At first in the worst-
affected parishes and then throughout the city the occupants of
infected households were ordered to remain indoors and to send

out on errands one person only who was to be identified with a
white stick. Eventually such families were totally segregated and
were ordered to keep all doors and windows closed for forty days.
In August special orders were made to keep those infected apart
from the crowds from all parts of the country attending the Bartholomew Fair. A proclamation attempted to enforce the segregation
of soldiers returning from Newhaven. Stray dogs were thought to
be capable of transmitting the plague and any dogs allowed to run
free were to be put down. In September all business in the courts
was suspended until the Hilary Term and the Court of Exchequer
transferred to Sion House, in the country. In December the Hilary
Term was transferred to Hertford and persons from infected
households were forbidden to attend, unless commanded to do
so by process.[47]

We have called the plague a 'visitation'. The conventional term
is the last relic of the conviction, still ostensibly universal in 1563,
which interpreted such an event as the judgment and correction of
God for the sins and unthankfulness of his people. The remedy to
avert the divine displeasure was prayer and fasting. In August
Grindal told Cecil that it had always been his opinion that the
papists had the advantage by their apparent devotion to these
disciplines 'which we utterly neglect'.[48] He now took a series of
rapid initiatives, ordering appropriate religious exercises, drawing
up a special form of common prayer and public fast, and engaging
Alexander Nowell to compose a special homily for the occasion,
'concerning the justice of God'. Through the close liaison which,
as always, he maintained with Cecil (eight letters are extant from
July and August 1563) these special forms of service were printed,
together with a letter from the queen to the archbishop as primate
of all England, requiring that 'universal prayer and fasting be more
effectually used in this our realm'; a warrant which Parker had also
requested.[49]

But Grindal's reactions to the crisis were also characteristically
practical. As early as 17 July he expressed surprise that the queen
had not already withdrawn from London, recalling that in Germany the proverbial advice in time of plague was 'fly quickly; fly
far off; return late'. He caused offence in some quarters by discouraging the mass gatherings often held at times of calamity and
ordering instead 'moderate assemblies' in parish churches, 'having
yet a prudent respect in such assemblies to keep the sick from the
whole'. Here he was at one with the city authorities who had
ordered the cleansing of churches and the removal of windows to
let in fresh air. Representatives from every household were to
attend services daily and to remain at least one hour, 'continually

serving God devoutly'.[50] Grindal suggested to Cecil that if the Court were to join in the fast, as it should for example's sake, the weekly provision saved could be distributed 'in the back lanes and alleys of London and amongst the poor strangers; for these are the sorest visited'. But it was something more than practicality which inspired him to complain to Cecil that nothing had done more to spread the contagion than the frequenting of plays by the idle youth, and to propose the suppression of all such plays and 'lewd interludes' for a year: 'and if it were for ever it were not amiss'. Perhaps it was the bishop's complaint which prompted a proclamation by the lord mayor condemning the large numbers of people attending plays, 'pressed together into small rooms', and introducing a form of theatrical licensing.[51] This was in February 1564 when weekly deaths from the plague were dropping to single figures and when a printed form of thanksgiving to God 'for ceasing the plague' had already been promulgated and celebrated at Paul's Cross with a sermon preached by Grindal.[52] The exchanges between Grindal and Parker about the religious exercises inspired by the plague illustrate the differences in their churchmanship. Parker had proposed a great communion service in St Paul's in thanksgiving. Grindal feared that this would become a mere public spectacle, all too reminiscent of a high mass. Parker for his part had earlier commented critically on Grindal's service of prayer and fasting as over-didactic and too remote from the forms of the Prayer Book.[53]

Cecil himself was ill in the grim autumn months of 1563, not with the plague but with that old enemy 'the stone' which he shared with the bishop. Grindal offered sympathetic advice on the treatment of this painful condition and towards the end of these taxing and terrible years urged the secretary, as he himself might have been exhorted, not to hurt his health 'with too much cogitation of evil successes of things which are in God's hands and without our compass'.[54] Grindal was not to know that there was worse to come: worse in the sense that the ecclesiastical crisis of 1565–7 was to undermine the authority which his outstanding leadership in 1561 and 1563 could only have enhanced.

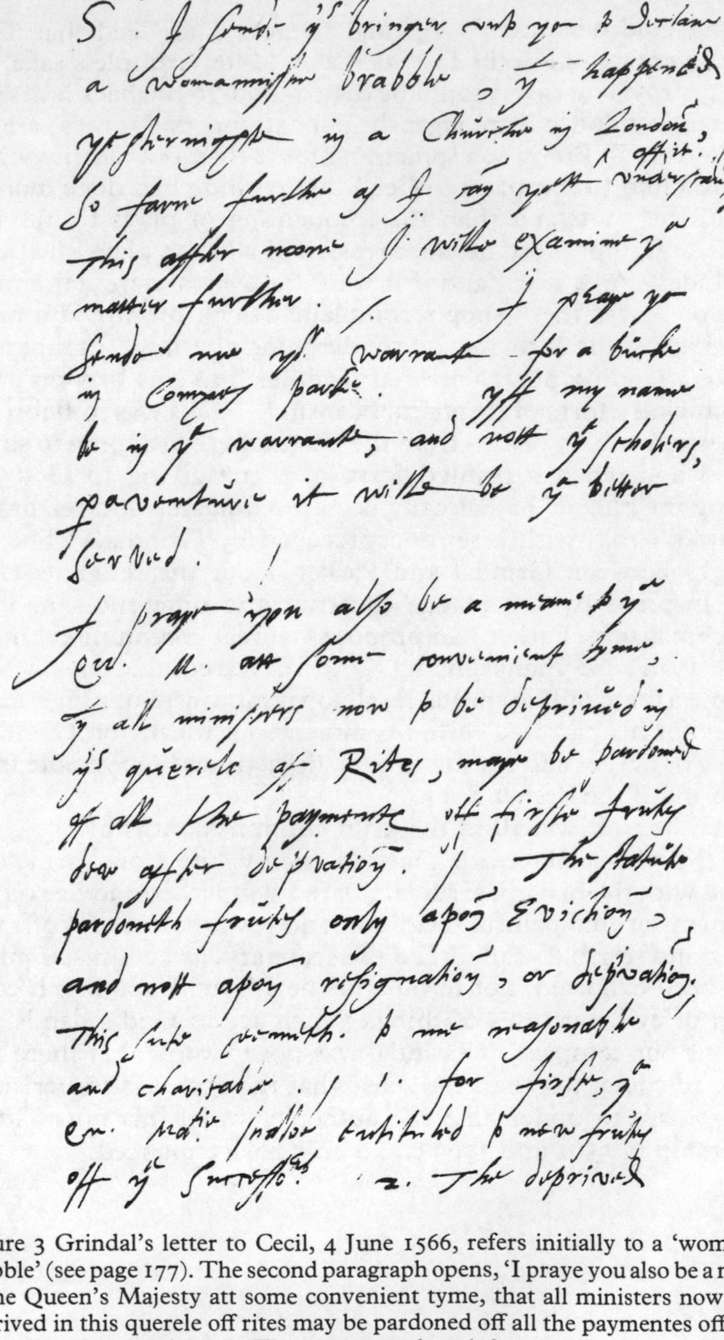
Sir. I sende this bringer unto you to declare a womanishe brabble that happened yesternighte in a Churche in London. So farre further as I can yett understand this after noone I wille examine the matter further. I praye you sende me your warrante for a bucke in Comptons parke. Yff my name be in the warrante, and nott the scholers, paraventure it wille be the better served.

I praye you also be a meane to the Q. M. att some convenient tyme, that all ministers now to be deprived in this querele off Rites, maye be pardoned off all the paymentes off firste frutes dew after deprivation. The statute pardoneth frutes only apon Eviction and nott apon resignation or deprivation. This sute seemeth to me reasonable and charitable. for firste the Qu. Matie shalbe entitled to newe frutes off the successor. 2. The deprived

Figure 3 Grindal's letter to Cecil, 4 June 1566, refers initially to a 'womanish brabble' (see page 177). The second paragraph opens, 'I praye you also be a meane to the Queen's Majesty att some convenient tyme, that all ministers now to be deprived in this querele off rites may be pardoned off all the paymentes off firste frutes dew after deprivation. The statute pardoneth frutes only apon eviction and nott apon resignation or deprivation. This sute seemeth to me reasonable and charitable.' Public Record Office, S.P. 12/40/1.

9

PURITANISM

THE early Elizabethan Church was an enforced coalition of contrary religious traditions and tendencies, crudely distinguishable as very protestant, not-so-protestant and crypto-papist. The terms and symbols of the coalition were contained in the Act of Uniformity and the Royal Injunctions of 1559, as interpreted by the bishops in a number of informal resolutions.[1] Among these symbols the outward appearance of the clergy acquired, as uniforms are apt to do, a special and emotive significance. The bishops agreed on the minimal requirement of the white linen surplice for all liturgical occasions and a long clerical gown and square cap (still familiar in a derivative form as the academic 'mortar board') for outdoor dress. This costume was supposed to be religiously nearly neutral, not invested with the teaching function of the catholic eucharistic vestments: in the words of the thirtieth Article, 'not thereby meaning to attribute any holiness or special meaning to the said garments'. The clergy were merely required to wear 'distinct habits', by 'temporal orders mere ecclesiastical, without any vain superstition, and as rules in some part of discipline, concerning decency, distinction, and order for the time'.[2] The ultra-protestant nevertheless objected either to the 'habits' as intrinsically antichristian, or to the 'tyranny' of 'worldly policy' by which things indifferent in themselves were imposed without respect for conscience, so effectively losing their indifference.

In January 1565 a royal letter reached Archbishop Parker complaining of episcopal connivance at 'open and manifest disorder' by 'diversity of opinions, and specially in the external, decent, and lawful rites and ceremonies to be used in the churches'.[3] For some time Parker had been attempting coercion with two of the most senior nonconformists, the Oxford heads Thomas Sampson, dean of Christ Church, and Laurence Humphrey, president of Magdalen. The queen's letter brought matters to a crisis, as Parker intended it should. With Grindal and four other episcopal members of the Ecclesiastical Commission he now drafted a collection of articles which codified many details of ceremonial, including vestiarian practice. In accordance with earlier resolutions, less was required of the parochial clergy than the strict terms of statutes and injunctions. Except in cathedral and collegiate churches the surplice was to be worn for all ministrations.[4] Consequently the struggle which followed concerned the surplice and square cap, not the vestments, properly so-called. Since these orders never received royal endorsement they are known to history by the somewhat diffident title of 'Advertisements'.

A year later, thirty-four London clergymen refusing to be bound to this standard were suspended from their ministry. Eventually a few of them, following the example already set by Sampson, were content to suffer a kind of martyrdom by ejection from their livings. The ensuing weeks and months witnessed serious ecclesiastical disturbances in the city: protests and riotous assemblies at churches temporarily bereft of their ministry or suffering the intrusion of unwelcome conformists; the first major pamphlet war between nonconformists and conformist protestants of the Church of England; and, finally, the withdrawal of some few hundred Londoners into conventicles, the beginnings of the separatist movement. 'And so', commented one of the nonconformists, 'the gracious knot of christian charity is broken.'[5]

John Stow recorded of the following year, 1567, that it was 'about that time' that there appeared in London congregations of 'anabaptists' who 'called themselves puritans'.[6] His account is confused. But ecclesiastical historians have never doubted that the name 'puritan' first came into use in connection with these events; or that it was in the mid-1560s that tension between nonconformity and conformity, puritanism and antipuritanism and, eventually, the schism between the Church of England and Dissent had its immediate origins, more especially in London.

This story has been told many times.[7] The intention here is not to tell it all over again but to investigate the nature and extent of Grindal's responsibility for the beginnings of this historic bifurcation in English protestantism. In the midst of the crisis of 1566 Archbishop Parker made a bitter comment, one of several:

> And now my lord of London by experience feeleth and seeth the marks and bounds of these good sprights which, but for his tolerations etc., had been suppressed for five or six years ago, and had prevented all this unquietness now taken, and both his reputation better saved and my poor honesty not so foully traduced.[8]

In Sir Sidney Lee's unfortunate phrase, Grindal 'feebly temporized with dissent'.[9] But did he? Grindal has been made to bear a threefold responsibility for what Dr Sacheverell in the reign of Queen Anne called 'the first plantation of dissenters'. It was his patronage which advanced the first nonconformists. More than that, he participated in their puritanism by his own negative disposition towards the distinctive features of the Anglican settlement. Finally he made little attempt to carry out his simple episcopal duty of enforcing conformity: or rather what he did was too little and too late. The first charge has already been substantiated in an earlier chapter.[10] The second contains an element of truth, although Grindal's attitude to the ceremonies in dispute and to the principle of what might be called Anglican loyalty requires careful definition. On the third count he has been misunderstood. His handling of the crisis was not lacking in pastoral responsibility or a sense of the political art of the possible. And he seems to have been motivated as much by respect for the integrity of the church as by zeal for the Gospel.

The London puritans were Grindal's doves, to adopt an image applied to a more recent maker of London clergy,[11] or, in brutal modern parlance, his mafia. At the second of his ordinations, in January 1560, he admitted to the diaconate one John Gough, at thirty-eight a seasoned London protestant with a background in the book trade, like the printer Robert Crowley, whom he collated to the wealthy vicarage of St Giles Cripplegate. These were the radical journalists of 1566. Ten days later he ordained Percival Wiburn, soon to be the agent for the disaffected puritan party in missions to Switzerland, and, on the same occasion, John Philpot, another of the hard and radical core. In the following year he ordained Richard Fittes, a Devon man who may well have been the 'Mr Fitz' known to the historians of nonconformity as the minister of one of the earliest organized separatist congregations. In 1562 Grindal again demonstrated his liking for mature ordinands when he admitted to the priesthood one Nicholas Crane, forty years of age, and to the diaconate Giles Seyntcler, aged forty-three. Two years later Nicholas Standon was ordained. These three were the leading names in the schisms and rumours of schism which were secondary to the troubles of 1566. And on 28 March 1566, when the storm had already broken, Grindal made a minister of the young John Field, soon to emerge as (so to speak) the Lenin of Elizabethan puritanism.[12]

Among the suspended nonconformists none commanded more respect than the aged Miles Coverdale, the translator of the first English printed Bible and a former bishop of Exeter, described by Grindal as one 'qui ante nos omnes fuit in Christo'. Between Grindal and Coverdale there was a special bond, which on

Grindal's side would have been filial. When the degree of Doctor of Divinity was conferred on Grindal by his old university (the conditions having been fulfilled by two sermons, one preached *ad clerum*, the other at Paul's Cross) the vice-chancellor was unable to confer the honour in person and tactfully nominated in his place the 'venerable father' Coverdale. It was in his own palace beside St Paul's that Coverdale admitted the bishop to his doctorate, on 15 April 1564, the little ceremony symbolizing the inheritance of the mantle of the first reformers. Not long before this Grindal had persuaded the nearly destitute Coverdale to accept the well-endowed parish of St Magnus the Martyr, at the foot of London Bridge. Coverdale did not expect to enjoy it for long, 'I going upon my grave'. Yet before his death in 1568, at the advanced age of eighty-one, he was to resume the way of life of a fugitive preacher, ministering in semi-clandestine circumstances; as an obscure separatist at that time described him: 'Father Coverdale, of whom we have a good opinion, and yet (God knoweth) the man was so fearful that he durst not be known unto us where he preached, though we sought it at his house.'[13]

The men of 1566 were the most sought-after of preachers in early Elizabethan London: frequently performing at Paul's Cross, at funeral sermons, and at the annual feats of liveried companies.[14] In mid-October 1562, for example, Londoners could have heard in the same week Robert Crowley at the Cross and John Gough preaching for the Master Painters. The following summer Gough preached for the Goldsmiths.[15] The oratory of this ultra-protestant élite was partisan, sometimes to the point of crudity. The conservative John Stow ironically observed 'a note of divinity' when Thomas Cole, an archdeacon, compared popish priests to apes, 'for, saith he, they be both bald alike, but that the priests be bald before, the apes behind.' Three weeks later Crowley used the same pulpit of Paul's Cross to 'inveigh against popish ceremonies'. Even the future Archbishop Whitgift tuned his Paul's Cross sermon of June 1565 to the London atmosphere of crude anti-popery.[16] Crowley later claimed that the matters in dispute had been regularly ventilated in London's pulpits for seven years 'without any great contradiction'.[17] We can well believe it. Either Grindal or others using his authority appointed Sampson and Humphrey to preach at the Cross at Easter 1565, just when Parker, having failed to bring them to heel, was moving towards their deprivation.[18]

Grindal made no secret of his personal distaste for the prescribed clerical attire and other ceremonies which implied to the uninstructed eye the continuity of the English Church with its past traditions rather than solidarity with the international reformed community. English congregations overseas, coming under his jurisdiction as bishop of London, were advised to conform in such respects to local custom. 'For ministry of baptism', he wrote to William Cole, preacher to the Merchant Adventurers in Antwerp, 'if the churches there use a baptistry, do you so, or if they use a basin, do likewise. Follow your Book except crossing. For the Lord's Supper, use the prayers of our Book. For rites, follow the manner of their churches. Place the table as theirs is. If they receive the sacrament standing, kneeling or sitting, do you the same. Neither need you use any surplice, whether they use it or no, for they know that the high Almayne churches use none.' Cole was to use only the Book of Common Prayer but he was to abbreviate the liturgy to make time for his sermon. 'Ye may take as much and as little thereof as to your discretion by the advice of your seniors shall be thought good.' The preachers attached to the English expeditionary force at Le Havre reported that Grindal had 'warned and charged' them not to employ any other order for ceremonies than they found among the reformed churches of France.[19] This was to agree with the doctrine attributed to St Augustine and preached in St Paul's in 1560 by William Alley, soon to be bishop of Exeter: 'There is no discipline better to a wise, grave and christian man (concerning these ceremonies) than to do after that manner as he shall see that church to do to which he shall happen to come.'[20] Ceremonies were things indifferent in which practice could legitimately vary, an area for christian liberty.

If to enjoy liberty had been to exercise a personal preference there is no doubt that Grindal would have held no brief for the disputed vestments. He was at one with the opinion expressed by Sandys as late as 1588 that some ceremonies 'by political constitutions authorized amongst us' were 'not so expedient in this church now' that 'they may better be disused by little and little than more and more urged'.[21] 'You see me wear a cope or a surplice in Paul's,' he told some radical puritans in 1567. 'I had rather minister without these things, but for order's sake and obedience to the prince.' The qualifying words indicate Grindal's acceptance of the need to be conformable in things of themselves indifferent, 'which lie in the prince's power to command for order's sake'.[22] This was the condition of his preparedness to serve as a bishop, in which he had the consistent support of the Zürich theologians: 'Things not forbidden of God may be used for order and obedience sake.' Although by no means an exclusively English doctrine this was to be the hallmark of an incipient Anglicanism,[23] in conflict with the puritan insistence that in matters of indifference the christian conscience was at liberty only to conform itself to what one Cambridge theologian called 'the constant sense of the general tenor of Scripture'.[24]

But there was another consideration, which for the sensitive conscience might take precedence over all others. In discussing with the Corinthians whether it was lawful to eat meat which had been offered to idols in sacrifice, St Paul had declared that while many things were lawful not all were expedient. To eat meat, any meat, was legitimate for the untroubled conscience. But if to eat would cause the conscience of a weaker christian brother to stumble then it was better not to eat. 'All things are lawful for me but all things are not expedient.' According to this pragmatic doctrine, which was the basis of the nonconformist position defended by Sampson and Humphrey, a minister who was himself relatively untroubled by what Bishop Jewel called 'ridiculous trifles' might feel bound to respect the consciences of his literal-minded flock, the 'weaker brethren' for whom these were matters of genuine offence. As John Knox observed to Sampson: 'It is evil to you to offend against your weak brethren to build again by your example that which your own tongues have destroyed by true doctrine.' And in his turn his superior, the pastorally responsible bishop, might wish to defer to the conscience of the minister. But there was a point where conscience became what Parker called 'timorous spiced conscience', or, more technically, scruple. There was little to be said in defence of the scruples of a minister who put his private integrity in a matter of indifference before the ultimate evangelical and pastoral objective of his ministry.[25]

These calculations influenced Grindal's attitude to the vestiarian question for as long as he enjoyed any freedom to manoeuvre, and to the limited extent that a policy of his own was compatible with the public function. Early in his episcopate he allowed one of his more unconventional ordinands, Thomas Upcher,[26] to minister without the surplice to a congregation near Colchester which, for understandable reasons, was deeply prejudiced against the 'popish attire'. Upcher was told to tolerate this situation 'for a time, till it be complained of, but yet in the mean time privately to exhort the godly so to frame their judgments that they conceive no offence if it be altered hereafter by authority'. But when other neighbouring clergy interpreted this as a general licence to abandon the surplice Grindal was angry:

I perceive they intend to make my diocese a place of liberty for every man to break the common orders at his own pleasure. But it may not be so, for as I wish reformation of orders, so the orders standing I will not bear the burden of licence in breaking them by private authority.

He told Upcher's archdeacon that if there were men of 'such straightness' that they would rather hide their talents than observe public order in a matter of indifference then 'habent suum judicem'. They had but themselves to blame for the consequences.[27]

Conform or face dismissal: Grindal was in no more doubt than his old mentor Martin Bucer that when the issue was stated as plainly as that the conscientious pastor should conform and remain pastorally available. But within the Tudor polity such stark choices were rare: evasion was often possible and perhaps legitimate. To enforce conformity on ultra-protestant London by an administrative act, in a spirit of 'thorough', might prove pastorally disastrous and alienating. Even Parker, whose motto was 'execution, execution, execution of laws and orders' admitted the need for 'moderations for times, places, multitudes, etc.' The Advertisements themselves represented a moderation of what the law in principle could exact. And even in March 1566 Parker doubted the wisdom of proceeding as far as deprivation of nonconformists.[28] So when required by the Privy Council in March 1563 to take action against certain persons who were said to have persuaded the people to break the orders set forth, Grindal took refuge in the generality of the order and did little.[29] Two years later not only Humphrey and Sampson and Crowley, Philpot and Gough, but also the dean of St Paul's, two of Grindal's archdeacons and Coverdale and Foxe were among a group of prominent clergy who protested against the implications of an uncompromising demand for conformity.[30] At this time John Knox was writing from Edinburgh in support of Sampson's 'refusal, which the curates of the Court call obstinacy'.[31] Meanwhile there was the paradox, with which Parker had to live for a year yet to come, and to some extent for the rest of his life, that 'the curates of the Court' lacked the active support of the Court in the implementation of a policy which the Court had supposedly initiated.

It has never been very clear who was making the running in the campaign for uniformity which was intensified in 1565. The queen certainly, but her intervention in the matter seems to have taken the form of occasional outbursts rather than sustained interest, while she was content that her ecclesiastics should taste the bitter fruits of ecclesiastical independence in carrying this burden, if in nothing else. As for the Council, several of its members were known to be sympathetic to the nonconformists. Parker implied that it was either Cecil personally or the Council collectively which had set the matter in train. But there is evidence that the royal letter of 25 January 1565 was requested and even its terms proposed by the archbishop himself, to strengthen his hand in a course of action which the queen had demanded only verbally. But no other support was forthcoming, no explicit governmental backing for the Advertisements. Parker warned Cecil that without this 'all that is done is but to be laughed at ... Better not to have begun, except more be done.'[32]

All this may help to explain why Grindal sat on the fence, or sought his own compromising formula, for so long. In March 1565 Parker thought that he was 'in a good mood to execute the laws' if directly so charged by the queen, in a private letter. But as Grindal subsequently reported, 'not six words' were spoken by the queen to that effect. Soon it was being said, to Parker's vexation, that 'my lord of London is their own ... and is but brought in against his will.'[33] At Grindal's second ordinary visitation of his diocese, held in May 1565, an example was made of a few of the more heterodox nonconformists but the ringleaders were left undisturbed.[34]

The immediate background to the crisis of Easter 1566 is full of obscurity. On 13 January (unless this letter should be placed in 1567)[35] Grindal wrote perhaps disingenuously to Parker:

Whereas your grace putteth me in remembrance for the state of my cure, I heartily thank your grace. In very deed my purpose was after this week ended ... to have prayed your grace's advice and aid for the same. For I must confess that I can hardly reduce things to conformity if I deal in it alone.

He proposed a meeting with the bishops of Winchester and Ely on 19 January to determine tactics, presumably to be followed by interviews with the offenders. 'I wish your chancellor present to direct us in matters of law.'[36] Some historians have placed in early February a gathering of London clergy before the bishop and archdeacon in the church of St Sepulchre. On this occasion all but a handful of Marian conservatives were persuaded to accept a felicitous compromise. They were to wear a distinctive but novel form of outdoor dress, with a round instead of a square cap, and in church, the surplice. Unfortunately the sole source of this information, a notebook compiled years after the event by a London clergyman, is far from reliable and obviously confused in its chronology. It is hard to reconcile this event with what Grindal wrote to Parker so shortly before it and it is possible that the Grindalian compromise was effected in 1565, or even 1564 where Strype and, following him, Dixon were inclined to place it.[37]

In early March Parker was still despondent, still urging the need for royal endorsement of the Advertisements, still (apparently) complaining of Grindal: 'I see how other men get their heads out of the collar and convey the envy otherwhere ... I have written and written oft that a few in London rule over this matter.'[38] Yet within eight days Parker and Grindal were agreed on a kind of final solution for the running sore of London nonconformity. In a joint letter to Cecil they announced their intention to summon the entire clergy of the city to Lambeth, to exhort them to conformity, 'presently to suspend' all who refused it, thereafter proceeding through sequestration of the fruits of their benefices to deprivation within three months of those remaining recalcitrant. They hoped that the queen would send some privy councillors in support, 'to authorize the rather her commandment and pleasure, as your honour signified unto me was purposed'. It may or may not be significant that this was primarily Parker's letter which the archbishop subscribed first, whereas a joint letter of the same month proposing the renewal of the licence to print the Geneva Bible was signed first by Grindal. Be that as it may, both prelates wrote separately to Cecil on the day before the fateful occasion, each in his own hand, each expressing the hope that Cecil himself and the lord keeper, Bacon, as well as other councillors, would be present to lend their authority to proceedings.[39] All to no avail. The comment of a privy councillor on a later occasion when the Council at least consented to interview a number of puritan ministers may shed some light on the non-cooperation of the laity: 'We see what they answer; we may not deal with them as in popish time.'[40] Within hours of the Lambeth meeting Parker was once more begging Cecil to put pressure on Grindal to execute order, agreeing with Cox of Ely that 'if London were reformed, all the realm would soon follow'. Within three weeks he gave vent to the most pointed of all his complaints against his apparently complacent brother. In a week of widespread disturbances Grindal had been inactive, engaged on the preparation of a sermon. Parker was doing the bishop of London's job for him. 'And must I do still all things alone?'[41] It was a full eight weeks after the Lambeth meeting that Grindal wrote to his dean and chapter ordering the same treatment for the clergy within their peculiar jurisdiction.[42]

Nevertheless, the action taken at Lambeth was extraordinary in its decisiveness, and in its timing. Easter Day was not far off and thirty-seven ministers had been suspended. Parker and Grindal foresaw the drastic consequences of their draconian initiative. 'What tumult may follow, what speeches and talks be like to rise in the realm, and presently in the whole city by this we leave it to your wisdom to consider.'[43] It was as if they were determined to rub the noses of the government in the consequences of what were supposed to be the queen's proceedings. (When Parker warned Elizabeth that 'these precise folk' would go to prison rather than submit she told him to imprison them.)[44] If so it was a futile gesture. The Ecclesiastical Commission was left to handle the consequences of 26 March unaided, and in virtually continuous session.

Much of the anticipated 'tumult' duly eventuated.[45] The suspended ministers may have represented a small proportion of the entire London clergy. But they were the élite of those preachers who were acceptable to 'the godly'. Their pulpits and congregations were placed under an almost total interdict. As anyone with experience of a modern 'confrontation', whether in industrial or academic life, would expect, the consequence of the punitive action taken was a radicalization of the situation. The suspended ministers, led by Crowley, took up their polemical pens, as a party: 'we consider', 'we have thought it our duty'. The defenders of ecclesiastical authority hit back at 'this small rout named London ministers'. The London ministers became cult figures. It was discovered that they had stuck by their posts in the plague years as good shepherds when the conformists fled to the country like hirelings. The old arguments about things indifferent were sharpened and some wounding and damaging insults were exchanged.[46] One anonymous reader of the puritan case revealed the strength and intolerance of underground opinion with his marginal notes: 'They rather serve their bellies, that are papists in outward show, to please men and maintain their kitchens... Gnats and parasites are content to admit any thing for princes' pleasures ... These lukewarm gentlemen.'[47] Soon the printed page itself would complain of 'the English mock-gospellers'.[48] Both sides hoped for vindication by the leaders of the reformed churches overseas, especially in Zürich. When Bullinger, the senior Zürich pastor, refused to approve the stand taken by the nonconformists and virtually accused them of concealing a contentious spirit under the name of conscience Grindal published in English and Latin the copy of his letter which had been sent for the sake of propriety to the English bishops.[49] This was more than decisive: it was opportunistic and later Grindal would be hoist with this particular petard himself.[50]

As commonly happens in a political free-for-all the original leadership was overtaken on the left by more obscure and less responsible agitators. And the so-called 'weaker brethren', the laity, whose tender consciences were supposedly the cause of all the fuss, took the law into their own hands. Now the victim of public denunciation and insult, Grindal ceased to 'feebly temporise', if that is what he had been doing, and emerged as a tough and resourceful opponent of the militants: but one who never abandoned his pastoral concern.

What Grindal was perhaps unprepared for was open defiance of his authority by some who ignored their suspensions and continued to preach, and to preach against their treatment. After one of these militants, John Bartlett, lecturer in Crowley's parish of St Giles Cripplegate, had been committed to house arrest, sixty women invaded the bishop's palace. Grindal refused to deal with them and suggested that they send half a dozen of their husbands, 'and with them I would talk etc.' Only the intervention of another suspended minister persuaded the women to leave, quietly but tearfully.[51] A month later Grindal had another 'womanish brabble' to report. And when in the following January he appeared in the church of St Margaret Fish Street wearing his square cap he was irreverently hooted at with cries of 'ware horns' — 'especially the women'. A preacher called Pattenson not only preached in spite of his suspension but publicly denounced the bishop as an antichrist, a traitor to God and the prince, and a heretic. On examination before the Ecclesiastical Commissioners Pattenson defended his words and refused to be bound by 'a popish licence'. When Grindal warned him that he could put him down for seven years Pattenson retorted: 'You know not whether you shall live seven days or not.' On the way back to custody he refused a cup of wine from the bishop's men because he thought Grindal to be 'a man accused before God'.[52]

There was no reasoning with such people. Yet Grindal continued to try, especially as it became clear that the sequel to the drive against nonconformity was to be a serious movement of schismatical separatism.[53] With the removal from London of the original leaders to enforced hospitality in other dioceses and the subsequent conformity of most of them the sectarian instincts of popular protestantism reasserted themselves. The roots were not far from the surface, but the taproot also ran deep. It was less than ten years since these same Londoners had gathered secretly in upper rooms and inns and even ships on the river to hold clandestine meetings and to manage the affairs of a well-organized underground church in separation from the Marian Church.[54] One of their number, John Harrydance, a Whitechapel bricklayer, had preached and taught in his own house and garden since the 1530s. Although illiterate, people said that 'he declared scripture as well as if he had studied at the universities'.[55] Now, as the godly went from church to church, looking for their favoured preachers and persuading them to disregard the bishop's ban, some of the conditions of those heroic years were replicated. It was said that the 'persecution grew so fast as that it brought many a hundred to know one another that never knew before'.[56] As one of their spokesmen told Grindal:

> But when it came to this point, that all our preachers were displaced by your law, that would not subscribe to your apparel and your law, so that we could not hear none of them in any church by the space of seven or eight weeks ... and then were we troubled and commanded to your courts from day to day for not coming to our parish churches: then we bethought us what were best to do; and we remembered that there was a congregation of us in this city in Queen Mary's days, and a congregation at Geneva ...[57]

The use of 'we' and 'us' and 'your' in this passage is surely very significant.

Recent scholarship[58] has established that the core of this new separation and a bridge between the parish system and the separatist conventicles was located in the church of Holy Trinity in the liberty of the Minories, not far from the Tower. Although a parish church, its congregation was not parochial but drawn from many parts of the city and suburbs, attracted by the ministrations of the more radical preachers, including Crowley and Gough. It enjoyed the patronage and protection of a radical of the highest rank: the formidable duchess of Suffolk, herself a former exile, and the owner of much property in the district. The irrepressible Pattenson was one of her protégés and another was Coverdale, who preached some of his last sermons in the Minories. This was also a forcing-ground for the extremists who were now coming to the fore: Nicholas Crane and William Bonham and, presently, John Field and Thomas Wilcox. When one of these preachers, Seth Jackson, died in prison in 1570 he specified that his body should be buried 'where the congregation shall think good'. The parishioners thought nothing of diverting funds from the poor box to sustain 'the preachers in prison'. John Stow seems to be a reliable witness when he tells us in an otherwise confused account that these first puritans 'kept their church in the Minories without Aldgate', and that it was 'afterwards' that they took to assembling in various private houses and on one occasion in a ship in St Katherine's Pool.

Grindal's first official encounter with separatism was on 20 June 1567, the day after a congregation of about a hundred had been surprised in Plumbers Hall, which had been hired for a wedding. Some of those taken were imprisoned in the Counter and eight of the ringleaders were examined before the Commissioners. They included an articulate baker called William White, a bitter critic of the bishop,[59] and a certain John Smith, whom Grindal insisted on making their spokesman: 'How say you, Smith? You seem to be the ancientest of them; answer you.' It is significant, as well as helpful to the historian, that those examined wrote up a kind of transcript of their interrogation, as the Marian martyrs had done before them. Even from this partisan record, Grindal's fundamentally pastoral rather than punitive concern is evident. Instead of proceeding peremptorily Grindal permitted a lengthy ventilation of the issues, often allowing the puritans to determine the course of the discussion. He was sometimes defensive, expressing regret for having said mass in his youth and explaining that he had no desire to wear a cope and surplice. He declined to condemn the Geneva liturgy when White thrust it under his nose. Other remarks suggest that he still favoured the kind of compromise which had prevailed before March 1566. If the puritans found their own parish clergy objectionable as crypto-papists they could go to other churches. Sampson and others had been allowed a hearing in the pulpit throughout their troubles. Bullinger and the learned of Geneva were against them. 'Therefore we desire and wish you to leave off and to be conformable.'[60]

But Grindal was taken aback by the truculence of White and his friends. 'I have talked with many men and yet I never saw any behave themselves so unreverently before magistrates.' And his deep abhorrence of the schism which the separatists had perpetrated emerges very clearly:

> In this severing yourselves from the society of other christians you condemn not only us but also the whole state of the Church reformed in King Edward's days ... There be good men and good martyrs that did wear these things in King Edward's days. Do you condemn them?

In the three years that he remained in London, as the new sectarianism threatened to become both endemic and institutionalized, Grindal proved himself among his fellow commissioners a relentless opponent of separatist puritanism, co-operating fully with the Council in a policy of repeated imprisonment. The interview of 20 June 1567 ended with the return of the leaders to prison, 'or the most part of them'. Nine months later six of the eight were among seventy-seven people arrested at a meeting in the house of a goldsmith near the Savoy. Some of these, including the preachers Bonham and Crane, were still in custody a year later.[61] At that time, in the spring of 1569, Grindal seems to have decided that since 'compulsion of imprisonment' had done little to convert the separatists a total reversal of policy was worth a trial. The Privy Council accepted his advice that those in prison should be released on the simple condition that they behave themselves in the future. And Bonham and Crane were not only released but licensed to resume their preaching after promising to conduct themselves within the law. But by the end of the year both preachers had broken their undertakings. Bonham had returned to prison and Crane was again inhibited from preaching. Some of the rank and file were back in custody and were being dealt with. 'Wherein my lord of Canterbury and I have had divers conferences.' The result was a petition to the Council from the separatists which seems to have grossly misrepresented the terms of their release. It was alleged that Grindal had advised them that they were free from attendance at their parish churches and might hear such preachers as they 'liked best'; and that he would tolerate the baptism of their children according to the Geneva Book and would 'appoint two or three to do it'.

This was the last straw. Grindal's advice to the Council was that 'all the heads of this unhappy faction should be with all expedition severely punished, to the example of others, as people fanatical and incurable; which punishment, if it proceed by order from your lordships, shall breed the greater terror.' Six of 'the most desperate' should be sent to the common jail at Cambridge, six to Oxford, and the rest to other country prisons. Nevertheless a few hardcore separatists seem to have remained more or less permanently in London prisons and some died there. Nicholas Crane, back in prison after many years at liberty, was buried from Newgate in 1588, in the context of the revived and more articulate separatist movement of later Elizabethan London.[62]

It is significant that Grindal was at some pains to emphasize the great difference between the separatists and such ministers as Humphrey and Sampson, who were now denounced as semi-papists and whose preaching was rejected. In writing to Zürich in 1568 he betrayed his continuing sympathy for the nonconformist pioneers with the comment that they had 'suffered so much to obtain liberty in respect of things indifferent'.[63] With some shrewdness he despatched a party of London separatists to Scotland which proved, as Grindal remarked with irony, 'not pure enough for our men'; and where they found that John Knox, who had approved of the stand taken by Sampson and his friends, agreed with the English ministers in condemning their schism.[64]

With some justification William White could complain not long before Grindal's departure from London of his policy of 'displacing, banishing, persecuting and imprisoning'.[65] As a result the phenomenon of separation was in recession by 1570, while most of the beneficed London clergy had either been induced to toe the line or had been displaced by conformists, a permanent change in the churchmanship of the capital.[66]

But the developing puritan controversy was now to take a new turn: a threat to the integrity of the Church of England more menacing than grassroots separatism in that it had scholarly support, in the universities and overseas, and involved not withdrawal from the Church but the ambition to alter radically its constitution and structure. This was the 'presbyterian' onslaught on the unreformed, hierarchical discipline of the Church in which the bishops were prime targets, in virtue of the inherently antichristian office which they were said to hold.[67] This had the effect of aligning Grindal less ambiguously with the established order, as well as creating some friction with Geneva where previously there had been none. In a letter to Grindal of June 1566 the senior Geneva pastor, influenced by the account of English affairs given by a puritan emissary, was as sharply critical as tact would allow of the role of the bishops and of much English ecclesiastical practice.

> If so be that the Apostle did rightly chide the Galatians ... how much more may it be lawful to say the same of you Englishmen, if peradventure after you have begun in the spirit you fall back again (as God forbid) ... to the trifles and trash of men's traditions.[68]

More frankly Beza had written to Zürich: 'If the case is as I hear it to be (and indeed these things can scarcely be invented) where did such a Babylon ever exist?'[69] Beza's subsequent attempts to maintain a constructive relationship with Grindal[70] were undermined when in 1572 Field and Wilcox printed the entire text of his original letter as an appendix to their tract to *An admonition to the Parliament*.[71] Beza was distressed[72] and Grindal cannot have been amused. Currency would later be given in England to Beza's published opinion that the episcopal office was an invention of 'the alone wisdom of man, besides the express word of God'. 'There is not to be found in the New Testament so much as one syllable whereby there may be least surmise of such a thing.'[73]

Not surprisingly Grindal held no brief for those who propagated these novel and subversive doctrines. At the time of Thomas Cartwright's sensational Cambridge lectures where they had their first academic airing in England his comment was: 'He hath a busy

head, stuffed full of singularities.' It was Grindal who first alerted
Cecil, as chancellor of the university, to the danger posed by
Cartwright and urged draconian measures: the silencing of Cartwright and his adherents, their expulsion from their colleges and
even from the university if necessary, and the refusal of
Cartwright's doctoral degree. 'The vice-chancellor and heads of
houses proceed not so roundly in this case as were requisite, in my
judgment.' So on the matter of Cartwright Grindal was entirely in
agreement with John Whitgift who became master of Trinity ten
days after this letter was written and later in the year, as vice-
chancellor, implemented some of the punitive measures which
Grindal had advocated. Three years later he wrote: 'They are
content to take the livings of the English Church and yet affirm it to
be no church.'[74] Once again Grindal's fundamental loyalty to the
Church is apparent.

In striking contrast Grindal retained benevolent intentions towards the original nonconformists, some of whom were as critical
of the new presbyterian teaching as he was.[75] Indeed he seems to
have been in sympathy with the more moderate puritans in all
matters save one, admittedly fundamental: the question of obedience to the prince in things indifferent. In 1574, as archbishop of
York, he was in correspondence with the original Elizabethan
nonconformist and one of his oldest friends, Thomas Sampson.
Only Sampson's letter survives, but from this it appears that
Grindal's letter was eirenical, speaking of his affection for 'some
godly brethren which do wish that such things as are amiss were
reformed' and for Sampson particularly; and expressing the disposition of his heart as 'not lordly, nor liketh lordly state'. Sampson
scorned the proffered olive branch with what sounds like inverted
pride: 'Ye do pity my poverty and lameness. To my remembrance
I complained neither of the one nor of the other to you.' Grindal
might disown his lordly state but he was a great lord none the less
and must learn to live with the consequences.

> And I say further of you, that to be in the fire and not to burn, to
> touch pitch and not to be defiled therewith, to walk among
> thorns and not to be pricked with them, argueth a special and a
> divine preservation ... And if you, whom policy hath made a
> great lord, be not lordly, but do keep the humble and straight
> course of a loving brother and minister of Christ's gospel, shall I
> say that you are a phoenix?[76]

Phoenix or not, it says much for Grindal's charity that he remained
accessible to a man whom the Zürich theologians had long before
found to be impossible, 'restless ... captious and unquiet'. It was

Bullinger and not Grindal who said of Sampson, as so many have since said of puritans in general: 'I have certainly a natural dislike to men of this stamp.'[77]

PART THREE

YORK

10

APOSTLE OF THE NORTH

IN June 1569, at a time when the filling of vacant bishoprics was
in the wind, Archbishop Parker advised Cecil that John Aylmer,
then archdeacon of Lincoln, would make 'a good, fast, earnest
servitor at London', whereas Grindal was 'as fit for York' and for
the 'heady and stout people' of the northern province, who were
'witty, but yet able to be dealt with by good governance, as long as
laws can be executed and men backed'. (Did this mean that Grindal as himself a northerner in speech and perhaps in 'wit' shared
that special kind of 'stoutness'?) Eight months later, on 20 February
1570, Cecil minuted the translation of the bishop of London to
York and his replacement by either Jewel of Salisbury or Sandys of
Worcester. Cecil's personal interest in the shuffle is implied in
Grindal's appointment of his controller Richard Ratcliff to attend
upon Cecil 'from time to time and to solicit for prosecution of the
matter intended towards me'. And two months later: 'I send my
man again herewith to solicit my suits, praying you to help me
forward as your leisure may serve.'[1] The date of Grindal's election was 11 April, of his translation 1 May, with the royal assent
sealed on 15 May, and of his installation by proxy in York Minster,
9 June. The temporalities were released to him on 6 June.[2] As to
the succession in London: Jewel was a dying man and it was
Grindal's boyhood friend Sandys who succeeded him, leaving
Aylmer to wait another six years before proving the truth of
Parker's accurate but premature testimonial.

In the light of the strained relations between the bishop of
London and his metropolitan three years earlier, Parker's letter
has often been taken to indicate that by being moved to York
Grindal was, in modern parlance, kicked upstairs. The bishopric
of London was the most onerous office in the Church, and Parker's
experience of Grindal suggested that a bishop who was sufficiently
affable to gain the approval of Londoners might have drunk too
deep of that dangerous cup 'popularity'. The northern province,
or so some have thought, was a sphere of minor consequence,
where a semi-puritan could be harmlessly employed in curbing the
papists. So Parker may have reasoned, although it is a mistake to

suppose that his relations with Grindal were permanently damaged by the events of 1566. He could write to Grindal at York in the
midst of a later round with the puritans: 'Her majesty hath written
me of late such a letter, and because you be a good fellow I send you
the copy, whereby you may know how she relents.'[3] As for Cecil, to
suggest that he promoted his old friend to York to get rid of him
would be to close the mind with southern provincialism to the
momentous events which were occurring north of the Trent.

1570 was a landmark in what has been described as 'the long and
gradual Tudor revolution in the North',[4] the wide march forming
the indefinite frontier between the medieval and the modern history of the region. In the closing months of 1569 the delicate
equilibrium of northern society under Elizabethan rule was shaken
by the rising of the northern earls and its suppression. This, with
the promulgation of the papal sentence of excommunication
against the queen a month or two later, marked the climax of a general political crisis which had begun with the flight of the Scottish
queen into England. Hitherto the government had handled the
north in the spirit of *quieta non movere*. The Council in the North
was a body adapted to local conditions and staffed by northerners,
or by men with long experience of the north, sensitive to the
realities of its regional politics. The same might be said of the other
major instrument of government, the Ecclesiastical Commission
for the Province of York. For four years Elizabeth had been
content that both institutions should be presided over by Grindal's
predecessor, Archbishop Thomas Young. As a trained civilian
Young was a competent and industrious official who put in hard
days on both Council and Commission. But he was no protestant
zealot and his régime placed little strain on the uncertain ties of
northern loyalty. When he died in 1568 he was replaced as lord
president by a nobleman of conservative outlook, the earl of
Sussex, while the archbishopric was left vacant for two years.[5] In
vain the dean of York alerted Cecil to the need for a 'good' archbishop: 'a teacher, because the country is ignorant, a virtuous
and godly man because the country is given to sift a man's life, a
stout and courageous man in God's cause because the country
otherwise will abuse him, and yet a sober and discreet man' — in
short, Grindal. And therefore do I wish that London were translated to York.'[6]

It took rebellion to expose the lack of a policy for the north, and
the need for the kind of administrative resolution which was only
to be looked for from strongly committed protestants. This, rather
than any desire to remove him from London, must explain the
queen's belated consent to Grindal's appointment to an office

which, if the conspiracies of 1570 had succeeded, might have gone to support the dignity of Lord Henry Howard, the future earl of Northampton.[7] Two years later, Sussex was replaced by that ardent puritan, Henry Hastings, third earl of Huntingdon. With this 'singular jewel'[8] Grindal vied in mutual admiration, sharing a trust not often encountered in the relations of Tudor prelates and politicians, and totally absent from Huntingdon's dealings with Grindal's successor, Archbishop Sandys. The significance of these two appointments was that a measure of 'thorough' was now to be introduced into the running of the north, somewhat reducing the element of 'indirect rule' which had obtained in the past. Given the slender resources of government the change was bound to be less than total. No more than Archbishop Young could Grindal and Huntingdon ride roughshod over local prejudice, or govern without the willing participation of local men of substance. Nevertheless the slow transformation of northern England was now accelerated. With Grindal's archiepiscopate and Huntingdon's lord presidency the Reformation in the north, in the sense of the effective protestantization of the region, began in earnest. It was also in Grindal's time, in 1574, that the influence of the catholic Counter-Reformation penetrated Yorkshire, in the person of the first of the missionary priests to enter the county.

The observation that much of this part of England remained attached to catholicism throughout Elizabeth's reign requires refinement. It leaves out of account immense local variations. The antiquary Camden, writing of Yorkshire alone, remarked upon its 'variety of parts'. By mid-century some parts accommodated distinct pockets of protestantism, notably the more economically and socially advanced localities, for example Hull and parts of the West Riding. (The city of York, by contrast, was an exceptionally conservative place.) It also ignores a conceptual distinction which many students of Elizabethan catholicism would wish to make between 'the old religion', or simple conservatism, and the forward-looking, dynamic sentiments associated with the mission of the seminary priests. The strength of the old faith lay in traditional observances and seasonal rites, contained within a framework of inherited social institutions and obligations, and especially those which were integrated in the life of the great household. In its organizational structure, its loyalties and spiritual heroism, the new catholicism, offered and accepted as a matter of deliberate choice, required no less than protestanism a leap out of received habits of mind and settled patterns of social behaviour.[9]

The old religion was capable of some adjustment to Elizabethan conditions, provided that no more was required of it than a minimal conformity and the fealty traditionally owed to the royal government. It was not necessarily distinguished by 'recusancy', that is, by conscientious absence from the parish church, nor, in many conservative parishes, was the conduct of public worship likely to offend those predisposed to compromise. The alterations in structure and ornaments required by royal and episcopal injunctions had not been carried out universally, and there must have been many clergy, Henrician or Marian ordinands, whose use of the Prayer Book approximated in external respects to the old service. The wafers administered in the communion were sometimes impressed with the same irons which had been used to make 'singing cakes' in the past. Rosaries and catholic books of private devotion were still in extensive private possession, and were carried to church. Even in Archbishop Young's later years it did not seem incongruous for the archbishop's register to contain the copy of a will in which a York incumbent bequeathed his soul to Almighty God 'and to our blessed Lady, Saint Mary, and to all the holy company of Heaven'.[10] On his arrival in Yorkshire Grindal would comment with astonishment on the survival of practices suggesting 'another church, rather than a member of the rest'.[11]

Grindal's archiepiscopate was marked by the most vigorous attack yet mounted against what has been called 'survivalism'. This was a campaign to hasten the disappearance of a catholicism which was assumed to be in decline, and to establish the reformed faith in a more than nominal sense. Recusancy, the hallmark of a more sensitive and resistant catholic allegiance, was hardly acknowledged in Grindal's time to be a new and advancing force, and Grindal did not deal with it as such. Only after his translation were its dimensions and potentialities understood, and preventive measures mounted on an appropriate scale.

Although the growth of recusancy is to be attributed primarily to missionary agencies, Grindal's attempt to bring the northern parishes to heel can only have contributed to the crystallization of the new catholicism. In place of the lethargy of a whole region the government was now to be confronted with the active dissent of an élite. Within a relatively short time of the arrival of the seminarists this minority was consolidated in a stable and numerically constant community, composed for the most part of gentry families and their dependants. In the short term, and for as long as recusancy could be regarded as politically dangerous, the thorough policies of Grindal and Huntingdon carried a risk, since they were calculated to harden the will to resist. But in the long term they would be vindicated. While the catholic community became neutralized by social and political isolation, reverting to the unadventurous leadership of its foremost laymen, the culture of the whole region became in a broad and general sense protestant, while certain areas, notably the towns of the West Riding, took on a puritan character. These momentous alterations in the civilization of the north of England may have owed as much to Archbishop Grindal as to any other person, with the exception of Huntingdon. If the saintly Bernard Gilpin will consent to the appropriation of a title traditionally his, Grindal may be called the apostle of the Elizabethan north.[12]

Grindal was not able to take charge of his new responsibilities until almost a year after his translation. In the early summer of 1570 he went down to Canterbury to be confirmed and inducted by Archbishop Parker 'in a great and honourable presence'. On Trinity Sunday he was entertained at a banquet, together with the bishops of Winchester and Rochester and Richard Curteys, who had been consecrated bishop of Chichester that morning. This was one of the great *convivia* at which Parker excelled, and which Grindal assured him (with irony?) no other archbishop would be able to emulate for a hundred years. The event was held to commemorate the new Henrician foundation of the cathedral. Everyone connected with the church was accommodated, 'even the children', and, 'at the remotest tables but in sight', the poor from the hospitals, so that those feasting at high table should be reminded of God's mercies in raising them to high estate 'out of their former dangers and calamities, when they themselves were poor and distressed'.[13] We know what Thomas Sampson would have thought of these instructively hierarchical arrangements. Was Grindal entirely at his ease? A month later there was occasion for a pleasant and perhaps rare jaunt in the country. While staying in Middlesex with Sir Thomas Wroth, an old friend from Strasbourg days and long before that, Grindal rode over to Waltham to inspect Cecil's building operations at Theobalds and to spend the afternoon with his children.[14] Since this is the only occasion in all of his correspondence when this bachelor bishop mentions children it is worth recalling that they included the young Robert Cecil, at that time seven years of age.

The departure for York was subsequently delayed by illness and uncompleted business, which included the tangled affairs of the Hospital of the Savoy. The famous reformer David Whitehead had earlier refused the mastership of this charitable foundation on grounds of conscience, with results which justified Grindal's suppression of similar scruples. The living had gone instead to the vice-master, Thomas Thurland, a man described accurately enough by an historian of Elizabethan industry as 'a company promoter'. Thurland applied not only his entrepreneurial talents but the revenues of his hospital to the speculative development of the copper mines at Keswick, in which his fellow-patentee was the German prospector, Daniel Hochstetter. The story of his activities involves actions for debt and bankruptcy and a series of more or less desperate financial expedients. This was not healthy for the Savoy and in April 1570 Grindal, as bishop of London, had received a bill of complaint which charged Thurland with such abuses as saddling the hospital with his private debts, selling or pawning the vestments, ornaments and other valuables, and filling the accommodation with his relatives and cronies. Complaints of this kind received a ready hearing from an old commonwealth man like Grindal, who when confronted with similar scandals in the management of Sherburne Hospital, Durham, wrote: 'I think often that those men which seek spoil of hospitals ... did never read the twenty-fifth chapter of Matthew.' When the Council took the view that Thurland had 'deserved well of the commonweal' he suggested that therefore he should be recompensed '*ex publico* and not *ex sanguine pauperum*'. Through Cecil a commission was obtained to visit the Savoy, which Grindal himself headed as archbishop-elect of York. By the end of July he was able to pronounce a formal sentence of deprivation, but Thurland's influence at Court ensured that this was not the last of the affair. Twice more, in 1572 and 1574, Grindal was obliged to intervene to frustrate the master's intrigues to secure reinstatement, and these were only terminated with Thurland's death.[15]

The day before leaving London, Grindal wrote apprehensively to Bullinger at Zürich. The northern counties were still unsettled, 'the feelings of the people ... much exasperated and panting for renewed disturbances'. Both he and Bishop Pilkington might yet find themselves in physical danger. 'But these things do not move me; the will of the Lord be done!' In the event, this new chapter began not with violence but with the anticlimax of tedium, discouragement and sickness. Grindal set out on 1 August 1570, but two days of unaccustomed exercise brought on a 'tertiary ague' which obliged him to rest for ten days. It was not until 17 August that he reached the archiepiscopal seat of Cawood Castle, seven miles along the Ouse from York. Eight months earlier it had been estimated that there were only ten gentlemen in Yorkshire who supported the queen's religious policy, so it was not surprising that Grindal met with a cool reception from the county. A small party of a dozen gentlemen met him near Doncaster, headed by Sir Thomas Gargrave. Gargrave was the leading lay member of the Ecclesiastical Commission and a staunch government man who on

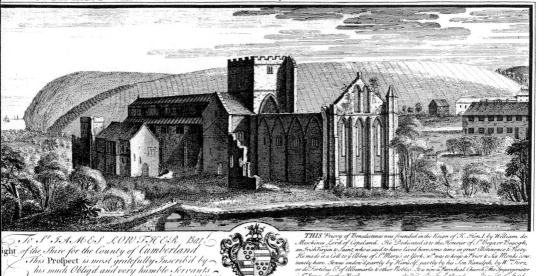

To St JAMES LOWTHER Bart
ight of the Shire for the County of Cumberland
This Prospect is most gratefully Inscrib'd by
his much Oblig'd and very humble Servants
Saml & Nathl Buck.

THIS Priory of Benedictines was founded in the Reign of K. Hen. I. by William de Meschines Lord of Copeland. He Dedicated it to the Honour of St Bega or Beaogh, an Irish Virgin & Saint, who is said to have lived here some time in great Abstinence & Piety. He made it a Cell to ye Abbey of St Mary's at York, nd was to keep a Prior & Six Monks constantly here. It was endow'd partly by Himself, partly by his Son Ranulph, by Wm Fortz or de Fortibus Et of Albemarle & other Nobles. It is now a Parochial Church. The Impropriator is St James Lowther Bart   dn. Val. 143: 17: 2. Dugd.—   143: 16: 6. Speed.

Saml & Nath Buck delin et Sculp. Publish'd according to Act of Parliament March 26. 1739.—£50. ye Man

1 St Bees Priory. This engraving, one of a series by Samuel and Nathaniel Buck, was published on 26 March 1739. It is not accurate in every detail. The school founded by Archbishop Grindal appears as the two-storey building on the extreme right.

2 The Old Court, Pembroke College Cambridge. The creeper-covered building known as the Old Library was the original college chapel. 'I have said mass. I am sorry for it,' Grindal remarked in 1567.

3 Bishop Nicholas Ridley, painted in the year in which he was degraded

MARTINVS BVCERVS.

Natales, Bucere, tuos Germania Jactat,
Natalibus felix tuis.
Quis verò et quantus fueris, tua scripta loquuntur,
Ad littus orbis ultimum.

cum priuillegio.

4 Martin Bucer. This engraved portrait first appeared in Theodore Beza's *Icones*, published at Geneva in 1580.

5 Archbishop Matthew Parker

receiving the news of Grindal's appointment had told Cecil: 'I am glad to hear we shall have a learned and grave archbishop' — and had immediately nominated him to every commission in the county for which he was eligible. Grindal stayed that night with Gargrave and the next day was met by the dean of York, his old friend Matthew Hutton, with other minster clergy, and by half a dozen other 'inferior gentlemen', and so brought to Cawood. Within the next few days other more substantial magnates straggled in to offer their apologies, pleading the sickness of themselves or their families. 'And indeed agues are universal throughout all this country.'[16]

Although Cawood had been favoured by Young, the valetudinarian Grindal found the river air 'very moist and gross' (his successor would describe the house as sometimes 'by reason of waters and ditches very unwholesome'),[17] and although Bishopthorpe was 'said to be an extreme cold house for winter', it was there, closer to York, that Grindal would choose to reside. He planned an early move to Bishopthorpe at Michaelmas, in order to be in touch with the business of the Ecclesiastical Commission, but on 2 September his fever returned in a severe form, reducing him to a state of weakness in which physicians and friends despaired of his recovery. 'I myself also received the sentence of death in myself.' On 7 November, in what was probably the first act of his archiepiscopate in which he participated personally, he conducted the collation of the vicar of Doncaster 'in quadam inferiora camera' in a south-facing portion of the castle. Three days later he was able to sign a letter to Cecil which reported the arrest of three 'mass priests' in the household of the countess of Northumberland and addressed itself to the legal claims against his predecessor's executors for dilapidations. On 7 December he sat in 'quadam camera vocata the withdrawing chamber' to receive the certificate of resignation of another incumbent. But he remained ill and confined to Cawood for the remainder of the winter.[18]

During these months Grindal's episcopal functions, as distinct from the ordinary administration of the diocese, were exercised on his behalf by Richard Barnes, bishop of Carlisle from July 1570. Barnes had received a commission to ordain from Young a month after he became suffragan bishop of Nottingham in 1567, and thereafter he had relieved the archbishop of this function entirely, in accordance with well-established provincial practice. Barnes continued to perform all the ordinations in the diocese until April 1571, and in the following summer he acted as Grindal's commissary in conducting the metropolitan visitation of the diocese of Chester. Somewhat later Grindal washed his hands of Barnes, probably after some experience of his reputation for venality and extortion, and he opposed his promotion to Durham in 1577. Grindal's aversion, which that other northern apostle Bernard Gilpin came to share, was to make Barnes his only enemy on the episcopal bench at the time of his troubles as archbishop of Canterbury.[19]

A more permanent and dependable member of Grindal's staff was his chancellor, John Rokeby. Rokeby was a seasoned civil lawyer, in his youth one of Henry VIII's legal counsel, a man with a European reputation for probity who had served two archbishops before Grindal. The chancellor of York combined the offices of vicar general and official principal, which were the presiding offices of the archbishop's courts, the Court of Audience (or Chancery) and the Consistory. To compare Rokeby to the permanent civil servant in charge of a government department and Grindal to the minister would if anything undervalue the role of the chancellor, for Tudor bishops, like their late-medieval predecessors, were not directly concerned with administration and the dispensing of justice. Although he might exercise an occasional right of intervention in the oversight of his court, it was only through the appointments in his gift that a bishop could greatly influence these processes. It was sufficient for Grindal to continue Rokeby in undisturbed enjoyment of his offices. When, presently, he relieved him of one of these, the position of commissary or presiding judge of yet another court, the Exchequer, it was to promote another skilled lawyer, Richard Percy, apparently on Rokeby's advice. Percy had decades of service at York ahead of him and with other experts, such as Rokeby's successor as chancellor, John Gibson, another Grindal appointment, perpetuated a tradition of sound diocesan government. (It was Grindal's successor Sandys who would disturb its even tenor with the flagrant nepotism which he exercised in favour of his sons.)[20]

In a study of the administrative institutions of the diocese of York in this period, such as Dr R. A. Marchant has written, Rokeby, Percy and Gibson loom larger than any of the archbishops they served. The biographer of one of these archbishops has to assume, and largely ignore, the existence of the institutional infrastructure, the machinery, the established circles of advocates, proctors and other officials with their expertise applied for the most part to the humdrum of social need and human failing. Even in those functions which were more immediately his own — ordination, institution to benefices, the consecration of churches — an archbishop could not easily proceed without the constant advice of a legal secretary.[21]

In March 1571 Grindal re-emerged from his imprisonment. On the 13th of that month he made his first appearance on the Ecclesiastical Commission, meeting in the deanery at York. It was perhaps the first time that he had entered the city. At about the same time he began to busy himself with the preparations for his metropolitan visitation. From this time onwards the itinerary which can be reconstructed from the various records of his administration suggests that his grip on the affairs of the diocese and province was rarely relaxed, and that he was probably continuously resident, except for one absence in London at the Parliament held in the early summer of 1572. In 1574 the earl of Shrewsbury, a staunch ally, made his London house of Coldharbour available to the archbishop 'to use it at his will during his abode in London. For I find his grace so dear a friend to me and mine as I would he should command anything that mine is.'[22] But it must be doubted whether Grindal ever had occasion to enjoy the earl's hospitality.

As soon as he was able to take his bearings Grindal discovered that he had exaggerated the instability of the north. He told Bullinger that he had found the people 'more complying than I expected, as far as external conformity is concerned', humbled as they had been by the calamities of civil war. The problems which faced him were not those of insurgency but of inertia. Within weeks of arriving in Yorkshire he had diagnosed three 'evil qualities' in its inhabitants: 'Great ignorance, much dullness to conceive better instructions, and great stiffness to retain their wonted errors.' Of these he had ample experience over the following years.

11

DELENDA AND AGENDA

A COMPREHENSIVE programme for the religious reform of the northern province was contained in the articles of enquiry and the injunctions published for Grindal's primary visitation, which began in May 1571.[1] Among other unexceptional matters, many of the injunctions had a special application to the backward state of northern religion. Every Sunday and holy day before evening prayer the clergy were to instruct children and servants in the Ten Commandments, the Articles of Belief and the Lord's Prayer, and to teach the Catechism. They were to repel from the communion not only 'notorious evil livers', as the rubric required, but any parishioner above the age of twenty-four who was ignorant of the Catechism. Registers were to be kept of those signifying their intention to receive communion and examinations of their fitness were to be held before each ministration. In the service itself the clergy were forbidden to use unauthorized gestures or rites, such as 'crossing or breathing over the sacramental bread or wine', or 'any showing or lifting up of the same to the people, to be by them worshipped and adored'. They were to deliver the bread into the people's hands, not into their mouths, and to use a communion cup, not a chalice nor yet a profane cup. Baptism was to be administered without 'oil or chrism, tapers, spattle, or any other popish ceremony'. The clergy were not to proclaim, observe or allow to be observed holy days or fast days which had been abrogated, nor were they to announce them 'by any indirect means'.

A further set of detailed orders, which cannot be precisely dated or placed, regulated the performance of public penance, providing a further illustration of Grindal's concern for discipline at the parochial level which, if royally endorsed would have done much to satisfy the puritans and to defuse attacks on the Church by presbyterian extremists. At every act of public penance there was to be a sermon or at least a homily, declaring the true doctrine of repentance, and after the sermon a procedure of interrogation to establish whether the parties were contrite. In the autumn of 1571 rural deans were enjoined not to commute acts of penance for money 'by any means to any manner of person whatsoever'.[2]

Much attention was paid to the fabric of the parish churches. Churchwardens were to erect a decent low pulpit in the body of the church for the saying of morning and evening prayer. Altars were to be 'utterly taken down and clean removed, even unto the foundation', all traces of their former presence erased and concealed with whitewash, and the altar stones 'broken, defaced and bestowed to some common use'. Where rood-lofts remained they were to be taken down, laying bare the cross-beam supporting any partition that there might be between nave and chancel. A special commission 'to discover and demolish rood-lofts' had been issued to the four archdeacons of the diocese of York and to the bishop of Sodor and Man on 23 March, together with articles which dealt with the same points and further required that each parish should provide a 'decent' communion table, that every minister should wear a 'comely' surplice, and that any linen cloths 'called altar cloths and before used about masses' should be replaced. Later in the same year the rural deans were instructed to visit the churches within their deaneries to confirm that these orders had been carried out.[3] At the visitation wardens were further asked whether antiphonaries, mass-books, portuises and other books 'which served for the superstitious Latin service' had been 'utterly defaced, rent and abolished', and whether such items of minor ecclesiastical furniture as mass vestments, handbells, censors, crosses, candlesticks, holy water stocks 'and such other relics and monuments of superstition and idolatry' had been defaced and destroyed, and, if not, in whose keeping they remained. The summer of 1571 in Yorkshire was no time or place to be a churchwarden or rural dean.

Other articles and injunctions related to traditional funeral customs, the telling of beads, the lighting of candles at Christmas, the use of the sign of the cross on entering a church, auricular confession, and such incidental aspects of late medieval culture as Christmas and May games, the presence of minstrels and morris dancers in church at rush-bearings, and the trade of pedlars in the church precincts during service time. The wardens were warned not to suffer 'any persons to walk, talk, or otherwise unreverently to behave themselves' in church, or to gamble or 'sit abroad' in the streets or churchyards or in taverns and alehouses in the time of divine service or sermons, 'whether it be before noon or afternoon'. Altogether, for anyone not subscribing to the religious premises on which it was based, a devastatingly comprehensive list of *delenda*.

But many of these requirements merely echo the canons approved in the Convocation of Canterbury at about this time, in April 1571, or reiterate the Royal Injunctions of 1559, or incorporate injunctions long since made by other bishops. For all that we know to the contrary they may even quote extensively from the articles and injunctions of Archbishop Young, which have not survived. 'Monuments of superstition' had been assiduously sought out in many parishes in Young's time, especially in his visitation of 1567 and by the Ecclesiastical Commission. Yet the impression which Grindal's injunctions convey is that in many parts of the north the Elizabethan Settlement was still at least in part a dead letter. They evoke a whole way of life in its rich diversity and disorder, and in spite of the sentence which had been passed against it, this folk religion was not to be easily eradicated. Even as late as the nineteenth century disconnected fragments of the old religious tradition persisted in parts of the North Riding.[4]

The occasion of the visitation was taken to require a general subscription from the clergy to the Thirty-Nine Articles in accordance with the recent parliamentary statute. The commissioners for the visitation also seem to have examined the clergy on their learning, Latinity and capacity to preach, catechize and keep parish registers. Those found wanting were summoned for further examination at the next visitation. In all these ways Grindal's primary visitation appears to mark a kind of primary implementation of the Reformation in the north.[5]

At eight o'clock on Tuesday 15 May 1571 the archbishop began the visitation of his cathedral church. The dean, precentor, canons and vicars choral presented themselves in the minster and, after the singing of the Litany and other prayers, heard their archbishop preach from an appropriate text in Acts chapter 15: 'Let us go again and visit our brethren in every city where we have preached the word of the Lord, and see how they do.' To ensure that the word should be constantly heard in the great church which dominated his metropolis, Grindal followed his visitation of the minster by making a 'perpetual order' for sermons. By this rota, beginning on Advent Sunday, the chancellor, dean, archdeacons and prebendaries were to take their turns in preaching on Sundays and holy days throughout the year, on pain of a fine for default. In October of the following year Grindal issued further injunctions which express the same concern to make his cathedral church before all else a place of instruction. The dean and chapter were to provide a notice-board in the chancel 'where it may easily be seen and read', containing the order for sermons. In addition, a learned preacher was to be appointed and supported from chapter funds who was to deliver a twice-weekly divinity lecture in the minster and to preach in the parish churches of York, especially those appropriated to the minster. The vicars choral and other inferior

ministers were bound to attend the cathedral lectures and to undergo monthly examinations of their knowledge, while the vicars
choral under the age of forty were to memorize every week one
chapter of St Paul's Epistles, beginning with Romans. These
orders, including the rota of preachers, reiterated the rather more
careful and detailed injunctions issued by the Edwardian Archbishop Holgate in 1552. But the opportunity now existed which
Holgate had been denied to settle the life of York Minster on a
securely reformed basis. Grindal's order for sermons was to stand
without alteration until 1685. In 1571 the prospects for converting
the minster into a power-house of reform were good. Matthew
Hutton was energetic, the only active, resident dean of York for a
century and a half. Between them Grindal and Hutton would
conspire to bring competent theologians and preachers on to the
staff, as vacancies occurred.[6]

The formal sessions of the visitation continued through the
summer, deanery by deanery. Finally, on 14 September, the archbishop's commissaries sat in the minster as a court for the correction of all persons presented throughout the diocese. (Only
under Grindal's successor would increasing business cause the
correction court itself to go on circuit.) With 'much weariness' the
still invalid archbishop had conducted the visitation in person,
travelling short distances and taking frequent rests. But the
visitation of the sprawling diocese of Chester, which ran from
Cheshire through the length of Lancashire to Westmorland, Cumberland and the North Riding, was deputed to Bishop Barnes of
Carlisle. Cheshire and Lancashire revealed a disturbing picture of
'dissolute living' and recusancy, but as Grindal explained to the
earl of Leicester: 'It is so far from me that I cannot do so much as
otherwise I would.' If his practice was no different from that of his
successors the visitation of the remaining dioceses of Durham and
Carlisle will also have been committed to the diocesans, or to
leading officials in those sees. No doubt Grindal regarded the
consolidation of the more populous and 'civil' areas of Yorkshire as
the immediate priority. The task of reconstruction in the Marches
could be left to Barnes in Carlisle and in Durham and Northumberland to Bishop Pilkington and perhaps to that apostolic man,
Bernard Gilpin, who, we are told, 'seemed even to supply the place
of a bishop' in his own winter visitations of the 'half barbarous and
rustic people' of Ridsdale and Tynedale.[7]

The court book which survives from the visitation of York
diocese only occasionally reflects the more remarkable of Grindal's
articles of enquiry. Leonard Latrie of Spofforth was examined for
retaining in his custody 'divers of the church goods serving for

Latin service'. The curate, churchwardens and others of Kildwick
in the remote country of Craven were charged with suffering
certain monuments of superstition to remain in their church undefaced, 'viz., two altar stones, which have hid in the church, a holy
water vat or trough, a cross and certain pieces of the rood-loft'. One
of these churchwardens explained that he had intended to use the
holy water stock for a pig trough, while a parishioner of Burnsall
presented for using 'a piece of a Latin primer called *Hortulus
animae*' claimed that he had employed it 'for a calendar and not
otherwise'. But such cases were greatly outnumbered by the presentments for sexual and other social offences which formed the
stock-in-trade of all ecclesiastical court proceedings.[8]

A court of correction following upon visitation or the consistory
court could proceed only on the basis of the presentments made to
it, and in spite of the pressures to which churchwardens were
subjected by the apparitors or summoners, information about
popish survivals may have been hard to obtain from those very
communities where they were most prevalent. In any event, it is
likely that Grindal relied less upon this traditional machinery than
upon a novel process of enquiry by commission, and of this there is
some evidence in the visitation court book itself. The churchwardens of Spofforth said that they had delivered the church goods in
question 'unto the queen's majesty's commissioners at Leeds',
who had defaced them. The incumbent of another parish alleged
that he had delivered a cope, already defaced, 'to the commissioners appointed for such purpose, and received an acquittance
for the discharge thereof'. These are references to action taken
under the authority of the Ecclesiastical Commission for the
Province of York, which held sessions at different centres of the
diocese during the months of the visitation and which was active on
its own account in the enforcement of the archbishop's injunctions.[9]

The act books of the York Ecclesiastical Commission, which are
unique in their continuity and volume, leave it in no doubt that it
was this body, a mixed clerical and lay tribunal appointed under
Letters Patent from the Crown, rather than the ordinary courts
spiritual which offered the best hope of making an impression on
the more serious irregularities in the diocese and province. It is
perhaps significant that in the semi-autonomous archdeaconry of
Nottingham, where in Grindal's time a local extension of the
Commission came to be inoperative, the effect of Grindal's primary visitation was to stimulate the archdeacon's court to unprecedented activity, so that the number of cases heard on a single day
rose from as few as six to more than fifty. For all that we know (and

only in the case of Nottinghamshire is the record in any way complete) Grindal may have issued a general mandate to step up the activities of the archdeacons' courts, the effect of which would have been to transfer the exercise of routine ecclesiastical discipline from the less efficient hands of the rural deans. This was a process which had occurred long since south of the Trent, but which seems to have been under way in the north only under the later Tudor archbishops. Be that as it may, unless serious distortion has resulted from the accidents of survival among the archives, it would appear that while the archdeacon's court was almost the only direct and regular instrument of discipline in Nottinghamshire, elsewhere the Ecclesiastical Commission increasingly assumed this function.[10]

The Commission was staffed by some of the same officials, notaries, proctors, apparitors, who served the regular spiritual courts, and among the quorum were the leading ecclesiastical adminstrators of the diocese, so that its forms and procedures in many ways approximated to those of the Consistory Court or the Court of Audience, or Chancery. But unlike the ecclesiastical courts the Commission had powers to imprison, to take bond and to fine, which made it the most effective weapon available for use against catholic recusancy in the years before the new penal laws of the 1580s made the secular courts primarily competent in this sphere. In the Elizabethan period more than half the total cases handled by the Ecclesiastical Commission of York involved recusancy in some form.

When Grindal assumed its presidency, the York Commission was already a seasoned institution, staffed by officials of the calibre of John Rokeby and Sir Thomas Gargrave. Its ascendancy over the Court of Audience dated from Young's time and by 1570 was complete. What the new archbishop seems to have brought to its deliberations was a characteristic personalizing influence, conveyed in the written record by the novelty of frequent transitions from formal Latin into a very full account of proceedings in English. He also made personal attendance a high priority. In four and a half years he spent at least 157 days on the Commission, no less than 55 of them between March and December 1571, so that it would hardly be an exaggeration to say it was from his seat at this table that Grindal governed his diocese and province.[11] Huntingdon, as lord president of the Council of the North, sometimes sat with him, after Grindal had secured new Letters Patent which included his name, and their co-operation effectively symbolized a complete identity of purpose between the chief representatives of church and state. 'Unanimous in God's and the Queen's business', as Strype puts it, their reciprocity was complete when Grindal was added to the Council of the North, on which he served from the close of 1572.[12]

In 1571 the Ecclesiastical Commission was busy with several aspects of 'survivalism': with two men of Richmond who had heard mass 'in the rebellion time'; with an alderman of York who was given to crossing himself; with persons who kept church vestments in their houses; with two men of Wilberfoss who had kept intact the timber and cross-stones from the rood-loft, claiming that they intended to use them to make a bridge; and with the churchwardens of Kirkby Malzeard who had done nothing to disturb either the rood-loft or the cross in their churchyard. In November 1572 the Commissioners wrote of the 'very rude and barbarous custom' whereby, on St Thomas's Day, 'two disguised persons' called Yule and Yule's Wife rode through the city of York 'very undecently and unseemly'.[13]

The Yule riding was only one part of the varied round of plays and seasonal entertainments which, for students and devotees of the medieval drama, represents the most appealing and lamentable casualty of the protestant campaign against the old religion and the folk traditions which were integral to it. With some reason this campaign is normally represented as an act of violent and arbitrary aggression against the popular culture. (But what, we may ask, was the standing in the third quarter of the sixteenth century of a dramatic tradition which depended upon the preservation a single, canonical manuscript text?) The great York cycle of Corpus Christi plays had apparently fallen into abeyance very shortly before Grindal arrived in the north, but up to 1572 the Paternoster play was still performed in the archiepiscopal city. In that year Grindal took possession of the copy of the play, ostensibly to bowdlerize the text, but in fact to impound it, effectively preventing any future performance. Four years later, in 1576, the Ecclesiastical Commission took action very shortly before Whitsun to prevent the performance of the Corpus Christi play cycle at Wakefield. And we know that Grindal exerted himself in successive years in ultimately unsuccessful attempts to use the authority of the Commission to suppress the Chester plays.[14]

For those who pertinaciously persisted in 'survivalism' Grindal and his colleagues meted out shrewd punishments. John Beckwith of Swinton in the North Riding parish of Masham, convicted of possessing 'certain superstitious monuments and images', was ordered to transport them to Richmond market place on market day, 'and when the most multitude of people shall be assembled' to burn them with his own hand, 'and stand by them until the same be wholly burned and consumed', publicly declaring his offence. After this he was to burn two other images in Masham market and do penance in church. Up to this point Beckwith's exemplary punishment resembled some meted out in Young's time. Grindal's touch is to be seen in the penalties imposed when Beckwith made his second appearance: a fine of ten marks and an order to erect 'a fair pulpit' in Masham church at his own charge, and to pay for a copy of Foxe's *Acts and Monuments* to be set up in the church.[15]

In more than one of these cases the figure of 'Ford the preacher' appears, as a watch-dog to ensure that the orders of the court were enforced. He was doubtless Anthony Ford, at this time vicar of Beckwith's parish of Swinton, whom Grindal promoted to the dignity of succentor in the Minster.[16] Mr Ford lived dangerously. At the burning of the images found in Long Marston, Leonard Atkinson ran out of his house with a pikestaff, crying that he trusted to see the day that those who plucked down the rood-lofts would be as glad to set them up again, and that the archbishop of York had no business to make such an order. Edward Ripley, with reference to the system of intelligence on which the drive for conformity depended, declared that 'my lord's grace had none about him but rascals ... to inform him of such idolatrous monuments as are undefaced in churches,' using his dagger to give point to a threat to put the vicar and curate 'out of the town by the ears'.[17]

It would be naive to suppose that the archbishop's purge could in itself have made an immediate and revolutionary change. In 1595 John Beckwith's parish of Masham would openly dispose of five sets of mass vestments and a quantity of other popish furnishings which had remained in the keeping of nine separate parishioners. The purchaser belonged to a family with known recusant leanings. At Grindal's ordinary visitation of the diocese of York begun in April 1575 it was found that at Gargrave the rood-loft was 'scarcely defaced'. At Huddersfield, where the demolition of the rood-loft had been resisted in 1571, it was seven years since the chancel roof had fallen in, killing the parish clerk and still 'the rain raineth into the church' and 'no amends any way'. (No amends either in several other parishes with ruinous chancels where the impropriator responsible for keeping the fabric in repair was none other than the archbishop himself!) At Gisburn in Craven the curate was quoted as saying before witnesses that 'the pope was and is the head of the Church.' At Scarborough a churchwarden, a bailiff and thirty-three other townspeople were presented for coming into morning prayer half-way through the service and refusing to pay their shilling fines for absence. Some of the same individuals preferred shooting and card-playing to attendance at evening prayer and a total of twenty-eight parishioners had refused to contribute to the poor. But such evidence has to be interpreted, and the interpretation which has been placed on the Scarborough case is that for some reason the churchwardens were presenting the irreligious behaviour of paupers and other classes of person who were often assumed by convention to lie beyond the discipline of the Church.[18]

In Grindal's view, the reform of towns like Scarborough could only come about through an effective ministry. For as long as the clergy were unlearned and incompetent, by a 'necessary consequence the people cannot be well instructed'. Yet contrary to what a reading of his correspondence might lead one to expect, the act books of the Ecclesiastical Commission do not record a purge of the more conservative and inadequate clergy of the province. The suggestion of one historian that the aftermath of the northern rebellion saw the deprivation of hundreds of clergy is remote not only from the facts but from the practical possibilities of Elizabethan administration.[19] It was not that Grindal entertained any illusions about the state of the ministry. He told the earl of Leicester that in his itinerary of 1571 he had found 'very few learned men'. In part this was owing to a 'want of due regard herctofore to place sufficient ministers', but Grindal knew that the problem was too intractable to yield to good intentions alone:

> Another cause not so easy to be remedied is the exility of stipends for ministers in many places, and especially in the greatest towns and parishes, where the profits were appropriated to religious houses; and so oftentimes where there are a thousand or fifteen hundred people in a parish there is neither parson nor vicar, but only a stipend of seven or eight pounds for a curate.

The alienation of much of the income of the parishes, now dispersed in the hands of countless lay owners of tithe, was 'a general inconvenience throughout the whole realm' but 'more common in these parts'. Consequently, as he wrote in his letter of 1576 to the queen, it was 'rather to be wished than hoped for' that every parish might have a preaching pastor. In such circumstances the simple and prime necessity of maintaining the parochial ministry, with the human material available, was not compatible with the root-and-branch reforms which puritans without administrative responsibilities glibly advocated.[20]

Between December 1570 and December 1571 only thirty-one clergy of the diocese of York and thirty-nine from the diocese of Chester were in trouble with the Commissioners, and not many of these cases ended in deprivation. The act books may tell only part of the story. The records of Grindal's institutions to livings reveal a growing number of resignations, rising from two in 1572 to eight in 1574 and seven in 1575. The circumstances of these may have amounted to deprivation. Yet no evidence survives to suggest a wholesale turnover of personnel. Only in one region do the clergy seem to have invited a general and searching inquisition, and this was in that sector of the vast and neglected archdeaconry of Richmond which lay closest to Grindal's native West Cumberland. In October 1571 a group of incumbents from the southern parts of the Lake counties appeared before the York Commission, together with a large number of recusants and other lay catholics who had been detected in the visitation of the summer and were now referred to York by the diocesan Commission at Chester. The clergy were variously described as 'malicious papists', 'simoniacs', and 'harbourers of priests', or else they were accused of more traditional offences, like the rector of Thornton in Lonsdale, 'no preacher, nor of sincere judgment', who was said to live incontinently 'with Mistress Canfield, and so has done six or seven years'. Among the offenders was the rector of the Cumbrian parish of Gosforth, seven miles to the south of Grindal's St Bees, who confessed to 'drunkenness and whoredom' and was deprived. The rector of Workington was also deprived, for simony committed with the patron of the benefice. When the patron took Grindal and his fellow Commissioners to law Grindal invoked the support of the chancellor of the Exchequer, Sir Walter Mildmay, and told him that he had procured 'a good preacher' to fill the cure which, like Gosforth, was 'but seven miles distant from the place where I was born'. There can be no doubt that Grindal was inspired by more than routine administrative zeal in seizing his opportunity to purge the corrupt ranks of the clergy who belonged to his native heath. The handling of these cases was marked by the shrewd realism which was the stamp of Grindal's government. The vicar of Kendal was discharged after preaching acceptable doctrine before the Commissioners in York Minster; but not before Grindal had enjoined him 'that he not behave himself doubly, professing here one thing and at home the contrary'.[21]

Four years later, at the time of an ordinary visitation of the diocese, Grindal sent out his domestic chaplains on a special tour of inspection into the state of the clergy. Their returns, cast in the conventional formulae of reports of this kind, provide a somewhat deceptively encouraging view of the quality of the Yorkshire clergy in the final year of Grindal's archiepiscopate. While the old Henrician and Marian priests are quaintly labelled 'sacerdos pontificius', and many others are described as 'mediocriter eruditus', a

high proportion appear as 'sufficienter eruditus' or at least 're-
ligiosus et pius'.[22]

It may be that this enquiry was meant to provide a basis on
which to launch a scheme of in-service training for the more
inadequate of the clergy of the kind which several bishops were to
employ in the next few years. In his injunctions of 1571 Grindal
had merely repeated the requirement of the Royal Injunctions that
ministers under the degree of M.A. should study the New Testament in Latin and English and undergo regular tests of their
ability. It was left to Archbishop Sandys and, following his lead, to
Barnes of Durham and Chaderton of Chester to provide for quarterly meetings of the clergy for learned conference and the examination of written tasks. In the diocese of Chester in 1584, thanks to
the initiative of the Lancashire preachers, 'exercises' of another
type were grafted on to these arrangements. These were enforced
monthly gatherings of the entire clergy of a deanery, at which the
'learned sort' preached and the 'mean sort' listened and took notes,
as well as undergoing examination. Conferences of this kind contained a promise of improving the existing clergy which was lacking from the penal procedures of the courts, or so much contemporary testimony would suggest. In all but name they were the
'prophesyings' which the queen suppressed in the southern province in 1577, and in view of Grindal's indignant non-cooperation
on that occasion it may seem odd that he had not done more to
establish preaching conferences as archbishop of York. Shortage
of the 'better sort' of ministers, of anything resembling the well-
organized cadre of Lancashire preachers, is the most likely explanation. In the market towns of Nottinghamshire, where conditions
were more favourable, preaching exercises were established early
in Grindal's archiepiscopate. But in the North Riding, even in the
1590s, an exercise at Northallerton was only prevented from col-
lapse by undergirding from the earl of Huntingdon, while in the
West Riding the great tradition of market town exercises began in
the early seventeenth century, with help from Lancashire.[23]

Evidently Grindal placed less reliance on improvement of existing manpower than on the importation of a new clerical élite. This
is where the emphasis was placed in that part of his famous letter to
the queen which referred to his experience in the north:

> I myself procured above forty learned preachers and graduates,
> within less than six years, to be placed within the diocese of
> York, besides those I found there; and there I have left them: the
> fruits of whose travail in preaching your majesty is like to reap
> daily, by most assured, dutiful obedience of your subjects in
> those parts.

Many and perhaps most of these preachers were in orders before they arrived in Yorkshire. Of the means used to attract them and place them we know very little. But so far as concerns Grindal's own ordinations a clear pattern emerges from his Register and Institution Act Books. These record two kinds of ordination: 'ordines generales', conferred on large numbers of candidates; and 'ordines speciales', involving a few, or even a single ordinand, and conferred on as many as a dozen occasions in the course of a year, usually in the chapel at Bishopthorpe, or, if it were near Christmas, at Cawood. (In the seven years of his archiepiscopate Young, or Barnes on his behalf, had conducted eleven general ordinations and only three described as 'special'.) Many of those ordained on these extraordinary occasions were admitted to deacon's and priest's orders on the same day, 'according to the wholesome order and rule of the Church of England in these parts'. A fair proportion were university men, or are described as 'literatus', and a detailed scrutiny might prove them to have been men of higher calibre than those ordained *en masse*.[24]

The very first of Grindal's special ordinands was Edmund Bunny, a bachelor of divinity and like his brother Francis prominent as a preacher, writer and administrator throughout the period of radical protestant ascendancy in the diocese. Bunny became Grindal's chaplain and a canon of the minster, where he later served as subdean. As with Grindal himself and his colleagues on the London chapter in Ridley's time, the dignitaries of the minster were to use their stipends to sustain them in an active apostolate beyond its walls. Grindal has been noted as 'the last archbishop to try to make the Elizabethan dean and chapter participate more actively in the life of the diocese'.[25] Another of Grindal's hand-picked ordinands was Christopher Shute, a Pembroke Hall man who was ordained in August 1572 and licensed to preach throughout the diocese and province.[26] As vicar of Giggleswick for half a century, from 1576 to 1626, Shute was to be one of the founding fathers of a radical religious tradition in the Craven district which in the seventeenth century tended to quakerism. No names of this quality occur in the general lists. With one hand, so to speak, Grindal brought in a better sort of minister, selected with some care. With the other he was content to keep patrons satisfied and parishes staffed with men of more ordinary attainments, while excluding the flagrantly unqualified.

Although the majority of Grindal's ordinands must have fallen well short of the best reformed standards, they may have undergone a more than cursory examination of their fitness. So one may infer from Grindal's institutions to benefices, which reveal that on

nine occasions institution was refused on grounds of insufficiency
to a clergyman holding valid letters of presentation from the patron. Entries of this kind in the records of Elizabethan ecclesiastical
administration are not common, and none occurs from York in the
times of Archbishop Young or Archbishop Sandys. Some of the
examinations were conducted by Grindal in person, as on one
occasion in the dean of Westminster's house when the archbishop
was attending the 1572 Parliament. At another time Grindal and
his chaplain took turns to catechize a certain William Ireland, whom
Barnes had ordained deacon during Grindal's illness and Grindal
himself had priested, and who held the presentation to Harthill.
Asked to construe the words in the document in his hand 'vestri
humiles et obedientes' Ireland rendered them 'your humbleness
and obedience', while in answer to the Old Testament question he
replied that it was King Saul who had led the Children of Israel out
of Egypt. Ireland coped no better with the remainder of the examination and was rejected as insufficient in doctrine and ignorant of
sacred scripture. On the failure of the patron to make an alternative
presentation Grindal exercised his right of collation and put in
Hugh Casson, whom he had ordained deacon and priest at a special
ordination a year before. Casson remained rector of Harthill for
the next fifty years.[27]

In every one of such cases Grindal incurred the risk of a *quare
impedit* suit brought against him in the secular courts by the
aggrieved patron. In 1575 he was sued at Chester by Sir Roland
Stanley — a name to conjure with, and impress juries — after he
had interfered with a simoniacal presention to a Cheshire living
and had engineered the substitution of 'Mr Gilpin of Cambridge'.
Grindal seems to have counter-attacked by hauling Stanley before
the Ecclesiastical Commission, with Huntingdon's co-operation
and the support of the Privy Council.[28]

In placing graduate ministers Grindal had an eye to the strategic, urban parishes. Where the urban magistracy had the will to
identify itself with the new-style preaching ministry Grindal was
quick to lend his good offices. At Hull in 1573 he negotiated a new
ecclesiastical settlement of a pragmatically protestant character.
The vicar surrendered his benefice with his parsonage into the
hands of the archbishop for the use of the mayor and aldermen of
Hull. The magistrates on their side were to provide a yearly
stipend of £40 for a preacher whom the archbishop was to appoint,
and in addition were to find the wages for a curate and to keep the
chancel of the parish church and the parsonage house in repair.
The vicar, Melchior Smith, consented to these arrangements, and
was no doubt reappointed on altered terms, exchanging his

parson's freehold for the goodwill of the archbishop and of the town. In the time of Grindal's predecessor a case had been brought against Smith in the High Commission from which it appears that he was an outspoken preacher in the puritan vein who admitted to having denounced the vestments as 'clouts and rags', to 'preaching against papistry and heresy', and to 'beating down of wicked vices reigning in these evil days amongst this sinful and adulterous generation'. In 1566, at the time of the controversy over vestments, Archbishop Young had resolved to make an example of him. The preacher appointed by Grindal under the 1573 treaty, one Griffith Brisken, would also find himself in trouble with the Commissioners for nonconformity. According to a recent historian of Elizabethan Hull, it was to these two, and especially to Melchior Smith, that the town owed its late Elizabethan reputation for militant protestantism. But some of the ultimate responsibility belongs to Grindal, whose co-operation with the town authorities permitted Smith to continue in an incumbency which ended only in 1591, and who imported the first of a line of town preachers.[29]

Elsewhere there were local difficulties. The Nottinghamshire parish of Stokesley was in the archbishop's gift but held *in commendam* by none other than Bishop Barnes. Grindal used his influence with Burghley (who was also Barnes's patron) to frustrate any attempt that Barnes might have made to perpetuate his hold on the parish, explaining: 'It is a market town, and hath been very evil served ever since he had it. I would place a preacher to be resident upon it.'[30]

A struggle with the patron of another Nottinghamshire living served to trigger off the *cause célèbre* of Grindal's quarrel with the archdeacon of Nottingham, John Lowth. Lowth was a not unsuccessful ecclesiastical careerist who enjoyed no less than four prebends, two benefices and an archdeaconry in which episcopal interference was by tradition only occasional. He was also contentious and autocratic. The paradox of the Grindal–Lowth affair was that it seems to have been the archbishop's policy to centralize discipline in the archdeacon's court at the very time that he was attacking the personal *folie de grandeur* of the archdeacon. No doubt the rock of offence was Lowth's pluralism and perhaps venality. But there were strong undertones of a clash of jurisdictions of the most traditional kind, for Lowth had pretensions to almost unlimited independence of the archbishop. The last straw seems to have been Lowth's presumption in adding to his livings a parish where Grindal had suffered a judicial defeat in his attempt to collate an incumbent of his own choice in place of the unsuitable clergyman originally presented. Displaying the resolution with which he is too seldom credited, and perhaps some malice too, Grindal employed both the Ecclesiastical Commission and the Chancery Court and indeed every other weapon at his disposal to destroy Lowth, probing into every weakness in his credentials and conduct, and seeking to deprive him of the more lucrative of his official functions. At the height of the quarrel Lowth suffered a short imprisonment in York Castle as the penalty for a slanderous letter comparing the Commission to the Spanish Inquisition. It was Corro all over again,[31] the human type that Grindal found least tolerable.

The sequel was inconclusive, but Lowth's ambitions were checked and he was only preserved in the safe enjoyment of his archdeaconry by Grindal's translation to Canterbury. Perhaps there was collusion between Lowth and Grindal's other great enemy, Bishop Barnes, a former suffragan of Nottingham. There is a hint of this in a letter from Archbishop Parker which in the context of the Lowth affair promises not 'to favour the suit that might be made unto me out of Carlisle etc'.[32] As for Lowth, he employed his considerable anecdotal powers to compose for John Foxe a circumstantial account of his experiences in the Marian persecution, and having reached the troubles of Archdeacon John Philpot at the hands of Bishop Stephen Gardiner allowed himself this comment: 'The like at this day is practised of our prelates under our noble Queen Elizabeth.'[33]

No doubt a more complete knowledge of these matters would reveal factional patterns in the opposition to Grindal. Conversely, there were social and political alliances which favoured his campaign to plant preachers in the towns and other neglected and strategic places. The principal promoter of such schemes was the earl of Huntingdon who, as his brother tells us, 'never set a straying foot in any place where he did not labour at the least to settle the preaching of the word to the people'. But for the wandering memory of an old man who made his will in 1642 we might not have known what mighty levers were sometimes pulled in order to bring this about. The memory belonged to Robert Moore, for sixty-one years rector of Guiseley, and with Christopher Shute one of the originators of the radical puritan tradition in Craven. At the age of twenty-four Moore came down from Cambridge to visit his friends in the north and to preach at Skipton Castle, by invitation of the Cliffords, earl and countess of Cumberland. After Moore had preached in and around Skipton for eighteen months, the rector of nearby Guiseley resigned the living, whereupon Huntingdon started a fund to purchase the advowson and so secure Moore's presentation. The subscribers were Moore's Clifford patrons, the earl of Warwick, Lord Willoughby of Eresby, the earl of Oxford and Sir Francis Walsingham, 'being all about the Court and having heard me preach'. The advowson was vested in Willoughby 'who did bear the greatest part of the charge'.[34] This happened in 1581, well after Grindal's time, but the circumstances are not likely to have been unique. It was not by accident, or because of something in the water, that protestantism took over some areas of the north, and by storm.

It is perhaps superfluous to record that little evidence survives of the prosecution of puritan nonconformists in the northern counties in Grindal's time. In December 1573, at the time of a general 'inquisition' in the south, directed against the early presbyterian agitators, Grindal told Parker that in his own diocese the Prayer Book was 'universally observed', although elsewhere in the province (Durham was probably meant) there were some 'novelties' which he had taken steps to restrain.[35] Yorkshire puritanism was embryonic in the 1570s,[36] but it must be reckoned the most considerable long-term consequence of the policies of Grindal and Huntingdon.

But the immediate fruit of Grindal's handiwork which he held out to the queen was the 'dutiful obedience of your subjects in those parts'.[37] He was back in the south when those words were written, and it was left to Archbishop Sandys and Huntingdon to respond with suitable severity to the wave of recusancy which appeared in the late 1570s to contradict him. Whereas Huntingdon is described by his biographer as 'a tireless persecutor', who committed prominent catholic prisoners to the harsh confinement of the blockhouses at Hull, Grindal hoped to effect the conversion of those not 'settled' by intermittent 'conference', combined with a milder form of detention in York, or enforced entertainment in a reliable protestant household. When Henry Neville appeared before the Commissioners in July 1571 and certified that he was 'not satisfied in conscience to come unto the church', he was licensed to confer concerning his doubts with Dean Hutton and others of the Commissioners. Thirty instances of this procedure are recorded for the period 1570-6, whereas the act books contain but one reference to 'conference' before Grindal's time. With recusants of some social consequence Grindal sometimes preferred to deal in person, as in March 1574, when the wife of Walter Calverley appeared at Bishopthorpe 'and had private conference with his grace', and in October of the same year when the act book records that in the case concerning John Rigmayden of Wedyton in Lancashire 'the said most reverend father himself hath condescended to confer with the said Mr Rigmayden for his better satisfaction'. Indeed Grindal was ready enough to fall into a leis-urely style of interrogation at formal sessions of the Commission itself. William Lacy of Sherburne, a hardened recusant well known to the Commissioners over many years, was asked 'whether he was one of that church whereof the pope was the head and the vicar-general under Christ in earth'. When he replied that he was, Grindal asked him 'whether he was resolved in such doubts of religion as he did stick upon or no'? When Lacy confirmed that he was not resolved Grindal further enquired 'whether he were a subject to the queen's majesty of England and believed in the Church of England and Ireland or no? Who answered and said that he believed in the catholic church.'[38] Bishop Creighton, generally less than enthusiatic in his judgments on Grindal, notes the 'good-will and considerable tact' which he displayed on these oc-casions.[39]

Mistaking a sullen quiescence for willing conformity, Grindal believed that gentlemen of Lacy's persuasion were neither num-erous nor dangerous. In April 1574 he assured Burghley: 'We are in good quietness (God be thanked) both for the civil and eccles-iastical state.' Seven months later Burghley was told that out of a whole term's business only five obstinate papists had been com-mitted. 'For the number of that sect (thanks be to God!) daily diminisheth, in this diocese especially.' One is reminded of Chamberlain's remark made in the spring of 1940 about Hitler having missed the bus. Within five years the Ecclesiastical Com-mission would be forced to deal with something approaching a mass movement of recusancy. Towards the end of 1580, special sessions held at Ripon, Beverley, Skipton and other centres dealt with over 400 recusants, and many more were cited to appear in York in the early months of the following year. In all it may be that as many as 350 families, perhaps a thousand individuals, were forced into conformity at this time, action on a scale never dreamed of by Grindal.[40]

Although he had not been forced to grapple with the problem of mass recusancy in the field, Grindal's northern experience made him something of an expert among his episcopal colleagues on catholic questions, and a persistent campaigner for more effective statutory penalties than the shilling fine incurred for absence from church under the 1559 legislation. In 1571 a bill had passed both houses of Parliament, only to receive the queen's veto, which would have imposed stiffer fines, linking them more closely with the purely ecclesiastical offence of failure to receive communion at least once a year. At the 1572 Parliament Grindal seems to have been at the centre of a movement to secure the enactment of an amended version of the same bill. On 1 June he led an episcopal delegation into Elizabeth's presence, and urged draft clauses which would have increased the penalties proposed in the previous year. As he told Burghley, the measure was especially needed 'in the north parts, where pecuniary mulcts are more feared than bodily imprisonment'. All to no avail: Elizabeth headed the bishops off, as she did four years later when Grindal, as archbishop of Canterbury, promoted the bill yet again in the House of Lords, and helped to guide it through committee.

During these years of legislative frustration, the bishops' policy, defined by Bishop Aylmer in 1577 and applied by the authority of the Ecclesiastical Commission, in both provinces, was one of 'round fines, to be imposed for contemptuous refusing the communion'. To fine for failure to communicate was a searching test of religious persuasion rather than of outward conformity alone, and, according to legal advice, a means of evading the objection that a man's recusancy had been sufficiently compounded by payment of the shilling fine. Grindal appears to have been an architect of this policy and consequently, if indirectly, of that part of the major new legislation of 1581 which raised the penalty for recusancy to £20 a month. This statute is properly taken as a landmark in the repression of Elizabethan catholicism, yet by a strange irony its effect was to remove from the front line the bishops and other ecclesiastical commissioners who, in the northern province at least and perhaps not only there, had hitherto provided the most credible response to the challenge of recusancy. Generally enforced, with the measure of imagination and resolution displayed by the York Commissioners in 1580, the 1581 Act must have broken the back of Yorkshire recusancy within a generation. But as the temporal magistrates and courts handled the new penal instrument, the majority of northern catholics knew it only as a general deterrent, not as a death sentence against their way of life. This at least was the conclusion of the modern historian of the penal laws, Father Walker.[41]

We have now passed beyond what after 1575 was of immediate concern to Edmund Grindal. At the end of that year, after the shortest reign of the five Elizabethan archbishops of York, he was called away to a more exalted and exposed station, where he would be confronted with a range of problems which were the exact reverse of his experience in the north. By his own account Grindal yielded to this ultimate preferment unwillingly and after 'many conflicts with myself about that matter', which were resolved by recollection of the example of Jonah, whose defiance of the heavenly vocation was as futile in its consequences as it was harrowing.[42] But if he could have foreseen what the next two years were to contain, and the six barren years which lay beyond, there would surely have been no conflict. Grindal would have moved heaven and earth to remain in York, to finish what he had so promisingly begun.

PART FOUR

CANTERBURY

12

GRINDAL'S HUNDRED DAYS

A<small>T</small> THE time of his death in May 1575 Archbishop Matthew Parker was approaching his seventy-first birthday, by the standard of the time an aged man and despondent. While Grindal had been otherwise engaged in the north the puritan agitation for 'further reformation' had taken a radical and, for the bishops, menacing turn. According to the pamphlet of 1572, *An admonition to the Parliament*, that bishops and their officers should take upon themselves the rule of God's Church was 'most horrible'. The very names of archbishop and bishop were 'drawn out of the pope's shop'.[1] Parker found to his dismay that political circles at Court were indifferent to this threat to the hierarchy of the Church. Finding the queen 'in constancy almost alone' offended with the puritans he was forced in his correspondence with Lord Burghley to insist that his efforts to repress the subversive writings and preaching of the presbyterians were not self-interested and to warn the politicians that what was at stake was the social order itself. 'The comfort that these puritans have and their continuance is marvellous; and therefore if her Highness with her Council (I mean some of them) step not to it, I see the likelihood of a pitiful commonwealth to follow.' 'I refer the standing or falling altogether to your own considerations, whether her Majesty and you will have any archbishops or bishops, or how you will have them ordered.' 'As for myself I care not three points.'[2] In the last year of his life he was prepared to believe on the evidence of crudely forged documents that the puritans were plotting revolution by violence, including the assassination of leading public figures. 'This deep, devilish traitorous dissimulation, this horrible conspiracy, hath so astonied me, that my wit, my memory, be quite gone.' When the forgeries were exposed it can have done his credit little good.[3]

In these last years Parker was morbidly suspicious of the Court and of courtly practices. He believed that the earl of Leicester was an enemy who 'purposed to undo' him. He suspected some of the bishops of working against him secretly 'for the satisfying of some of their partial friends'. 'The world is subtle.' When he spelt out his fears and suspicions to Burghley he added: 'I am a fool to use this plainness with you in writing.'[4] Yet on another occasion he was more unguarded still, denouncing 'this matchivel [Machiavellian] government' to Burghley who, after all, was its principal executive, and openly regretting having ever consented to serve as archbishop: 'Yea if I had not been so much bound to the mother [Queen Anne Boleyn] I would not so soon have granted to serve the daughter in this place ... I fear her Highness shall be strangely chronicled.'[5] His last recorded utterance consisted of a line of classical verse, converted into a prophecy of impending doom which he expected to follow the queen's death.[6]

In this depressed state Parker was not capable of the positive and creative policies which might have offered a more convincing response to subversive agitation. He expressed little interest in institutional or pastoral reform. Instead his preoccupation was with the traditions of his own great office and their perpetuation. 'I toy out my time, partly with copying of books, partly in devising ordinances for scholars to help the ministry, partly in genealogies, and so forth.' He planned a major new building at his manor of Bekesbourne outside Canterbury, not so much for his own satisfaction as for 'the commodity of the see'.[7] And with the help of his scholarly secretary John Joscelyn he completed a notable antiquarian work, the *De Antiquitate Britannicae Ecclesiae*, a history of the English Church seen through the careers of seventy archbishops of Canterbury, from Augustine to Parker himself. He professed some embarrassment about his 'ambitious fantasy' in decorating presentation volumes of his history with the illuminating arms of prelates living and dead.[8] A puritan pamphleteer was cruelly successful in capturing and turning to account Parker's mood and the climate of public opinion in the title he gave to a pirated version of Parker's own life out of this 'legend of Canterbury tales', the *Matthaeus: The liffe off the 70 archbishopp of Canterbury presentlye sitting Englished ... This numbre of seventy is so compleat a number as it is greate pitie there should be one more: But that as Augustine was the first, so Matthew might be the last.*[9] Such was Grindal's inheritance as the seventy-first archbishop of Canterbury.

It was on the cards that Parker would be succeeded by a metropolitan who would point the Church still more firmly in the direction of conformism and anti-puritan repression. This was to be the logic of several episcopal appointments of the late 1570s and early 1580s, culminating in the elevation to Canterbury of John Whitgift, the hammer of the puritans, after Grindal's death. In his last letter to Burghley Parker had drawn up a short list of three for the vacant and sensitive diocese of Norwich, consisting exclusively of conservative churchmen of this stamp: Gabriel Goodman, dean of Westminster (his first choice, a man of 'sad and sure governance'), John Piers, later to preside at York when Whitgift was at Canterbury, and Whitgift himself. He felt it necessary to explain that his preferences were not influenced by 'any displeasure that I bear to my lord of Leicester's chaplains'.[10] Writing to the queen soon after the demise of Parker, that 'shining star', Bishop Cox of Ely urged the need to avoid delay in appointing his successor in view of the threat posed by schismatics. He spoke of his old chaplain, Whitgift, as an 'athleta Dei fortissimus' who would repay honour by successfully coercing the Church's enemies. But Cox did not directly nominate Whitgift for the primacy, and as a senior member of the hierarchy and a sometime royal almoner he may have expected it for himself.[11] However, Cox was out of favour and Whitgift, not yet a bishop, would have been as unlikely and divisive an appointment as one of Leicester's semi-puritan chaplains.

It was far from the natural order of events for an archbishop of York to be translated to Canterbury. But in the circumstances of 1575 Edmund Grindal was the obvious choice. The fact that he shared the outlook of the more moderate puritans and was known to favour further reform rather than blind repression made him the candidate of those very forces at Court by which Parker felt threatened, including Leicester. The puritanical earl of Huntingdon, his colleague in the north, knew 'none worthy to be preferred before him to that place for many respects.'[12] Even those who were no hot gospellers may have seen the advantage of an escape from the siege mentality which had guided Parker in his later years. Most protestants of the governing class seem to have been sufficiently preoccupied with the supposed menace of popery, to the exclusion of concern about anti-episcopal, puritan propaganda. But it would be a mistake to regard Grindal's elevation as a partisan, puritan coup. The day before Parker's death Alexander Nowell, dean of St Paul's and the personification of the typical, central virtues of the Church of his day, spoke of the need to appoint in his place 'a man of great government', and advised Burghley that 'of all the clergy I think the archbishop of York to be a man of the greatest wisdom and ability to govern, and unto whom the other bishops with best contentation would submit themselves.'[13] Cox rather pointedly failed to mention Grindal in his letter to the queen written a week later. Nevertheless there is no reason to question the soundness of Nowell's analysis, which is borne out by the nearly solid support which Grindal would later receive from his episcopal colleagues, not excluding Cox, even in the depths of his disgrace. As for Burghley, whom we know to have been the 'principal procurer' of all Grindal's preferments,[14] he told Walsingham even before Nowell's letter reached him that the archbishop of York was the 'meetest man to succeed'. 'Take my proxy for my poor voice.'[15]

But although bishops and archbishops, then as now, 'emerge' by a complex and usually hidden process, and even if what we may call the secondary patronage of courtiers was often decisive, it was the queen who in the last resort made the appointment. It may be that on this occasion she was reluctant to endorse Burghley's choice. Not until six months after he had cast his 'poor voice', and was known to have done so,[16] was Burghley able to tell Grindal that 'I think assuredly her Majesty will have your Grace come to this province of Canterbury to take care thereof, and that now, at this Parliament.'[17] This letter was rushed north, arriving (if Grindal is to be believed) the day after it was written. It was then that Grindal undertook 'many conflicts with myself about that matter'; only after two weeks responding, on 10 December, with a suitable formula of disabling acceptance:

> Yet have I in the end determined to yield unto the ordinary vocation, lest in resisting the same I might with Jonas offend God, occasion a tempest etc.; beseeching God to assist me with his grace, if that weighty charge be laid upon me, to the sustaining whereof I find great insufficiency in myself.[18]

On Christmas Eve Elizabeth at last signed the *congé d'élire*.

The delay was not out of the ordinary but given the rapidity and decisiveness of Burghley's choice it provokes our curiosity. Huntingdon made a half-hearted attempt to detain Grindal in the north, but that can hardly have been the cause.[19] One motive for an extended vacancy was always the profit accruing to the Crown from the temporalities. But in all probability the queen was prejudiced against Grindal by what she knew of his churchmanship. How was her opposition overcome? One answer might be, by courtly manoeuvres better understood by those who practised them than by us. The fact that Grindal was unmarried may have helped to tip the scales in his favour. When Whitgift succeeded him seven years later it was said that Elizabeth was 'resolved to admit none but a single man'.[20] Grindal may also have benefited from his relationship, whether real or supposed, to the queen's old tutor William Grindal, for whose memory she may, for all that we know to the contrary, have entertained respect and affection. Above all it was desirable to have an archbishop of Canterbury in place before the sessions of Parliament and Convocation expected early in 1576, and which in fact opened on 8 February.

'Her Majesty told me that I had supreme government ecclesi-astical; but what is it to govern, cumbered with such subtlety?'[21] It was to Parker, not Grindal, that the queen uttered these reassuring but apparently empty words. But since Grindal too was to become the victim of courtly 'subtlety', and so soon, it is necessary to recall the hopeful circumstances with which his primacy began, con-ditions typical of the first 'hundred days' of any reformist adminis-tration which succeeds the stultifying barrenness of an ageing régime. In Burghley's letter of intimation to Grindal of his im-pending election the point was reached only after some Cecilian ruminations about the corruptions of the ecclesiastical courts and the need for some *via media* between the unacceptable face of ecclesiastical administration and puritan subversion:

And truly though I like not the unruly reprehenders of our clergy at this time, yet I fear the abuse of the ecclesiastical jurisdiction both by bishops [and] archdeacons doth give over great a cause to these stoical and irregular rovers, to multiply their invectives against the state of our clergy. And therefore I wish there was more caution and circumspection in all their canonical jurisdictions and consistories, that the exercise thereof might be directly *ad edificationem*, and not to make gain of that which was meant to punish or prevent sin.[22]

The courtier who wrote to inform Grindal of the signing of the *congé d'élire* was on the same wave-length, but less oblique and more enthusiastic in his message: so direct in fact that his letter must be reproduced in its entirety:

Your lordship's certificate directed unto my fellow and to me we have received and have made my lords understand the diligence ye have used therein, the same being the first certificate that hath been sent hither by any of your lordship's brethren. On Christ-mas Even last her Majesty signed the congé d'élire directed to the dean and chapter of Canterbury for the choosing of your lordship archbishop: It is greatly hoped for by the godly and well-affected of this realm that your lordship will prove a profit-able instrument in that calling, especially in removing the cor-ruptions in the Court of Faculties, which is one of the greatest abuses that remain in this Church of England. For that it is determined that Parliament should hold at the day prefixed, I could wish your lordship to repair hither with as convenient speed as ye may, to the end that there may be some consultation had with some of your brethren, how some part of those Romish dregs remaining in [the Church?],[23] offensive to the godly, may be removed. I know it will be hard for you to do that good that you and your brethren desire. Yet (things discreetly ordered) somewhat there may be done. Herein I had rather declare unto your lordship at your repair hither frankly by mouth what I think than to commit the same to letters. And so in the mean time I commit your lordship to God's good protection etc.[24]

But Grindal proved to be incapable of 'convenient speed'. He may have been Parker's junior by fifteen or sixteen years but he shared some of the same ailments ('the stone', particularly) and his expedition southward, like the journey to York five years before, was interrupted by illness. The dean of Canterbury had set off for London, no doubt early in January, to certify the queen and the archbishop himself of his election, and, as the chapter accounts have it, 'to meet my lord his grace'. But the chapter later doubled his expenses to cover the time spent 'attending and waiting for the coming of the said archbishop of York, which happened by reason the said archbishop was stayed by sickness'.[25] By the time Grindal reached London the parliamentary session must have been only days away and there would have been little time for political consultation. But by 19 February the new archbishop was sufficiently at home in Lambeth House to throw a party, or, in Strype's eighteenth-century term, 'a treat', attended by great numbers of the nobility and gentry.[26] It was the night before his installation and enthronement in Canterbury Cathedral.[27]

Grindal was absent from these solemnities and represented by proxy. That was the long-established custom and in no way remarkable. But what is more curious is that it cannot now be proved that Grindal ever so much as visited Canterbury as archbishop, to sit in Augustine's chair, or to preach in Christ Church, or to inspect the continuing building operations at Parker's favoured seat of Bekesbourne. In the first year there was hardly time to go down into Kent and after that year there was no longer liberty to do so. As Easter 1576 approached, the chapter resolved to present the new archbishop with twenty fat wethers 'in token of the chapter's good will at his new entry into the archiepiscopal see', 'against this next Easter'.[28] It sounds as if Grindal was expected to keep Easter in his diocese, and that this present anticipated some lavish entertainment at his expense. (In 1570 Parker had written, four days after Easter: 'I am now preparing to repair into Kent, mine own diocese, where I have not been a good while, and I am looked for.')[29] But Easter Day 1576 fell on 22 April, and Grindal's Register shows him to have been at Lambeth on the 16th and 28th, which will allow for no more than a week in Canterbury or

6 The interior of St Paul's Cathedral. A nineteenth-century impression of what had become, in Grindal's time, a general meeting place for Londoners (see page 156).

7 Archbishop Edmund Grindal, artist unknown. Grindal's arms impale those of the see of Canterbury. An inscription reads 'TURRIS FORTISSIMA NOMEN DOMINI PRO. 18' ('The name of the Lord is a strong tower, Proverbs 18:10'). This appears to be a reference to Grindal's legendary fortitude.

8 Queen Elizabeth I, c. 1575, attributed to Hilliard

9 The archbishop's house at Croydon. A nineteenth-century view of the house where Grindal died.

10 Archbishop Edwin Sandys and his second wife. This portrait, by an unknown artist, was drawn in the sitters' lifetime for Sir Edwin Sandys, the archbishop's second son. It is now at Bishopthorpe Palace.

Edwyn Sandys
A:B. 1576

Bekesbourne. In the treasurer's accounts the twenty wethers have turned into two oxen, which may indicate a change of plan.[30] In the following month of May the archbishop's visitation of the cathedral took place, but this was performed by the dean and the bishop of Dover, as commissioners.[31] In the city records one single, trivial circumstance links Grindal with Canterbury: the existence of a loan-fund, 'my lord of Canterbury's money'. Ten pounds of this money was loaned out to a certain William Collinson.[32] Nevertheless Grindal's archiepiscopate was not without incident for the ecclesiastical history of Kent. It was Grindal who took the important and salutary step of freeing the archdeaconry of Canterbury from the bishopric of Rochester with which it had previously been held *in commendam*.[33] No doubt it was his own enforced absence from the scene which prompted the archbishop to strengthen the office of archdeacon, traditionally *oculus episcopi*.

In the 'quiet and pliant'[34] Parliament of 1576 the 'somewhat' which Grindal's anonymous correspondent had asked for was at least attempted, if little enough was accomplished. In the first week of the session, perhaps within a fortnight of the archbishop's arrival in London, the bill to increase the financial penalties for non-attendance at church and to enforce participation in the communion by secular, statute law was reintroduced into the House of Lords. Grindal had been the principal sponsor of this anti-catholic measure in the previous Parliament of 1572 and he now headed the prestigious group of bishops and peers to which the bill was committed after its second reading, and which otherwise included Burghley, Sussex, Bedford and Leicester. With such a committee it could only have been the queen who prevented the matter from making further progress. New and stiffer laws against popish recusancy were to wait until 1581, when Elizabeth would temper rather than veto the protestant zeal of her parliamentarians.[35]

In late February some members of the House of Commons, led by Tristram Pistor, seized the initiative in directing attention towards such notorious and fundamental imperfections of the Church as 'the unlearnedness of the ministry, abuses of excommunication, want of discipline, dispensations and tolerations for non-residency and such like'. Since Pistor and other participants in the debate were already seasoned campaigners in the cause of religious reform, Sir John Neale not unreasonably gathered that this was the latest chapter in a radical and wholly unauthorized attempt to complete the Reformation of the Church on the puritans' terms. 'And the odds are that the clerical friends of the Presbyterian party were in the background.'[36]

However, most of the evidence is unfavourable to such an interpretation. The abuses detailed by Pistor were capable of reform within the established, episcopal constitution of the Church. There was no implication that that constitution was in itself popish. It was agreed to proceed diplomatically, by way of petition to the queen rather than by bill, and the petition was drafted by a committee which included all the privy councillors in the Commons. Although the wording of the petition was replete with zealous jargon its propositions in their substance would have commanded the assent of the great majority of those calling themselves protestant in the Elizabethan political nation. It was said that vast numbers of the queen's subjects were deprived of the preaching of the word of God, 'the only ordinary means of salvation of souls', both by the admission of great numbers of unqualified men to the ministry and by the abuses of non-residence and pluralism among the qualified. Behind the scandal of the insufficient clergy stood the lack of true 'discipline'. Pluralism and non-residence were tolerated by dispensations, excommunication was abused, sin unpunished and papists unrestrained. It was a diagnosis from which few honest, public-spirited protestant laymen would have dissented.[37] And it was entirely in harmony with the sentiments of the letter which Grindal had received from his well-connected correspondent. The same concern for grass-roots parochial reform is evidenced by a bill 'for the relief of vicars and curates' which reached its second reading less than forty-eight hours before the prorogation of this Parliament, and which in two of its surviving drafts is heavily annotated by none other than Lord Burghley himself.[38] This measure was designed to assist anyone possessed of the impropriate tithes of a parish who might feel constrained to restore all or a proportion of the income to the vicar or curate of the church. And if the vicar or curate were to be an absentee, it authorized the parishioners to withhold their tithes and to pay them to such other persons as the impropriator might present to the bishop in his place, 'to preach and teach and minister the sacraments to the people of the said parish'. Whoever drew up this abortive bill had located the very nub of the Church's pastoral debility, but showed insufficient respect for the absoluteness of property rights at common law for his measure to have any hope of success.

Meanwhile the petition arising from Pistor's initiative had been presented to the queen by a delegation of privy councillors from both houses, including Burghley and Leicester. Elizabeth's response, communicated through Mildmay, was sympathetic, even if its intention was to deflect further discussion of these matters towards Convocation, 'considering that reformation hereof is to be principally sought in the clergy'. It was almost without precedent (or sequel) for Elizabeth to declare that she intended to use her authority 'to the increase of the honour of God and to the reformation of the abuses in the Church'.[39] Her words, which were taken in an anticlerical sense which was probably not intended, made a profound impression and were long remembered by puritan parliamentarians.[40] In her statement the queen explained that she had already conferred with the principal bishops 'in the beginning of her Convocation', 'such as she thought were best disposed to reform these errors in the Church'. This is the full extent of our knowledge of what passed between Grindal and his royal mistress in his first hundred days.

The consequences were contained in the collection of thirteen articles (or canons) approved in Convocation and presently published by royal authority.[41] These articles addressed themselves to the same problems which had exercised Parliament, but for the most part by a simple underlining of established canonical procedure. Candidates for orders were to be of canonical age, were to be certified of sound religion and life, and were to provide evidence of adequate Latinity. Unless they belonged to the ordaining bishop's diocese they were to bring letters dimissory from their own diocesan and they were to enjoy a title to a benefice. Those admitted to benefices were to be sufficiently qualified. There was to be a review of preaching licences. Bishops were to ensure that the preachers within their dioceses 'do earnestly and with diligence teach their auditors sound doctrine of faith and true religion, and continually exhort them to repentance and amendment of life'. The catechism was to be taught and the homilies read. Clergy below the degree of master of arts were to be supervised by the archdeacons and their officials in the systematic study of the New Testament. There was to be no commutation of penance for money 'unless the same be done upon great and urgent causes'. Archdeacons and their subordinates were to exercise their corrective jurisdiction 'effectually'.

This was the 'somewhat' which the Parliament and Convocation of 1576 yielded, and it was not very much. By comparison with the detailed articles in which the next Parliament of 1581 rearranged the grievances of 1576[42] they did little to touch the nerve of lay discontent with the state of the Church and the ministry. In a literal sense the canons of Convocation did not speak the same language. And could the bishops and archdeacons be trusted to observe their own self-imposed standards? Whereas the canons merely reinforced procedures for the control of entry to the ministry which had been tried and found wanting, the 1581 articles of the Commons proposed novelties which would bring the practice of the English Church somewhat closer to that of other reformed churches; principally by associating learned preachers with the bishop in the public examination of candidates, and in allowing to parishes the right to object to the incumbent provided for them. Whereas the canons were silent on 'abuses of excommunication', the articles would have restored the credibility of this ultimate sanction of pastoral discipline by confining it to 'enormous crimes' and entrusting it not to lay officials but to the bishops in person, assisted by 'grave persons of calling in the Church', that is, learned preachers. And whereas the abortive articles of 1581 severely restricted the granting of dispensations by the Court of Faculties, the canons of 1576 made no mention of the subject, to which Grindal's correspondent had drawn particular attention. It is probable that the 1581 articles contained too many unacceptable innovations even for Grindal, as they certainly did for Whitgift, by then bishop of Worcester. At one point Grindal's hand appears alongside that of his successor in the critical annotations appended to Whitgift's copy of the articles.[43] But perhaps the archbishop would not have entirely disagreed with Sir Walter Mildmay (and was Mildmay the correspondent of Christmas 1575?) when he later described the 1576 canons as 'little or nothing to the purpose'.[44] The likelihood is that the queen's conference with her bishops had ensured that the canons would contain little of an innovatory character.

But in the months following the prorogation of Parliament not only Mildmay but the entire Privy Council joined in administrative action to clean up that little Augean stable, the archbishop's Court of Faculties, 'one of the greatest abuses that remain in this Church of England'. The Faculty Office provided for the national Church, within the jurisdiction of the archbishop of Canterbury, facilities for relief from the constraints of the canon law not unlike those which in the past had been provided by the papal *curia*. For the puritan conscience this popish ancestry was enough to condemn the institution out of hand. For the Admonitioners it was 'the filthy court', 'the filthy quavemire and poisoned plash of all the abominations that do infect the whole realm': which according to Thomas Cartwright was to speak 'nothing of it but that the streets and highways talk of'.[45] On more rational grounds the dispensations in which it dealt could appear a grave obstacle to effective ecclesiastical reform. And in the eyes of suspicious laymen the fees charged by the Court for its services provided the true and sinister rationale for the entire operation. In defending his right to full restitution of the temporalities of the archbishopric,[46] Grindal was to note that 'the late archbishop had many occasions of wealth the possibilities whereof are now taken away from his next successor.' In particular, by calling in Cardinal Pole's dispensations and issuing his own, Parker had made 'great sums', 'and every year after made a more profit than hereafter is convenient by admitting children to cures'. However a statement of the archbishop's likely income put the matter in proportion by predicting that 'upon reformation intended of that Court' the archbishop's revenue from faculties was likely to fall from £60 a year to £30.[47] In fairness to Parker he had reacted to earlier criticism of the Court of Faculties by declaring his own dislike of it. 'I have a long time offered in Convocation to my brethren to procure the dispatchment of this offensive court.' But he was also capable of defending it and of proposing less than radical reforms of its procedures, which were presumably intended to preserve it.[48]

Strype assumed that it was on Grindal's initiative that radical reform of the Faculty Office was now proposed.[49] Be that as it may, in form the measures were described as 'orders taken by the Lords of the Council touching faculties', and dated 20 June 1576.[50] What was involved is perhaps best described as a kind of treaty between the archbishop and the Privy Council. The document made a basic distinction between dispensations which were to be 'utterly abolished, as not agreeable to christian religion, in the opinion of the Lords of the Council', and 'dispensations left to the consideration of the Lords of the Council and by them allowed as they be here qualified'. In the first category were included faculties to hold three benefices, 'trialities', which were taxed at £9, and for more than three benefices, which were more expensive; for ordination or presentation to a benefice at less than the canonical age, for ordination in another diocese, or to take the orders of deacon and priest on the same occasion; and for marriage without the calling of banns and outside the parish church. (Years earlier this last species of dispensation had adversely affected Grindal's own family fortunes.)[51] Among the classes of dispensation 'to be considered' were licences for the bishops of the poorer dioceses to hold livings *in commendam*; 'dualities', that is, licences to hold two livings simultaneously, subject to certain conditions; dispensations for the ordination of bastards; for non-residence for a limited season 'for recovery of health and such like urgent cause'; and for exemption from fasting. In these cases the fees were to be subject to a new scale of distribution, sharing the proceeds between the queen, the lord chancellor, and the archbishop and his responsible officers. There is no evidence that the queen was involved in this reform, or even informed of it. But in January 1578, on the occasion of a controversy concerning Irish faculties, the Council caused to be 'registered and entered into the Council Book' the order 'taken and subscribed by their lordships ... with the lord archbishop of Canterbury at his first coming to that see', and took other action which implied that the order was considered to be in force. This is striking evidence of the desire of the governing class to take religious policy in hand, and of what is sometimes pejoratively described as 'lay intervention' in the Church's affairs. It must always be remembered that protestant magistrates in no way accepted the principle of their exclusion from the affairs of the Church, of which they were as properly members as the clergy. The orders bear the names of nine councillors: Bacon, Burghley, Lincoln, Sussex, Arundel, Bedford, Knollys, Croft and Mildmay. Mildmay, whose name was appended last, was perhaps the moving spirit.[52]

Meanwhile Grindal was concerning himself with the state of his remaining courts spiritual, the Court of Arches, the Court of Audience, and the Prerogative Court of Canterbury. Since he intended to reform these institutions on the basis of reports submitted by leading civil lawyers who included the judges who presided over them[53] the approach was very different from that of prejudiced and ignorant puritan criticism, although that criticism may have served to alert the archbishop to the need of reform in the first instance. What he found to be wrong was not 'popery' but professional self-interest, amounting to corrupt practice, poor service to the customer, intolerable delays. As Strype has it, the reports, which date from April and May 1576, have to do with 'justice', 'equity', and 'despatch'. The subject is one of intractable technicality and it would be inappropriate to attempt to go much beyond the opening words of the report made by Dr Yale, Grindal's chancellor, who by virtue of his office was presiding judge of the Court of Audience: 'In your Grace's Court of Audience, as in all other your courts, so things be out of order that few things be as they should be.'[54] By common consent the existing statutes of the Court of Arches were sufficient, if only they could be faithfully observed. The way forward was thought to lie in bringing these statutes up to date and extending their application, with suitable modifications, to the remaining courts which were not so well served; and especially to the Prerogative Court of Canterbury, the seat of the archbishop's testamentary jurisdiction and consequently an institution with immense capacity for both good and harm. But Dr William Aubrey, the author of the longest report (fifty-five numbered paragraphs) was responsible for perhaps the most honest of all the observations prompted by this exercise: 'I am not so able to advertise your Grace how to remedy the disease of these delays as to make them known to you.'[55] The verdict of a recent historian of the Prerogative Court is terse: 'Grindal's projected reforms did not materialize.' Whitgift was later rather more successful.[56] But 'men being men', as Parker was wont to remark, the enquiry was immediately productive of a keen contest for precedence between Dr Yale, as chancellor and official principal, and Dr Bartholomew Clark, the official of the ancient Court of the Arches.[57]

Irrepressible concern for the reformation of the Church and the repair of its pastoral institutions made the Elizabethan age a great age of abortive reform. In the event renewal of religious life, the formation of a 'godly preaching ministry' and a profoundly moral transformation of society was to come about not through legislation and the overhaul of institutions but by the religious force of protestantism itself in its apostolate at the grass roots. It was a case of:

> For while the tired waves, vainly breaking,
> Seem here no painful inch to gain,
> Far back through creeks and inlets making
> Comes silent, flooding in, the main.

Grindal's archiepiscopate was later remembered by puritans as a time of advance in the creeks and inlets of the Church. It must be a matter of opinion whether this arose from the failure of Parker's repressive policies, or through Grindal's positive encouragement, or as a consequence of the administrative confusion which prevailed in the years of his sequestration; or whether these only seemed to be green years, in contrast to the Whitgiftian régime which followed. Josias Nicholls of Kent and of Grindal's own diocese looked back to 'a golden time, full of godly fruit':

> There was such unity between the ministers, and they joined in all places so lovingly and diligently in labour: that not only did the unpreaching minister and non-resident quake and prepare themselves in measure to take pains in the Church: but also many thousands were converted from atheism and popery and became notable christians.[58]

The most important vehicle of the protestant revolution which Nicholls described was the English Bible in the Geneva version. It was from the Geneva Bible that the preachers expounded and to its text and apparatus of 'profitable annotations' that they pointed their hearers, who were learning to carry their bibles to the sermons and at home to exercise themselves and their families in its study. In the prefatorial matter the owner of the Geneva Bible was exhorted to 'diligently keep such order of reading the scriptures and prayer as may stand with his calling and state of life', a habit to be observed 'at the least twice every day'. He was to mark and consider the 'coherence of the text, how it hangeth together' and the 'agreement that one place of Scripture hath with another, whereby that which seemeth dark in one is made easy in another'. And he was to 'take opportunity to read interpreters, if he be able; confer with such as can open the Scriptures; hear preaching and to prove by the Scriptures that which is taught'. Someone in Norfolk was so far provoked by the incessant Bible-thumping as to wish to see all that carried Geneva Bibles hanged.[59]

The Geneva Bible was not printed in England for as long as Parker was alive, although it is not quite clear whether, as some embittered puritans supposed, it was deliberately suppressed.[60] But what is certain is that between Parker's death and the advent of Whitgift no less than eighteen editions were printed by Christopher Barker, the queen's printer, who also enjoyed the patronage of Sir Francis Walsingham and displayed Walsingham's device of the tiger's head outside his premises in St Paul's Churchyard. Many of these Bibles were intended for private and domestic use, but some were folios, Bibles 'of the largest volume', which can only have been intended for the lecterns of parish churches, where they would compete with the authorized Bishops' Bible. Some editions even contained a puritanical version of the Book of Common Prayer which omitted altogether such doubtful ceremonies as private baptism, confirmation and the churching of women.[61] Whether the cause of 'further reformation' prospered at Westminster or not was almost irrelevant to the onward progress of protestantization, by means such as these.

The cause of Grindal's personal disaster was his conscientious inability to take action to impede this often quiet and insidious process, not a confrontation with the queen over reform in the sense of laws and canons to change the Church. Specifically, the crisis arose from Grindal's hostile reaction to a suggestion that the number of preachers might be 'abridged' and from his outright refusal to transmit a royal command for the suppression of the learned 'exercises' of preaching and conference known as 'prophesyings'.

13

A SCRUPLE OF CONSCIENCE

THE first tremor of the earthquake which was to bring the archbishop down was felt at Lambeth in early June 1576, only five months after Grindal had taken up residence. Letters crossed the river from the earl of Leicester, from Lord Burghley, and from Sir Francis Walsingham, all bearing the same news of certain 'disorders' involving preachers in Northamptonshire and Warwickshire. Leicester's letter was the first to arrive, the queen having 'first of any' mentioned the matter to him. His message was perhaps intended as a friendly warning of what was likely to follow. Warwickshire was the earl's country and in puritan circles it was soon rumoured that it was Leicester who had betrayed them. Walsingham wrote 'by her Majesty's commandment' and Burghley supplied the names of the 'stirrers', Paget and Oxenbridge. Eusebius Paget was a deprived Northamptonshire minister, John Oxenbridge rector of the south Warwickshire township of Southam, the scene of the alleged incidents. Grindal was at once in urgent communication with the bishops of Peterborough and Coventry and Lichfield, ordering the preachers to be sent up to London, presumably to face the Ecclesiastical Commission. Summoned himself to Court to account for his stewardship, the archbishop was quick to point out to Burghley that since it was notorious that the offenders were sustained by 'some men of countenance in those countries' it was equally a matter for the Privy Council. That was a tactic in which his predecessor had grown weary.[1]

The 'disorders' in question arose from what Elizabethan protestants knew as 'the godly exercise of prophesying', as it had been practised in the midland shires. Anyone who has ever heard the name of Archbishop Grindal knows that he came to grief for refusing to suppress the 'prophesyings'. But the somewhat exotic associations of the term have often misled historians, as perhaps they misled the queen, into imagining enthusiastic and disorderly assemblies in which puritan bibliolatry held unbridled sway and a serious threat was posed to the doctrine and discipline of the Church. Grindal's sympathy for something so anarchical was sufficient to demonstrate to the satisfaction of many Anglicans of later generations his total unfitness to lead the Church of England as it faced this grave challenge to its integrity. But in reality prophesying was a sober affair. Modelled on the practice of some of the continental reformed churches, and deriving ultimately from the order of things in Zwingli's Zürich, it comprised a gathering of clergy for collective edification through the preaching of two or three sermons on the same passage of Scripture. The end served by the 'exercise' might be to educate the brethren of meagre talents, encouraging them to qualify in their turn as preachers: an open university, as it were. Sometimes the ministers sustaining the exercise were all established preachers, a circle of near equals, but subject to the authority of two or three of their seniors, as moderators. The sermons were delivered before a lay audience which, like the ministers, came in from the surrounding country to occupy a large and centrally located church, often in a market town, perhaps on market day. After the public proceedings the ministers would retire for formal 'censure' of the doctrine preached, to discuss other matters of common and professional interest, and to dine together. There were occasional excitements and upsets as men of diverse talents and backgrounds addressed their minds to controverted texts. Sometimes, as no doubt in Southam in 1576, the occasion was exploited for polemical and even subversive purposes. But the orders regulating the conduct of the prophesyings were discouraging to public disagreement and the participation of laymen was not permitted.

By 1576 this institution was very widely established in most dioceses of Grindal's province and it was soon to spread to the north. Throughout the vast see of Lincoln, in East Anglia, in Essex and many other counties, including Kent in Parker's later years, much of the population must have lived within riding distance of an exercise. The Prayer Book and Injunctions were silent on the topic of prophesying and the bishops were rarely the true initiators of these undertakings. But some bishops had approved and issued in their own names the orders which regulated them and had even taken part themselves as preachers or moderators or in other ways supported them.[2]

But to those with conservative religious inclinations or no love of religion at all the prophesyings were an irritant and a provocation. Grindal was to tell the queen: 'Only backward men in religion and contemners of learning in the countries abroad do fret against it.' The conspicuous attendance of magistrates and other men of substance made a show of protestant strength, as, for example, in Shrewsbury where the members of the Council in the Marches, when sitting in the town, were 'always present at this exercise'.[3] Since the queen had not authorized such assemblies and perhaps had no more than a vague sense of their existence, opponents of the godly party had an easy remedy to hand. Tales carried into her presence, perhaps when on progress in the counties affected, would be sure to work wonders. Bishop Cooper of Lincoln was to warn Grindal that an exercise in his jurisdiction was threatened by 'one or two of some countenances and easy access unto the prince, that have small liking to that or any other thing whereby religion may be further published'.[4]

Such incidents had occurred once or twice before the crisis of 1576. In 1574 reports of the activities of suspended puritan preachers in two of the Norfolk prophesyings had led to the issuing of a general order to all the bishops by Archbishop Parker for the suppression of 'these vain exercises'. This was at the queen's command. Yet Bishop Parkhurst of Norwich received letters from Bishop Sandys of London and three councillors (Smith, Knollys and Mildmay) which assumed that the exercises were threatened by 'some not well minded towards true religion' and required him to ensure that 'so good an help and mean to further true religion may not be hindered and stayed, but may proceed and go forward, to God's glory and the edifying of the people'. This was on the condition that no heretical or seditious doctrine could be proved to have been taught or maintained. This letter was procured by some of the Norfolk gentry who were the preacher's patrons and whom Parkhurst was loth to cross. In desperation he grasped at one word in Parker's letter and proposed to suppress only such exercises as might prove to be 'vain'. This was to pursue the strategy which Grindal would adopt in 1576: to proceed against manifest disorders but otherwise to defend the exercises 'which surely have and do daily bring singular benefit to the Church of God'. Parker's reply was tart. Parkhurst's friends had advised him to 'stand upon that word *vain*'. 'It is pity we should show any vanity in our obedience.' But soon afterwards Bishop Freke of Rochester, who was to be Parkhurst's successor, told him that nothing was known of the archbishop's order in his diocese, nor in London, but that Sandys's advice was to take action only to prevent the abuse of public controversy. 'And so by this means the exercise is continued to the comfort of God's Church, increase of knowledge in the ministry without offence.'[5]

It seems to have been a few days later that Sandys was belatedly informed of the queen's wishes in a postscript to a letter from his metropolitan: 'Because your lordship may fortune not know the queen's commandment uttered unto me, to signify that her Highness thinks it convenient that these exercises in your diocese called the prophesyings should stay, this is to declare unto you her pleasure.' But instead of acting as Parker expected, Sandys merely referred the matter to the Privy Council, 'praying to know her Majesty's pleasure herein by your Lordships'. And he reported that his diocese was quiet and orderly and that to suppress 'such profitable exercises' which enjoyed so much acceptance would breed unquietness.[6] Grindal later noted that Sandys had in effect ignored Parker's instructions, apparently on the advice of the Council.[7] A year later it was the turn of Cooper of Lincoln to adopt evasive tactics when a similar royal order reached him. He was advised by his friends at Court to dissolve the exercises 'in such sort' as he could 'conveniently'.[8]

Why did Grindal not play the same game? There were many ways of quietly thwarting the queen in which her servants were expert. If he had merely evaded her orders it is unlikely that *de facto* toleration of the prophesyings would have ended, or that he would have suffered much personal inconvenience. But Grindal did not believe that in good conscience the issue could be dodged. The queen for her part was exasperated, perhaps more so than on earlier occasions, and the letters which Grindal received from three senior councillors in June 1576 were so many signals that they could not do for him what had earlier been done for Sandys. The reports from the midlands were out of the ordinary. The puritan movement in Northamptonshire and neighbouring districts of Warwickshire and Oxfordshire tended to extremes.[9] Some deprived ministers, including Eusebius Paget, continued to preach up and down the country as 'posting apostles' and perhaps to dominate the exercises with their radical presbyterian doctrine. The Southam exercise was remote from the centres of ecclesiastical administration and an unknown quantity so far as Bishop Bentham of Coventry and Lichfield was concerned. It is significant that such an extreme puritan as Thomas Wood should have described it as 'undoubtedly without exception... the best exercise in this realm'. In Wood's correspondence with his Dudley patrons, the earls of Warwick and Leicester, it is clear that the earls feared that the excesses at Southam would bring into disrepute the whole 'cause of religion' as they knew and valued it:

> I fear the over-busy dealing of some hath done so much hurt in striving to make better perforce that which is by permission good enough already as we shall neither have it in Southam nor any other where else, and do what we can all, and those all you think more zealous than I.[10]

In the absence of the records of the Ecclesiastical Commission we do not know what was done with Paget and Oxenbridge, except that Paget's friends found him a new niche in the West Country and that Oxenbridge continued to enjoy the rectory of Southam. But the fears of the earls proved to be fully justified. When Grindal went to Court on 12 June the queen confronted him with the reports which she had received and ordered him to enquire into the matter, 'saying if it were so she would discharge them all generally'.[11] Strange as it may seem given the indelible association which events were now to establish between the name of Grindal and the prophesying movement, the archbishop may have had little direct experience of the exercises. So far as the diocese of London was concerned, prophesying had long been established in several Essex towns and in St Albans, but it was the responsibility of the archdeacons, while in London itself the favourable pastoral situation made the practice unnecessary. And in Grindal's time there were few exercises in the northern province, except in the virtually autonomous archdeaconry of Nottingham.[12] On returning from Court Grindal wrote to the bishops of the province, calling for factual and evaluative reports. Sandys responded with alacrity, thinking that Grindal intended to deal with the queen in the matter before her departure on summer progress. By 9 July he was able to forward detailed and favourable reports from his archdeacons, backed up in the case of St Albans by letters from the magistrates of the town and the schoolmaster. Bishops more remote from the centre replied more tardily, and aged Bishop Guest of Salisbury as late as 15 December!

Of the fifteen bishops whose replies are known,[13] only four, Cox of Ely, Scory of Hereford, Guest of Salisbury and Hughes of St Asaph, were hostile, Cox's peremptory note contrasting with the detailed reports of the favourable bishops: 'To what end your questions tend I cannot tell. This I can tell: the world is full of new fangles and fancies ... Execute severely the orders which are already established.'[14] Eight were in favour of the exercises.[15] It is noticeable that from all the dioceses where the practice was strongly entrenched the reports were positive, and for the most part prompt and richly informative. Cooper of Lincoln, Bentham of Coventry and Lichfield, Curteys of Chichester and Bradbridge of Exeter were eloquent in their support.[16] Bradbridge told how his predecessor, Alley, had encouraged the exercises, taking pains 'to travail in the work himself'. He himself took the part of moderator 'if I be nigh to the place':

Many gentlemen and other zealous desire the continuance.

Great profit groweth thereby, I do persuade myself, for that I see the people delight to hear and gladly do resort, the clergy become studious in the tongues and grow ripe in the Scriptures.

He considered their continuance 'right necessary, and for that it is a monument of the like practices holden in the primitive Church', in proof of which he proceeded to quote Tertullian. 'And surely there is no danger in this work if ambition may be excluded and prevented.' Grindal had an analysis made of these letters, which would have been helpful if episcopal opinion had counted for anything in the Elizabethan scheme of things.[17] But the queen's attitude to such presumption was expressed in a memorandum later composed in justification of Grindal's deprivation: 'A thing not sufferable that any shall set up any things in the Church without public authority: neither hath the bishop such power.'[18]

It would later be argued on the queen's behalf that prophesying was a case of *adiaphora*, 'not of necessity to be used'. It was not used in Edward VI's time, nor in many reformed churches overseas, nor 'in christian churches many hundred years'.[19] Grindal set out to prove the contrary, that it was a necessary institution, marshalling his scholarship and that of his chaplains in the composition of a learned treatise on the subject, perhaps prompted by Bishop Bradbridge's appeal to the example of the primitive Church. Many folios survive,[20] containing the sources for a large-scale 'tractatus de exercitiis', planned in four books and culminating in the case for retention: 'Quod prophetia sit retinenda'. The material consists of the comments and glosses of theologians ancient and modern on relevant places of Scripture, of which the most germane was St Paul in 1 Corinthians 14: 'But he that prophesieth speaketh unto men to edifying, and to exhortation, and to comfort… Let the Prophets speak, two, or three, and let the other judge' (Geneva version). It was necessary to establish that the prophesying of which the apostle spoke was interpretation of the Scripture, not prediction of the future, 'which gift is not now ordinary in the church of God', and that it was an ecclesiastical resource instituted for all time, not an exceptional and miraculous grace granted to the apostolic Church. Ambrose, Augustine, Chrysostum and Jerome jostle with Thomas Aquinas, Erasmus, Zwingli, Calvin, Peter Martyr and Beza. The hand is that of a secretary or chaplain, with Grindal's pen frequently intruding. Precedents ranged from the ministry of Christ himself in the Temple to an otherwise unrecorded episode of the first year of Elizabeth's reign: a disputation held with certain 'Pelagians' (or 'free will men') in Grindal's house beside St Paul's in the presence of the citizens of London, which had contributed to the speedy extirpation of that heresy. The conservatism of the scholarship is implicit in the total absence of any historical sense of anachronism, the 1560 episode sharing equal status with a similar case recorded in the fourth century by Eusebius of Caesarea.[21]

The last of the defensive posts which Grindal hammered into place was a collection of 'Orders for reformation of abuses about the learned exercises and conferences amongst the ministers of the Church'.[22] These had the effect of subjecting the prophesyings to close and effective episcopal surveillance, as to places and times, arrangements for moderation, the names of the participating speakers and the parts of Scripture to be expounded. The non-preaching clergy were to be set written tasks which were to be discussed privately among the ministers. And 'ante omnia, that no lay person be suffered to speak publicly in those assemblies'. The moderators were not to tolerate any words spoken against 'any state, or any person public or private', or 'any invection against the laws, rites, policies and discipline of the church of England established by public authority'. Speakers so offending were to be barred from the exercise until readmitted by the bishop's approbation. The last of the orders closed the stable door against the participation of suspended and deprived ministers such as Paget and the other 'posting apostles'.

All this proved to be so much wasted ink and effort. When Grindal returned to Court with his report the queen did not want to listen to him. His letter later referred to 'the speeches which it hath pleased you to deliver unto me', not to anything which he may have said to her. According to an account of the affair, probably composed by Sir Walter Mildmay, Elizabeth was by now 'so incensed' against the exercises that 'down she would have them', and Grindal was commanded to proceed against them by his own authority.[23] We do not know whether this second interview took place in the summer of 1576 or as late as December, when most of the episcopal letters had come in. In his letter to the queen Grindal referred only to what was said 'when I last attended on your Highness'. The matter is of some consequence and affects the view we are likely to take of what now followed. If Grindal's letter was his response to an order already some months old his action was magnificent but it was not war, still less diplomacy. But if Elizabeth had very recently confirmed her peremptory command then perhaps he had no choice but to meet his mistress head on, in deliberate confrontation. This is the most likely order of events, if only because we should not expect the archbishop of Canterbury to have been absent from the Court for half a year. Nevertheless the letter was no hasty and intemperate improvisation of the kind which Archbishop Parker had regretted as soon as it was sent,[24] Rather it reads as a measured statement which had matured over the months and, in a sense, from the beginnings of the queen's reign. In length it runs to more than 6,000 words, a veritable 'book to the queen' as contemporaries knew it.[25]

Grindal addressed himself initially to the queen's orders, 'those two articles then propounded', which seem to have concerned not only the 'utter suppression of all learned exercises and conferences among the ministers of the Church, allowed by their bishops and ordinaries', but more vaguely the 'abridging' of the number of preachers, the queen having expressed the opinion that three or four were sufficient for a shire, leaving the remainder of the clergy to read the common prayers and the homilies. On this point Grindal administered a schoolmasterly reproof:

> But surely I cannot marvel enough, how this strange opinion should once enter into your mind, that it should be good for the Church to have few preachers. Alas, Madam! is the Scripture more plain in any one thing, than that the gospel of Christ should be plentifully preached; and that plenty of labourers should be sent into the Lord's harvest; which, being great and large, standeth in need, not of a few, but many workmen?

After citing a number of biblical precedents and texts Grindal reminded the queen of the two great purposes served by preaching. 'Public and continual preaching of God's word is the ordinary mean and instrument of the salvation of mankind ... By preaching of God's word the glory of God is enlarged, faith is nourished, and charity increased.' In the second place preaching planted in the hearts of subjects due obedience to christian princes and magistrates. 'For obedience proceedeth of conscience; conscience is grounded upon the word of God; the word of God worketh his effect by preaching. So as generally, where preaching wanteth, obedience faileth.' This sounds like a current proverb, and indeed it was proverbial wisdom among protestants that loyalty and obedience were active qualities, to be aroused by the lively preaching of the word of God; whereas Queen Elizabeth found more safety in passive conformity and submission. Grindal hoped that recent history might serve to make his point. London, with 'continual preaching', overflowed with loving loyalty. The ignorant north had risen in rebellion. Yet even in the north protestant Halifax had sent three or four thousand men into the field to serve the queen against the rebels.

But the queen should not imagine that her bishops had entrusted the delicate and onerous responsibility of preaching to the unworthy and insufficient. 'We admit no man to the office that either professeth papistry or puritanism.' Normally only graduates were licensed, 'unless it be some few which have excellent gifts of knowledge in the Scriptures, joined with good utterance and godly persuasion'. Grindal himself had procured more than forty learned preachers and graduates to serve in the diocese of York in the six years which he had spent there. God forbid that the queen should hearken to the hostile critics of preaching who were either religious conservatives, 'mislikers of the godly reformation in religion now established', or 'altogether worldly minded', bent on serving not God but Mammon. Homilies had their uses. 'It is an old and a true proverb, "better half a loaf than no bread".' But 'if every flock might have a preaching pastor, which is rather to be wished than hoped for, then were reading of homilies altogether unnecessary'. This was one homily which made no impression. Eight years later Elizabeth would assure Grindal's successor and other bishops that there was more learning in one of the homilies than in twenty of some of their sermons.[26]

Grindal then moved to the second and major issue, which he was careful to define as 'concerning the learned exercise and conference amongst the ministers of the Church', only introducing the word 'prophesy' in Latin, in the context of a careful exposition of terms 'very odious in our days to some, because they are not rightly understood'. The root of the matter was in 1 Corinthians 14: 'St Paul also doth make express mention that the like in effect was used in the primitive Church, and giveth rules for the order of the same: as namely, that two or three should speak and the rest should keep silence.' 'The ground of this or like exercise is of great and ancient authority.'

> I have consulted with divers of my brethren, the bishops, by letters; who think the same as I do, viz., a thing profitable to the Church and therefore expedient to be continued. And I trust your Majesty will think the like, when your Highness shall have been informed of the manner and order thereof; what authority it hath of the Scriptures; what commodity it bringeth with it; and what incommodities will follow if it be clean taken away.

According to Mildmay's account of the affair, there was a further ground for Grindal's resistance to the royal command, namely 'that his authority would not stretch so far by law', since every bishop had 'the proper and only power himself within his diocese over all such causes'.[27] But this dubious doctrine has no place in the letter.

What did follow was a measured but defiant statement, the heart of the letter and as it were the pivot of the writer's entire career:

And for my own part, because I am very well assured, both by reasons and arguments taken out of the holy Scriptures and by experience (the most certain seal of sure knowledge) that the said exercises for the interpretation and exposition of the Scriptures and for exhortation and comfort drawn out of the same are both profitable to increase knowledge among the ministers and tendeth to the edifying of the hearers: I am forced, with all humility, and yet plainly, to profess that I cannot with safe conscience and without the offence of the majesty of God give my assent to the suppressing of the said exercises; much less can I send out any injunction for the utter and universal subversion of the same. I say with St Paul, 'I have no power to destroy, but to only edify'; and with the same apostle, 'I can do nothing against the truth, but for the truth'. If it be your Majesty's pleasure, for this or any other cause, to remove me out of this place, I will with all humility yield thereunto and render again to your Majesty that I received of the same... Bear with me, I beseech you, Madam, if I choose rather to offend your earthly Majesty than to offend the heavenly majesty of God.

Strype was moved by this passage to exclaim: 'O episcopus vere apostolicus!' And there will be few who will read Grindal's spirited words without a sense of admiration that they were uttered. The dismissive remark of a later historian of the Elizabethan Church, himself a bishop, appears cruelly insensitive: 'a particular piece of characteristically puritan crankiness'.[28] However it was not so much 'puritan crankiness' as respect for ancient precedent which disposed Grindal to end his letter with 'two short petitions', couched in words of that most apostolic of bishops, St Ambrose of Milan, as they were recorded in certain letters addressed to the Roman emperors of the late fourth century, the great Theodosius and Valentinian II. For a peroration with which to round out a rhetorical exercise on the theme of the integrity of the Church the voice of Ambrose was almost too apt. Theodosius had been instructed that there was nothing in a bishop 'so perilous before God or so disgraceful before men as not to speak his thoughts freely ... You are imperilled by my silence, you are benefited by my freedom. I am not an officious meddler in matters outside my province, intruding myself in the affairs of others. I am doing my duty, I am obeying our God's commands.'[29] Grindal had found the ecclesiastical counterpart to Peter Wentworth's rhetoric of parliamentary free speech and in the ears of Queen Elizabeth such sentiments could only add insult to the injury already administered by the archbishop's disobedience. They were echoes of a polity foreign to Tudor England, with its adulation of godly princes and its royal supremacy, a constitutional fact which Grindal had acknowledged in offering himself for deprivation. In the days of Ambrose it could be said that 'palaces belong to the emperor, churches to the bishop'; and that as christians even emperors were within the Church, not above it. It was not like this in Elizabeth's realm.[30] In adopting Ambrose as his model, in set-piece confrontation with the imperial purple, Grindal had little sense of the anachronism he was perpetrating. The memorial to his magnificant folly, once as it were a keg of dynamite, reposes on the shelves of the Library of the Queen's College Oxford to which he later bequeathed it: his own copy of the Erasmian edition of the *Opera* of Ambrose, in the Basle impression of 1538.[31]

Grindal was only an occasional annotator of his books. The numerous observations entered in the margins of his copy of the Epistles of Ambrose are exceptional and are matched only by his annotation of the chapter on the duties of bishops in Martin Bucer's *De regno Christi*.[32] The implication is clear. The citations in the letter to the queen had a more than decorative purpose. Ambrose had inspired the letter in the first place and had provided the epistolary models. Grindal *was* Ambrose, and Elizabeth Theodosius. The 'book to the queen' in its very form was an Ambrosian oration, making of 'prophesying' an issue in church–state relations equivalent to those disputed claims to basilicas which had exercised the bishop of Milan in the fourth century. The marginal notes show how Grindal's obstinate mind was impelled by this great father of the Church in an adventurous direction. In his reading of Erasmus's dedication of the edition to John à Lasco he noted that Theodosius had been praised for suffering himself to be subdued, 'vinci', by Ambrose. From Epistle 40 Grindal gathered that it was the part of bishops freely to declare their minds: 'speculatores, non adulatores', watchmen, not flatterers; from Epistle 21 that priests were to be judged by priests; from the sermon of Ambrose preached in the midst of the 'battle of the basilicas' three pregnant words — 'Imperator filius Ecclesiae' — and from Ambrose's account of the episode sent to his sister in Letter 20 three more — 'Imperator Deo subditus'.[33] One minor mystery remains. Grindal made a particular note of the fact that Ambrose had written Epistle 51 with his own hand, 'manu mea', so that Theodosius alone might read it, 'ut solus legas'.[34] The words are quoted in the letter to the queen. Yet the copy endorsed and filed by Burghley[35] is not in Grindal's hand and bears no signature, and indeed no holograph or autograph copy of the letter survives.

To return to the letter itself: the first of the two petitions for which the voice of Ambrose was borrowed was to the effect that Queen Elizabeth should follow the example of all godly christian emperors and princes in referring ecclesiastical matters touching religion or church doctrine to the bishops and divines of her realm. 'If you consult your ministers in matters of finance, it is surely more fitting that you should consult the bishops of the Lord on matters of religion.' That was Epistle 40, to Theodosius, but rendered for the benefit of an erudite queen in the original Latin, as were all of Grindal's quotations. Here he had noted in the margin of the *Opera*: 'Causa religionis episcopi consulendi.'[36] 'What will happen next if a bishop is to be instructed by a layman? ... In a matter of faith, I repeat, it is the practice for bishops to judge christian emperors, and not emperors bishops.' This passage, which Grindal had marked out in the original context with especial emphasis, had been uttered to the young Valentinian who, under the influence of his mother Justina, had presumed to arbitrate between Ambrose and a rival Arian bishop, after Ambrose had refused a demand to surrender church property to the Arians 'with a deferential but categorical refusal'.[37]

The second petition was that in matters of faith and religion or touching the Church Elizabeth 'would not use to pronounce so resolutely and peremptorily, *quasi ex auctoritate*, as ye may do in civil and extern matters'. 'Remember, Madam, that you are a mortal creature. "Look not only (as was said to Theodosius) upon the purple and princely array, wherewith ye are apparelled; but consider withal what is that that is covered therewith. Is it not flesh and blood? Is it not dust and ashes? Is it not a corruptible body, which must return to his earth again, God knoweth how soon?"' This was to trespass on still more dangerous ground. For Grindal was here freely adapting the account given by the church historian Theodoret of the oration made by Ambrose when he excommunicated Theodosius and obliged him to do penance after his massacre of the inhabitants of Thessalonika.[38] But the final words were Grindal's own. And if not precisely puritanical their flavour was that of the Reformation, not patristic. God had blessed Queen Elizabeth with great felicity for many years. But let her not impute these benefits to her own deserts. The only reason was the goodness of the cause of true religion which she had set forth, and the sighs and groanings of the godly in their prayers, 'which have hitherto, as it were, tied and bound the hands of God, that he could not pour out his plagues upon you and your people, most justly deserved':

Ye have done many things well; but except ye persevere to the end, ye cannot be blessed. For if ye turn from God, then God will turn away his merciful countenance from you. And what remaineth then to be looked for, but only a terrible expectation of God's judgments, and an heaping up of wrath against the day of wrath?

Strong and tactless language. But did Grindal in his Ambrosian role dethrone Elizabeth, or at least deprive her of her ecclesiastical supremacy? Did he depart significantly from the Tudor tradition of reverent non-resistance to the christian emperor, the doctrine of John Jewel and John Foxe which would cast such a long shadow over the century to come? According to Jewel: 'Constantine called the Council of Nicaea. Theodosius the First called the council at Constantinople... Continually, for the space of five hundred years, the Emperor alone appointed the ecclesiastical assemblies and called the councils of the bishops together.'[39] Foxe made Constantine the hero of his great story and the hinge of his scheme of church history (the scheme of the Apocalypse, its mysteries revealed to him, lying in bed one Sunday morning): 'A singular spectacle for all christian princes to behold and imitate, and worthy of perpetual memory in all congregations of christian saints', prototype of Elizabeth as deliverer of God's people in a line which began with Moses. 'No less beneficial was his godly care also in quieting the inward dissensions and disturbance within the Church, among the christian bishops themselves.' According to Foxe, Constantine was the son of a British princess, and it was none other than Ambrose, in his funeral oration over Theodosius, who began the rumour that his mother Helena was in fact nothing but a common inn-keeper's daughter.[40]

In a sense Grindal subscribed to, even reinforced this christian imperial ideology. That after all was the point of casting Elizabeth as Theodosius, whose claims to be revered as a founder of christian empire was as worthy as Constantine's. Christian emperors and christian bishops were meant to complement one another. Grindal had not refused to obey the royal order suppressing the prophesyings: he had merely declined to lend his person and office to the transmitting of it. He had not defied the queen from a perch of 'popish' independence of the temporal power, and certainly he had not as much as threatened to excommunicate her. He acknowledged that he owed his office to her appointment and he offered to surrender it back into the hands which had bestowed it. But the Ambrosian model suggests if not a recasting of the royal and episcopal roles another set of stage directions from those to which

Elizabeth and still more her royal father had been accustomed. Grindal noted from Ambrose that he was to defer to emperors, not to yield to them.[41] If he was not claiming to be a bishop *iure divino*, like some Anglican bishops who would later make such a claim, he believed that fathers of the Church had a duty, under the royal supremacy, to order ecclesiastical affairs according to their understanding of the divine will.

Queen Elizabeth never received such another letter as this, and with good reason. The 'problem of counsel', how to convey unwelcome truths to princely ears hard of hearing, had long been debated, and if the debate had produced agreement on any one thing it was that mere prophetic utterance was not enough. That much Sir Thomas More, the author of *Utopia*, never doubted.[42] 'Hold your tongue', Sir Thomas Elyot repeated as a monotonous refrain in his essay on the same problem, published in a sensitive year of the reign of Elizabeth's father, 1532.[43] Not long after Grindal's letter was written a Dutch divine and man of affairs had occasion to issue this warning to an English correspondent:

> I cannot refrain from saying that the way to pacify kings is not to oppose them, or announce by writings, signatures or remarks that one does not approve their doings. It is necessary to be humble, or at least to hold one's tongue. You know why I say this and there is no need of longer discourse.[44]

What then are we to conclude? That Grindal was deaf to the wise voice of policy, taking his stand on a robust churchmanship which had emancipated itself from politics? Or that in writing his letter he was not in the business of pacifying but of coercing the queen? Or had he concluded that he lacked all leverage within the situation so that his sole remaining concern was to preserve the integrity of his own conscience? The events of the months and years which followed the perpetration of this bombshell of a 'book' will shed some light on this problem without entirely dispelling it.

Grindal's letter was taken to Court by the earl of Leicester. If he knew its contents and did nothing to prevent it reaching the queen's eyes then this was not the least ambiguous of Leicester's friendly offices to the archbishop. But perhaps the letter was not delivered to the queen immediately. More than a week after he had sent it on its way Grindal was like a man who has lit a fuse and waits in vain for the explosion. He told Burghley on 16 December that he did not yet know whether the queen had read his letter, 'much less whether she like or dislike of it'.[45] This remark had a naivety not present in the letter itself, unless indeed it was made disingenuously. Within the next twenty-four hours word came from both Leicester and Burghley. Leicester had a compromise to propose. Would Grindal consent to the exclusion from the prophesyings of the popular element, converting the meetings into learned exercises of the ministers only?[46] It would be widely assumed in the years to come that it was chiefly the presence of 'the people' which had rendered the prophesyings obnoxious, and sometimes it was suggested that the royal ban did not extend to purely clerical conferences. Francis Bacon was one of those who later reported that 'the only reason of the abuse [in prophesying] was because there was admitted to it a popular auditory, and it was not contained within a private conference of ministers.'[47] But Grindal closed off this way of escape. 'I see no reason why the people should be excluded, seeing St Paul giveth so great commendation to that which was used in the primitive Church; especially for the benefit that groweth thereby to the hearers.'[48] After this there was no hope. Probably the queen had no knowledge of Leicester's diplomatic initiative. And perhaps she still knew nothing of the letter. But Burghley's endorsement of his copy with the date '20th December' suggests that it was then and no earlier that the decision was taken, perhaps with reluctance, to reveal its contents to her.[49] At least one other privy councillor, Sir Walter Mildmay, preserved a copy which resembles Burghley's closely and which equally carried the heading 'To her Majesty, 20mo Decembris 1576'.[50]

Still nothing happened. For five months no action was taken against the archbishop, while the business of the province proceeded without interruption. On 8 March a notable event was recorded in the chapel at Lambeth: the formal confirmation of the election of Grindal's boyhood companion Edwin Sandys as archbishop of York. Two weeks later John Aylmer was consecrated bishop of London, and in mid-April John Whitgift bishop of Worcester. Grindal presided at all these ceremonies, which determined the leadership of the Church of England in the years of his eclipse and beyond.[51] In the early months of 1577 he continued to promulgate the inhibitions and commissions relating to his metropolitan visitation of various dioceses and cathedral churches.[52] The injunctions of Bangor Cathedral survive and include instructions for a preaching roster of the kind which Grindal had earlier established in York Minster. These are dated 25 February.[53] On 30 January normal and seasonal procedure had been followed in forwarding to the earl of Sussex, as lord chamberlain, a list of names for the preachers of the Lenten sermons at Court, Grindal 'praying your lordship to understand her Majesty's pleasure therein and to certify me of the same by this bringer'.[54]

But the atmosphere was menacing. On 27 February Burghley

thanked Grindal for a letter and 'other writing concerning the reformation of the exercises amongst the ministers'. This may have contained the archbishop's 'Orders for reformation of abuses about the learned exercises', which have already been noticed. On these matters Burghley proposed further consultation, through 'any of your advised chaplains'. But the archbishop was warned to stay away from Court. 'I could be content your coming to speech with her Majesty were delayed a while longer, and to that end I wish my lord of Leicester were your intercessor, to excuse your absence by reason of your sickness. This I wish for your respects, and yet I refer the order to yourself.'[55] Last-ditch efforts were being made to rescue Grindal from the consequences of his letter, while other parties were perhaps exploiting it to bring about his undoing.

By early May the battle had been lost. In April drafts had been made of a royal letter to the bishops, containing a tendentious account of the prophesyings as 'a certain public exercise or (as they call it) prophesying, by certain persons pretending a more purity, by the manner of the doing whereof evil effect hath ensued in some places, to our grief, among the unlearned sort, easy to be carried with novelties'. The bishops, 'forthwith, upon the receipt hereof', were to take express order throughout their dioceses for the suppression of 'all such prophesying', and they were to inform the Privy Council of the places where prophesying was held, and of the names of the participants and of any disregarding the queen's order; 'and what you shall have done herein from time to time'.[56] The draft of a version of this letter intended for the bishop of Lincoln suggests that there may have been a plan to write to every bishop, or to certain bishops, individually, naming the places where prophesying was known to have occurred.[57]

This was peremptory but perhaps not sufficiently peremptory for Queen Elizabeth. On 7 May Burghley endorsed and annotated the draft of a wholly different royal letter which embodied a more rounded but even more hostile account of prophesying as a social institution. It spoke of 'assemblies of a great number of people, out of their ordinary parishes and from places far distant, and that also of some of our subjects of good calling (though therein not well advised), to be hearers of their disputations and new devised opinions upon points of divinity, far unmeet for vulgar people'. This 'manner of innovations' brought the vulgar sort to idleness and bred schismatical division within towns and parishes and even in families, to the breach of common order and the offence of 'all other our quiet subjects': 'whereof the sequel cannot be but over-dangerous to be suffered'. This was to stand Grindal's argument about obedience ('where preaching wanteth obedience faileth') on its head. The bishops were to make sure that no services or rites were to be 'in any sort used in the Church' beyond those established by law. Preaching was to be confined to duly qualified and licensed persons, 'conformable to the ministry in the rites and ceremonies of this Church of England'. Others were to read the public homilies. As for the prophesyings, 'for that the same are not nor have been appointed or warranted by us or our laws', the bishops were to cause them to cease forthwith. They were to imprison any who infringed the order, informing the queen or the Council of their names and those of their 'maintainers and abetters': 'that thereupon, for better example, their punishment may be made more sharp for their reformation.' The bishops were to so conduct themselves that the queen would not be forced 'to make some ensample in reforming of you according to your deserts'. There was no more arbitrary exercise of the royal supremacy in the history of the Church of England than this. The letter went out over the royal signet on 7 May. The copy received by Whitgift as bishop of Worcester survives.[58] The order was later said to have been obeyed in Grindal's own diocese and peculiars.[59] If so it helps to clarify his position as one not of simple disobedience but of passive resistance in the matter of the promulgation of the queen's mandate.

Some time in May, probably towards the end of that month, Grindal was formally sequestered and confined as a virtual prisoner to Lambeth House. The order seems to have been taken after the archbishop had made an appearance before the Council, and, in spite of persuasion, had refused to retract: 'a second offence of disobedience, greater than the first'.[60] The text of the order of sequestration (if text there ever was) has not survived and its terms are uncertain. But the archbishop's register suggests that its principal effect was to render invalid any of those written instructions which would normally be issued over his own hand and seal. The first registered evidence of an abnormal state of affairs belongs to 1 June when Dr Yale, as official principal and vicar general, issued in his own name a commission for the metropolitan visitation of the cathedral and diocese of Salisbury and of the archdeaconry of Dorset.[61] Yale continued to act in this special and unusual sense as the archbishop's vicar until November 1577, when he took to his deathbed, Grindal informing the Privy Council that he was 'so dangerously sick as there is no help of his recovery'. In response to his request, the archbishop was now authorized to choose 'two sufficient persons' to take Dr Yale's place as presiding judges of the Court of Audience 'with all other things incident to Dr Yale's office ... until further order shall be taken in that behalf by her

Majesty'. Grindal accordingly appointed Dr William Drury and Dr Lawrence Hussey by his own commission as auditors of the Court of Audience, vicars general in spirituals and officials principal.[62] But on 20 January he was informed by Mr Secretary Wilson that their places as vicars general were to be taken by Dr William Aubrey and Dr William Clark. After legal advice had been sought, Aubrey had been nominated by the queen, Clark by the Council. Both were to occupy jointly during her Majesty's pleasure the office described at one point in the register as 'the vicarageship of the archiepiscopal see of Canterbury'. From September 1581 Aubrey appears to have acted alone in the execution of this office.[63]

Sequestration was intended by Elizabeth as only the first step. No sooner was the sentence imposed than she set in train a more radical process for his dismissal from office. The ostensible motive, as reported by Walsingham to Burghley on 31 May 1577, was doubt whether the proceedings of those acting under the archbishop's seal were 'of validity', 'in this time of sequestration'. Walsingham had been told to write to two ecclesiastical and civil lawyers, Dr Lewyn and Dr Dale, ordering them to examine the patents of appointment of the archbishop's officers; and also to confer with the principal law officers of the Crown 'touching the order is meet to be had in the deprivation of the said archbishop.'[64] In reality we may suspect that the reason for these moves was that the queen's anger with her recalcitrant archbishop was of an intensity which could only be appeased by his removal from the great office to which she had elevated him. This was a personal animus which Walsingham and Burghley in their private and discreet exchanges deplored. At the end of May Walsingham had bad news from overseas to share with Burghley and with his mistress:

> But yet it worketh not that effect, to make her stay her proceeding against the archbishop (which at this time, howsoever he hath offended, were in true policy most requisite), a matter that doth greatly grieve as many as truly love her Majesty.

Burghley had a sour comment: 'I think the persons appointed to consult for deprivation of the archbishop shall be much troubled to find a precedent.'[65]

But it was something more than the prospect of dubious precedents and legal tangles which deterred these two most senior members of Elizabeth's régime. Both were agreed, or professed to agree, that the threat to the archbishop was a threat to the security of the queen and of the realm because it offered a challenge to the divine benevolence on which safety depended. 'Thus my good

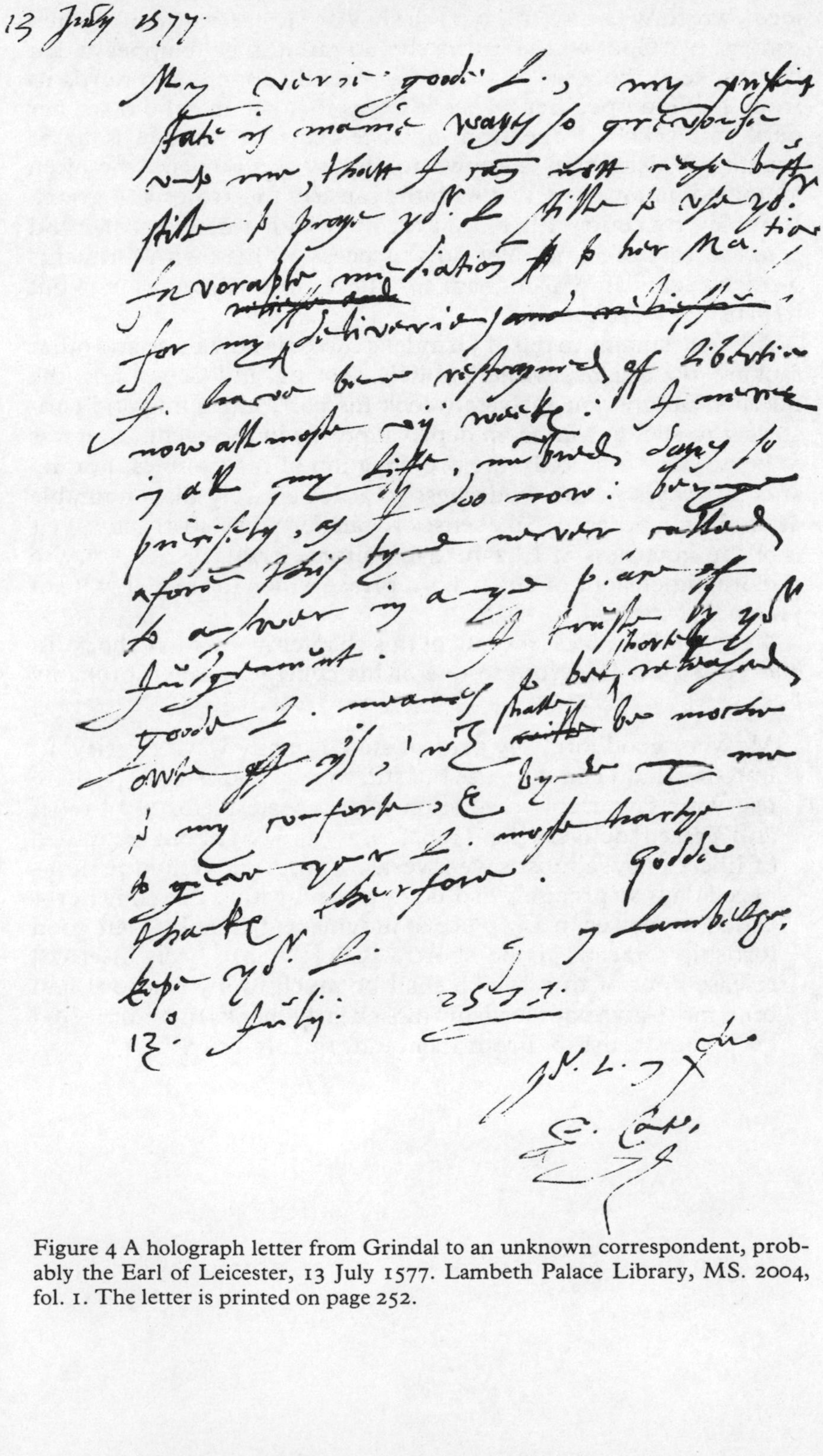

Figure 4 A holograph letter from Grindal to an unknown correspondent, probably the Earl of Leicester, 13 July 1577. Lambeth Palace Library, MS. 2004, fol. 1. The letter is printed on page 252.

lord', wrote Walsingham, 'you see how we proceed still in making war against God: whose ire we should rather seek to appease that he may keep the wars that most apparently approach towards us from us. God open her Majesty's eyes that she may both see her peril and acknowledge from whence the true remedy is to be sought.' Walsingham is known to history as a puritan who often identified national interest with the cause of the protestant gospel. Burghley by contrast has been credited with a more secular and *politique* cast of mind. Yet on this occasion his own sentiments were an echo of Walsingham's: 'These proceedings cannot but irritate our merciful God.'

All that remains to tell of Grindal's career is how these and other ranking politicians, while publicly sharing and expressing the queen's indignation, privately took his part, intriguing and conspiring to shelter him from deprivation. So in the event there was to be no dismissal, only the prolongation of his troubles, leading after six years in the wilderness to a not entirely dishonourable death. But in order to make sense of a tangled story, instructive as it is of the innerness of Elizabethan politics, it will be necessary to explore dimensions of Grindal's disgrace which the reader will not yet have suspected.

We leave Grindal at the end of this chapter in a state of shock. In mid-July 1577 he wrote to one of his courtly patrons, probably Leicester:

> My very good lord, my present state is many ways so grievous unto me that I cannot cease but still to pray your lordship still to use your favourable mediation to her Majesty for my ['relief and' erased] delivery ['and relief' erased]. I have been restrained of liberty now almost seven weeks. I never in all my life numbered days so precisely as I do now: being afore this time never called to answer in any place of judgment. I trust by your good lordship's means to be shortly ['shortly' has been inserted] released out of this, which shall be much to my comfort, and bind me to give your lordship most hearty thanks therefore. God keep your lordship. From Lambeth, 13 July 1577.[66]

14

POLICY AND INTRIGUE

HITHERTO the narrative has assumed that Grindal's disgrace and sequestration arose simply from his act of conscientious disobedience. But in the view of early Elizabethan annalists this was not the real reason, or at least not the only reason for his troubles. No less an authority than William Camden alleged that it was by 'the cunning artifices of his adversaries' that the archbishop forfeited the royal favour:

> as if he had countenanced the conventicles of some turbulent and hot-spirited ministers and their prophecies (as they called them); but in truth because he had condemned the unlawful marriage of *Julio*, an *Italian* physician, with another man's wife, while *Leicester* in vain opposed his proceedings therein.[1]

Other writers followed this lead and embroidered the story, which was a requisite part of the early seventeenth-century legend of Grindal's immovable constancy.[2] Sir John Harington in a gossipy character book of the Elizabethan bishops knew nothing of the prophesyings but had 'heard by some (that knew somewhat in those days) that [Grindal] kept his house upon a strange occasion, the secret whereof is known to few, and the certainty is not easy to find out, but thus I was told ...' In Harington's version the '*Italian* doctor' becomes the bigamist, against whom 'this good archbishop' took resolute legal action. The physician's patron, 'some great lord' whom Harington chose not to name, wrote to Grindal asking him 'to stop the proceedings, to tolerate, to dispense, or to mitigate the censures'. But the archbishop proving 'still unmoved and unmovable' the queen was induced to intervene, whereupon 'this *John Baptist*' not only persisted in his judgment against the doctor but in a reverent fashion required her to give an account of her faith, since she had advocated a course expressly against the word of God: which the queen might have yielded if the same great lord had not dissuaded her and so incensed her against the archbishop that he was privately commanded to keep his house.[3] In due course Thomas Fuller in his more weighty and authoritative *Church History of Britain* cited as evidence of Grindal's impartial judicial rigour his 'sharp reproving of Julio, the Italian physician, for marrying another man's wife; which bitter but wholesome pill the physician himself not being able to digest, incensed the earl of Leicester, and he the queen's Majesty against the good archbishop. But all was put on the account of Grindal's nonconformity for favouring the factious meetings called prophesyings.' Fuller suspected a still more hidden motive. Leicester had covetous designs on Lambeth House, as Ahab had for Naboth's vineyard and, as we may recall, Christopher Hatton for Bishop Cox's Ely Place.[4] Still later Peter Heylyn made the possession of 'his goodly house and manor of Lambeth' the main issue in the breach between the archbishop and 'that mighty favourite'.[5]

In spite of the general atmosphere of informed hearsay at which Harington hinted it is likely that all these reports have a single origin in the libel published against the earl of Leicester in 1584, known since the seventeenth century as *Leicester's Commonwealth* and described not unreasonably by Sir Francis Walsingham as 'the most malicious written thing that ever was penned since the beginning of the world'. Harington, who continued to aim his poisoned darts at Leicester long after he was dead, confessed to having read the libel, and in sufficiently embarrassing circumstances. Leicester himself caught him at it, in the tiltyard at Greenwich, and asked him what he was reading. 'I blushed and (God forgive me for lying) I answered they were certain Cantoes of Ariosto.'[6]

In the course of probing into the alleged circumstances of Leicester's marriage to the widow of the earl of Essex the author of *Leicester's Commonwealth* found an intriguing parallel in the marital trials of Dr Julio, and perhaps more than a parallel, since he insinuated that it was by 'Italian art' and through 'an Italian recipe' that Essex had met his end.

> You must think that Dr Dale will dispense in that matter as he did (at his lordship's appointment) with his Italian physician Dr Julio, to have two wives at once: at the leastwise the matter was permitted, and borne out by them both publicly (as all the world knoweth) and that against no less person than the archbishop of Canterbury himself, whose overthrow was principally wrought by this tyrant for contrarying his will in so beastly a demand.

This was called Leicester's 'intolerable tyranny upon the last archbishop of Canterbury for Doctor Julio his sake'.[7]

Unless we are to believe all the wilder charges made in this sensational book we may decide to reject the story of Dr Julio out of hand, having traced it to this tainted source. However, that the court physician Giulio Borgarucci had married a woman who was already in some sense another man's wife, and that Leicester had an interest in the case as the friend and patron of 'Dr Julio,' are facts for which there is independent testimony. According to Strype, the case had lingered in the courts for years before it reached Archbishop Grindal and had concerned the Master of the Rolls and, in 1573, a commission of delegates presided over by Bishop Sandys of London. That the distinguished civilian and dean of Wells Dr Valentine Dale was willing to give judgment for Julio, and that Grindal intervened to determine the case the other way seem also to be matters of more than hearsay.[8] On 4 December 1576, in the very week that Grindal composed his 'book' to the queen, Julio wrote to Leicester, complaining of the 'hard dealing' of the archbishop's vicar general, Dr Thomas Yale, and of the archbishop himself, who 'had sworn I should never obtain this gentlewoman I have married, nor enjoy her'. Accordingly Yale had gone back upon his word and was handling the case partially. With the advice of his learned counsel Julio invited Leicester 'to be so good and gracious' that 'with her Majesty's favour' he might have impartial justice.[9] It may stretch credibility too far to suggest that the response to this plea was effectively to deprive the archbishop of Canterbury of his power to function, not only in this case but in the totality of his jurisdiction. Yet when on 31 May of the following year Walsingham and Burghley exchanged news on the queen's intention to proceed to Grindal's deprivation Burghley had the following titbit of information to impart:

> In the evening after that we had delivered to the archbishop her Majesty's message I understood that Mr Julio had that morning told a doctor of the law what should be done. So as I see he was more of her Majesty's counsel than two or three that are of present Council.[10]

'They that will beat a dog shall want no weapon.' That was a proverb which Leicester could quote against himself.[11] The earl had many enemies of whom the author of *Leicester's Commonwealth* was merely the most publicly damaging. Professor Trevor-Roper considers that Camden's dislike of the earl was sufficient to distort his otherwise impeccable historical judgment.[12] At this very time the puritans themselves were doubting Leicester's integrity and were suspecting him of duplicity in the matter of the prophesyings.[13] As early as February 1578 the rumour was abroad that the earl had furthered the archbishop's troubles.[14] But although Leicester's behaviour was not always free from ambiguity we cannot disregard the securely documented fact that he was Grindal's 'intercessor' at Court, nor suppress our knowledge that he was publicly identified with the progressive protestant cause, at home and abroad, which was equally Grindal's cause and that of his well-wishers. Giulio Borgarucci may have been Leicester's physician and intimate[15] but he was also the queen's physician with access to her chamber.[16] Moreover he also tended the health of that rising star in the courtly firmament of the late 1570s, Christopher Hatton. In 1573 he had accompanied Hatton on an extended visit to the Spa, just as he later attended Leicester when he took the waters at Buxton, and he sent the queen regular reports on her current favourite's progress.[17]

So was it the Italian connection with Hatton which was at the root of Grindal's troubles? It is possible. The transcriber of a copy of the archbishop's letter to the queen thought that she had been 'moved by Hatton and some other' to restrain the number of preachers and to put down the exercises.[18] The godly had as much cause to suspect Hatton as papists had to resent Leicester and there is no doubt that as Hatton advanced, as courtier and statesman, he carried with him those conformist forces in the Church which in the 1580s were to conduct an anti-puritan campaign which satisfied the queen but which was unacceptable to almost all leading members of the protestant governing class, Hatton alone excepted. Their leaders were the three bishops, John Aylmer, who was Hatton's client, John Whitgift, to whom he gave invaluable encouragement, and Richard Bancroft, his chaplain and on occasions his speech-writer.[19] If Hatton was Grindal's hidden enemy in the Court (and there is no positive evidence that he was) it would make all the more significant the later success of Bishops Cox and Aylmer in persuading him to become the archbishop's advocate.[20]

The general truth to be extracted from these ultimately impenetrable details is that Grindal was the victim not simply of a specific issue of conscience but of courtly intrigue. His fall was recognized to be a portent of reaction against the progressive protestantism which he symbolized, at a time when protestant and conservative, even crypto-catholic forces were in contention for the mastery, at Court and in the direction of domestic and foreign policy. The policies favoured by the leading progressive politicians, those of the Leicester–Walsingham axis, were coherent and grounded on a protestant world-view which saw the active restraint of a popish, antichristian conspiracy as an urgent necessity, if the safety of the queen and the security of the realm were to be preserved.[21]

At home the times required the promotion of protestant religion through preaching and effective discipline, backed by the repression of native catholics; abroad the securing of Scotland against the queen's enemies, solidarity with those 'of the religion' in France, and, above all, a policy of creative intervention in the volatile politics of the Low Countries, underwriting the Prince of Orange and the protestant cause. The conservative forces were passively or actively opposed to these ideologically motivated policies: either on grounds of rational rejection of the protestant political analysis, or through some measure of participation in the contrary, catholic interest. The prevailing atmosphere was one of intense mutual suspicion, and of crisis. Within the next ten years the crisis would mature through a series of political sensations: the queen's abortive marriage negotiations with the French prince, the duke of Anjou; the entry of the first Jesuit missionaries into England; the draconian anti-catholic penal laws of 1581; the assassination of Orange in 1584, and in England the reaction to that event in the Oath of Association; the beginnings of open hostilities with Spain; the execution of Mary Stuart. Each of these events tended to resolve the issues of the time in favour of England's historic role (as it would appear to generations still to come) of the elder child and champion of protestant Europe. But the queen's personal conservatism and disinclination to respond as her ultra-protestant subjects responded to apparent threats promised to complicate, if not to frustrate, the otherwise ascending protestant cause. So the factional struggles in the Court may have concerned the affairs of such trivial people as Dr Giulio Borgarucci, but even these trifles bore upon what has been called 'a political and military watershed in European history'.[22]

The Grindal affair has not hitherto been recognized as a step along this, the main road of Elizabethan history. But contemporaries were aware of its general coherence with the great issues of the day. In January 1578, for example, the veteran Sir Francis Knollys, already a superannuated figure in the Council but, as the queen's remote cousin, a privileged one, summed up the agenda for the benefit of Secretary Wilson:

> The avoiding of her Majesty's danger doth consist in the preventing of the conquest of the Low Countries betimes; secondly, in the preventing of the revolt of Scotland from her Majesty's devotion unto the French and to the queen of Scots; and, thirdly, in the timely preventing of the contemptuous growing of the disobedient papists here in England.

Also, if the queen would be safe, she must 'comfort the hearts of those that be her most faithful subjects, even for conscience sake' — the godly. 'But if the bishop of Canterbury shall be deprived, then up starts the pride and practice of the papists ... And then King Richard the Second's men will flock into Court apace and will show themselves in their colours.'[23] 'King Richard the Second's men' served as useful shorthand for the 'flatterers and parasites' whom Knollys and his kind suspected of creeping into the queen's bosom. As Burghley's brother-in-law Henry Killigrew wrote in April 1578 to the godly William Davison, the queen's ambassador in the Netherlands: 'Her Majesty hath some that do mar more in a day than all her godly councillors and servants can persuade in a week.'[24] Of course it was no part of protestant policy that the archbishop of Canterbury should write to the queen as he had written. That was an impolitic letter and its theme was the radical incoherence of politics, 'civil and extern matters', and religion, 'matters that touch the Church of Christ'.[25] But once Grindal fell victim to his own conscience, and perhaps to more sinister forces, it became an important consideration of protestant policy to save him from the worst consequences of his action: partly for fear of the depressing effect of his deprivation, symbolically, on the hearts of the queen's most faithful subjects; partly for fear of the actual damage which such an event would do to the fabric and well-being of the Church and to its sister churches. Consequently, Grindal's fluctuating fortunes, especially in the first year of his disgrace, provide a kind of index of the state of the political and ideological struggle in courtly circles. It seems to be no accident that news about them occurs in the correspondence passing between London and the Netherlands, which was otherwise preoccupied with the greater cause of Dutch liberties, and with the prospects for English intervention.

Some of these letters were written by a certain Edward Cheke, who seems to have been acting as Grindal's secretary but who was impatient to join his cousin Davison in the Low Countries. On 8 August 1577 Cheke reported from the Court at Richmond that he was in daily attendance 'about my lord's business, and do forward it so much as possibly I can by the means of my best friends, because I would most gladly be with you'. Leicester and Hatton had assured him that 'it shall take end very shortly.' The queen had been so troubled with Dutch and French affairs that this had been 'the only let of my lord's cause'.[26] A fortnight later Henry Killigrew, a prominent official of puritan sympathies, advised Davison that the archbishop had been released from house arrest. 'My lord of Canterbury is at liberty to go where he will.'[27] Grindal was now free to commute between Lambeth and Croydon, but seems to have made no attempt to retreat into his diocese, as disgraced bishops might have done in earlier times. On 19 September Cheke hoped for early release from his 'long travail': 'for before I go home from the Court I am surely promised to have my lord's liberty, which once had I come over with all speed. I presume the more because my lord of late hath had some enlargement and her Majesty since well pacified.' In the same letter he included a report that Leicester was to go over as general of all the forces which the queen would send into the Low Countries. 'This is his full determination, but yet unknown unto her Highness.'[28]

In October Grindal made the first of many formal requests to the Council to be 'means for me to her Majesty to receive me again into her gracious favour', and acknowledged his particular debt to the earl of Leicester 'who hath from the beginning most carefully and painfully travailed for me to her Majesty'.[29] As the autumn moved on into November he was 'put in assured hope of liberty'. But then arose 'a sudden contrary tempest' and it was appointed that he should appear before the Council in the Star Chamber at the end of the month.[30] We know from a remarkable account of these events, almost certainly composed by Sir Walter Mildmay and surviving among his papers,[31] that the queen had communicated her pleasure that on his appearance Grindal should either 'confess himself faulty for refusing to do her commandment in that kind' or else 'receive his deprivation'. The very phraseology expresses the impatience and lack of legal finesse with which Elizabeth consistently approached the problem. When the Council assembled for this purpose on two successive days, 29 and 30 November, they were supported by the judges and charged 'to hear and determine certain matters between her Highness and the archbishop of Canterbury'. There can be no doubt that the queen supposed that it was possible to dismiss her archbishop there and then, without further ado.

But as we learn from the Mildmay memorandum, the Privy Council had previously met at the house of Sir Nicholas Bacon who, as lord keeper, would be obliged to preside at the formal hearing in the Star Chamber. The stark alternatives presented by the royal message needed discussion before the councillors found themselves confronted by a recalcitrant archbishop, in public and flanked by the judges. Mildmay himself made a speech in which he called the proposed procedure 'a very strange course'. Grindal did not have benefit of counsel. No formal commission had been issued for the examination of the cause or for the proceedings envisaged, nor was it clear that the Council had any jurisdiction in such a matter. In effect, Mildmay complained that a crude administrative solution was being applied to a most complex problem of jurisprudence. He suggested that it was necessary to know in advance whether Grindal was likely to confess himself to have offended or not, and he made his point with a striking reference to the popularity of the archbishop's cause: 'For otherwise if he should be brought into the face of the Court and there stiffly maintain his doings he desired them to consider what might thereupon follow, the people addicted to the matter as they were.' It was concluded that Mildmay and Sir Ralph Sadler should go to Grindal to persuade him to confess himself at fault, or to require him to appear in the Star Chamber to undergo deprivation.

While Mildmay and Sadler set off for Lambeth, Burghley sent his own private message through the dean of Westminster, with detailed information about the procedure likely to be followed in the Star Chamber and advice on how the archbishop should conduct himself.[32] He would be told, in public, that his many private expressions of regret for having offended the queen and his pleas for forgiveness were not enough. He must approve the queen's proceedings, praise her as a prince whose doings were invariably above reproach, and condemn her critics. 'And in this point the archbishop should do well to use the more large speech, as in good reason he may do without offence of his conscience.' More briefly, or such was the implication of Burghley's counsel, he was to acknowledge his fault, crying pardon. 'If the archbishop would consider hereof, and set down in writing his answer, or the sum thereof, that it might be seen aforehand, it is thought that thereby some good might follow.'

But Grindal was equally unmoved by the advice of his old patron and friend, and by the visit of Mildmay and Sadler. The two councillors found him 'so settled in his opinion as before he would yield himself guilty he would be torn in pieces with horses'. Such extravagant language was foreign to Grindal and may have been Mildmay's gloss on the archbishop's resolute refusal to offer what was required:

> for his conscience did assure him that they [the prophesyings] were necessary and he was able to prove it by Scripture and by example of other reformed churches that they were so needful among the people, and he was fully persuaded never to find mercy at God's hands if he should confess the contrary.

He was sorry to have incurred the queen's displeasure, he was content that his lands, life and goods should be at her disposal, and he would 'most willingly appear at the day appointed before the lords in the place beforesaid'. Mildmay returned with a written statement which elaborated this stand: 'The humble submission of Edmund, archbishop of Canterbury, to the lords of her Majesty's Privy Council in Star Chamber.'[33] This protested that his noncompliance was a matter not of wilful refusal but of conscience, and that it implied no more than his own inability to be made the 'chief instrument' of the royal will and meant no condemnation of those who were of contrary judgment. Far from complaining of his six-month restraint and sequestration he acknowledged that the queen could have dealt with him more severely, but professed that his greatest grief was the loss of her favour. He again begged the Council to be a means for his rehabilitation. There was no endorsement of the queen's actions, no acknowledgment of the infallibility of her judgment, above all no confession of fault, no plea for pardon. Moreover, in continuing to ask the Council to use its mediating offices, Grindal failed to recognize it as a tribunal before which he must answer and tactlessly drew attention to the possibility of a policy difference between the queen and her closest advisers.

Apparently Grindal had chosen to be a kind of martyr. If he had kept his appointment with the Council in this frame of mind only technical and procedural difficulties could have stood in the way of his deprivation. But his old enemy 'the stone' intervened, and on two successive days, the last in November, he was too ill to make his appearance in the Star Chamber. This was more than a diplomatic illness but given the uncertain mood of the Council it was highly convenient. Perhaps even the queen did not find it inconvenient. Sir Nicholas Bacon told the assembled company on the second day that the council had received a royal message to the effect that 'she would not proceed against any man, the cause being never so just, the party himself absent.'[34] So perhaps Elizabeth had been bluffing after all, and had only wanted the public spectacle of the archbishop's self-abasement. Copies of two speeches prepared by Bacon for use in the Star Chamber survive in more than one collection of the lord keeper's oratory. Both betray some sense of unease in a statesman famous for his rhetorical powers. In a short statement made on 30 November,[35] Bacon explained the queen's unwillingness to proceed against the archbishop in his absence, warned the company to disperse with dutiful minds, and then admitted, in effect, where the sympathies of many present might lie:

> Some no doubt are apt enough to marvel why her Majesty should so proceed against him. But if it were as well known to you as to my lords here present what reasons her Highness had to lead her hereunto I should not need so many words in this matter.

But according to an account of his speech in Mildmay's papers[36] some words were used, to the effect that Grindal had been 'accused of great and weighty causes neither in secret nor by any private person, but by magistrates, judges, men of good calling and bishops, and that both by letters and messages'. This passage is absent from two identical copies of what Bacon purportedly said.

The second speech, elements of which seem to be conflated with the first in Mildmay's account, was perhaps prepared for this occasion and not used, or just possibly it was delivered if and when Grindal eventually appeared in the Star Chamber in the following term.[37] In it Bacon addressed himself to the archbishop directly. He vindicated the queen's actions, after she had been informed by bishops and judges of the 'great inconveniences and disorders' occasioned by the prophesyings. Without the queen's intervention 'it was like that religion, which of his own nature should be uniform, would against his nature have proved milliform, yea in continuance nulliform, specially in rites and ceremonies and some-time also in matters of doctrine.' He next spoke of the disobedi-ence of Grindal, 'her principal minister in those causes', which had been compounded by a subsequent refusal to yield to the reason-able persuasions of the Council 'to condescend to perform this her Majesty's commandment': 'whereby you committed a second offence of disobedience, greater than the first.' This was Bacon at his vigorous best. But instead of coming to a climax with a warning to the archbishop to expect to 'receive deprivation' if he failed to confess his fault the speech ended with reflections on the many delays in the hearing, 'partly by reason of your own infirmity, partly by her Majesty's greater business, partly by the adjourn-ment of the term, and sometime the absence of councillors'. Hav-ing then considered that there were probably aspects of the case which he had neglected to mention he offered to hand over to other councillors. From Bacon it was, or would have been, a broken-backed performance. But Mildmay's account implies that Grindal never did appear in Star Chamber to hear this or any other speech, 'but from that time forward he remained in his house as prisoner, continuing in his opinion ...'

The queen was not amused. On 29 January Killigrew reported to Davison that 'the bishop of Canterbury is now more like to be deprived than *at the first*.'[38] A week before this Mildmay had dated a series of notes of matters which might be dealt with in a mem-orandum 'touching the archbishop of Canterbury in the matter of the exercises'.[39] This paper reflects an official rather than personal viewpoint, in justification of the queen and her 'disposition in religion' and in condemnation of the archbishop for defending an institution for which there was neither necessity nor sure pre-cedent: 'a thing not sufferable that any shall set up any things in the

Church without public authority. Neither hath the bishop such power.' The most telling and menacing element in the memorandum related to the matter of conscience. Since prophesyings were of the nature of *adiaphora* rather than an essential part of the religion it was 'no matter of conscience to disallow them'. Burghley was absent from Court at this time and Walsingham was ill,[40] which may explain why Mildmay rather than the lord treasurer or secretary was employed to sketch out an argument which may have been intended to justify Grindal's deprivation.

The next day, 23 January, Sir Thomas Wilson informed Burghley that the queen was 'much offended with the archbishop, and disliketh our darings for dealing with him so at large, whom her Highness would have deprived for his contempt committed'. Wilson had told her that 'a deprivation of an archbishop cannot be done so soon' and had warned her that Grindal was likely to ask for benefit of law, appoint counsel and contest the issue, 'whereby the matter will grow long before it be decided'. (Since Grindal had never shown any preparedness to defend his office and in his original letter had offered to surrender it this may have been disingenuous.) Wilson hoped that on his return to Court Burghley would succeed in persuading the queen to 'take that course which is more safe, more easy, and as honourable as the other, which is his resignation'.[41] And indeed Elizabeth must have been overruled for there was to be no more talk of deprivation. On 22 February Killigrew could report that 'there is hope that the bishop of Canterbury shall do better and better daily' and coupled this with a rumour that the Council had resolved to despatch the earl of Leicester to the Low Countries with 10,000 men. 'I would this were a true prognostication.' But God was able to defend his own cause 'against the expectation of the wise politiques of this age'.[42]

Cheke had advised Davison in a postscript to one of his letters: 'You should not do amiss to remember Mr Hatton when you send over.'[43] In the spring of 1578 it occurred to at least one of Grindal's well-wishers, Bishop Cox of Ely, that salvation might lie in that quarter of increasing influence. For Christopher Hatton had been elevated to the office of vice-chamberlain, admitted to the Privy Council and knighted, all in the closing months of 1577. Cox had already addressed the queen directly and eloquently on Grindal's behalf on two occasions.[44] To Bishop Aylmer he expressed his concern, 'if by any means we may possibly help our brother. Ye know the man to be wise, zealous and godly.' His own efforts had met with no success. But Aylmer had praised his patron Hatton (no friend in the past to Cox) and Cox was prepared to believe that 'he is the man that ye write of.'

I pray enter into consideration with me. In case Mr Vice-Chamberlain could by any prudent means mitigate and assuage her Majesty's displeasure I am persuaded that he should do God high honour and her Majesty very good service, deserve at the hand of those that be zealous and godly infinite thanks and win their hearts forever.[45]

This was as much as to incite Hatton to poach for allies and clients in Leicester's godly preserves.

Hatton duly responded to this prompting, for within eight weeks Grindal wrote him an especially effusive letter of thanks:

Although your long and instant travail to her Majesty for my benefit is not yet come to such fulness of effect as you desire and I have long wished for, yet do I think myself especially bound to give you most hearty thanks, and that in as ample manner as if I presently enjoyed the fruition of the end of my suit.[46]

It was a case of so near and yet so far. According to the earl of Huntingdon, writing in the same month of May 1578 to Dean Hutton of York and quoting verbatim from his informant:

My lord of Canterbury did stand now at this present upon his delivery by the good means of Mr Vice-Chamberlain, and now at this present the bishops of Durham and York have written to her Majesty of such sects and puritans that is in those countries that hath made a stay of his deliverance.[47]

More intrigue! Barnes of Durham and Sandys of York were on bad terms with both Huntingdon and Hutton and Huntingdon was doubtless prepared to believe the worst of both of them. But he further reported that Sandys had cleared himself by explaining that in a letter to the queen he had reported two isolated instances of inflammatory puritan preaching, one of them at Hull, but had otherwise written of the increase of popery in his diocese. 'By this I see some sparks have flown abroad.'[48] That left Bishop Barnes, whom we know to have been no friend to Grindal, nor Grindal to him. The enmity dated from Grindal's time in York, when Barnes was his suffragan bishop of Nottingham. Grindal suspected him of corrupt careerism and attributed his elevation to a cynical move on the part of Hutton and Sir Thomas Gargrave. 'Ye two commended him to be rid of him, and now Simon is as good as Peter.'[49] But Barnes was Burghley's man[50] and in February 1578, when Grindal's deprivation was still very much on the cards, he wrote to his great patron in self-defence against what he assumed to be a damaging report that he did not 'have a good mind to the archbishop of Canterbury in the time of his trouble'. He also found it politic to explain to the queen's first minister why on a recent visit to London he had avoided a call at Lambeth House, having been warned 'by those I will obey' to keep clear. Finding attack the best means of defence Barnes was unsparing in his criticism of the archbishop for 'his wilfulness and contending with the regal majesty, and obstinacy in not yielding to that which your honours set down'. Making obedience dependent upon 'conscience' was reminiscent of 'the malapertness of brainless men' in their conventicles (puritans) and smelt of anabaptism. So Barnes had not feared to declare 'in defence of my gracious sovereign' and of the Council that the occasion of Grindal's troubles was his own wilfulness and undutifulness. But Barnes was exceptional and seems to have found himself at odds with the prevailing opinion that the archbishop had been 'cruelly dealt withall and had not deserved to be straitened'.[51]

tie deus noster admonet,signis cœlestibus,prophetarū præceptis,uisionibus etiam
peccatorē uult nos intelligere, quo rogemus eū,ut pertubatiōes auferat,pacē uobis
imperātibus seruet,fides ecclesiæ & trāquillitas perseueret,cui prodest Christianos
& pios esse imperatores.Certe uis probari deo:omnis rei tēpus,ut scriptū est: Tem
pus,inquit,faciēdi dñe.Et tempus beneplaciti deus.Tūc offeres, cū sacrificādi acce   Psal.118
peris facultatē,quādo hostia tua accepta sit deo.Nōne me delectaret habere grati   Psal.68
am imperatoris,ut secundū uoluntatē tuam agerem, si causa pateretur? Et simplex
oratio sacrificiū est, hæc ueniā refert, illa offensionē, quia hæc habet humilitatē, illa
contemptū.Dei enim uox est,quod malit ut fiat mandatū eius quàm deferatur sa
crificiū.Clamat istud deus,ad populū Moyses annūciat,ad populos Paulus prædi   Osee.6
cat.Id facito quod intelligis in tēpore plus placere. Misericordiā inquit malo quàm   Mat.9 & 12
sacrificiū.Quare non illi magis sint Christiani qui peccatū condemnant suū,quàm
qui defendere putāt? Iustus enim in exordio sermonis accusator est sui.Qui se accu   Prouer.18
sat cum peccauerit iustus est,nõ ille qui se laudauerit.Vtinam imperator etiam an
te mihi potius credidissem quàm consuetudini tuæ:dum puto quod cito ignoscis,ci
to reuocas,ut sæpe fecisti,& tu præuentus es,& ego non declinaui quod cauere non
debuerā.Sed gratias domino qui uult seruulos suos castigare ne perdat. Istud mihi
commune est cum Prophetis,& tibi erit cõmune cum sanctis.An ego Gratiani pa
trem non oculis meis præferam? Debent ueniā sancta alia pignora tua . Dulce mi
hi nomen antetuli, quibus amorem communiter detuli. Amo, diligo, orationibus
prosequor.Si credis sequere.Si inquā credis,agnosce quod dico.Si non credis,igno
sce quod facio in quo deum præfero. Beatissimus & florentissimus cum sanctis pi
gnoribus fruaris tranquillitate perpetua imperator Auguste.

　　　　Diui Ambrosii ad Theodosium imperatorem uindicari iubentem in
　　　　episcopum & Christianos qui synagogam incenderunt, uehementer
　　　　eum ob hoc arguentis,atᵭ ut aliam epistolam dictari iubeat, & quod
　　　　prius iussum fuerat emendet,exhortantis,　　Epistola.　　XXIX

CLemētissimo principi ac beatissimo imperatori Theodosio Augusto,Ambro
sius Episcopus.Exercitus semper iugibus ferè curis sum imperator beatissime,
sed nunquam tanto in æstu fui quanto nunc, cum uideo cauendū ne quid sit quod
ascribatur mihi etiam de sacrilegij periculo.Itaque peto ut patienter sermonem me
um audias. Nam si indignus sum qui à te audiar, indignus sum qui pro te offeram,   *offerre*
cui tua uota,cui tuas committas preces,Ipse ergo non audies eum quem pro te au
diri uelis? Non audies pro se agentem,quem pro alijs audisti? Nec ueteris iudicium
tuum, ne cum indignum putaris quem audias , indignum feceris qui pro te audia
tur . Sed neque imperiale est libertatem dicendi negare, neque sacerdotale quod
sentiat non dicere. Nihil enim in uobis imperatoribus tam populare & tam amabile
est,quàm libertatem etiam in ijs diligere qui obsequio militiæ uobis subditi sunt. Si
quidem hoc interest inter bonos & malos principes, quod boni libertatem amant,   *differētia inter*
seruitutem improbi. Nihil etiam in sacerdote tam periculum apud deum,tam tur   *bonos & malos*
pe apud homines, quàm quod sentiat non libere denunciare. Siquidem scriptum   *principes*
est: Et loquebar de testimonijs tuis in conspectu regum, & non cõfundebar.Et ali   Psal.118
bi: Fili hominis speculatorē te posui domui Israel, in eo inquit, ut si auertatur iustus   Ezech.3
à iusticijs suis & fecerit delictum quia non distinxisti ei, hoc est,non dixisti quid sit
cauendum, non retinebitur memoria iusticiæ eius, & sanguinem eius de manu tua
　　　　　　　　　　　　　　　　　　　　　　　　　　　　　　exquiram

Figure 5 Grindal's annotation of what modern scholarship knows as Epistle 40 of
St Ambrose, in his copy of the 1538, Basle edition of the *Opera*, preserved in the
Library of the Queen's College, Oxford. See page 243.

15

OUR ENGLISH ELI

'I NOTHING doubt but in time her Majesty, who of her own nature is inclined to deal graciously with everybody, will see her error.' So wrote Sir Francis Walsingham in May 1580, to comfort not Archbishop Grindal but Lord Burghley, who was receiving 'hard measure'. Walsingham reminded Burghley of 'the late afflictions and crosses' which he himself had endured. Not long before this the earl of Leicester had been disgraced by the news of his marriage to the widow of the earl of Essex and wrote: 'Her Majesty I see is grown into a very strange humour, all things considered, toward me.'[1]

With the weathercock of Elizabeth's favour turning now this way and now that it should not surprise us if little more was done to persuade her to 'deal graciously' with her obstinate primate. After Hatton's intervention no major initiative seems to have been exercised upon his behalf for some time. In November 1578 Grindal wrote again to the vice-chamberlain to renew what he called 'my old suit unto you for the continuance of your honourable intercession for me', but, as we must presume, without effect.[2] In February 1579 he told his old friend Dean Hutton that 'my case dependeth long, as you see', and referred to some recent discouragement. 'And yet, if a man may believe court promises, I was at no time so near an end of my troubles as this present.'[3] The archbishop continued to address regular appeals to the Privy Council. One such petition, 'to be means for me to her Majesty for my liberty and restitution to her Majesty's favour', dates from 30 March 1580 and refers to an earlier approach on 23 January in the same year. Between these two petitions 'occasion of sickness and other accidents' had intervened to prevent the active prosecution of his suit.[4]

In January of the following year, 1581, with the first parliament since 1576 assembled at Westminster and most bishops in town the queen may have had wind of their intention to present petitions on the archbishop's behalf as members of Convocation. According to Sir Walter Mildmay, the day before Parliament met, 16 January, Bishop Whitgift 'was by the queen sent unto him', doubtless with new persuasions to confess his fault, 'whose answer I never understood'.[5] It must have been in connection with this démarche that a new form of submission was devised by Whitgift and his ally John Piers, the bishop of Salisbury, and sent to Grindal on 21 January. This formula was carefully tailored to fit both the occasion and the narrow measurements of the archbishop's conscience. It placed the best of constructions on the motives of all parties: the archbishop, whose 'offence began rather of some scruple of conscience'; the queen, who 'did nothing but with the advice and allowance of certain bishops, his brethren' and who 'had herein a sincere and godly meaning'; the bishops, some of whom had found the prophesyings 'more hurtful than profitable'. Nevertheless it contained a retraction. Grindal was to express himself sorry for offending the queen in not executing her command and in proof of his essential obedience Elizabeth was to be informed of the implementation of her order in the archbishop's own diocese and peculiars.[6] Strype, who saw another copy of this document without endorsement or date, placed it in 1582, assuming that it represented a submission which Grindal actually made. This enabled him to explain a minor puzzle of the archbishop's register. On 20 January 1583 (although Strype dated the entry 'new style', 1582) Grindal issued in his own name a commission to visit Lichfield Cathedral.[7] Coupled with evidence which in fact has no bearing on the matter that from September 1581 Dr Aubrey occupied solely the office of vicar general,[8] a development which he also placed in the supposedly critical year of 1582, this suggested to Strype that Grindal's submission had the desired effect, 'and that from henceforth our archbishop had his sequestration taken off, and was restored to the exercise of his ecclesiastical jurisdiction'.[9]

In fact there is no reason to think that Grindal made a submission in the terms proposed by the future archbishops, Whitgift and Piers, or that his sequestration was ever formally lifted. In effect the Church of England was bereft of normal metropolitan leadership for the full six years which elapsed between Grindal's initial suspension and his death. The principal impact was felt through his absence from those settings and great occasions which most required his participation. In his place the bishop of London presided over the Ecclesiastical Commission,[10] and when Convocation met in 1581 the presidency of that assembly devolved on the same bishop.[11] Aylmer also assumed responsibility for the appointment of court preachers,[12] reminding us that it must have been at Court that the archbishop's absence would have been particularly noticeable, and scandalous. At the 1581 Parliament the archbishop of York took precedence, but Whitgift made an impression which implies that his advancement to the primacy was already anticipated.[13]

But Grindal was not totally detached from the business of this Parliament, since his hand occurs along with Whitgift's in the annotation of the major programme of church reform advanced by the House of Commons on this occasion.[14] Noting the concern expressed by these articles for the reform of excommunication and its restriction to genuinely 'enormous crimes', Strype suspected that the 1581 Convocation was equally occupied with the reform of ecclesiastical discipline and that Grindal was responsible for arousing this concern, presumably exercising his influence from the sidelines. 'The handling of this weighty subject of *excommunication*, which had been so abused hitherto ... was owing in a great measure to our archbishop, who earnestly recommended the consideration and reformation of it to this synod.' Strype thought he also 'contributed his pains' to the equally salutary business of the reform of public penance in the context of ecclesiastical discipline.[15] His evidence was in a number of documents in the Petyt MSS.[16] Grindal would certainly have approved of the general tendency of these drafts. Excommunication was to be preserved as a genuinely spiritual and rigorous penalty for grave sins by creating a new and distinct offence of contempt of ecclesiastical jurisdiction and providing a special procedure for dealing with it. And the pronouncement of excommunication was to be reserved to the archbishops and bishops in their own persons, 'with such assistance as shall be thought meet, as it was wont to be in the primitive Church'. But all these papers appear to belong to Archbishop Bancroft's time and relate to proposals to legislate in the late Elizabethan and early Jacobean parliaments and convocations. 'A form of penance devised by my lord himself'[17] may well be of Grindal's authorship. It was a scheme for restoring due solemnity to the often farcical ritual of public penance in open congregation. But there is no reason to believe that any of these papers related to the business of Convocation in 1581.

Apart from his most public disabilities, Grindal's sequestration applied to his jurisdiction and administration and prevented him from determining and confirming with his own hand and seal all those matters of correction which belonged to him as visitor and judge. Since his vicar general and other officers would have dealt with much of this business as a matter of course, the practical effect of the archbishop's incapacity, as reflected in his register, was not necessarily great: although it was calculated to reduce to a mere formality the metropolitan visitation on which Grindal was embarked when the sequestration was imposed. But the archbishop's more properly spiritual, episcopal functions were not impeded by his sequestration. He participated in the consecration of bishops in March 1578, August 1579, September 1580 and September 1581, and issued mandates to confirm the election of other bishops and for their installation.[18]

Moreover he was frequently instructed by the Privy Council to take administrative action 'notwithstanding your present sequestration'[19] in a variety of miscellaneous and occasional matters. These included the investigation of popish recusancy;[20] the transmitting of a Council order directed against radical puritanism and requiring unbeneficed preachers to celebrate the communion;[21] the ordering of special prayers 'for the turning of God's wrath from us' after the alarming earthquake of 1580;[22] and the issuing of a licence to permit the removal of the bones of Lord Cheyney's ancestors from a chapel in the church of Minster in Kent.[23] He was also called upon with some regularity to promulgate to the other bishops of his province royal briefs for charitable collections in aid of distressed individuals and communities.[24] In the early 1580s the greatest and worthiest of such charities was the collection of funds for the relief of the beleaguered city of Geneva, under military threat from the duke of Savoy. In January 1583 the Council not only followed its normal procedure in forwarding through the archbishop its order for a collection of money from the clergy for this purpose but noted that it had 'especially recommended the care hereof' to Grindal. Moreover by the Council's special order the agent of Geneva was brought to visit the archbishop and to seek his advice. Grindal wrote at more than usual length to the bishops and deans about this matter, 'considering that under her Majesty and their lordships of her most honourable Privy Council the immediate charge of the province doth appertain to me, and especially of the clergy', and recommending the strategy to be adopted in organizing the collection.[25]

At about the same time, in mid-March 1583, Sir Francis Walsingham was in close touch with Grindal over the weighty matter of the reform of the calendar. The queen was anxious that England should fall into line with the recent change on the continent, initiated by Pope Gregory XIII. After taking appropriate advice from the mathematician Dudley Digges and the magical polymath Dr Dee she proposed to publish the new calendar by proclamation on 1 May. But this momentous business was recognized to be as much in the competence of divines as of astronomers and Grindal was invited to confer with as many of his brethren as could be found in London at short notice. On 4 April he joined with Aylmer of London, Piers of Salisbury and Young of Rochester in signing an adverse report. The new calendar would serve to realign the English Church with the Romanists and against other protestant churches. Even internally it might provoke a new schism of the kind which had occurred over other issues which, like the calendar, were indifferent but not expedient: in plain words, the puritans would repudiate it as they had rejected the surplice and other ceremonies. There should be no decision until the matter had been discussed not only in Convocation but with other reformed churches 'which profess the same religion that we do'. By the time that this was written the queen had changed her mind. It was left to the Age of Reason to reform the English calendar, making 1 January the first day of the year and robbing the simple-minded of those eleven days of their lives which should have fallen between 2 and 14 September 1752.[26]

Grindal was also kept busy with the arbitration of disputes arising from the tensions and rivalries of institutional life, in which he expended energies which in happier times might have been fully employed in routine administration. In the summer of 1579 he acted as mediator in a controversy over certain rents owing to his own dean and chapter by Queen's College Cambridge, both parties waiting upon him at Lambeth. This was upon Lord Burghley's 'motion' and the order he took in the matter was issued under his own hand and seal.[27] In 1580 Burghley referred to Grindal's arbitration an internal Cambridge controversy between the vice-chancellor and the heads of houses concerning certain decisions (technically 'graces') made by the vice-chancellor which were allegedly contrary to university statutes. After investigating the matter with the assistance of the dean of Westminster Grindal prepared a summary of the dispute and a definitive judgment in favour of the heads which demonstrates that lawyer-like practicality which would lead Bishop Wren to suspect some formal training 'in judiciis'.[28] This episode also suggests that the understanding and trust between the archbishop and the lord treasurer were as firm as ever. Burghley told Grindal that he knew more about the university and its statutes than he himself did. Grindal for his part assured Burghley: 'I count the university happy that it hath you for chancellor in these unquiet times. Your wisdom and authority may work more good with them than could be done otherwise. Notwithstanding I will most gladly impart mine opinion.' It was this 'opinion' which the chancellor proceeded to implement.[29]

In the affairs of two Oxford colleges Grindal intervened by his own mere authority as visitor and patron. In 1581 the warden of Merton (Thomas Bickley, a future bishop) with the vice-master and fellows disregarded the archbishop's mandate in choosing to make their own interpretation of the statutes of their house by depriving of his fellowship a certain William Wilkes who had gained presentation to an Oxford vicarage. Bickley and his colleagues were summoned before Grindal in person and then handed over to the Court of Arches. The outcome was a humble submission in which they apologized 'that in execution (as we take it) of our statutes we have committed a contempt against your grace's authority'.[30] A year later, as patron of All Souls, Grindal exercised his right to appoint to two scholarships which had not been filled by election within the time allowed by the statutes, and he gave detailed attention to raising the weekly allowances for the warden and fellows to keep pace with inflation.[31]

In 1582 Grindal acted as arbitrator in a major dispute of long duration between the dean and chapter of York and the civil lawyer Dr John Gibson, whom Grindal had appointed to the chancellorship of the diocese during his time at York. Although a layman, Gibson held in addition the precentorship of York and a prebend in the Minster, which was contrary to statute. The dean and chapter contested the matter and referred it to Grindal, presumably because Gibson held appropriate dispensations from the archbishop's Court of Faculties. But it was with the consent of both parties that Grindal arbitrated. Gibson was a coming man with court connections who would perhaps have found his way around Grindal's verdict if it had gone against him. But Grindal cautiously declined to make a definitive judgment, perhaps because he was the friend and patron of both parties, of Dr Gibson as well as of Dean Hutton, and was at this very time making Gibson dean of his Shoreham and Croydon peculiars. But the case involved the archbishop in much correspondence with York and long discussions with Gibson, which had to be fitted into an otherwise busy schedule: 'much writing and some business of great weight'. And this at a time when Grindal was apparently approaching total blindness.[32]

Sufficient evidence has been produced to suggest that the extent to which Grindal was incapacitated by his sequestration is far from clear and might tax a historian learned in the laws. But the anonymous author of a paper headed 'Inconveniences by the sequestration of the archbishop of Canterbury'[33] was in no doubt that the situation was unhealthy for the Church, and in ways which for the historian are somewhat imponderable. It was alleged that processes which normally went out over the archbishop's name and title would be 'less esteemed' and their validity even doubted if these were lacking; and that the metropolitan visitation would be more than ordinarily ineffective, and the Ecclesiastical Commission impoverished without the archbishop's credit and authority. We cannot tell how far all this was so. It was further alleged that the archbishop was unable, as he was accustomed, to arbitrate personally in major disputes. As we have seen, this was not necessarily the case. But we gain a credible insight into the archbishop of Canterbury's often unrecorded role in this quarrelsome and litigious society when the writer complains (and perhaps he wrote in the early days of Grindal's physical confinement) that the whole province was suffering from the archbishop's inability to 'appease' the many 'controversies and occasions of strife and slander' which arose daily, and which in normal times would fall into his lap.

When the Convocation of Canterbury met in 1581 the assembled bishops and representative inferior clergy seem to have agreed that the absence of their metropolitan was a wound through which the whole Church bled, and to which as a body they must address themselves. However, the suggestion of some early historians that the synod was in a militant mood and prepared to make the relief of the archbishop a condition of granting the queen their clerical subsidies does not seem to be well founded. Tobie Matthew, dean of Christ Church and a future archbishop of York, was the most eloquent of Oxford rhetoricians and as something of a court favourite, no militant. It was therefore appropriate that he should be chosen to turn to the burning issue of the day in the closing periods of a speech made at the formal ceremony of presenting the prolocutor of the Lower House, the dean of Windsor, to the assembled bishops in the Upper House.[34] This was a plea both polished and passionate for an initiative leading to the reconciliation of queen and archbishop. Matthew made bold play of the 'he' and 'she', 'ille' and 'illa', of this tragedy: 'ut pro illo apud illam, pro praesule apud principem, pro subdito apud reginam, pro patre et fratre apud matrem intercedatis.' His rhetorical device may suggest to the biographer how little material there is to hand from which to reconstruct the personal encounter of queen and archbishop: no letter from Elizabeth to Grindal, no record of a conversation between them, no evidence of a human relationship.

Matthew was subsequently employed to compose the supplication with which both houses of Convocation, 'observantissimi episcopi, decani, archidiaconi et reliqui ministri Ecclesiae Anglicanae', addressed their queen: a unique document in the annals of the Elizabethan Church. This was a shining testimonial to the character of an archbishop who had lived innocent of even the suspicion of wrongdoing, had preserved his religion free from both popish corruption and schism (puritanism), and had undergone persecution for righteousness' sake and exile for the cause of the gospel. Only on one occasion had he offended, and that in a matter not of wilfulness but of tender conscience. The terms were fulsomely laudatory, with promises of the gratitude and praise which Elizabeth would win by a characteristic gesture of clemency and charity. The conclusion was an eloquent plea that she would not only raise up an archbishop broken and feeble with grief ('archepiscopum maerore fractum, ac debilitatum ... iacentem') but restore the Church to him and him to the Church ('Ecclesiam ipsi, ipsum Ecclesia'), to her subjects, to his brethren, to foreign nations and, in short, to all men of piety and goodwill.[35]

Meanwhile twelve of the bishops of the southern province memorialized the queen on their own account:[36] Aylmer of London, Watson of Winchester, Cox of Ely (with but six months to live),[37] Scory of Hereford, Overton of Coventry and Lichfield, Young of St Davids, Scambler of Peterborough, Cooper of Lincoln, Freke of Norwich, Piers of Salisbury, Whitgift of Worcester and Young of Rochester. With Oxford and Gloucester vacant, the bishop of Bath and Wells ailing and Curteys of Chichester himself under suspension, this number included the entire effective strength of the episcopate of the province, Woolton of Exeter and most of the Welsh bishops excepted. The letter was carried to Court by another erudite and eloquent Oxonian, Cooper of Lincoln, author of the standard Latin dictionary of the time. That their metropolitan, 'summus in Ecclesia Anglicana sacerdos Dei', should remain in the queen's heavy displeasure was described by the bishops as not only a cause of shame but of injury ('detrimentum'), an encouragement to the Church's enemies and depressing to its friends, indeed a matter of consternation to other reformed churches. Once again, much was made of Grindal's impeccable record as a man of total integrity, a victim of his own evangelical fidelity and in his time an exile for the sake of the gospel. But the bishops thought that the archbishop had found the despondency of exile easier to bear than his present troubles and bitterness. The times were full of peril, the governors of the Church in contention with popish enemies on the one hand and pertinacious innovators on the other. Earnestly and at great length the bishops besought their mistress to exercise her wonted mercy and to spare the man and spare the Church.

But by 1581 there was little hope of a formal rehabilitation if this was to mean Grindal's full resumption of the primatial office. For one thing, his constitution, never robust, was now breaking down altogether. The process of physical degeneration can be chronicled from letters to friends and patrons. In February 1579 he could still inform Hutton of his 'reasonable good health'. But in the following winter there was a severe illness which may have been the 'great sickness' he was to refer to in 1581, but followed again in the spring with 'reasonable health'. In August 1581 Grindal supplied the earl of Leicester with a detailed account of his symptoms, including the first mention of the grievous legacy of recent illnesses:

> My strength of body increaseth very slowly; my appetite is very weak and (which grieveth me most by reason of the rheum which hath ever haunted me since the beginning of the recovery of my great sickness) mine eyesight is so dim and dull that I have small or almost no use of the same for reading or writing, or other my necessary affairs. I am put in hope that as my strength increaseth, so the brightness of my sight will also increase.

But in July 1582 he put his frail signature to a brief note to Walsingham excusing his failure to deal with his correspondence. 'My purpose is to make answer as soon as my weak health will serve me.' Finally in January 1583, six months before the end, he wrote to Burghley of 'some hope of recovering my sight, as some other in like case have done'. It was not to be. [38]

Here was the legendary Grindal of his immediate posterity, a passive and immensely sympathetic figure. Thomas Fuller turned him into 'our English Eli', aged, like the high priest of old, 'whereby both were blind' (but Grindal died in his early sixties), and heartbroken with sorrow.[39] For Raphael Holinshed he was truly called 'Grind-all':

> This good man in his lifetime was so studious that his book was his bride and his study his bridechamber, whereupon he spent both his eyesight, his strength and his health, and therefore might very well not actively but passively be named (as he was) Grindal: for he ground himself even to his grave by mortification.[40]

Most memorable of all the literary evocations of Grindal was Edmund Spenser's gentle pastor, Algrind.[41] In the tightly integrated imagery and emblematic symbolism of *The shepheardes calender* Spenser conveyed a sense of Grindal's role as victim of the politics of the time:

> Ah good *Algrin*, his hap was ill:
> but shall be better in time.

Applying an old and famous fable, the poet represented Queen Elizabeth as a soaring eagle who had let fall a shellfish on the whitened head of this ancient shepherd, mistaking it for chalk:

So now stonied with the stroke,
he lyes in lingering payne.

By the winter of 1582–3 there were signs of a slow thaw in the
queen's attitude to her archbishop. For the first time since his
entry into the see she sent him a New Year's gift of a 'standing
cup'.[42] But events were now moving towards the honourable resignation which Secretary Wilson had looked for in the first year of
the archbishop's troubles, and which Grindal says he had offered
'before, in the time of my better health'.[43] The resignation was
discussed and its terms negotiated in a series of letters from Grindal to his original and consistent patron, Lord Burghley, written
between the end of January and early April 1583.[44] As Grindal saw
it his resignation and its timing were subject to a number of
circumstances which were not easily brought into conjunction. It
was necessary that he should despair of recovering the queen's
favour and so of returning to full and ordinary archiepiscopal duty:
but for many years he had not abandoned that hope and, it appears,
would not have relinquished it now, but for the loss of his sight. It
was also necessary that the queen should overcome her reluctance
to accept his resignation. Grindal had been told that she did not
desire it and had refused it in other cases of age and debility. This
referred to Bishop Cox of Ely whose resignation had been actively
canvassed four years before. Bishop Freke of Norwich had received formal intimation of his appointment as Cox's successor,
the terms of Cox's pension had been agreed and the instruments of
his resignation drafted. But there the matter had rested and the
bishop of Ely had died, still in harness, in 1581. Probably the Privy
Council fought shy of the legal and canonical uncertainties surrounding the sufficiently unusual circumstance of a bishop's resignation.[45] But Grindal was now advised that it was the queen's
pleasure that he should resign 'and thereby enjoy her Majesty's
favour, which I esteem above all other worldly things'. But Grindal seems to have hoped for some token of favour to be shown to
him *before* his resignation, enough to enable him to put his diocese
into order, to see to its finances, clear up outstanding suits and so
'to make a perfect account of all things, to the satisfaction of
my successor'. He expected these matters to occupy him until
Michaelmas 1583, and that this remission would also enable
him to attend to other things close to his heart: the foundation of a
school in his birthplace of St Bees, the safeguarding of various
leases intended as pensions for his servants, and the negotiation
of an 'honest pension' for himself.

In February Grindal was in touch with Burghley over the details of his pension. Since he had no house of his own 'to put my head in after I be removed from this place', he asked that he might be allowed to retain the archbishop's manor of Croydon, together with other property in the district. Croydon was not a favoured residence, but it was close to London where Grindal would require regular medical attention. He also hoped that he might enjoy the immunity from dilapidation suits normally enjoyed, according to legal opinion, upon resignation of a see. 'Because I have been so much troubled with suits for dilapidations, I am fearful.' Later in the month his vicar general and steward supplied Burghley with the evidence required for the 'proportioning' of his pension. We know from the undated draft of a letter that Grindal's continuing confidence in his old friend was not misplaced. Noting that the queen was to be informed of Grindal's willingness to resign at Lady Day, 25 March, Burghley declared his personal wish that the pension should be 'large and honourable'. This might prove burdensome to his successor. 'But he that shall have it must shape his garment with his cloth for the time.' Was Burghley already disclosing the animosity which would grow between himself and Archbishop Whitgift within a year?[46] Having valued the archbishop's income at £2,680 from the Book of First Fruits and from the accounts of actual annual receipts, 'which groweth somewhat but not much above', he was disposed to recommend a pension for Grindal of £700 or £800.[47] In April, while these matters were still under negotiation, Grindal sent Burghley a draft of his formal act of resignation, a document without precedent in the history of the English Church.[48]

In early May Walsingham's secretary Nicholas Faunt described the anticipated scenario in a letter to Anthony Bacon which provides evidence of the unique esteem with which Grindal was regarded in puritan circles which otherwise had little room for bishops.

The good archbishop of Canterbury is presently to resign his place, being now altogether blind in body but most vigilant in mind to do good so long as he liveth. And therefore having made great suit to be removed and so obtain licence to found certain schools and places of learning in the university hath to that purpose discharged his train and employed all the profits he hath spared of his living besides his ordinary expenses, reserving some little to maintain him and a few servants the rest of his life, which cannot be long. It is thought that Whitgift now bishop of Worcester shall succeed him: but wherein besides his place it is easily guessed. And all the rest will hold on the like course for the maintenance of their lordly estates.

Later Faunt wrote caustically that Whitgift would be Grindal's successor 'and so must there be a removing of that crew from place to place'.[49]

But Grindal having narrowly escaped the unique fate of deprivation by judicial process was not allowed to become the first archbishop of Canterbury to resign his great office. That privilege was left to Archbishop Randall Davidson, in 1928. In his last correspondence with Burghley Grindal knew that he was not far from the end, referring to 'the short time that I have to live'. On 25 March Walsingham wrote to the solicitor general, Thomas Egerton, asking him to rush through the legal formalities connected with the archbishop's foundation of a grammar school at St Bees: 'the more speed the better, in respect of the archbishop's weak state of body'.[50] The Letters Patent were duly signed on 24 April and revised on 15 June, less than a month before Grindal's demise. On 8 May he composed his will. On 6 July he died, at Croydon, still archbishop of Canterbury.

According to Archbishop Whitgift's secretary and biographer, Sir George Paule, no other end to the story was ever to be looked for, since his master, whom Queen Elizabeth had 'designed' as Grindal's successor and in whose favour Grindal was willing to resign, 'utterly refused, and in presence of the queen herself besought pardon in not accepting thereof upon any condition whatsoever in the lifetime of the other'. Whereupon, according to Paule, the queen, 'commiserating the good old man's estate (being a grave and learned father of the Church and at that time blind with years and grief), was graciously pleased to say, *That as she had made him an archbishop, so he should die an archbishop*, as he did shortly after.'[51] It is a good story which reflects honourably on both Whitgift and the queen, but there is a tincture of evidence against it. For it was through Whitgift's ally Bishop Piers of Salisbury, later archbishop of York in the time of Whitgift's primacy, that Grindal had learned of Elizabeth's willingness to receive his resignation.[52] Since Piers, as royal almoner, was a suitable messenger for the purpose this may be of no significance. But the suggestion that Grindal proposed to resign in favour of a named individual, Whitgift, does not ring true and must be dismissed as Paule's invention.

In making his characteristically protestant will,[53] Grindal required to be buried in the choir of Croydon parish church, 'without any solemn hearse or funeral pomp'. But it was also in character that he should add the proviso that if he were to die in office the heralds should not lack their accustomed fees in such cases. In the event it was the funeral of an archbishop of Canterbury which was

celebrated on 1 August, and while in scale it was more modest than
Parker's solemn obsequies of eight years before,[54] it was most
honourable. In accordance with the will Grindal's executors compounded with the heralds for their fees of £100. But against his
wishes they authorized the preparation of an elaborate hearse with
palls, carpets, pillows and other coverings, requiring no less than
seventy-eight yards of black velvet, besides 'a cloth of estate of
three breadths of velvet' and fringes of gold and black silk, with
much other furniture including twelve ells of lockram (linen
fabric) 'to let the body into the grave'. An observer of the funeral
procession would have seen seventy poor men at the head, going
two by two. Then followed sixty gentlemen mourners, members
of the archbishop's household, kinsmen and officers, eighteen of
lesser rank in cloaks, forty-two of greater consequence in gowns: a
list of names before which Grindal's biographer stands re-
proached, unable as he is to put a face to more than a few of them.
Next came the archbishop's eight chaplains and two secretaries,
and the preacher of the funeral sermon, the refreshingly familiar
figure of Grindal's old friend and fellow-exile Alexander Nowell,
dean of St Paul's, himself a septuagenarian, but with twenty years
of his life still ahead of him. (The sermon is sadly not extant.)
Then followed the archbishop's steward, treasurer and controller,
and after them the heralds, preceding the bishop of London, by
tradition the chief mourner. Last of all walked a group of ecclesiastics, the bishop of Rochester and the bishop suffragan of Dover,
the deans of Canterbury, Westminster and Windsor, the archdeacon of Canterbury and Dr Gibson, dean of Croydon. With the
exception of the master of requests and a stray sergeant, the
judges, so prominent at Parker's funeral, were absent. Evidently
it was not the custom for the most senior of the crown's servants
to be present at an archiepiscopal funeral. So Burghley was
not there, nor Walsingham, nor any other representative of that
ardently protestant element in the ruling class which had held
Edmund Grindal in such high regard.[55]

Grindal was the first of six archbishops to be interred at Croydon, his example being followed by Whitgift, Sheldon, Wake,
Potter and Herring. Of the six splendid sepulchral monuments
which once flanked the choir and aisles only those commemorating
Whitgift and Sheldon survived the disastrous fire which destroyed
the old parish church of Croydon in 1867, and the subsequent
reconstruction. Fortunately Strype described Grindal's monument and, in addition, an account of the effigy was communicated
to the Surrey Archaeological Society before the calamity occurred.[56] The archbishop is described as recumbent, 'a pretty height

from the ground', with hands conjoined and uplifted in the conventional devotional attitude, vested in his rochet, under a scarlet doctoral gown. The surviving effigy of Whitgift is similarly positioned, and vested. According to Strype the sculptor recorded 'a comely face, a long black beard somewhat forked and somewhat curling'. The antiquary reported a face 'portrayed according to the fashion of the age, with a long flowing beard and moustache over the upper lip', eyes blank to suggest blindness (in Strype's words, 'a kind of white in the pupils to denote his blindness'), and on the head a cap: which was not a square cap, still less a mitre, Archbishop Harsnet of York being the first post-Reformation prelate to be so represented, in 1631. Rubbings exist of the associated heraldic brasses: three shields, bearing the arms of London, York and Canterbury respectively, impaling those of Grindal.[57] Strype transcribed the 'large and historical' epitaph and the three sets of verses which also adorned the tomb. The epitaph to 'Edmundus Grindallus Cumbriensis' is all that survives and is now set in the wall of the choir, below a simple brass plate which states that 'close to this spot lies the body of Edmund Grindal, Archbishop of Canterbury from November A.D. 1575 to July A.D. 1583'.

A more enduring monument proved to be the educational endowments which the archbishop settled before his death. Of these the most substantial was the free grammar school which he founded in his native heath of St Bees, where he had not been for perhaps forty-five years. The school was to be built and furnished at a cost of £366. 13s. 4d. and endowed with annual revenues of £50. Only three days before his death Grindal had published his statutes for the school, a series of minute and specific regulations which have often been exploited by historians of Tudor education. Although the foundation was to be sometimes at risk in its early years a school building had been erected by 1588 and a tradition of learning and pedagogy begun which has continued without a break for almost four centuries. Grindal linked the school with his own college of Pembroke Hall by founding two scholarships for St Bees boys as well as a fellowship. Another St Bees scholarship was founded at Magdalene College with an endowment of £100. But the largest and most significant benefaction outside St Bees was made to the Queen's College Oxford, a society with strong Cumbrian connections. A fellowship and two St Bees scholarships were endowed and the Queen's was linked in perpetuity with the school through the provision that its provost was to serve as a governor and appoint the headmaster.[58] To the Queen's Grindal further bequeathed 'all such books as I have assigned unto them, to be kept in their library, contained in a catalogue subscribed with my hand'.

And there they are still to be found: some eighty volumes, each bearing a printed label inserted at the time of the bequest.[59] From Grindal's will we learn of the careful disposition of other portions of his library to further beneficiaries: some to Pembroke Hall (mostly Greek books, together with a Hebrew Bible, annotated by Archdeacon Watts of Middlesex during the Marian Exile), some to a fellow of Pembroke, some to his chaplain Mr Wilson (and these may later have crossed the Atlantic to Boston),[60] and others to a servant.

It cannot be said of Grindal's bequests as Strype said of Parker's that they were 'very noble and very large'.[61] A careful modesty pervades his will, the last written thing from his hand. It provides a good place to take our last leave of Edmund Grindal, with its intimate record of the many pieces and connections of which his life was composed, towards its end. 'Having nothing worthy to be presented to her Majesty' (did he mean worthier?) the queen was asked to accept the New Testament in Greek 'as an argument of my dutiful and loving heart towards her Highness, whom I pray Almighty God long to prosper and preserve to the benefit of his Church'. Burghley was to receive the queen's belated token of returning favour, the standing cup which was her New Year's gift in 1583; and was asked to be 'supervisor' of the will. Sir Francis Walsingham got his best standing cup which he brought from York, with a request to be 'good and favourable towards the accomplishing of this my testament'. 'My faithful friend Mr Nowell, dean of Paul's' was to receive 'my ambling gelding, called Grey Olephant'. 'My gelding called Old Marshall' went to the steward of his household, 'my white hobby called York' to the archdeacon of Canterbury and to his favourite nephew William Woodhall 'my black stray nag called Nix'. He further bequeathed to Woodhall 'the bed wherein I use to lie in Lambeth' with the pillows, sheets and other bed furniture, including a tapestry coverlet wrought with green leaves, 'my signet of gold, my great nut, my best salt, double gilt' and other plate. More pieces of plate were distributed to Pembroke Hall, the Queen's College, St Bees parish church, Dr Gibson, and to various nephews and nieces. £100 was left to the mayor and citizens of Canterbury as a loan stock for the use of the poor, to set them on work, and further sums were given to the poor of Lambeth, Croydon and St Bees. Seventeen servants were remembered by name with sums ranging from £5 to £40, and no servant received less than half a year's wages. Eight nieces received £50 each. The executors were instructed in some detail how to provide for the preferment of Grindal's chaplains. The remainder of the estate was to be bestowed upon 'the poorest of my kinsfolk and servants, and upon poor scholars'. The earl of Leicester was not remembered, still less Sir Christopher Hatton. Perhaps Grindal died as he had learned to live: disillusioned with 'court promises'.[62]

EPILOGUE

'**S**UCH bishops would have prevented our contentions and wars.'[1] This was the verdict on Grindal pronounced by the great divine Richard Baxter in the aftermath of civil war and revolution, in 1656. The remark was prompted by memory of 'that excellent letter' which was perhaps all or most of what Baxter knew about Grindal. No matter. Grindal was important as a symbol of all that was best and of so much that might have been in the episcopal leadership of the English Church and Reformation.

Modern historians of the 'contentions and wars' of the seventeenth century are increasingly disinclined to seek their roots deep in the history of earlier reigns. It would not now seem plausible to suggest that Archbishop Grindal might have prevented the Civil War. The temptation must nevertheless be strong to end this biography with the historian's self-indulgence of half-claims based on might-have-beens. If Grindal had secured the confidence of the queen as well as of the protestant nation ... If he had been followed by archbishops of like persuasion and equal quality ... If the thirst for godly reformation which remained so powerful for three-quarters of a century after Grindal's death had been satisfied within the national Church, by a perfect harmony of godly prince and godly bishop, presiding over godly magistrates and ministers and willing people ...[2] Then the Reformed Church for which Grindal had striven would have assumed more solid form, without the fatal tendency to ideological fracture which was to beset its future. The reform of institutions and of finance might have been negotiated with the co-operation of the propertied classes, rather than against the grain of lay prejudice. Controversy there would surely have been, but perhaps not Dissent as an institution, challenging and undermining the national religious establishment. Radical thought would not have flowed from the springs of resentful dissidence. The margin of tolerance allowed to catholics would have been narrower, perhaps non-existent. English civilization would have been more monolithic, less diverse and perhaps less creative. The role of seniority and leadership in Protestant Europe accorded to England in Foxeian mythology might have become a fact, with a correspondingly reduced interest in North America: no New England. Dr Christopher Hill, not to mention a host of American historians of puritanism, would have had nothing, or something different, to write about.

To proceed any further with such fantasies, if as far, would not be profitable. The reader will not be asked which version of English history he finds more inviting, and if he thinks that Grindal's importance is in danger of being blown out of proportion he is probably right. Better to rest with the observation, as valid for this as for any other moment of high aspiration in human affairs, that the future was the product of the failure rather than of the success of the English Reformation, a failure which Grindal's career seems to epitomize. However the ultimate failure to bring to creative fruition what Grindal would have recognized as a church rightly reformed was not foreseen in 1583. Indeed, the vision of a godly church and commonwealth was as bright in the 1640s as at any time in the earlier history of the Reformation. The 'contentions and wars' of that decade had their positive as well as negative motivation.

How far Grindal's archiepiscopate should itself be considered a disastrous failure was and still is a matter of opinion, and prejudice. The secretary and first biographer of his successor wrote vividly of 'that crazy state of the Church' at Whitgift's coming to the archbishopric 'and a long time after', and characterized his master as a gentle and moderate physician, prescribing 'conserves and electuaries and some gentle purges' to his fractious patient.[3] It would not be difficult to compose a superficially coherent account of the sickness of the Church of England in the years of Grindal's lame-duck primacy. Not to look beyond the bishops, it was a time of scandal and grave political embarrassment. Bishop Curteys of Chichester was a preacher and a patron of preachers who made a brave onslaught on the backwardness of his impenetrably rural diocese. But when he attempted the public coercion of the catholic and crypto-catholic gentry of Sussex in full consistory, in his cathedral, the Privy Council could not defend such folly. Like his metropolitan, Curteys ended his career disgraced and suspended, removed from the commission of the peace and the local ecclesiastical commission.[4] In the diocese of Norwich Edmund Freke challenged strong factions of puritan gentry in both Norfolk and Suffolk and suspended and deprived their preachers. Since Freke had hitherto enjoyed a good reputation with puritans he may have done no more than obey the queen's orders when he stumbled into these confrontations. But Sir Thomas Heneage expressed the view of the Privy Council when he wrote of 'the foolish bishop' who had complained of 'divers most zealous and loyal gentlemen'. After years of futile strife, Freke secured escape to a quieter diocese.[5] According to Whitgift, as bishop of the neighbouring diocese of Worcester, Coventry and Lichfield in Grindal's time was 'in sundry parts ... out of frame'. It was served by one of the least admirable of Elizabethan bishops, William Overton, and disturbed by a squalid battle for the chancellorship of the diocese.[6] In Hereford the aged Bishop Scory was suspected of 'certain matters of very foul disorder' and professed to find his bishopric 'a purgatory'.[7]

In the north Archbishop Sandys quarrelled with everyone who mattered, including the lord president, Huntingdon, and the deans of both York and Durham. He told Burghley that as long as Huntingdon and Hutton, the dean of York, banded together against him he could do no good. His only hope lay in the preferment of Hutton to a bishopric. 'Verily my lord I receive great wrong. My faithful and upright service is ill requited.' But there was much worse to come. In 1582 one of his enemies framed him in a morally compromising situation in a Doncaster inn, where it was made to appear that the archbishop of York had at least attempted adultery with the landlord's wife. It was a criminal conspiracy, crudely contrived, but the efforts of Sandys to buy the conspirators off did his credit little good.[8]

The near-paranoia expressed in Sandys's letters to Burghley was echoed by his brother and successor of London, John Aylmer. Aylmer came badly out of an enquiry into the wasting of episcopal timber and seems to have been threatened with deprivation. In a desperate letter to the lord treasurer he declared rashly that 'your lordship can have no great victory for me'. Whether or not Burghley had a hand in his promotion he professed not to know. 'But if you would procure to bring me out I assure you I would thank you... And to be plain with your lordship you are the man that doth most discourage me. Not in these points ... but in that by your words and countenance my government is hindered. For when such words shall pass from you, that such and such things be not of the substance of religion, that the ecclesiastical jurisdiction (which you yourself by statute have confirmed) is mere papal, that you would such and such should preach which are disturbers etc., it cannot be my lord but three words from your mouth *huius generis* shall more embolden them and hinder our labour than our toil and moil shall in many years be able to help and salve.'[9]

Sandys and Aylmer were not so preoccupied with their several political troubles as to be without the energy to go to law against each other over dilapidations. The cause was arbitrated by Sir

Francis Walsingham, whose ears were filled with rancorous and unseemly complaints of mercenary conduct, one bishop against another. No wonder Walsingham's secretary spoke in his letters of 'that crew' and of their 'offensive conversations' of which the Court was 'too much and often a witness'.[10]

Grindal can hardly be held responsible for all this, if for any of it. None of these scandals was directly attributable to his sequestration unless, as a contemporary document suggests, through his inability to offer the leadership expected of an archbishop in the arbitration of quarrels.[11] But the one element which was common to most of these otherwise unrelated affairs was the humiliation of the bishops by members of the secular governing class, or in their sight. If the interests of the Church lay in the defence of its integrity, dignity and financial independence as a separate ecclesiastical corporation, then Grindal's archiepiscopate represents a very low point in its condition, if not the nadir of the Elizabethan Church. The aim of Archbishop Whitgift and of his successor Richard Bancroft was to lift the Church out of this depression and to an extent they were successful. Within three years of his arrival at Lambeth Whitgift sat on the Privy Council, to which his predecessor had addressed deferential and futile appeals. But since the dignity of the clergy was a principle not easily squared with what might be called the primitive spirit of protestantism and was certain to provoke lay susceptibilities, the policies of Whitgift and Bancroft threatened to be counter-productive. Whitgift was told by an aged and indignant Kentish gentleman who had seen six archbishops that he was the first to set himself against the gentry.[12] So the effort to redeem the disaster of Grindal's archiepiscopate increased the disequilibrium in relations between the Church, in the sense of the hierarchy, and society.

At a more basic level the 'state of the Church' was tending to improve in the Grindal years and the improvement was sustained on an ascending curve in the quarter-century which followed. That is to say that the parish ministry was being taken over by university men, so that by the second decade of the seventeenth century the Church of England had acquired in all but the more remote dioceses a largely graduate clergy, with competition among well-qualified candidates for even the poorer livings. This was less the consequence of a deliberate campaign of reform than of an enlarged intake at Oxford and Cambridge, since the Church still provided the only available professional outlet for the majority of graduates. In this way the growing wealth and stability of society, as well as the high fertility of gentry and clergy families, was converted into a more learned ministry. But in itself this transformation held no guarantee of a more effective parochial ministry. And in the absence of radical financial reform to improve the income of thousands of impoverished benefices it was far from solving all problems. In some ways it increased them, since it may be that clerical arrogance based on superior education and an enhanced professional *esprit de corps* was at the root of much seventeeth-century anticlericalism. 'The re-formation of the clergy seems a surface reformation only.'[13]

When Baxter suggested that bishops like Grindal could have prevented the Civil War he meant that Grindal would not have provoked and alienated puritan consciences like his own. In the opinion of some puritans who lived through it, Grindal's archiepiscopate was a time of blessed relief from harassment, when the godly preachers were free to labour for conversion and reformation, and when the kingdom of God was visibly growing. Josias Nicholls, a Kentish minister of Grindal's own diocese, remembered it as 'a goodly space of quietness', 'a golden time, full of godly fruit'. 'Many thousands were converted from atheism and popery and became notable christians.'[14] The radical activist John Field, never happy except in a fight, seems to testify to the same atmosphere of relaxation when he wrote of 'this unhappy time of looseness and liberty gaining upon me and choking those good things which I thank God I was wont to feel in greater measure'.[15] It is not quite clear whether this laxity should be attributed to a positive factor, Grindal's moderation and sympathy for the preaching ministry, or negatively, as the consequence of disrupted administration during his sequestration. In any case quietness was by no means the universal experience of the puritan ministry in the Grindal years. In some dioceses, notably London under Aylmer and Norwich under Freke, the queen had already installed bishops who acted on instructions to proceed with impartial severity against both papists and puritans. The battle was joined in East Anglia and in London itself while Grindal was still archbishop, and it was at this time that 'Brownism', the name by which sectarian separatism was to be known for ever afterwards, had its origins, around Norwich and Bury St Edmunds. Yet there is ample evidence of a kind of informal agreement prevailing in many quarters that 'civil wars of the Church of God' would be abandoned in favour of an affirmation of those things in which all protestants assented, against papists, against such sectarian threats as the Family of Love, and positively, in the pursuit of a more fruitful, less superficial practice of religion. All this is reflected in the Paul's Cross sermons and other publications of the period.[16]

The onslaught which Whitgift mounted against puritanism within months of assuming the primacy made a watershed in English church history. It was directed not only against non-conformity and subversive activity but against the most private of conscientious scruples, since the entire clergy were required to subscribe to articles which endorsed the Prayer Book as containing 'nothing in it contrary to the word of God', as well as the royal supremacy and the articles of religion. Although the new arch-bishop was soon persuaded to become more realistic in his objectives and to concentrate on the more patently factious of puritan dissidents the civil wars of the Church of God were re-newed with a vengeance.[17] Richard Bancroft, whose career was largely erected on the paranoiac resourcefulness and toughness of his own anti-puritanism, later succeeded Whitgift in the primacy and in the prosecution of nonconformity by means of subscription. In the early years of James I he embarked on a reconstruction of the laws and institutions of the Church which was grandly con-ceived and had its enduring qualities, but which alienated a very substantial body of opinion which was both puritan and Calvinist, but not necessarily disloyal to the Church.[18]

Whitgift's policy was not without its contradictions since he participated in the broadly Calvinist, vigorously anti-Roman div-inity which represented the true gravitational centre of the Eliza-bethan Church.[19] If he promoted Bancroft he was also the patron and friend of the most learned Calvinist theologian of late Eliza-bethan Cambridge, William Whitaker. When questions of the-ology were in dispute, as they were in Cambridge in the 1590s, Whitgift was bound to come down on the side of Whitaker's Calvinism, which was subjected to only minor modifications in his Lambeth Articles of 1595.[20] Andrew Melville's attack on Bancroft as 'the capital enemy of all the reformed churches in Europe' was excessive, but it indicates the much greater detachment of Whitgift's successor from the Calvinist mainstream. In Dr Tyacke's words, he 'lacked the restraining influence of a the-ology shared with his nonconformist opponents'.[21] But in this he was a somewhat isolated figure, not typical of the Jacobean episcopate.

The case against the zeal for Anglican conformity and discipline of both Whitgift and Bancroft, and still more of Archbishop Laud in the next generation, has nothing to do with its intrinsic merits or its consistency with the laws and symbols of the Church. Their policies stand condemned in the perspective enjoyed by the his-torian for their narrow basis of support, their lack of practicality. These archbishops were at odds, Whitgift partially, Bancroft largely, Laud wholly, with a consensus of Calvinist opinion characterized by one historian as 'the protestant mind of the English Reformation' and regarded by another as 'establishment orthodoxy'.[22] By contemporaries it was never doubted that their 'formal' policies were court policies and lacking in 'popularity'. (And since James I was himself a convinced Calvinist, revisionist theology was on an uncertain footing even at Court so long as his reign lasted.) Grindal may not have been, as William Temple was said to have been in the twentieth century, a 'people's archbishop'. In the context of the sixteenth century the description would be meaningless. But in a sense wholly meaningful in that age he was a 'popular' archbishop. At the time of his troubles Sir Walter Mildmay had asked the Privy Council to consider the consequences of forcing the matter to the issue of deprivation, 'the people addicted to the matter as they were'.[23] In every aspect of his churchmanship, piety and social and political outlook Grindal made a perfect fit with the consensus, sharing its protestant mind. This is why he was so much more important than historians have hitherto allowed.

Grindal's predecessor, Parker, had a dread of 'popularity'. 'God keep us from such visitation as Knox have attempted in Scotland: the people to be orderers of things.' 'I am not now to learn how to fawn upon man.'[24] The analysis of history so far proposed in these concluding pages can be countered with an alternative series of might-have-beens. If Parker had not been succeeded by Grindal, with his dangerous tendency to succumb to 'popularity', and if the pressure brought to bear against the puritans in the early 1570s had not been relaxed, Whitgift would not have had such a difficult time in the 1580s. Dr Sacheverell spoke no more than the truth when he held Grindal responsible for 'the first plantation of dissenters'.[25] And if Bancroft had not been replaced by the complacent Archbishop George Abbot, puritanism would not have been allowed to fester until it provided the ideology for rebellion. It might have been suppressed. Obedience need not have faltered. If Baxter as a puritan thought that Grindal or bishops like him could have prevented 'our contentions and wars', Clarendon in his *History of the Great Rebellion* suggested that if Bancroft had only lived (and he was sixty-six when he died in 1610 and would have been nearly a hundred when the Civil War broke out) he would 'quickly have extinguished all that fire in England which had been kindled at Geneva'. For Clarendon the 'never enough lamented' death of Bancroft was one of the earliest events to which it was profitable to refer in any discussion of the origins of the Civil War.[26]

If I prefer Baxter's analysis to Clarendon's it is not out of partial affection for Grindal, in whose company I have spent so many hours. It is because I share with other students of politics and religion in the seventeenth century the sense that if the Civil War was provoked by anything on the religious front it was by the 'counter-revolution' against 'the protestant mind of the English Reformation' mounted by Archbishop Neile of York, Archbishop Laud and other bishops of the 'Arminian' school in the later 1620s and 1630s.[27]

One consequence of the renewed interest in the historic role of the innovating and provocative Arminian episcopate of Charles I has been the recognition that up to about 1630 most bishops were of a different persuasion, and, for that matter, not much like Bancroft or even Whitgift. From a vantage point in the early 1620s, when the Calvinist George Abbot was still archbishop, albeit, like Grindal, a lame-duck archbishop, the Parker–Whitgift–Bancroft sequence appears less than central, even somewhat deviant from a norm for which the model of Grindal has more relevance. In the northern province there was, until 1628, an unbroken tradition of moderate, Elizabethan, Calvinist churchmanship: after Matthew Hutton, close friend of both Grindal and Whitgift, Tobie Matthew, an indefatigable preacher and patron of the preaching ministry.[28] Most Jacobean bishops of London were Calvinists. One of the most influential of James's bishops, a privy councillor and the editor of the king's collected literary *Works*, was James Montague, who died as bishop of Winchester. Montague was one of the Cambridge heads who had alerted Whitgift in the 1590s to the threat to Calvinist orthodoxy contained in the doctrine of the proto-Arminian, Peter Baro. He was the first master of Sidney Sussex College, like Emmanuel as much a puritan seminary as a college, and he had preached at the funeral of the most famous of all Cambridge puritan divines, William Perkins. He was the brother of a Northamptonshire magnate who was a consistent patron of puritan ministers.[29] Montague was bishop of Bath and Wells for eight years, where he succeeded Bishop John Still, previously noted for his friendly relations with the Suffolk preachers when he was archdeacon of Sudbury, and he was followed by Bishop Arthur Lake, yet another bishop in the moderate tradition who was at Wells until 1626. Grindal would have approved of Lake. He was a regular preacher in his cathedral and in the country parishes. He personally examined candidates for ordination. And he believed in a rigorous and truly pastoral discipline. He sat in his consistory in person and refused to allow the commutations of penance. There were dramatic occasions in Wells Cathedral when he preached and pronounced absolution at the public penance of 'notorious' offenders.[30] This is the other face of the Jacobean episcopate, not acknowledged by Professor Trevor-Roper in his brilliant indictment of Milton's 'swan-eating and canary-sucking prelates' and of bishops who were nothing more than 'lay courtiers holding clerical sinecures'.[31] So long as bishops of this persuasion and quality ruled puritanism was not much spoken of, still less made the object of inquisition and penal repression. John Pym, the parliamentary leader of the future, would have been surprised and affronted in the 1620s to have been called a puritan and he had a good opinion of bishops.[32]

But what would surely have pleased Grindal most was that the prophesyings which he had defended in his letter to the queen were alive and well and remained one of the most distinctive institutions of the reformed Church of England in what was, in some sense, its Jacobean heyday.[33] In the Bath of Bishops Montague and Lake, for example, something like the old prophesying, the 'ancient weekly lecture', continued to attract to the abbey church the nobility and others who congregated in the spring and autumn to take the waters. There was a difference. The word 'prophesying' was abandoned after the royal ban of 1577 and although the vaguer and more elastic term 'exercise' was still in use the nature of the exercise was usually defined, as at Bath, as a 'lecture'. The change of name indicates a transposition from a public conference of as many as three preachers to a single sermon on each occasion. But there were special features distinguishing these lectures from ordinary sermons, and even from the offerings of the clergymen styled 'lecturers' and employed by town corporations and parishes as professional, salaried preachers. They took place on a regular weekly or fortnightly basis, as often as not in a market town and on market days. Like the prophesyings they drew their audience from a large catchment area within riding distance of the town. And they were supplied by a panel or 'combination' of preaching clergy from the surrounding country and came to be known as 'lectures by combination'. There was little to distinguish these combinations from the groups of preachers who had sustained the prophesyings of Elizabethan days, and it was common practice for the combination to be present on each occasion and for the lectures to be followed by dinner and a clerical conference. In this way the collegiality which was such a marked feature of the prophesyings continued. Indeed, in such centres as Bury St Edmunds and Leicester there is evidence of a nearly continuous history of 'lecture days', involving the preaching clergy of the neighbouring parishes and running from the beginnings of prophesying in the 1560s to the 1630s and even beyond. It was in connection with his own Worcestershire Association and the business of commending it as a model to other counties that Richard Baxter, in the 1650s, acknowledged the indebtedness of this kind of ecclesiastical organization to the 'ministerial meetings and exercises' of which Grindal had written to Queen Elizabeth.

The assumption of historians that lectures and lecturers were always subversive and a threat to the integrity of the Church misses the point, at least the point about combination lectures. Lectures by combination and the meetings of ministers associated with them were typical of the Church of this period, not of alienation from it, and they satisfied a number of dominant interests in early seventeenth-century provincial society. Most obviously they met the insatiable demand for preaching, especially where it was otherwise scarce, and they answered to a popular taste for variety.[34] They favoured the learning and the growing professionalization of the clergy: in the words of a contemporary document, 'advancement to the clergymen when their gifts shall be known'. They were popular with the ruling gentry as a valuable instrument of popular religious education and, doubtless, of social control. And they served the bread-and-butter interests of the towns: 'benefit also to the inhabitants for their market, by concourse of people'.[35] By their sympathetic responses some Jacobean bishops identified themselves with these aspirations and acknowledged social realities. In inviting a group of Norfolk clergy to mount a combination lecture Bishop Jegon of Norwich was satisfying the ministers, gentlemen and townsmen who had made their several, formal approaches to him. He addressed them in a civil manner, as Grindal might have done, but with a touch of pomp and circumstance which was more Jacobean than Elizabethan: 'I have presumed upon my credit with you to name you thirteen to assist that exercise, every man once a quarter.'[36]

It was the Laudian successors of such bishops who believed, with how much justification is a matter to be discussed rather than assumed, that by making itself beholden to the laity and by working with the grain of provincial society the Church placed itself at risk. As an ecclesiastical official of Norwich diocese put it in the 1630s: 'The lay contribution and support hath made the ecclesiastic persons and ceremonies wag and dance after their pipe from whom they receive the livelihood.'[37] But the laity were 'ecclesiastic persons' too, according to Reformation principles first enunciated by Luther himself. Did it make sense to oppose their massive and not always irresponsible interest in religion as foreign and dangerous?

Because recent events had tended to invest all recent bishops with an evil reputation the puritans and parliamentarians of the mid-seventeeth century sometimes looked back as far as Grindal for their image of a bishop whom they could find tolerable, even admirable.[38] Yet when the dust had settled, in the 1680s, Richard Baxter recalled that he had known a bishop in the flesh perhaps as admirable as the legendary Grindal. As a boy he had run out of school with his friends to kneel on a path and receive confirmation, in the casual manner of the time, from Bishop Thomas Morton, then of Coventry and Lichfield and later of Durham. And Morton, he recollected, was 'one of the learnedest and best bishops that ever I knew'.[39] Morton was classed by Clarendon with 'the less formal and more popular prelates'.[40] Recent historians have been tempted to confer on this 'less formal and more popular' episcopal tradition the honorific label 'Grindalian', a term which in 1971 appeared for the first time in a textbook for schools,[41] and which is perhaps no less justified than 'Laudian' as a term of convenience and art.

The biographer would naturally prefer to eat his cake and have it. He would like to agree with John Milton that Grindal was the best of all bishops, entitled to a lonely eminence. But he must also recognize that he was not the last of his kind. Grindal's immediate failure was nearly total. And in the long term the English Church experienced what he could only have regarded as a long succession of tragic failures in which it missed if not its way his way. But in the fifty years which intervened between Grindal's death and the onset of crisis and civil war in the 1630s and 1640s, Grindalian episcopacy continued to moderate the affairs of the Church of England, and more markedly towards the end of this half-century than in the immediate aftermath of Grindal's abortive archiepiscopate.

APPENDIX

GETTING AND SPENDING: GRINDAL'S STEWARDSHIP

T HE most unflattering of all possible portraits of the Elizabethan bishops can be painted with the aid of the letters in
which they angled for preferment or complained of the greed and
opportunism of other churchmen. In 1559 John Aylmer asked the
future earl of Leicester: 'Good my lord, if the deanery of Winchester be not already swallowed up let me among the rest of the small
fishes have a snatch at the bait: if it be gone, I beseech your good
lordship cast a hook for the deanery of Durham... '[1] Twenty years
later, when the same John Aylmer had risen to be bishop of
London, Archbishop Sandys accused him of 'unsatiable desire',
'coloured covetousness' and 'an envious heart'.[2] This was written
in the heat of litigation between the two prelates which, to say the
least, suggested no indifference on Sandys's part to his own
pecuniary interest.

Grindal never wrote in such a spirit. In a letter to Cecil he made a
withering comment on ecclesiastical careerism: 'Those men that
sue for bishoprics do in that declare themselves unmeet for the
room.'[3] Nor is there any evidence that he actively pursued his own
great preferments. When his translation to York was mooted he
wrote to Cecil of the 'prosecution of the matter intended towards
me'.[4] Cynics may conclude that such unworldliness was a re-
flection as much of Grindal's bachelor status as of superior virtue.
It is also true that the man whose career opens before him without
apparent effort has no need for careerism. The fact remains that
Grindal, for whatever reason, betrayed no strong attachment to
what Elizabethans called 'worldly commodity'.

Nevertheless, like it or not, he was possessed of commodity.
This book is not a study of episcopal finance or of 'the economic
problems of the Church'[5] and it has no pretension to investigate
with any thoroughness Grindal's financial affairs or estate and
household management. But it would outdo Grindal himself in
unworldliness to disregard altogether these aspects of his career.
The bishopric of London, which he held for ten years and a few
months, was valued 'in the queen's books' at £1,019. 13s. 4d., with
other contemporary valuations ranging from a round £1,000 to

295

£1,119. 8s. 4d. Probably the gross revenue was somewhat higher since those unpredictable and often unrecorded sources of income known as 'casualties' were said in 1579 to be 'of good value' in London.[6] In the later 1560s it is thought to have averaged £1,385, although actual cash receipts fluctuated and were usually less.[7] Perhaps we shall not be far wrong if we add up Grindal's total receipts in his first see to a round sum of £12,000, although this may be an underestimate. The archbishopric of York was valued with some precision early in Elizabeth's reign at £1,789. 14s. 3¾d., and at the end of the century was thought to average £1,866 annually. Grindal himself put his income at York, 'taking one year with another', at £1,300, but this is considered to be an understatement.[8] Perhaps we should credit him with a gross York revenue of £8,500 to £9,000, received during his five years and some months in the see. Wide variations occur in the contemporary valuations of Canterbury. One document of 1559 considered it to be worth £3,233. 18s. 8d., while another reduced it to £2,900.[9] At the time of Grindal's translation yet another figure quoted was £3,093. 18s. 8d., and a year later still this precise sum was repeated.[10] In Grindal's last months Burghley looked into the records of the first fruits and tenths in order to find a sum on which to base his pension, found the figure of £2,680 quoted, and formed the impression from the archbishop's own accounts that this was an underestimate but not a gross underestimate of actual income.[11] Grindal's own financial officers reckoned that after the subtraction of tenths fees and pensions the see was worth in the first year of Grindal's incumbency in 'the clear yearly value of the profit which he shall receive' £2,230. 14s. 6d. and, counting the depleted income expected from the Court of Faculties, £2,260. 14s. 6d.[12] Assuming that that was somewhat disingenuously pessimistic, we may put Grindal's total Canterbury receipts at a round £20,000. Computed in this rough and ready fashion it looks as if between 1559 and 1583 he acquired at least £40,000, and perhaps considerably more; in sixteenth-century terms a large enough sum in all conscience.

There is no reason to suppose that Grindal was indifferent to his temporalities, or that the professional estate managers and accountants who served him were unduly conservative or careless in the collection of his dues. Lax administration Grindal was unlikely to tolerate, in whatever department, and his interests in remaining solvent and in rewarding his kindred and servants were not different from those of other bishops. At one point in his career good fortune enabled him to maximize his profits and to exercise much valuable patronage. The register of leases made in his time as archbishop of York shows that an unusually large number of leases fell in, especially during his last two years in the diocese. In 1575 no less than forty-two leases expired, compared with only four in each of the two preceding years. The leases were for twenty-one years, so that the entry fines would not have been large. Nevertheless, they must have added up to a useful nest-egg to help Grindal on his way to Canterbury. It was more significant that many of these leases were bestowed on members of the archbishop's household, and on his favourite nephew William Woodhall and a Woodhall kinswoman. His steward, John Scott, and another senior household officer, William Marshall, each received three leases, Richard Ratcliff the controller and Grindal's secretary Richard Frampton two each, while eighteen other household servants received a total of nineteen further leases.[13] Out of a total of eighty leases recorded for Grindal's time in York, as many as thirty-three seem to have benefited servants and kinsmen, while the leasing of the remaining forty-seven appears to have been governed by other considerations, among them Court pressure, including in one instance the 'special request' of the earl of Leicester.[14] But the allegation made by his successor, Sandys, that Grindal had corruptly seized six score leases for his kinsmen and servants was inaccurate and exaggerated, and coloured by the self-interested malice which characterized Sandys in later life.[15] After all, the leases, which were mostly for twenty-one years, were not especially 'beneficial' (to use the technical term appropriate to these matters) or injurious to Grindal's successors.

By this time much of the income of the archbishop of York, between a third and a half, was derived from rectories which the Crown had exchanged for episcopal manors. They owed their wealth, it has been said, to the relative privation of some thirty-three vicars of livings of which they were the impropriators.[16] There is no evidence that Grindal's conscience found this an uncomfortable way to make a living, or that his record was any better than that of other episcopal impropriators in keeping the chancels of these parish churches in repair.[17] In affairs of this kind Grindal was not capable of transcending the conditions and conventional practices of his time.[18]

When Grindal arrived at Lambeth he had to fight for the full restitution of his Canterbury temporalities, which the Crown had administered during the vacancy. The case had been made that Parker's wealth argued that the see had some other 'secret commodities' not specified in the bill of temporalities. The reply which Grindal prepared (and the document is endorsed in his hand) reveals an expert knowledge of the intricacies of episcopal finance.[19] He was able to detail the peculiar pecuniary advantages which Archbishop Parker had enjoyed in the circumstances obtaining immediately after the Elizabethan settlement. These included the granting of new dispensations, after calling in all those granted by Cardinal Pole; conducting visitations *sede vacante*, consecrating bishops and then holding his own metropolitan visitation, with fees payable on all three occasions; disposing of offices and letting a good number of beneficial leases, against entry fines. The implication was that in the absence of such opportunities Grindal should not be deprived of any proportion of his legitimate temporalities. On the other hand the document sounds an unmistakable note of moral idealism. Grindal did not intend to profit by the dubious dispensations in which the Faculty Office had dealt under Parker. Parker had collected substantial entry fines by leasing benefices of which he was the impropriator, 'which his successor never did, nor cannot do, nor would do if he could'. (But it is not true that Grindal had never leased rectories. He had done so both at London and York, where he had leased the great tithes of one Yorkshire parish together with the site of the tithe barn to his cook and his butler.)[20] Grindal further declared his high-minded intention not to make money out of his metropolitan visitation but rather to bestow on it charges of his own.

This document seems to epitomize Grindal's attitude to matters of revenue: a firm and practical resolve to lay claim to whatever was lawfully his, indeed a concern to maximize his cash income; but little trace of those devious financial devices with which both Sandys and Aylmer and some other Elizabethan bishops are credited.

So much for the getting. What of the spending? The first fact to establish is that all but a small residue of Grindal's very substantial revenues were apparently used up in his lifetime. Including the educational endowments, we may roughly compute the archbishop's residual estate at something more than £3,000 and considerably less than £4,000: a figure not greatly in excess of a single year's income from the see of Canterbury.[21] In composing his character of Grindal that most felicitous but not always reliable of seventeenth-century writers Thomas Fuller found cause for wonder in 'the mean estate' which this bachelor prelate, 'living and dying sole and single', left behind him.[22] The implied suggestion that he should have died rich is not entirely justified. Some bishops ended in bankruptcy so that their executors were unable to pay the dilapidations claimed by their successors or to compound with the Crown for taxation revenue still owing.[23] Winchester was one of the richest bishoprics, valued at £3,700 in 1559 and at £2,491 in

1576. Yet Robert Horne died after twenty years in possession with private debts of £300, a personal debt to the Crown of £200 and arrears for first fruits and tenths from the diocese amounting to more than £900. In addition the unfortunate executors had to find £200 for payments to the bishop's servants and other legacies. Their only remedy, an inadequate one, was to melt down his plate.[24]

But Fuller was entitled to raise at least one eyebrow. Horne had to make provision for four daughters. And the contrast between Grindal's 'mean estate' and what his boyhood friend Edwin Sandys made, materially speaking, out of twenty-eight years of episcopal life is striking. Far from living 'sole and single' Sandys fathered seven sons and two daughters. Fuller remarked that Grindal could not be accused of 'cockering to his own children'. But no one of this generation 'cockered' more assiduously and successfully than Sandys. He established his sons in the ranks of the gentry 'and he managed it out of church revenues'.[25] What, Fuller wondered, had wasted Grindal's assets? Not prodigality: more likely contempt of the world. He was 'unwilling to die guilty of much wealth'. Yet the money must have gone somewhere and Fuller had his suspicions: 'not to speak of fat servants made under a lean master'.

From figures which were later assembled for the purpose of litigation from Grindal's decade as bishop of London it appears that Fuller's suggestion of lax domestic administration cannot be entirely discounted.[26] The single item of 'hospitality' accounted for the expenditure of a gross sum of £12,534 7s. 4d., or an annual outlay of at least £1,200. This was more than the see was officially supposed to be worth. 'Hospitality' covered a multitude of virtues, if not of sins, and a variety of incidents in the daily life of a great household such as Grindal, for all his personal simplicity and austerity, was obliged to maintain. It included the wages and maintenance of the many members of this large and diverse community, from chaplains and secretaries and stewards to menial servants. In a censorious letter of 1574, the puritan Thomas Sampson instructed Grindal that Christ's patrimony ought not to be spent to maintain 'a sort and company of idle serving men, which do only serve the pomp of one person':

> But yet your state, your port, your train of men waiting on you in the streets, your gentleman usher going before you with bare head, your family full of idle serving men, and so the rest of your *apparatus* in the world and sight of men is very lordly

and, we may add, costly.[27]

Hospitality also embraced entertainment and all that was consumed in Grindal's household by outsiders: the poor, certainly, to
an extent which there is no way of measuring, but also by all kinds
of people on every kind of business. On 14 July 1562 the London
parish of St Gregory's in Paul's Churchyard had its annual archery
match, 'the one half against the other', red scarves versus yellow
scarves, drums and flutes. 'And so to my lord of London's place to
sup, a hundred messes.'[28] At other times the guests at Paul's or
Fulham included foreign diplomats, or the quarrelsome ministers
and elders of the London stranger churches, settling their differences with toasts drunk in the bishop's wine.[29] One one occasion
a puritan fanatic who had just called Grindal a heretic and an
antichrist was offered wine by the bishop's servants on his way
back to jail.[30]

How freely did the wine flow? Was Grindal's household an
institution for extensive outdoor relief? Not to put too fine a point
upon it, did legs of mutton walk out of the back door, at Fulham, at
Bishopthorpe, at Lambeth? We cannot be sure. But we are entitled
to doubt whether Grindal was a careless master of his household.
And comparisons can be made which will suggest that his expenses
in 'hospitality', while on the high side, were not dramatically out of
line with those incurred by other bishops. Sandys alleged that his
annual expenditure on hospitality as bishop of London was £800,
or two-thirds of that recorded for Grindal. To run the risk of
generalizing from a couple of examples, this may suggest that a
bachelor bishop was liable to spend more than a married bishop
who could recruit his wife as quartermaster. But the role of bishops' wives in household management is a subject of almost total
obscurity. And Sandys had no more success than Grindal in keeping his gross expenditure within the limits of his nominal income.
His outlay on all items in six years and nine months amounted to
£8,431. 7s. 4d., or £1,681 more than the sum of the annual revenues of £1,000 which he claimed to have received.[31] The experience of Grindal's predecessor had not been different. In 1558
Bonner had confessed to spending 'a great deal more than is my
livelihood, wherein though I do play the fool, yet such is the place
that I am in that I cannot otherwise do.'[32]

But perhaps both Grindal and Sandys understated their true
incomes as bishops of London by a substantial margin. On the
figures returned Grindal would have been out of pocket for the
single item of housekeeping alone. But there were other large sums
to be found: particularly for the satisfaction of the Crown. Grindal
as bishop of London was rated to pay the queen £1,000 in first
fruits and £111 annually in tenths: more than £2,000 out of his

total London receipts of perhaps £12,000. Three years after his
entry into the see he had paid only a quarter of the sum owing in
first fruits.[33] First fruits and tenths at York may have cost him
£2,400 and at Canterbury £4,730. The global sum owing in first
fruits and tenths may have been more than £9,000 out of total
revenues of some £40,000. Perhaps Grindal was excused some of
these payments, as it was said other bishops had been excused, in
whole or part.[34] But there is no evidence of this and in his last year
at York, when he was expecting the arrival of the queen on progress, Grindal told Parker that he was due to make the last (and
presumably the fifth) payment of his first fruits in the coming
Michaelmas Term, the sum of £380. There is no suggestion that
he was hoping to avoid this levy, although he allowed himself the
wry comment: 'How well it will stand with a progress your Grace
may consider.'[35] In the event Elizabeth never crossed the Trent
on progress. On his translation to Canterbury Grindal made a case
against being required to pay first-fruits within either two years or
three, but not to escape them altogether.[36]

Over and above their liability for first fruits and tenths the
bishops, in common with the other clergy, were taxed under the
subsidy, normally at 6s. in the £, payable over three years. Subsidies were granted in 1563, 1572, 1576 and 1582.[37] As bishop of
London Grindal would have had to find more than £100 for the
subsidy in three successive years. In calculating the implications
for his Canterbury income if first fruits were demanded in the first
two or three years he had to take additional account of the subsidy
granted in 1576, payable in instalments of £268. 5s. 2d. If the first
fruits were paid over three years his disposable income would be
only £1,332. 10s. 6d. in the first year, dropping to £1,164. 5s. 9d.
in the two following years. If they were required in two instalments, this would depress his effective income to £968. 9s. 1d. in
the first year and to a derisory £700. 3s. 11d. in the second.[38] What
made matters worse for the bishops was their personal responsibility to answer for all the clerical taxation, first fruits, tenths
and subsidies, owing from their diocesan clergy: a liability which
found many of them in arrears with the government from time to
time.[39] As late as 1564 Grindal was still toiling under an unwelcome obligation to collect the remains of a Marian subsidy
from his London clergy at the same time as a new subsidy was due.
He explained to the lord treasurer, the marquis of Winchester, that
the current subsidy was being collected 'with much difficulty ...
and many complain of want of money'. He hoped that the Council
might spare the bishops the debts of their predecessors, 'but will
be content if we pay our own'.[40]

It begins to look less mysterious than it did to Fuller that Grindal should have left a somewhat 'mean estate'. Yet we still have to face the further demands on his resources represented by the obligation to maintain in good repair the fabric of his episcopal residences and of other structures, not to speak of the colossal and extraordinary expenses occasioned by the great St Paul's fire of 1561.[41] Since it was in the interests of bishops to enquire narrowly into the performance of their predecessors in this regard the facts of Grindal's expenditure on repairs and maintenance are readily accessible.[42] According to ecclesiastical law, a bishop entering upon his see could recover from his predecessor, or from his executors, 'dilapidations', the duly authenticated expenses of repairing the decay of those edifices for which he had assumed responsibility: principally houses, but also the chancels of parish churches where the bishop was impropriator and rector, and even bridges and sea defences. Although the bishops had already forfeited many of their late medieval residences, both in London and in the country, the maintenance of those that remained was an unwelcome legacy of the energetic building activities of their early Tudor predecessors, as much of this property matured into middle age or beyond.[43] Handled with tact and restraint claims for dilapidations and their settlement were a normal incident of the transition from one incumbency to another. As Bishop Aylmer of London pointed out in 1579:

> All bishops in her Majesty's time hath been answered by their predecessors' executors or of themselves if they have been translated, viz.: Archbishop Grindal at Archbishop Young's widow's hands, Matthew Cantuar at Pole's hands, Edmund Cantuar at Matthew's hands, Lincoln at Bullingham bishop of Worcester his hands, Norwich at Parkhurst's hands, etc.[44]

Cooper of Winchester made a 'friendly composition' with Bishop Watson's executors for all the dilapidations of both Watson's and the bankrupt Horne's times.[45] But in conditions of financial stringency and buoyant litigation bishops did not always find it possible to act with restraint, or to reach informal agreements on these matters. If there was a failure to settle liability for dilapidations at a personal, informal level, then it was necessary to go to law, and the law made the contending parties of necessity antagonists.

When Edwin Sandys followed his friend Grindal as bishop of London he neither claimed nor received as much as a farthing in dilapidations, thinking that it would be 'great greediness' to charge his predecessor for the consequences of the fire of St Paul's. But in the jaundiced view of his own successor, John Aylmer, this was negligence on Sandys's part, not generosity.[46] When Sandys succeeded Grindal at York he commended Aylmer to the Queen and gave him 'all friendly encouragement', participating in his consecration when it proved difficult to find sufficient bishops from the southern province to officiate. Or so Sandys later alleged, claiming that Aylmer in gratitude, 'considering that I had been his friend and what cost I had been at in repairing these houses', promised that he would claim no dilapidations against him. Sandys's brother Miles thought that he ought to have got that promise in writing. For by the time Sandys was preparing to leave for the north Aylmer was mentioning a figure of a hundred pounds and later raised his bid. 'Now I hear that he gapeth after thousands.' 'So soon as the bishop of York had holpen him on with his rochet he was transformed and showed himself in his own nature.' Perhaps Aylmer's change of heart was prompted by the discovery of how much he would have to pay to the Crown in his first two or three years as a bishop. Be that as it may, Aylmer's ungrateful and uncharitable demands, as they appeared to Sandys, forced him to make belated demands against Grindal for dilapidations at both London and York.[47] So far as Aylmer was concerned, this was normal procedure, and a necessary one if a bishop was to protect himself and his heirs and executors against future litigation. But it was admittedly a scandal that 'three of the chief bishops should go to law'.[48] And once Aylmer had successfully agitated for the appointment of a special royal commission of delegates to hear the tripartite suit[49] the scandal was prolonged, outlasting Archbishop Grindal himself.

From the defence offered first by Grindal and later by his executors we learn that at the time of Bonner's deprivation of the bishopric of London there were 'divers great ruins and decays' in the three principal episcopal residences, in London, at Fulham, and at Hadham in Hertfordshire. Bonner was sued for dilapidations and subsequently excommunicated and denounced at Paul's Cross for failing to appear. Presumably it was his proxies who were contumacious, since Bonner himself was forcibly detained in the Marshalsea Prison. Bonner subsequently died intestate, there was no administration of his goods, and Grindal had no remedy. As bishop of London Grindal maintained builders 'continually in his livery' and spent on repairs no less than £1,964. 7s. 1d., at an annual rate of some £185, or almost 20 per cent of his nominal income. Aylmer alleged that all bishops had a canonical duty to spend a quarter of their revenue in maintenance of their property but, as Sandys's advocates were not slow to point out, it was doubtful whether this canon was still in force. Certainly no bishop, least of all Aylmer himself, observed it. But Grindal's outlay of nearly £2,000 did not fall far short of the £2,500 for which he was liable according to this quite unrealistic criterion.[50]

By far the largest share was accounted for by repairs to St Paul's after the fire of 1561: £1,184. 18s. 11d. from the bishop's own pocket. £147. 2s. 2d. was spent on the bishop's house beside St Paul's, where inherited decays were estimated at £457. 8s., and £356. 15s. 7d. at Fulham, where the house was left in great decay by Bonner and 'very sufficiently repaired' by Grindal. The accounts are confused when they come to Hadham, where the total expenditure may have been £200. 10s. 9d., but the itemized accounts suggest that this was the sum required to make 'windtight and watertight' a structure at Hadham known as the Oxhouse which Sandys later demolished, and that the enormous sum of £500 was spent on reroofing Hadham Hall itself, which Grindal found in 'utter ruin', with not a dry room in the house except for a caretaker's cubbyhole. Smaller sums were spent on minor properties, including the upkeep of chancels and parsonage houses in some Essex parishes. It is with no surprise that we learn that 'by this great charge the said lord archbishop while he remained in London, after the burning of Paul's, became in debt and was enforced to borrow money yearly the latter years of his abiding in London next before his translation.'[51]

Quite apart from the heroic response which he made to the calamity of St Paul's there is no reason to doubt what was alleged on Grindal's behalf: that as bishop of London he was 'a very careful man and vigilant to maintain and repair his houses and to preserve his woods'. What Sandys alleged in a letter to Walsingham, that at his entry to the diocese he found the bishop's houses 'in marvellous great ruin and no show of reparations done in my predecessor's time' is implausible, given that Sandys made no claim against Grindal in 1570. Indeed he elsewhere inconsistently conceded that since Grindal had taken timely steps to deal with the damage from the fire 'there happened no great decays in my time nor necessity of greater sums than I expended'. Aylmer's advocates made convincingly specific allegations that the building works which Sandys did undertake consisted of new embellishments rather than the repair of old buildings, 'matters rather of pleasure than of necessity', and this in itself suggests that the essential fabric was in good order when Sandys took it over. Sandys himself claimed to have spent no more than £232. 13s. 4d. on repairs in his six years in London. Aylmer thought that the true sum was 'not £100'. And it was plausibly alleged that Sandys had spent little or nothing on St Paul's, which indeed was notoriously neglected after Grindal's time until William Laud took it in hand in the reign of Charles I.[52]

When Grindal arrived in York he found that Archbishop Young had made 'great waste and destruction' of his houses, and especially of the palace at York. Sir John Harington later knew and repeated the story of how Young stripped the lead from the roof of this building, valued at £1,000, and made the proceeds over to 'a great lord in the Court', almost certainly the earl of Leicester.[53] Grindal failed to obtain a satisfactory settlement in respect of these dilapidations and explained to Cecil that he was forced to go to law, 'otherwise if I die the next successor hath his action against mine executors'. When Grindal wrote this, in November 1570, he was seriously ill and probably did not expect to survive the winter. Young's widow lived in York and the two remaining executors outside the province of York so that it was not possible to sue them jointly before an ecclesiastical judge in either province. So the archbishop's controller Richard Ratcliff came south to solicit for the appointment of a commission of royal delegates to determine the matter. The commission was appointed within a month and reads like a roll-call of the most distinguished Elizabethan lawyers, a testimony to the leverage which Grindal exerted at Court through his friendship with Burghley. The commission included Sir Thomas Smith, Sir Thomas Wroth, Dr Walter Haddon, Thomas Bromley, solicitor general, George Bromley, attorney of the duchy of Lancaster, Dr Thomas Wilson and others.[54] We must assume that Grindal obtained speedy satisfaction. Aylmer later reported as much. According to the same witness, when Sandys succeeded him Grindal for his part made a generous settlement for dilapidations which were not as considerable as Sandys left behind in London. And in his turn Grindal was 'answered' at the hands of Parker's executors, claiming and receiving the sum of £350, whereas Parker himself had received £600 from Pole's executors.[55]

When Grindal was negotiating the terms of his resignation, early in 1583, he asked that he should be spared the distraction of a claim for dilapidations and quoted legal opinion that these were not due in cases of resignation. It was not that he doubted the equity of his successor but because he had been 'so much troubled with suits for dilapidations'.[56] But Grindal died in office and in due course his estate was endangered by Archbishop Whitgift's claims against it. Moreover the commission hearing the major tripartite dilapidations suit seems to have found in favour of Aylmer against Grindal as well as Sandys. John Scott, the archbishop's steward and now one of his executors, was alarmed at the threat to Grindal's pious and educational benefactions and in July 1584 addressed himself to Walsingham, whom Grindal had prudently appointed, with Burghley, an overseer of his will. Evidence was supplied to show that Grindal was to be discharged of the dilapidations awarded to Aylmer and 'rightly laid upon the archbishop of York in respect of his small expense bestowed in reparations'. In another paper the executors alleged that Whitgift's demands were unreasonable. 'Archbishop Grindal was in his lifetime for all his sees that he enjoyed always known and taken to be the most diligent repairer of his houses, and was otherwise *bonus paterfamilias* for preserving the commodity of his sees.' Grindal, 'having very good experience and understanding in what state of repair bishops ought to leave their houses', had so ordered these things that he had thought his successor would have cause to demand little or nothing for dilapidations, and the provision for his servants had been made on this assumption. The conclusion was an offer to Whitgift of £250 'in full satisfaction', which Walsingham and Burghley were asked to approve as reasonable.[57] And thus much, as Strype would have said, of dilapidations matters. Even granted the origin of most of the evidence in the partial circumstances of litigation there appears no reason to deprive Grindal of the reputation, if not of 'vir architectonicus', as was said of a future archbishop of York, Richard Neile,[58] then at least of 'a very careful man', *bonus paterfamilias*.

Finally, as an appendix to this appendix, something must be added on the subject of woods and timber. The timber growing on an episcopal estate was a standing temptation to a bishop who wished or felt constrained by necessity to convert the capital resources of his benefice into ready cash. Even Archbishop Cranmer was said by his secretary, Ralph Morice, to have been driven to exchange and sell his woods by the expenses of hospitality, although he had allegedly replaced them with woods 'more commodious for his houses'.[59] Woods were available to be cropped, for fuel and building materials, but a 'good husband' was supposed to hand on to his successor a stock of timber at least equivalent to that which he had himself inherited. So when Aylmer included in a list of Sandys's assets at York woods to the value of £3,000 Sandys indignantly retorted that 'he might as well rate the houses there to pull down and sell.' 'If it be lawful for the bishop of York to sell all his woods at £3,000, then is it lawful for the bishop of London to do the like, who hath as much wood left him as is at York.'[60] It was to become somewhat notorious that Aylmer took the hint, making such a waste of his timber that he won from Martin Marprelate the anagrammatic nickname of Mar-Elm: 'for you have marred all the elms in Fulham, having cut them all down.'[61] Sandys, for that matter, had been accused of making 'spoil' of his timber as bishop of Worcester, making more than £2,000 out of sales to his brother Miles Sandys and in other scarcely reputable transactions.[62]

In 1580, with the national resources of timber increasingly scarce and expensive, the Privy Council launched a general enquiry into the felling and sale of episcopal woods and issued strict instructions against further spoliation. In their certificates[63] the bishops blame their predecessors and tenants, allege that they themselves have felled trees only for the furnishing and repairs of their own houses, but in some cases admit the details of sales. Bishop Piers of Salisbury, for example, confessed to selling wood worth £172 to meet various expenses, whereas Young of Rochester reported that the only trees felled had been used to repair his manor house at Bromley.[64]

From the large number of papers which survive[65] it looks as if the government was particularly interested in Bishop Aylmer's activities as forester and timber merchant, and that these may have prompted the general enquiry. As early as May 1579 Aylmer was obliged to account for his wasting of woods and was being threatened with deprivation by Burghley. 'This grieveth me', he wrote, 'that my lord treasurer is counted to have a miscontented mind toward the bishop of London.'[66] Later it was disclosed that in three to four years he had sold to various named parties more than 300 acres of coppice and at least 1,000 timber trees, amounting in total value to £1,000. 'It is also supposed that all the woods belonging to the bishopric are so wasted and spoiled by the said bishop that by the time all is felled that is already sold small or no wood will be left growing.' In his defence Aylmer confirmed some of the alleged transactions, disputed others and estimated his total sales at £600. 'Note that in these three years I have and must pay to her majesty £1,800, besides my house-keeping.' Predictably, Aylmer accused Sandys of destroying 400 acres of woodland in his time as bishop of London.

But no such charge was levelled against Grindal, the papers containing references only to woods which had been stocked by him, or to moderate sales. In his own certificate of 22 March 1580, signed somewhat ostentatiously 'your majesty's most humble subject and daily orator', Grindal reported that he had sold no timber since his entry into the see of Canterbury, 'no, not so much as one timber tree', and had not caused any trees to be felled except as required for repairs to buildings and bridges, although he had given away twelve small trees from the Blean, outside Canterbury.

And as for my doings in this behalf in the bishoprics of London and York during my incumbency in them: I was no spoiler but a careful preserver of the timber, as will be testified (I am sure), if the case require, by a number that know my doings in those places.[67]

The provisional conclusion of this superficial investigation of Grindal's stewardship is that he was indeed 'no spoiler', and not covetous; and that only by forfeiting this reputation, and by a policy of rigorously parsimonious house-keeping, could he have contrived to leave anything but a somewhat 'mean estate' behind him. But surely Grindal managed things very well. He died virtually free of debt, with enough money to make his educational benefactions, pension his servants and do a little good for his kinsfolk, without turning them into upstart gentry. The final irony is that Queen Elizabeth had helped to make this possible by forcing her archbishop into a life of semi-retirement.

ABBREVIATIONS

A.P.C.	*Acts of the Privy Council of England*, n.s., ed. J. R. Dasent, 32 vols, 1890–1907.
B.I.H.R.	*Bulletin of the Institute of Historical Research*
BL	British Library
	MS. Add. Additional Manuscript
	MS. Harl. Harleian Manuscript
	MS. Lansd. Lansdowne Manuscript
Bodl.	Bodleian Library
CUL	Cambridge University Library
CS	Camden Society
CALC	Cathedral Archives and Library Canterbury
CLRO	Corporation of London Record Office
D.N.B.	*Dictionary of National Biography*
Elizabethan Puritan Movement	Patrick Collinson, *The Elizabethan Puritan Movement*, 1967.
E.H.R.	*English Historical Review*
Foxe	*The Acts and Monuments of John Foxe*, ed. G. Townsend and S. R. Cattley, 8 vols, 1837–41.
Fuller	Thomas Fuller, *The Church History of Britain*, 5 vols, Oxford 1845.
GLRO	Greater London Record Office
GLL	Guildhall Library London
ITL	Inner Temple Library
J.E.H.	*Journal of Ecclesiastical History*
J.T.S.	*Journal of Theological Studies*
LPL	Lambeth Palace Library
Letters of Thomas Wood	Patrick Collinson, ed., *Letters of Thomas Wood, Puritan, 1566–1577*, *B.I.H.R.* Special Supplement v. 1960.
O.L., i	*Original Letters Relative to the English Reformation*, 2 vols,
O.L., ii	ed. H. Robinson, PS, 1846, 1847.
Parker Correspondence	*Correspondence of Matthew Parker*, ed. Bruce and Perowne, PS, 1853.
PS	The Parker Society for the Publication of the Works of the Fathers and Early Writers of the Reformed English Church, Cambridge
PRO	Public Record Office
Remains	*The Remains of Edmund Grindal*, ed. W. Nicholson, PS, 1843.
Strype	John Strype, *The Life and Acts of the Most Reverend Father in God, Edmund Grindal* (1710), Oxford 1821.

Strype,   John Strype, *Annals of the Reformation and Establishment*
  Annals   *of Religion, and Other Various Occurrences in the Church of*
                     England During Queen Elizabeth's Happy Reign, 3 vols in
                     6 pts, Oxford 1824.
Z.L., i   *Zurich Letters 1558–1579*, ed. H. Robinson, PS, 1842.
Z.L., ii   *Zurich Letters (Second Series) 1558–1602*, PS, 1845.

NOTES

Unless otherwise stated, the place of publication is London.

Introduction

1 Creighton's article on Grindal in *D.N.B.*; W. H. Frere, *A History of the English Church in the Reigns of Elizabeth and James I*, 1904, p. 192; W. P. M. Kennedy, *Studies in Tudor History*, 1916, p. 260; Sir Sidney Lee in *Cambridge Modern History*, iii. 1907, p. 341; H. M. Gwatkin, *Church and State in England to the Death of Queen Anne*, 1917, p. 255; P. A. Welsby, *George Abbot, the Unwanted Archbishop*, 1962, p. 1.

2 Frere, op. cit., p. 192; *Remains*, p. 387.

3 Thomas Rogers, *The Catholic Doctrine of the Church of England*, ed. J. J. S. Perowne, PS 1854, p. 9; Raphael Holinshed, *The Third Volume of Chronicles*, 1587, p. 1354; John Hayward, *Annals of the First Four Years of the Reign of Queen Elizabeth*, ed. John Bruce, CS 1840, p. 89.

4 John Milton, *Of reformation, touching church discipline in England*, 1641, p. 15; William Prynne, *The antipathie of the English lordly prelacie both to regall monarchy and civil unity*, 1641, pp. 147–9; Daniel Neal, *The History of the Puritans*, 1793 edn, i. 346–7.

5 Fuller, v. 58.

6 *The tryal of Dr Henry Sacheverell*, 1710; *The bishop of Lincolns and bishop of Norwichs speeches in the House of Lords, March the 17th*, 1710. For the circumstances, see Geoffrey Holmes, *The Trial of Doctor Sacheverell*, 1973.

7 (John Strype), *A brief and true character and account of Edmund Grindall*, 1710; (Henry Sacheverell?), *Memorials of Archbishop Grindal: wherein the true causes of his suspension and disgrace are impartially related*, 1710; *Strange news from the dead: or, Archbishop Grindal's letter of thanks to the honourable M...rs and others, who strenuously vindicated affronts done to him above an hundred years after he was dead* (1710?).

8 *A brief and true character*; *Letters of Eminent Men Addressed to Ralph Thoresby FRS*, 1832, ed. Joseph Hunter, ii. 257; *Memorials of Archbishop Grindal*, pp. 33–5. There are modern accounts of Strype in W. D. J. Cargill Thompson, 'John Strype as a Source for the Study of Sixteenth-Century English Church History', in *The Materials Sources and Methods of Ecclesiastical History, Studies in Church History*, xi. ed. D. Baker, Oxford 1975, pp. 237–47; and by Cecile Zinberg, 'The Usable Dissenting Past: John Strype and Elizabethan Puritanism', in *The Dissenting Tradition: Essays for Leland H. Carlson*, ed. C. R. Cole and M. E. Moody, Athens Ohio 1975, pp. 123–39.

9 *Letters to Thoresby*, ii. 257; various letters of Strype in vol. 6 of the Baumgartner MSS. in CUL and in William Cole's transcripts (with polemical glosses) in BL, MS. Add. 5853; list of subscribers printed in the first edition of the *Life of Grindal*, 1710.

10 *The Lives of John Bradford, Edmund Grindal and Sir Matthew Hale*, p. 237.

11 There is a modern unpublished thesis: V. C. Greer, 'The Place of Edmund Grindal in the Elizabethan Church', M.Litt., Cambridge 1963.

1 That Little Angle

The principal sources for the genealogical and family history contained in this chapter include (1) biographical information in a memorandum composed by Archbishop Sandys (PRO, S.P. 15/12/92), supplemented by further details relating to the Sandys family kindly supplied by Miss N. M. Fuidge of the History of Parliament Trust; (2) a number of Grindal's letters (*Remains*, pp. 256–7, 267–8, 321–3); (3) the parish registers of St Bees, and a number of articles by William Jackson based on these registers and on wills and other documents. The St Bees registers, 1538–1837, were transcribed by H. B. Stout and published in 1968 for the Parish Register Section of the Cumberland and Westmorland Antiquarian and Archaeological Society (cited hereafter as *Registers*). Jackson's articles, including 'Archbishop Grindal and his Grammar School of St Bees' and 'Extracts from the Parish Registers of St Bees with Comments upon the Same' were reprinted in *Papers and Pedigrees Mainly Relating to Cumberland*, Cumberland and Westmorland Antiquarian and Archaeological Society Publications, e.s., vols 5, 6, 1892. I am also indebted to the modern historian of St Bees, John Todd, for information imparted in correspondence and verbally, including details from the Ministers' Account of 1539 relating to the dissolution of St Bees Priory (PRO, Augmentations, S.C.6.7382). The wider background has been supplied from the following authorities: C. M. L. Bouch and G. P. Jones, *The Lake Counties, 1500–1830*, Manchester 1961; C. M. L. Bouch, *Prelates and People of the Lake Counties*, Kendal 1948; *The Agrarian History of England and Wales*, iv. ed. Joan Thirsk, Cambridge 1967; D. W. L. Tough, *The Last Years of a Frontier*, Oxford 1928; *The Register of the Priory of St Bees*, ed. J. Wilson, Surtees Soc., cxxvi; Henry Barnes, 'Visitations of the Plague in Cumberland and Westmorland', Cumberland and Westmorland Antiquarian and Archaeological Society, xi; G. Elliott, 'The System of Cultivation and Evidence of Enclosure in the Cumberland Open Fields in the Sixteenth Century', ibid., n.s., lix; and last, but not least, on appreciative explorations of West Cumberland, shod, as R. H. Tawney directed, in boots.

1 Tobie Matthew to Francis Mylles, 9 Jan. 1587(/8); BL, MS. Cotton Titus B VII, fols 424–6.
2 *Letters of Eminent Men Addressed to Ralph Thoresby FRS*, 1832, ed. Joseph Hunter, i. 186–90, ii. 56–8; CUL, MS. Baumgartner 6. In September 1694 Thoresby recorded his visit to the place 'where worthy Bishop Grindall was born'. (*The Diary of Ralph Thoresby*, ed. J. Hunter, 1830, i. 269.)
3 *The Story of St Bees 1583–1939: A Souvenir of the 350th Anniversary of the Opening of St Bees School*, 1939, p. 15.
4 Mr John Todd of St Bees, whose wife is a native of Hensingham, has assisted me with these details.
5 *Registers*, i. 5, 7, 8, 11, 12, 36, 37, ii. 6, 12, 13, 15, 20, 21, 31, 37, 41, iii. 13; Jackson, *Papers and Pedigrees*, ii. 187–8.
6 *Registers*, ii. 38.
7 William Hutchinson, *History of the County of Cumberland*, Carlisle 1794, i. 551.
8 For a sensitive appreciation of changing values in north-eastern England in the sixteenth century see the various writings of Dr M. E. James of Durham University and especially his *Family, Lineage and Civil Society*, Oxford 1974.
9 Grindal's will, in *Remains*, pp. 458–63; Grindal to Sir Walter Mildmay, 4 June 1571, PRO, S.P. 46/29, fol. 36; York Minster Library, MS. W6, fols 173ᵛ–5, 196ᵛ–8, 203, 204 (references supplied to me by Dr W. J. Sheils of

the Borthwick Institute of Historical Research of the University of York); information on John Wilson of Boston, Mass., imparted by Dr H. C. Porter of the University of Cambridge.

10 Jackson, *Papers and Pedigrees*, ii. 187.
11 *Cal. S.P. Dom. Add., 1566–1579*, pp. 347–8.
12 Jackson, *Papers and Pedigrees*, ii. 7.
13 Grindal to Challoner, 20 Feb. 1563; PRO, S.P. 70/51/301.
14 LPL, MS. F I/A/B, fol. 21ᵛ. I owe this reference to Dr J. I. Daeley.
15 Grindal's account of these events (*Remains*, pp. 321–3) has been corrected from the entries in the *Registers* and other data cited by Jackson, *Papers and Pedigrees*, i. 59–72. The proclamation 'Offering Pardon to Followers of Leonard Dacres' is in *Tudor Royal Proclamations*, ed. P. J. Hughes and J. F. Larkin, ii. New Haven 1969, 329–32. Grindal's purchase of the lease is recorded in *Cal. of Patent Rolls, Eliz. I*, v. 1569–72, no. 2046, p. 251.
16 Jackson, *Papers and Pedigrees*, ii. 199–200.
17 W. R. D. Jones, *The Tudor Commonwealth, 1529–1559*, 1970; G. R. Elton, *Reform and Renewal: Thomas Cromwell and the Common Weal*, Cambridge 1973, and *Reform and Reformation: England 1509–1558*, 1977; W. K. Jordan, *Edward VI: the Threshold of Power*, 1970, p. 225.
18 Grindal to Burghley, 9 March 1574; BL, MS. Lansd. 18, no. 27, fol. 52.
19 W. K. Jordan, *The Social Institutions of Lancashire: A Study of the Changing Patterns of Aspirations in Lancashire 1480–1660*, Chetham Socy Publications, 3rd ser. xi. 1962, esp. pp. 28–75, 112–14.
20 G. Elliott, op. cit., 103; W. M. Williams, *The Sociology of an English Village: Gosforth*, 1956, esp. chapter 10.
21 Hutchinson, op. cit., i. 551.
22 *Cal. S.P. Dom., 1598–1601*, p. 363.
23 Jordan, *Social Institutions of Lancashire*, p. 32.
24 Foxe, vii. 287.
25 Mr John Todd of St Bees informs me that neither the Ministers' Account of 1539 relating to the Priory (PRO, Augmentations, S.C.6.7382) nor an account roll of 1516–17 (Carlisle Record Office, D/Lons/W/St Bees 1.1) contains any mention of a school. However, Jackson seems to have assumed that Sandys and Grindal were privately educated at Rottington, which certainly may have been the case.
26 CUL, MS. Baumgartner 10, no. 21 (Thomas Baker's transcript of Bishop Matthew Wren's history 'De Custodiis Pembrochianis', of which the original is in Pembroke College Library); Martin Bucer, *Scripta Anglicana*, Basle 1577, dedicatory epistle addressed to Grindal by the editor, Conrad Hubert, Sigs α 2–4ʳ.

2   The Glory of Pembroke Hall

The principal sources for this chapter are as follows: Thomas Baker's transcript of Bishop Matthew Wren's history 'De Custodiis Pembrochianis', CUL, MS. Baumgartner 10; Aubrey Attwater, *Pembroke College, Cambridge: A Short History*, Cambridge 1936; J. Bass Mullinger, *The University of Cambridge*, ii. Cambridge 1884; H. C. Porter, *Reformation and Reaction in Tudor Cambridge*, Cambridge 1958; and material in the following volumes of the Parker Society: Nicholas Ridley, *Works*, 1843, John Bradford, *Writings*, i. 1848, ii. 1853, and Thomas Becon, *Works*, ii. 1844.

1 *Letter-Book of Gabriel Harvey, 1573–1580*, ed. E. J. L. Scott, CS n.s. xxxiii.

1884, pp. 53–4; Strype, pp. 606–7; *Parentalia: or, Memoirs of the Family of the Wrens*, 1750, p. 2.

2 Lever, *Sermons*, ed. E. Arber, English Reprints, 1895, pp. 121–2; Raphael Holinshed, *The Third Volume of Chronicles*, 1587, p. 1354.

3 In his will (*Remains*, p. 459) Grindal bequeathed to the provost and fellows of the Queen's College 'all such books as I have assigned unto them, to be kept in their library, contained in a catalogue subscribed with my hand, and ten pounds towards the clasping, bossing, and chaining of the same'. The books are listed in the seventeenth-century record of bequests, Queen's College Oxford MS. 556. Sears Jayne states in *Library Catalogues of the English Renaissance* (Berkeley and Los Angeles 1956) that the books no longer survive (pp. 20, 125). This is happily not the case and I am grateful to the Assistant Librarian, Miss Helen Powell, for help in locating most of the books on the shelves of the upper library. Each bears a small printed bookplate, apparently contemporaneous with the bequest: 'Liber Collegii Reginae ex dono Reverendissimi D. Edmundi Grindalli Archiep. Cantuar'.

4 References to German books in Grindal's correspondence (*Z.L.*, ii. 24) and to Greek books in the minor bequests in his will (*Remains*, p. 459).

5 Corpus Christi College Cambridge, MS. 106, no. 100, fol. 318.

6 Foxe, v. 4–5. A. B. Emden doubts the truth of this story in so far as it applied to Clerk. (*A Biographical Register of the University of Oxford A.D. 1501 to 1540*, Oxford 1974, pp. 118–19.)

7 C. E. Raven, *English Naturalists from Neckham to Ray*, Cambridge 1947, pp. 48–137.

8 Hakluyt, *Voyages*, 1599, II.i. 165; Fuller, v. 59–60; John Ray, *Historia plantarum*, ii. 1688, 1704; *Gentleman's Magazine*, lxxxiii. pt I, 241, lxxxvii. pt I, 426, and lxxxviii. pt I, 506. Cf. Turner's account of tamarisk, *The seconde parte of William Turners herball*, 1562, fols 58–60.

9 Raven, op. cit., pp. 112–13.

10 *English Reformers*, ed. T. H. L. Parker, Library of Christian Classics xxvi. 1966, pp. 262–71; Richard Hooker, 'A Learned Discourse of Justification', in *Works*, ed. Keble, Oxford 1874, iii. 490; John Davenant, *A Treatise on Justification*, i. 1844, 165; *Remains*, p. 211.

11 The Cambridge disputation is printed in Foxe, vi. 319–36. The London disputation was printed by John Strype, from a Corpus Christi College Cambridge MS., in *Life of Sir John Cheke*, Oxford 1821, pp. 70–86

12 'An Epistle to the English Church' (at Frankfurt?) in *Martyrs divine epistles*, appended to *Common places*, tr. Anthonie Marten, 1583, pp. 136B–139A.

13 Peter Brooks, *Thomas Cranmer's Doctrine of the Eucharist*, 1965; D. G. Selwyn, 'A Neglected Edition of Cranmer's Catechism', *J.T.S.*, n.s. xv, 1964, 76–91; C. C. Richardson, 'Thomas Cranmer and the Analysis of Eucharistic Doctrine', ibid., xvi. 1965, 421–37. For a radically different view, see C. W. Dugmore, *The Mass and the English Reformers*, 1959.

14 J. C. McLelland, *The Visible Words of God: An Exposition of the Sacramental Theology of Peter Martyr Vermigli*, 1957, p. 278 and passim.

15 *Z.L.*, i. 182.

16 The book formed part of Grindal's bequest to the Queen's College Oxford. The work in question was Bullinger's *De origine erroris in negocio eucharistiae ac missae*, first published in 1526, and not *De origine erroris in divorum ac simulachorum cultu*, 1529.

17 Foxe, vi. 336–49. Foxe does not identify the author, except as 'a certain learned and reverend person of this realm'. The ascription depends upon the

Wren MS. 'De Custodiis Pembrochianis'. The work is reprinted in *Remains*, pp. 35–74.

18 Strype, *Annals*, I.i.499. I have been unsuccessful in attempts to verify this report from the references which Strype gives to the controversy between Thomas Dorman (*A proufe of certeyne articles*, 1564) and Laurence Nowell (*Confutation as wel of M. Dorman*, 1567).

19 *Remains*, pp. 247–52; Grindal to Cecil, 24 Jan. 1563, BL, MS. Lansd. 7, fol. 133; *Correspondance de Théodore de Bèze*, vi. (1565), ed. Meylan, Dufour and Henseler, Travaux d'humanisme et renaissance cxiii, Geneva 1970, no. 410.

20 *Remains*, p. 402.

3 Bucer and Ridley: the Edwardian Standard

1 W. K. Jordan, *Edward VI: the Young King*, 1968, p. 436; G. R. Elton, 'The Good Duke', *Studies in Tudor and Stuart Politics and Government*, Cambridge 1974, i. 231–7.

2 M. L. Bush, *The Government Policy of Protector Somerset*, 1975; D. E. Hoak, *The King's Council in the Reign of Edward VI*, Cambridge 1976. For a less than fully convincing attempt to rehabilitate Northumberland, see B. L. Beer, *Northumberland: the Political Career of John Dudley, Earl of Warwick and Duke of Northumberland*, Kent Ohio 1973.

3 Hoak, op. cit., p. 266; G. R. Elton, *Reform and Reformation: England 1509–1558*, 1977, p. 358.

4 Joan Simon, *Education and Society in Tudor England*, Cambridge 1966, pp. 269–70.

5 Quoted, W. R. D. Jones, *The Tudor Commonwealth 1529–1559*, 1970, p. 78.

6 For the constructive concern, see much material in W. K. Jordan's *Philanthropy in England 1480–1660*, 1959, and in Jordan's related regional studies.

7 Simon, op. cit., pp. 268–91. Cf. Jones, op. cit., and G. R. Elton, *Reform and Renewal: Thomas Cromwell and the Common Weal*, Cambridge 1973.

8 Sampson to Burghley, 8 March 1573, BL, MS. Lansd. 18, fols 55–6; Sampson's preface to *Two notable sermons made by ... John Bradford*, 1574, in *Writings of John Bradford*, ed. A. Townsend, i. PS 1848, p. 37; George L. Blackman, 'The Career and Influence of Bishop Richard Cox, 1547–1581', unpublished Cambridge Ph.D. thesis, 1953, p. 48.

9 *Remains*, pp. 202–3.

10 Martyr to Peter Sturmius, 13 April 1561, in *Martyrs divine epistles*, appended to *Common places*, tr. Anthonie Marten, 1583, p. 148A. The paragraphs that follow draw upon material in Martin Bucer, *Scripta Anglicana*, Basle 1577, and on the letters of or relating to Bucer in *Original Letters*, ed. H. Robinson, 2 vols, PS 1846–7, *Zurich Letters*, ed. H. Robinson, 2 vols, PS 1842–5, and in *Gleanings of a Few Scattered Ears During the Reformation in England*, ed. G. C. Gorham, 1857. Further reference will be found in my article 'The Reformer and the Archbishop: Martin Bucer and an English Bucerian', *Journal of Religious History*, vi. 1971, 305–30.

11 James Pilkington, *Works*, ed. J. Scholefield, PS 1842, p. 656.

12 On Peter Martyr and the 'Christ Church Circle' in Edwardian Oxford see Jane E. A. Dawson, 'The Early Career of Christopher Goodman and his Place in the Development of English Protestant Thought', unpublished Durham Ph.D. thesis, 1978.

13 Pilkington, *Works*, pp. 651–2.

14 Pembroke College MS. 217, presented in 1589 by Lancelot Andrewes and described by François Wendel in his introduction to the edition of *De regno Christi* in *Martini Buceri Opera Latina*, xv. Paris 1955, liv-lv.

15 *De obitu doctissimi et sanctissimi theologi Doctoris Martini Buceri*, Basle 1551; reprinted, *Scripta Anglicana*, pp. 867–82.

16 *Historia vera de vita, obitu, sepultra …*, ed. Conrad Hubert, Basle 1562; reprinted, *Scripta Anglicana*, pp. 902–14, 946–58.

17 Ibid., pp. 803–4; English translation, Gorham, op. cit., pp. 163–7.

18 I remain unconvinced by the argument of Mark E. Vandeschaar, 'Archbishop Parker's Efforts Toward a Bucerian Discipline' (*Sixteenth-Century Journal*, viii. 1977, 85–103), who minimizes the differences in pastoral outlook between Parker and Grindal and in the impression made on the two future archbishops by Bucer.

19 Printed in *Historia vera* (op. cit.) and in *Scripta Anglicana*, pp. 915–44; English translation by Arthur Golding, *A briefe treatise concerning the burn-ynge of Bucer and Phagius*, 1562.

20 *Z.L.*, ii. 24, 72–4.

21 W. P. Stephens, *The Holy Spirit in the Theology of Martin Bucer*, Cambridge 1970; *Common Places of Martin Bucer*, tr. and ed. D. F. Wright, Courtenay Library of Reformation Classics 4, Appleford 1972.

22 *Martyrs divine epistles*, pp. 62–3; whence printed, Gorham, op. cit., pp. 19–27.

23 François Wendel published a scholarly modern edition as vol. xv of the *Opera Latina* of Bucer, Paris 1956 (French text in vol. xv *bis*). The greater part has been translated into English by Wilhelm Pauck and included in *Melanchthon and Bucer*, vol. 19 of the Library of Christian Classics, 1969.

24 Bernd Moeller, *Imperial Cities and the Reformation: Three Essays*, tr. and ed. H. C. E. Midelfort and M. U. Edwards, Philadelphia 1972. Cf. M. U. Chrisman, *Strasbourg and the Reform*, New Haven 1967.

25 A somewhat broader context to what follows is provided in my 'Episcopacy and Reform in England in the Later Sixteenth Century', *Studies in Church History*, iii. ed. G. J. Cuming, Leiden 1966, pp. 91–125.

26 In the letter cited in n. 8 above.

27 J. H. Primus, *The Vestments Controversy*, Kampen 1960, pp. 16–67; C. Hopf, 'Bishop Hooper's Notes to the Council', *J.T.S.*, xliv. 1946, 194–9; Ridley's arguments in *Writings of John Bradford*, ii. ed. A. Townsend, PS 1853, 373–95. On the underlying issues, see most recently Bernard J. Verkamp, *The Indifferent Mean: Adiaphorism in the English Reformation to 1554*, Studies in the Reformation vol. 1, Athens Ohio 1977.

28 See pp. 176–83.

29 Gorham, op. cit., p. 200.

30 Private communication from Professor Rupp.

31 Corpus Christi College Cambridge, MS. 106, no. 100, p. 318; University of Cambridge to Andrew Perne, Edmund Grindal and John Ponet, 15 May 1552, BL, MS. Add. 5813, no. 89, fol. 89.

32 *The Lamentacyon of a Christen Agaynst the Cytye of London*, ed. J. M. Cowper, Early English Text Society, e.s. xxii. 1874, 93.

33 Ridley to Cheke, 23 July 1551, BL, MS. Add. 19398, fol. 54 (Ridley, *Works*, ed. H. Christmas, PS 1843, pp. 331–4); Ridley to Cecil and Gates, 18 Nov. 1552, BL, MS. Lansd. 2, fol. 220 (ibid., pp. 336–7).

34 *Writings of Bradford*, ii. 192.

35 BL, MS. Harl. 416, fol. 132 (Ridley, *Works*, p. 493); Grindal to Ridley, 6 May 1555, *Remains*, pp. 238–40, Ridley, *Works*, pp. 386–8; Ridley to Grindal, n.d., *Works*, pp. 388–95. The source for both these letters is Coverdale's *Certaine most godly letters of such true saintes as gave their lyves*, 1564. For further discussion of the content of Ridley's letter to Grindal, see pp. 75–6.

36 This paragraph is indebted to the unpublished London M.A. thesis of Mr E. L. C. Mullins, 'The Effects of the Marian and Elizabethan Religious Settlements upon the Clergy of London, 1553–1564', 1948, pp. 79–87.

37 *Valor Ecclesiasticus*, i. 1810, 363–5.

38 Ridley, *Works*, p. 408.

39 Ibid., pp. 337–42, 391.

40 E. R. Adair, 'William Thomas: a Forgotten Clerk of the Privy Council', *Tudor Studies*, ed. R. W. Seton-Watson, 1924, pp. 133–60; P. J. Laven, 'The Life and Writings of William Thomas, d. 1554', unpublished London M.A. thesis, 1954; W. K. Jordan, *Edward VI: the threshold of Power*, 1970, pp. 25, 415–19.

41 *A.P.C.*, iii. 53, 58; Ridley, *Works*, pp. 331–4; *John Le Neve Fasti Ecclesiae Anglicanae 1541–1857*, i. *St Paul's London*, comp. J. M. Horn, 1969, pp. 18, 25, 43, 50; Jordan, *Edward VI: the Threshold of Power*, pp. 468–70.

42 Ridley, *Works*, p. 59.

43 *Literary Remains of King Edward the Sixth*, ed. J. G. Nichols, Roxburghe Club, 1857, ii. 376–7; *A.P.C.*, iv. 148; *Calº. of Patent Rolls*, ix. 382, 311; P. Lorimer, *John Knox and the Church of England*, 1875, p. 80; John Le Neve, *Fasti Ecclesiae Anglicanae*, Oxford 1844, iii. 353.

44 *A.P.C.*, iv. 148; PRO, S.P. 10/15/28.

45 Ridley, *Works*, pp. 336–7.

46 *O.L.*, i. 89, ii. 399.

47 Hoak, op. cit., pp. 241–58.

48 See my *Letters of Thomas Wood*.

49 *De regno Christi*, II.v.

50 Ridley, *Works*, p. 59; Knox, *Works*, ed. D. Laing, iii. Edinburgh 1854, 175–6, 269–70, 277, 281–2, iv. Edinburgh 1855, 566; Jasper Ridley, *John Knox*, Oxford 1968, pp. 115–29; *Letters of Thomas Wood*, p. 23; *Writings of Bradford*, i. 31.

51 PRO, S.P. 10/15/35. What follows is based on Northumberland's correspondence with Cecil, S.P. 10/15/62, 63, 66, 18/1, 3, 9. Some of these letters are printed in P. F. Tytler, *England under the Reigns of Edward VI and Mary*, 1839, ii. Cf. Lorimer, op. cit., pp. 149–52; Charles Sturge, *Cuthbert Tunstall*, 1938, pp. 285–96; H. R. Trevor-Roper, 'The Bishopric of Durham and the Capitalist Reformation', *Durham University Journal*, xxxviii. 1946, 45–58.

52 Jordan, *Edward VI: the Threshold of Power*, p. 28.

53 Ridley, *Works*, p. 336.

54 Jordan, *Edward VI: the Threshold of Power*, pp. 374–5.

55 PRO, S.P. 10/15/63; *D.N.B.*, art. Harley.

56 Jordan, *Edward VI: the Threshold of Power*, esp. chs 8, 10, 14.

57 PRO, S.P. 10/18/9, 27; Ridley, *Works*, p. 405.

58 Thomas Rogers, *The Catholic Doctrine of the Church of England*, ed. J. J. S. Perowne, PS 1854, p. 9; Tobie Matthew to Francis Mylles, 9 Jan. 1587(/8), BL, MS. Cotton Titus B VII, fols 424–6; PRO, S.P. 10/18/28.

4   A Germanical Nature

This chapter is founded on correspondence in Grindal's *Remains*, Ridley's *Works*, Cf Ch. 2 intro., and the two volumes of *Original Letters (O.L.)*, all Parker Society publications; on the biographical information collected by C. H. Garrett in *The Marian Exiles*, Cambridge 1938; and on the documents printed by the anonymous Elizabethan editor of *A brieff discours off the troubles begonne at Franckford*, Heidelberg 1575, cited from J. Petheram's edition of 1846.

1 *Parker Correspondence*, p. 125.
2 Garrett, op. cit., p. 1.
3 *A piteous lamentation of the miserable estate of the Church in England*, in *Works*, pp. 47–80. Knowledgeable English protestants would have been instructed by Peter Martyr's *De fuga in persecutione*, a work inspired in part by personal experience, and, no doubt, by a treatise by Tertullian with the same title, printed at Basle in 1521. (I owe this suggestion to Dr Marvin W. Anderson.) For Martyr's own experience, see P. McNair, *Peter Martyr in Italy: An Anatomy of Apostacy*, Oxford 1967, pp. 239–68.
4 *Remains*, pp. 238–40; Ridley, *Works*, pp. 386–8.
5 *D.N.B.*, art. Alley, quoting John Vowell, alias Hooker, *A catalog of the bishops of Excester*, 1584.
6 Alley, Πτωχομυσεῖον. *The poore mans librarie. Rapsodiae G.A. byshop of Exceter upon the first epistle of S. Peter*, 1571 edn, fols 72ᵛ–3; Edwin Sandys, *Sermons*, ed. J. Ayre, PS 1841, p. 335.
7 Ridley, *Works*, pp. 380–1.
8 *Z.L.*, i. 224.
9 He wrote to Cecil on 22 July that so far as he could understand French the proposals of a group of French protestants in Southampton appeared reasonable. (PRO, S.P. 12/43/29.)
10 Martin Bucer, *Scripta Anglicana*, Basle 1577, Sig. α2ʳ.
11 Foxe, viii. 598.
12 *Z.L.*, ii. 22–4, 27–8, 74, 107; *Remains*, pp. 286–7; BL, MS. Lansd. 7, fol. 133.
13 *Remains*, pp. 220–1.
14 *Z.L.*, ii. 24, 73.
15 *Remains*, p. 250.
16 BL. MS. Lansd. 7, fol. 133.
17 *Z.L.*, ii. 52.
18 G. D. Ramsay, *The City of London in International Politics at the Accession of Elizabeth Tudor*, Manchester 1975, pp. 229–43. See also p. 129 below, and references there.
19 Foxe, viii. 597–8.
20 Corpus Christi College Cambridge, MS. 106, no. 207, p. 512; *John Le Neve Fasti Ecclesiae Anglicanae 1541–1857*, i. *St Paul's London*, comp. J. M. Horn, 1969, p. 18.
21 Bucer, *Scripta Anglicana*, Sig. α2ʳ; *Z.L.*, ii. 52.
22 *Remains*, pp. 275, 220, 228.
23. M. U. Chrisman, *Strasbourg and the Reform*, New Haven 1967.
24. Laurence Humphrey, *J. Juelli ... vitam*, 1573, p. 87; W. M. Southgate, *John Jewel and the Problem of Doctrinal Authority*, Cambridge Mass. 1962, pp. 20–1; *Remains*, p. 239; Martyr to Grindal, 28 Jan. 1560, LPL, MS. 2010, no. 73, fol. 114.
25 *Martyrs divine epistles*, appended to *Common places*, tr. Anthonie Marten, 1583, pp. 136B–139B; Bentham to Lever, 1557, BL, MS. Harl 416, fol. 63.

26 ITL, MS. Petyt 538/47, fols 380, 380X.

27 See my article, 'The Authorship of *A brieff discours off the troubles begonne at Franckford*', *J.E.H.*, ix. 1958, 188−208. The matter is further discussed, but with increasing eccentricity, by M. A. Simpson in 'Of the Troubles Begun at Frankfurt, A.D. 1554', in *Reformation and Revolution*, ed. D. Shaw, Edinburgh 1967, and in *John Knox and the Troubles Begun at Frankfurt*, Edinburgh 1975.

28 A MS. copy of Ridley's letter to Grindal (the only such letter extant) survives in its integrity among the 'Letters of the Martyrs' in Emmanuel College Cambridge, MS. 260, fol. 114*. The passage omitted by Coverdale in *Certaine most godly letters*, 1564, pp. 51−6, and by Foxe, vii. 434−6, was supplied by the editors of Ridley's *Works*, partly from William Covell, *A briefe answer unto certaine reasons by way of an apologie ... by M. Iohn Burges*, 1606, p. 69, partly from Gloucester Ridley's *Life of Dr. Nicholas Ridley*, 1763, and, perhaps, from the Emmanuel MS.: without however appreciating, or at least disclosing, that it belonged to the letter printed elsewhere in the same volume. (Ridley, *Works*, pp. 388−95, 535−5.)

29 LPL, MS. 2523, fol. 3ʳ.

30 *Liturgia sacra ... per V. Pollanum*, 1551; reprinted, Leiden 1970.

31 *O.L.*, ii. 769. The foregoing account has followed the *Brief Discourse of the Troubles Begun at Frankfort*, supplemented by Knox's narrative in *Works* (ed. D. Laing, iv, Edinburgh 1954), and the letters from Frankfurt in *O.L.*, ii. 753−71.

32 *Z.L.*, i. 256.

33 Foxe, i. 520; Foxe to Martyr, n.d., John Strype, *Ecclesiastical Memorials*, Oxford 1822, III.ii. 310−11.

34 Ridley, *Works*, pp. 533−5, 386−8; *Troubles at Frankfort*, p. 51; *O.L.*, ii. 753−5.

35 *O.L.*, i. 183.

36 Jewel, *Works*, iv. PS 1850, 1192−3. The letter is dated 1 June, without year. The PS editors prefer 1557, before Goodman wrote *How superior powers oght to be obeyed*, while M. M. Knappen (*Tudor Puritanism*, Chicago 1965 edn, p. 148) opts for 1558.

37 Haller, *Foxe's Book of Martyrs and the Elect Nation*, 1963, pp. 53−4.

38 P. M. Little, 'The Origins of the Political Ideologies of John Knox and the Marian Exiles', unpublished Edinburgh Ph.D. thesis, 1972.

39 Frank Isaac, 'Egidius Van der Erve and his English Printed Books', *Library*, 4th ser. xii. 1932, 336−52.

40 James Pilkington, *Works*, ed. J. Scholefield, PS 1842, p. 655.

41 Haller, op. cit.; J. F. Mozley, *John Foxe and his Book*, 1940; E. G. Rupp, 'John Foxe and his "Book of Martyrs"', in *Six Makers of English Religion 1500−1700*, pp. 53−73.

42 BL, MS. Harl. 416, fols 113, 112, 102, 119, 114, 102; all printed in *Remains*, pp. 219−38.

43 BL, MS. Harl. 417, fol. 92.

44 GLL, MS. 9535/1, fol. 87ʳ; BL, MS. Harl. 417, fols 95ᵛ, 102ᵛ, 119ᵛ, 125ᵛ, 129.

45 Foxe, viii. 598; *Z.L.*, i. 6.

46 A few of the books in Grindal's Queen's College bequest (see above, p. 36) bear his signature in the form 'Ed. Gr.' or 'Edm. Grindallus' and were consequently in his possession before his elevation to the episcopate in late 1559. These include the Castellio Bible and the first volume of the Musculus

Commentaries. It is likely that many of the other books in the collection, of which a good proportion were printed in the 1550s, most of them at Basle, were also acquired in exile.

47 See p. 40.

5   In the Wings: the Elizabethan Settlement

1 Simonds D'Ewes, *Journals of all the Parliaments of Queen Elizabeth*, 1682, p. 34.
2 *The Seconde Parte of a Register*, ed. A. Peel, Cambridge 1915, ii. 60.
3 *Puritan Manifestoes*, ed. W. H. Frere and C. E. Douglas, 1954 edn, p. 9. On the significance of 'scarce', see *Elizabethan Puritan Movement*, p. 120, n. 24.
4 Grindal to Bullinger, 27 August 1566; *Z.L.*, i. 169.
5 *Parker Correspondence*, pp. 66, 68; *Z.L.*, i. 10, ii. 13–14.
6 'The Elizabethan Acts of Supremacy and Uniformity', *E.H.R.*, lxv. 1950, 304–32. The argument is restated in *Elizabeth I and her Parliaments, 1559–1581*, 1953, pp. 51–84.
7 N. L. Jones, 'Faith by Statute: the Politics of Religion in the Parliament of 1559', unpublished Cambridge Ph.D. thesis, 1977. I am grateful to Dr Jones for permission to refer to his thesis. No doubt his views will be ventilated more publicly and will lead to lively discussion.
8 *Letters of Thomas Wood*, p. 13.
9 Marquess of Bath MSS. at Longleat House, Dudley Papers, i. fol. 139.
10 Text of the 'Device' in H. Gee, *The Elizabethan Prayer-Book and Ornaments*, 1902, pp. 195–202.
11 *Z.L.*, i. 6.
12 See G. L. Blackman, 'The Career and Influence of Bishop Richard Cox, 1547–1581', unpublished Cambridge Ph.D. thesis, 1953.
13 *The Diary of Henry Machyn, Citizen and Merchant-Taylor of London from A.D. 1550 to A.D. 1563*, ed. J. G. Nichols, CS xlii. 1848, p. 190.
14 Accounts of the disputation in Strype, *Annals*, I.i. 128–38, R. W. Dixon, *History of the Church of England from the Abolition of the Roman Jurisdiction*, v. Oxford 1902, 74–89, and W. P. Haugaard, *Elizabeth and the English Reformation*, Cambridge 1968, pp. 96–104.
15 Philip Hughes, *The Reformation in England*, iii. 1954, 26–8.
16 *Z.L.*, ii. 19, i. 169.
17 Ibid., ii. 3–8; duchess of Suffolk to Cecil, 4 March 1559, PRO, S.P. 12/3/9; Calvin, Correspondance nos 3170, 3199, repr. F. de Schickler, *Les Églises du réfuge*, iii. Paris 1892, 47–8.
18 *Commentaries on the Twelve Minor Prophets*, ii. Calvin Translation Socy, Edinburgh 1846, 351.
19 Ibid., 349.
20 James Pilkington, *Works*, ed. J. Scholefield, PS 1842, p. 416.
21 *Z.L.*, i. 169.
22 *Parker Correspondence*, p. 66.
23 *Z.L.*, i. 21, 23, 31–2; *Parker Correspondence*, p. 58.
24 A. F. Pollard, *History of England from the Accession of Edward VI to the Death of Elizabeth (1547–1603)*, Political History of England, vi. 1910, 208–9.
25 *Parker Correspondence*, p. 65.
26 Sandys to Cecil, 26 April 1570, BL, MS. Lansd. 12, no. 82, fol. 179; Edwin Sandys, *Sermons*, ed. J. Ayre, PS 1841, p. 334.
27 Edmund Allen, at the time of his death in August 1559 bishop elect of

Rochester. (See E. L. C. Mullins in *E.H.R.*, lxii. 1957, 213–17.) Allen's letter to John Abell is printed in Ralph Churton, *Life of Alexander Nowell*, Oxford 1809, pp. 392–8, and in *Cal. of State Papers, Foreign, 1558–9*, p. 287, Cf. Charles Wriothesly, *Chronicle*, ed. W. D. Hamilton, ii. CS n.s. xx, 1877, p. 145.

28 H. Gee, *The Elizabethan Clergy and the Settlement of Religion 1558–1564*, Oxford 1898, pp. 34–5; E. L. C. Mullins, 'The Effects of the Marian and Elizabethan Religious Settlements upon the Clergy of London, 1553–1564', unpublished London M.A. thesis, 1948, pp. 166–7; PRO, PROB/34/2/2.

29 *Remains*, pp. 307–8; Foxe, viii. 667.

30 *Z.L.*, ii. 24.

31 LPL, MS. 2010, nos 82, 83, fols 133–5.

32 1 Eliz. cap. 19; *Cal. of Patent Rolls, Eliz. I*, i. 422, 441, 453, ii. 306–8.

33 L. Stone, 'The Political Programme of Thomas Cromwell', *B.I.H.R.*, xxiv. 1951, and G. R. Elton, 'Parliamentary Drafts, 1529–1540', ibid., xxv. 1952, 117–32.

34 What follows is based on Felicity Heal, 'The Bishops and the Act of Exchange of 1559', *Historical Journal*, xvii. 1974, 227–46, which supersedes much earlier discussion. But see also Heal, 'The Tudors and Church Lands: Economic Problems of the Bishopric of Ely During the Sixteenth Century', *Economic History Review*, xxvi. 1973, 198–217, Claire Cross, 'The Economic Problems of the See of York: Decline and Recovery in the Sixteenth Century', in *Land, Church, and People*, ed. J. Thirsk, Agricultural History Review Supplement, 1970, pp. 64–83, P. M. Hembry, *The Bishops of Bath and Wells, 1540–1640*, 1967, and Gina Alexander, 'Victim or Spendthrift? The Bishop of London and his Income in the Sixteenth Century', in *Wealth and Power in Tudor England: Essays Presented to S. T. Bindoff*, ed. E. W. Ives, R. J. Knecht and J. J. Scarisbrick, 1978, pp. 128–45.

35 Richard Curteys, *Two sermons*, 1576, pp. 118–19.

36 *Z.L.*, i. 29, 61, 40.

37 The Letter Book of Bishop Thomas Bentham, National Library of Wales MS. 4919D. Publication in a *Camden Miscellany* volume is forthcoming. I am grateful to Dr M. R. O'Day for supplying me with xerox copies of the MS., which is discussed in her article 'Thomas Bentham: a Case Study in the Problems of the Early Elizabethan Episcopate', *J.E.H.*, xxiii. 1972, 137–59.

38 Felicity Heal, 'Clerical Tax Collection under the Tudors: the Influence of the Reformation', in *Continuity and Change: Personnel and Administration of the Church in England 1500–1642*, ed. R. O'Day and F. Heal, Leicester 1976, pp. 97–122.

39 Parker and four other bishops elect to the queen, n.d., *Parker Correspondence*, pp. 97–101.

40 Strype, pp. 41–8; *Z.L.*, i. 1–2, 62–5, 75–6, ii. 25–7, 32–3, 38–41, 47–9, 152.

41 Grindal to Bullinger, 27 August 1566, Grindal and Horne to Bullinger and Gualter, 6 Feb. 1567, *Z.L.*, i. 168–70, 175–82.

42 Grindal's copy of Bucer's *De regno Christi* in the Queen's College Library, p. 106.

43 LPL, MS. 2010, no. 73, fol. 114. I follow the translation of Martyr's letter in Marvin W. Anderson, *Peter Martyr: A Reformer in Exile 1542–62*, Nieuwkoop 1975.

44 John Field to Anthony Gilby, 10 Jan, 1572; CUL, MS. Mm.1.43, p. 447.

45 *Parker Correspondence*, pp. 79–95; *Z.L.*, i. 55, 67–8, 73–4; Haugaard, op. cit., pp. 185–200.

46 See pp. 239–46.

47 Corpus Christi College Cambridge MS. 105, art. 11, pp. 201–15, printed *Parker Correspondence*, pp. 79–95; another copy of the letter, without the treatise, LPL, MS. 2002, no. 5, fol. 29. Foxe's edition of the treatise in *Acts and Monuments*, viii. 701–7, whence printed in Ridley's *Works*, pp. 81–96. I have discussed the difficulties surrounding this document in 'If Constantine, Then Also Theodosius: St Ambrose and the Integrity of the Elizabethan *Ecclesia Anglicana*', *J.E.H.*, xxx, 1979.

48 *Z.L.*, i. 73–4.

49 J. E. Neale, *Essays in Elizabethan History*, 1958, pp. 9–20.

50 *Seconde Parte of a Register*, ii. 53–4.

51 W. H. Frere, *Visitation Articles and Injunctions of the Period of the Reformation*, iii. Alcuin Club Collections xvi. 1910, 8–29.

52 Printed by Strype, *Annals*, I.i. 237–41, from ITL, MS. Petyt 538/38, no. 9, fols 29–31. The copy bearing Grindal's endorsement is in LPL, MS. 2002, no. 18, fols 107–10.

53 PRO, S.P. 12/10 is an act book of the royal visitation in the northern province: printed in *The Royal Visitation of 1559: Act Book for the Northern Province*, ed. C. J. Kitching, Surtees Socy, clxxxvii. 1972. PRO, PROB 34/1 and PROB 34/2/2 are two volumes containing acts of the visitors for the dioceses of London, Norwich and Ely. The fullest account of the visitation is in Gee, *Elizabethan Clergy*, pp. 41–136. Cf. Mullins, 'The Effects of the Marian and Elizabethan Religious Settlements', pp. 167–207.

54 Strype, *Annals*, I.i. 249–54, drawing on a 'register book' no longer extant; Wriothesly, *Chronicle*, ii. 146.

55 'The Interpretations of the Bishops' in Frere, op. cit., iii. 59–73; W. P. M. Kennedy, *The Interpretations of the Bishops*, 1908, and 'The Early History of the Elizabethan Compromise in Ceremonial', in his *Studies in Tudor History*, 1916, pp. 143–64; *Orders taken the x. day of October in the thirde yere of the raigne of ... Elizabeth quene of Englande*, 1561.

56 *Machyn's Diary*, p. 207; Wriothesly, *Chronicle*, ii. 146.

57 *Z.L.*, i. 44.

58 *The English Church in the Reigns of Elizabeth and James I*, 1904, p. 55.

59 Kitching, op. cit., p. 3; Gee, *Elizabethan Clergy*, p. 92.

60 Ibid., pp. 147–52.

61 Wriothesly, *Chronicle*, ii. 146.

62 Gee, *Elizabethan Clergy*, pp. 152–4; BL, MS. Egerton 2350, fol. 39. I owe this last reference to Mr E. L. C. Mullins.

63 Kitching, op. cit., passim; PRO, PROB 34/1, PROB 34/2/2. (PROB 34/1 is an act book primarily occupied with suits for the restitution of married clergy. PROB 34/2/2 is mainly a register of wills proved before the visitors.)

64 See Dr Philip Tyler's Introduction to the 1969 reissue of R. G. Usher's *The Rise and Fall of the High Commission*, correcting Usher on these points.

65 PRO, S.P. 15/11/45.

66 PRO, S.P. 12/39/18.

67 BL, MS. Lansd. 10, no. 48, fols 152–3.

68 PRO, S.P. 12/48/26I.

69 PRO, S.P. 12/22/5, 6, 7.

70 PRO, S.P. 12/40/45, 46. See Mortimer Levine, *The Early Elizabethan Succession Question, 1558–1568*, Stanford 1966, pp. 13–29 and passim, and *Tudor Dynastic Problems, 1460–1571*, 1973.

71 Grindal to Cecil, 15 Oct. 1563, *Remains*, pp. 280–1, 8 Sept. 1568, PRO,

S.P. 12/47/62. Cf. the bishop of Ely and his strawberries, Shakespeare's *Richard III*, Act III, Scene iv.

72 *Registrum Matthei Parker*, i. ed. W. H. Frere, Canterbury and York Socy, xxxv. Oxford 1928, 38–53; GLL, MS. 9531/13 (Grindal's register), fols 1–2ʳ.

6 This Cumbrous Charge

1 Edwin Sandys, *Sermons*, ed. J. Ayre, PS 1841, p. 331.
2 Recent comments on the population of London in W. K. Jordan, *The Charities of London, 1480–1660*, 1960, p. 16, F. F. Foster, *The Politics of Stability: A Portrait of the Rulers of Elizabethan London*, 1977, p. 7, n. 2, and G. D. Ramsay, *The City of London in International Politics at the Accession of Elizabeth Tudor*, Manchester 1975, p. 33.
3 CLRO, JOR 18, fols 145ᵛ, 151ᵛ–2, 153ʳ, 204.
4 Sir William Dugdale, *The History of St Paul's Cathedral in London*, 1716, p. 137.
5 Foster, op. cit., p. 160.
6 Sandys, op. cit., p. 331.
7 Said of Richard Vaughan, bishop from 1604 to 1607, by John Williams, later bishop of Lincoln and archbishop of York; BL, MS. Harl. 6495, art. 6, fol. 102ᵛ.
8 Grindal to Parker, 9 Dec. 1573; *Remains*, p. 347.
9 Grindal to Cecil, 8 Sept. 1562; PRO, S.P. 12/24/24.
10 Statistical and structural details from the diocesan certificate returned to the Privy Council in 1563; GLL, MS. 9531/13 (Grindal's register), fols 27ᵛ–33ʳ. (Another copy is in BL, MS. Harl. 595, fols 61–78.)
11 *Parker Correspondence*, p. 45; BL, MS. Harl. 417, fol. 129.
12 The fullest record of this 'chain of command' and of the business which passed down it is in the rich collection of correspondence and other documents of the archdeaconry of St Albans, preserved in the Hertfordshire Record Office. A selection is calendared in H.R. Wilton Hall, *Records of the Old Archdeaconry of St Albans*, St Albans and Hertfordshire Architectural and Archaeological Socy, 1908.
13 R. G. Usher, *The Reconstruction of the English Church*, 1910, ii. 383.
14 The Letter Book of Bishop Thomas Bentham, National Library of Wales MS. 4919D (discussed by Dr M. R. O'Day in *J.E.H.*, xxiii. 1972, 137–59); the Letter Book of Bishop Parkhurst, CUL, MS. Ee.11.34, edited by R. A. Houlbrooke as *The Letter Book of John Parkhurst Bishop of Norwich Compiled During the Years 1571–15*, Norfolk Record Socy, 1974 and 1975.
15 Preserved in the Minster Library, York, in a transcript by Thomas Wilson.
16 M. R. O'Day, 'Clerical Patronage and Recruitment in England in the Elizabethan and Stuart Periods, with Special Reference to the Diocese of Coventry and Lichfield', unpublished London Ph.D. thesis, 1972; and her article, 'The Law of Patronage in Early Modern England', *J.E.H.*, xxvi. 1975, 247–60.
17 E. L. C. Mullins, 'The Effects of the Marian and Elizabethan Religious Settlements upon the Clergy of London, 1553–1564', unpublished London M.A. thesis, 1948, p. 206.
18 F. J. Fisher, 'Inflation and Influenza in Tudor England', *Economic History Review*, 2nd ser. xviii. 1965, 120–9.
19 BL, MS. Lansd. 109, fol. 67; Strype, *Annals*, I.i. 203; William Harrison, *Description of England*, ed. F. J. Furnivall, 1877, p. 37.

20 What follows is based on Grindal's ordination register, GLL, MS. 9531/13, fols 1–74.
21 *Parker Correspondence*, pp. 120–1.
22 Strype, pp. 58–60.
23 John I. Daeley, 'The Episcopal Administration of Matthew Parker, Archbishop of Canterbury, 1559–1575', unpublished London Ph.D. thesis, 1967, pp. 178–89.
24 V. J. K. Brook, *Life of Archbishop Parker*, Oxford 1962, pp. 90–1.
25 BL, MS. Add. 19398, fol. 59. For another reference to the same (?) meeting, called a 'synod', see Sandys to Lord Robert Dudley, 20 July 1560, BL, MS. Add. 32091, fol. 185.
26 GLL, MS. 9537/2.
27 BL, MS. Royal 18 B VI, fol. 288ᵛ.
28 The ordination register has been compared with C. H. Garrett, *The Marian Exiles*, Cambridge 1938. Miss Garrett was sometimes more positive in her identifications than the evidence warranted.
29 Minutes and letters relating to this congregation in LPL, MS. 2523.
30 Grindal to Archdeacon Pulleyn of Colchester, 5 June 1560; Corpus Christi College Oxford, MS. 319, no. 54, fol. 183. For Upcher, see J. Oxley, *The Reformation in Essex*, Manchester 1965, pp. 165, 192–3, 195, 204; and J. F. Davis, 'Heresy and the Reformation in the South-East of England, 1520–1559', unpublished Oxford D.Phil. thesis, 1968, p. 344. For information about the conventicles from which Upcher came, see J. W. Martin, 'English Protestant Separatism at its Beginnings: Henry Hart and the Free-Will Men', *Sixteenth-Century Journal*, vii. 1976, 55–74.
31 Corpus Christi College Oxford, MS. 319, no. 54, fol. 183.
32 Gough's identity is established by *The Diary of Henry Machyn, Citizen and Merchant-Taylor of London from A.D. 1550 to A.D. 1563*, ed. J. G. Nichols, CS xlii. 1848, p. 269.
33 Corpus Christi College Oxford, MS. 319, no. 54, fol. 183.
34 *A.P.C.*, vii. 87–8. See the account of Colchester in Marian days in William Wilkinson, *Confutation of ... the familye of love* (1579), quoted, Strype, *Annals*, II.ii. 282–6.
35 GLL, MS. 9537/2 (Call Book of 1561 Visitation), fol. 63ᵛ, MS. 9531/13 (Grindal's register), fols 28³–33ʳ. In 1561 five of these churches were without any ministry whatsoever. It appears that some were derelict, and later made over to Dutch protestant immigrants. Colchester was over-supplied with churches. I have benefited from discussing Colchester with Dr J. P. Anglin.
36 Strype, *Annals*, II.ii. 282.
37 Biographical information in these paragraphs based on *D.N.B.*, Garrett, op. cit., and the unpublished theses by E. L. C. Mullins (op. cit.) and H. G. Owen, 'The London Parish Clergy in the Reign of Elizabeth I', Ph.D. London, 1957. Details of appointments from George Hennessy, *Novum Repertorium*, 1898 and *John Le Neve Fasti Ecclesiae Anglicanae 1541–1857*, i. *St Paul's London*, comp. J. M. Horn, 1969, pp. 8, 5, 11, 9, 41, 36, 40, 43.
38 Philippe Denis, 'John Veron: the First Known French Protestant in England', *Proceedings of the Huguenot Socy. of London*, xxii. 1973, 257–63.
39 *Cal. S.P. Dom.*, vi. *1547–1580*, 155.
40 *Miscellanea*, i. Catholic Record Socy, 1905, 44; Albert Feuillerat, *Documents Relating to the Office of the Revels in the Time of Queen Elizabeth*, Louvain 1908, pp. 241–98.
41 GLRO, Vicar General Book 'Huick', fol. 77ʳ; Grindal to Lord Robert Dudley, August 1563, *Remains*, pp. 261–4.

42 Mullins, op. cit., p. 212.
43 Anthony Gilby, *A pleasaunt dialogue betweene a souldior of Barwicke and an English chaplaine*, 1581, Sig. C 5.
44 BL, MS. Add. 35831, no. 86, fol. 184.
45 CALC, MS. X.1.2, fols 27–8. The parish was Elmstead.
46 GLL, MSS. 3476/1, fol. 64ʳ, 9537/2, fol. 23ʳ, 4956/2, fol. 66ʳ, 4071/1, fol. 61ᵛ; *Tudor Royal Proclamations*, ed. P. J. Hughes and F. J. Larkin, New Haven, ii. 1969, 146–8; *Machyn's Diary*, pp. 228, 247; *Z.L.*, i. 71; *Victoria County History of London*, i. 307; Owen, op. cit., p. 478.
47 W. H. Frere, *Visitation Articles and Injunctions of the Period of the Reformation*, iii. Alcuin Club Collections xvi. 1910, 108–10.
48 Corpus Christi College Oxford, MS. 319, no. 54, fol. 183.
49 GLRO, Vicar General Book 'Huick'.
50 Ibid., fols 45ʳ, 63ᵛ, 89, 148ᵛ, 153, 237, 46ʳ; *Machyn's Diary*, pp. 272–3.
51 Call Book of the visitation, GLL, MS. 9537/2. See H. G. Owen, 'The Episcopal Visitation: its Limits and Limitations in Elizabethan London', *J.E.H.*, xi. 1960, 179–85.
52 *Parker Correspondence*, pp. 115–17.
53 See ch. 8.
54 GLRO, Vicar General Book 'Huick', fol. 44ᵛ.
55 *Tudor Royal Proclamations*, ii. 177–9.
56 GLRO, Vicar General Book 'Huick', fols 70ᵛ, 77ʳ.
57 By Dr Owen in *J.E.H.*, xi. 1960, 179–85.
58 BL, MS. Sloane 1317, fol. 115ᵛ–16ʳ is a certificate of excommunications arising from this visitation, bearing the names of eight clergymen of the archdeaconry of Middlesex.
59 J. van Dorsten, *The Radical Arts: First Decade of an Elizabethan Renaissance*, 1970, p. 15.

7 Calvinism with a Human Face

This chapter is based on the following printed sources and authorities: Theodore Beza, *Epistolarum theologicarum Theodorii Bezae Vezelii liber unus, secundo editio*, Geneva 1575; and *Correspondance de Théodore de Bèze*, vi (1565), vii (1566), ed. Meylan, Dufour et al., Travaux d'humanisme et renaissance cxiii, cxxxvi, Geneva 1970, 1973. Eduard Boehmer, *Bibliotheca Wiffeniana: Spanish Reformers of the two Centuries from 1520*, 'According to the late Benjamin B. Wiffen's plans and with the use of his materials', ii, iii. Strasbourg and London, 1883, 1904. John Calvin, *Opera*, ed. Baum, Cunitz and Reuss, xvi–xx, *Epistolae* (being vols xliv–xlviii of the *Corpus Reformatorum*). Paul J. Hauben, *Three Spanish Heretics and the Reformation*, Études de philologie et d'histoire, iii. Geneva 1967; and articles by Hauben in *Church History*, xxxiv, xxxix and *Historical Journal*, ix. J. H. Hessels, ed., *Ecclesiae Londino-Batavae Archivum*, 3 vols in 4, Cambridge 1887–1897. A. Gordon Kinder, *Casiodoro de Reina: Spanish Reformer of the Sixteenth Century*, 1975. Elsie Johnson, ed., *Actes du consistoire de l'église française de Threadneedle Street, Londres*, i. (1560–1565), Huguenot Socy of London, Quarto Ser. xxxviii. 1937. J. Lindeboom, *Austin Friars: History of the Dutch Reformed Church in London, 1550–1950*, The Hague 1950. A. A. van Schelven, ed., *Kerkeraads-Protocollen der Nederduitsche Vluchtelingen-Kerk te Londen 1560–1563*, Werken uitgegeven door het Historisch genootschap ser. 3, 43, Amsterdam 1921. A. A. van Schelven, *De Nederduitsche Vluchtelingen-kerken der XVIe Eeuw in Engeland en Duitschland*, 's-Gravenhagen 1909. Baron F. de Schickler, *Les Églises du réfuge en Angleterre*, 3 vols, Paris 1892.

1 R. F. G. and E. F. Kirk, *Return of Aliens in London*, Huguenot Socy of London, Quarto Ser. xii. 1–154; cf. Boehmer, op. cit., iii. 33, Lindeboom, op. cit., p. 30 seq.

2 *An epistle or godlie admonition of a learned minister of the gospel of our Saviour Christ sent to the pastoures of the Flemish church in Antwerp (who name themselves of the Confession of Auspurge)*, 1569, fols 25–6, 30.

3 *History of the Church of England from the Abolition of the Roman Jurisdiction*, iii. 1885, 236.

4 *Actes du consistoire*, i. 54; *Kerkeraads-Protocollen*, p. 209; Grindal to Cecil, 8 Sept. 1562, PRO, S.P. 12/24/24.

5 *Correspondance de Théodore de Bèze*, vi. no. 410.

6 Writing to Calvin on 10 Feb. 1561 Grindal referred to Beza 'cum quo aliquam familiaritatem Argentinae contraxi'. (Calvin, *Opera*, xviii. cols 357–9.)

7 Basil Hall, *John à Lasco 1499–1560: A Pole in Reformation England*, Friends of Dr Williams's Library 25th Lecture, 1971.

8 Schickler, op. cit., i. 85–6.

9 Frederick A. Norwood, 'The Strangers' Model Churches in Sixteenth-Century England', in *Reformation Studies: Essays in Honor of R. H. Bainton*, ed. F. H. Littell, Richmond Va., 1962.

10 Letters from Micron and Utenhove to Bullinger of Zürich in *O.L.*, ii. 557–604. Cf. W. M. West, 'John Hooper and the Origins of Puritanism', *Baptist Quarterly*, xvi. 1955–6, 24–30.

11 F. Pijper, *Jan Utenhove: zijn Leven en zijne Werken*, Leiden 1883.

12 A comparison of the letters from Calvin to des Gallars of June 1560 and from des Gallars to Calvin of 2 August 1560 (Calvin, *Opera*, xviii. cols 116–17, 161–7) undermines the suggestion of the editor of this volume of Calvin's letters that it was des Gallars whom some would have preferred as superintendent.

13 Grindal to Cecil, 4 August 1562, PRO, S.P. 12/24/3; Utenhove to Cecil, 20 Dec. 1563, PRO, S.P. 70/66/1319; Grindal to Utenhove, 10 Feb. 1564, Hessels, op. cit., ii. 210–13; Utenhove to Cecil, 17 March 1564, ibid., ii. 213–17; Grindal to Cecil, 11, 18, 21 March 1564, BL, MS. Lansd. 7, nos 64–5, 68, fols 149–51, 157; George Needham to Cecil, 13 April 1564, PRO, S.P. 70/70/256; Utenhove to Cecil, 17, 27 July 1564, PRO, S.P. 12/34/38, 41. Cf. G. D. Ramsay, *The City of London in International Politics at the Accession of Elizabeth Tudor*, Manchester 1975, pp. 229–43.

14 Patrick Collinson, 'The Elizabethan Puritans and the Foreign Reformed Churches in London', *Proceedings of the Huguenot Socy of London*, xx. 1964, 528–55.

15 *Actes du consistoire*, i. 97.

16 See pp. 97–9.

17 Calvin to Grindal, 15 May 1560; Calvin, *Opera*, xviii. cols 87–8. English translation by G. C. Gorham, *Gleanings of a Few Scattered Ears*, 1854, pp. 415–17.

18 *Correspondance de Théodore de Bèze*, vii. 229.

19 Calvin to des Gallars, June 1560, *Opera*, xviii. cols 116–17; Grindal to Calvin, 10 Feb. 1561, 19 June 1563, ibid., xviii. cols 357–9, xx. cols 43–5; des Gallars to Calvin, 1 July 1560, 14 Feb. 1561, ibid., xviii. cols 91–2, 366–8.

20 The still definitive account of what follows will be found in Schickler.

21 Remembered in the seventeeth century as 'ce grand Alexandre, qui fut titré des siens la merveille d'Arras'. (*La muse chrestienne du sieur Adrian de Rocquigny*, 1634, p. 77.)

22 On predestination and on matrimony, Corpus Christi College Cambridge MSS. 115, 126; on ecclesiastical discipline and excommunication and on purgatory, BL, MS. Add. 48040, no. 3.

23 R. M. Kingdon, *Geneva and the Consolidation of the French Protestant Movement 1564–1572: A Contribution to the History of Congregationalism, Presbyterianism and Calvinist Resistance Theory*, Madison 1967.

24 Published in French and Latin editions, the Latin with a dedication to Grindal. What may be the sole surviving copy of the Latin edition was in the possession of a London puritan activist John Field. (BL, MS. Add. 48096.)

25 'Apologia Petri Alexandri adversus animadversiones Domini Galasii ad reverendum patrem et dominum episcopum Londinensem', Corpus Christi College Cambridge MS. 340, no. 19, pp. 425–33; 'In scripto domini Petri inquit haec sunt animadvertanda' (signed by des Gallars), ibid., p. 433; 'Responsio Petri Alexandri ad animadversionem domini Galasii', ibid., p. 434.

26 Des Gallars to Grindal, 29 Oct. 1561; PRO, S.P. 70/31/486.

27 Most of the copious documentation for the van Haemstede affair will be found in the second and third volumes of Hessels's edition of the correspondence of the Dutch church, *Ecclesiae Londino-Batavae Archivum*, and in van Schelven's edition of the consistory minutes, *Kerkeraads-Protocollen*.

28 See the study by A. J. Jeslmas, *Adriaan van Haemstede en zijn Martelaarsboek*, The Hague 1970; and cf. the title of J. F. Mozley's *John Foxe and his Book*, 1940.

29 J.-F. Gilmont, 'la Genèse du martyrologe d'Adrien van Haemstede (1559)', *Revue d'histoire ecclésiastique*, lxiii. 1968, 379–414. See the heading on p. 23 of *Kerkeraads-Protocollen*: 'De Adriano bibliopola'.

30 J. van Dorsten, *The Radical Arts: First Decade of an Elizabethan Renaissance*, 1970, ch. 4.

31 There is a considerable literature on Acontius, not much of it in English. But see W. K. Jordan, *The Development of Religious Toleration in England*, i. 1932, 303–64.

32 Philip McNair, 'Ochino's Apology: Three Gods or Three Wives?', *History*, lx. 1975, 355. Professor McNair remarks that the Italian exiles mixed with the 'severe and doctrinaire divines' of northern Europe like oil with water. 'Wherever there was trouble, there was an Italian behind it.'

33 There is a modern edition by W. Koehler, Tübingen 1927; and an English translation of Books I–IV with an Introduction by C. D. O'Malley, Sturo Branch, California State Library, Occasional Papers, English Series no. 5, pt 1, San Francisco 1940.

34 *Tudor Royal Proclamations*, ed. P. L. Hughes and J. F. Larkin, ii. New Haven 1969, no. 470, pp. 148–9. Was a formal petition presented? The archives of the Dutch church contain a letter from Grindal to Utenhove and Deleen, dated 4 Sept. 1560, referring to a supplication submitted by certain anonymous persons, 'apparently anabaptists'. Grindal goes on to report the opinion that the author was 'Adrianus'. But Hessels knew of evidence which identified this man as a certain Adrianus Gorinus rather than as van Haemstede. (Hessels, op. cit., ii. 139–41.)

35 Hessels, ii. 522–3, 552–8; Foxe, i. 198–201.

36 G. H. Williams, *The Radical Reformation*, 1962, pp. 325–37.

37 Calvin, *Opera*, xviii. cols 340–2.

38 van Dorsten, op. cit., pp. 27–33; B. Rekers, *Benito Arias Montano*, 1972, pp. 70–104; Library of the French Protestant Church, Soho Square, London, MS. Livre de Coetus 1575–1598, p. 3.

39 Philippe Denis, 'Un combat aux frontières de l'orthodoxie: la controverse entre Acontius et des Gallars sur la question du fondement et des circonstances de l'église', *Bibliothèque d'humanisme et renaissance*, xxxviii. 1976, 55–72.
40 *Actes du consistoire*, i. 16.
41 Denis, op. cit., 56.
42 *Kerkeraads-Protocollen*, pp. 293–4.
43 Ibid., p. 331.
44 Included in Grindal's *Remains*, pp. 441–5.
45 Hessels, op. cit., ii. 206.
46 Velsius's 'Christiani hominis norma', with other documents, including Grindal's critique, Hessels, op. cit., iii. 17–29. Grindal to Cecil, reporting on Velsius, with a dossier of documents, 20 March 1563, PRO, S.P. 12/28/6–8.
47 The principal source is the correspondence of the Dutch church printed by Hessels, with additional information supplied from the *Actes du consistoire* of the French church. Cf. the accounts of this major crisis in the history of the London Dutch community in van Schelven and Lindeboom. Lindeboom gives a misleading account of Grindal's role.
48 *Remains*, pp. 247–52.
49 *Actes du consistoire*, i. xxviii; *Cal. of State Papers, Spanish, 1558–1567*, no. 458, p. 690. On van Winghen's hostility to iconoclasm and other forms of 'direct action' in the Netherlands see P. M. Crew, *Calvinist Preaching and Iconoclasm in the Netherlands 1544–1569*, Cambridge 1978, pp. 44–50. Dr Crew reports that the issue which preoccupied the Dutch ministers in England more than any other was that of violence in the home country (pp. 98–9).
50 *Actes du consistoire*, i. 87.
51 Yet Grindal is reported as having assured the dissidents that their refusal to admit godparents was not a sin but merely an offence against church order which ought not to be a cause for excommunication. (Ibid., i. 88.)
52 See pp. 174–81.
53 See pp. 181–2; and *Elizabethan Puritan Movement*, pp. 79–82.
54 The documents occur in the *Registres de la compagnie des pasteurs de Génève*, iii. (1565–1574), ed. Olivier Fatio and Olivier Labarthe, Travaux d'humanisme et renaissance, cvii. Geneva 1969, Appendix nos 48, 50–3, 56–7. The articles were printed as Epistola 24 in Beza's *Epistolae*, Geneva 1575, pp. 137–54. Strype provided an English translation from a text in the Moore MSS., now in CUL. (Grindal, App. xviii, pp. 519–27.)
55 Schickler, op. cit., i. 167.
56 The fundamental account, with documents, in Boehmer, op. cit.; copious documentation in Hessels, op. cit., iii; Kinder's study of Casiodoro de Reina and the monograph and articles by Hauben; and Schickler.
57 Hauben, *Three Spanish Heretics*, p. xii.
58 E. M. Wilson in *The Cambridge History of the Bible*, ii. Cambridge 1963, 127–8.
59 *Cal. of State Papers, Spanish, 1558–1567*, no. 170, p. 247.
60 Grindal's copy, endorsed (possibly in 1578) 'De causa Cassiodori Hispani, Confessio Hispanica' in LPL, MS. 2002, fols 31ᵛ–48ᵛ.
61 Denis, op. cit., 63.
62 *Actes du consistoire*, i. 13.
63 BL, MS. Lansd. 11, no. 67, fol. 150, printed, Boehmer, op. cit., iii. 89–91.
64 The depositions of de Reina's accuser Balthasar Sanchez and his own evi-

dence survive in the archives of the French church in Frankfurt. (Boehmer, op. cit., iii. 30n, ii. 220–1.) Details of the London enquiry of 1564, Hessels, op. cit., iii. 35–6. Cf. Kinder, op. cit., esp. p. 27.

65 Ibid., pp. 29–31, and Appendix.
66 The charge may have arisen from de Reina's dependence upon Servetus, or on a rabbinical source which he shared with Servetus, for certain marginal notes on the Old Testament. De Reina himself suggested this in writing to Beza, 1 March 1566. (*Correspondance de Théodore de Bèze*, vii. 48–51.)
67 Kinder, op. cit., p. 19.
68 Beza to Cousin, 14 Feb. 1571, Hessels, op. cit., ii. no. 106, 370–6.
69 Boehmer, op. cit., ii. 172. I am grateful to the Assistant Librarian of the Queen's College Oxford for helping me to trace Grindal's Bear Bible.
70 Schickler, op. cit., i. 231–5.
71 Ibid., i. 169 n. 1 prints the relevant sections of the fateful letter, with bibliographical details of the extant copies.
72 In Epistle 59; *Epistolae*, p. 253.
73 Hessels, op. cit., iii. 32.
74 Bochmer, op. cit., iii. 40.
75 Kingdon, op. cit., pp. 86–8.
76 A version of this *Epistle or godlie admonition* was published in London in 1569. See above, n. 2 to this chapter.
77 *Remains*, pp. 313–14. The French version is printed from a copy in Geneva by Schickler, op. cit., iii. 73–4.
78 A list in BL, MS. Lansd. 10, no. 61, fol. 177 of 'those which are of the Italian church being born in Flanders and other places under the dominion of the king of Spain' lists 57 names, of which only 12 are self-evidently Italian.
79 Boehmer, op. cit., iii. 91.
80 Corro to Parker, 16 Jan. 1569; *Parker Correspondence*, pp. 339–40.
81 Sentence printed from a Genevan source by Schickler, op. cit., iii. 84–5.
82 Beza to Cousin, 11 March 1569, no. 57 of *Epistolae*, in Hessels, op. cit., ii. 308–10; Schickler, op. cit., i. 172, n.2.
83 Grindal to Cecil, 20 Sept. 1569, *Remains*, pp. 309–12; Grindal to Cousin, 7 Nov. 1569, Hessels, op. cit., ii. 328–9; Consistory to Grindal, 22 Nov. 1569, ibid., iii. 95–8. Hauben (*Three Spanish Heretics*, p. 49) finds it 'mysterious' that Grindal sat on Corro's 'semi-apology' for two months. But in the light of the plague orders of 1562–3 (see pp. 163–5) Grindal's letter to Cousin provides an adequate explanation.
84 One copy of the printed text extant in CUL. Printed from a MS. copy by Hessels, op. cit., iii. 75–80.
85 *Remains*, pp. 309–12.
86 Details in the MS. minutes of the Consistory of the Italian church, which record a bitter dispute between Corro and Cypriano de Valera. (BL, MS. Add. 48096, no. 2, fols 21–31^v.)
87 Pierre Loiseleur, seigneur de Villiers, present in London from 1572 and a successor to Cousin, who died in 1574.
88 Killigrew to Davison, 23 August 1577, 29 Jan. 1578; PRO, S.P. 83/2/43, S.P. 15/25/71.
89 Corro's progression and significance for English Arminianism are discussed in two unpublished doctoral dissertations: W. McFadden, 'The Life and Works of Antonio del Corro, 1527–1591', Queen's University of Belfast Ph.D. thesis, 1953; N. R. N. Tyacke, 'Arminianism in England in Religion and Politics from 1604 to 1640', Oxford D.Phil. thesis, 1969, pp. 83–8.

90 Boehmer, op. cit., iii. 74.
91 Acontius to Grindal, 1564, Hessels, op. cit., ii. 224–34. The letter has been printed more recently in Koehler's edition of *Stratagematum Satanae*, pp. 235–42.

8   Fire and Pestilence

1 The following account draws on these primary and secondary authorities: *Documents Illustrating the History of St Paul's Cathedral*, ed. W. Sparrow Simpson, CS n.s. xxvi. 1888; W. Sparrow Simpson, *Chapters in the History of Old St Paul's*, 1881; Sir William Dugdale, *The History of St Paul's Cathedral in London*, 1716; *A Survey of London by John Stow*, ed. C. L. Kingsford, 3 vols, Oxford 1908; H. H. Milman, *Annals of S. Paul's Cathedral*, 1869; *A History of St Paul's Cathedral*, ed. W. R. Matthews and W. M. Atkins, 1957.
2 CLRO, JOR 17, fol. 328^v.
3 James Calfhill, *An Answer to John Martiall's Treatise of the Cross*, ed. R. Gibbings, PS 1846, p. 180.
4 *Narratives of the Days of the Reformation*, ed. J. G. Nichols, CS lxxvii. 1859, 154–6.
5 GLL, MS. 9531/13 (Grindal's register), fols 23–4^r; *The true report of the burnyng of the steple and churche of Paules in London*, 1561 (repr. in *Documents Illustrating the History of St Paul's*, pp. 113–25); *The Diary of Henry Machyn, Citizen and Merchant-Taylor of London from A.D. 1550 to A.D. 1563*, ed. J. G. Nichols, CS xlii. 1848, p. 259; *Three Fifteenth-Century Chronicles with Historical Memoranda by John Stow*, ed. J. Gairdner, CS n.s. xxvi. 1880, p. 116; *Annals of the First Four Years of the Reign of Queen Elizabeth by Sir John Hayward*, ed. J. Bruce, CS 1840, pp. 87–8; Peter Heylyn, *Ecclesia restaurata*, 1661, p. 140; Dugdale, op. cit., pp. 135–6.
6 *Hayward's Annals*, p. 88.
7 James Pilkington, *Works*, ed. J. Scholefield, PS 1842, p. 483.
8 Quoted, Milman, op. cit, p. 281, n. 9.
9 Pilkington, op. cit., p. 539.
10 John Earle, *The Autograph Manuscript of Microcosmographie* (Scolar Press Facsimile), Leeds 1966, p. 143.
11 Pilkington, op. cit., pp. 540–1.
12 *Henry IV* Pt 2, Act I, Sc. ii.
13 A practice complained of in 1572 in *An admonition to the parliament* by John Field and Thomas Wilcox, *Puritan Manifestoes*, ed. W. H. Frere and C. E. Douglas, 1954 edn, p. 31.
14 Michael Hickes, quoted in Alan G. R. Smith, *Servant of the Cecils: the Life of Sir Michael Hickes*, 1977, p. 107.
15 Earle, op. cit., pp. 142–6; *Documents Illustrating the History of St Paul's*, p. 131.
16 *Tudor Royal Proclamations*, ed. P. J. Hughes and J. F. Larkin, ii. New Haven 1969, 177–9. The proclamation was copied in Grindal's register (GLL, MS. 9531/13, fol. 23^v) and in the Journal of the Common Council of the City (CLRO, JOR 18, fols 1–2^r).
17 *Machyn's Diary*, p. 273.
18 Matthews and Atkins, op. cit., p. 151.
19 *Reports of Cases in the Courts of Star Chamber and High Commission*, ed. S. R. Gardiner, CS n.s. xxxix. 1886, 280–1, 298.
20 PRO, S.P. 12/19/64.

21 *Machyn's Diary*, p. 265.
22 PRO, S.P. 12/17/34, 35, 36, 37, 39.
23 CLRO, JOR 17, fols 316ᵛ–18, 328ᵛ; *Machyn's Diary*, pp. 259, 262, 267, 271; PRO, S.P. 12/17/35, S.P. 12/20/4; *Stowe's Survey*, i. 332.
24 Draft of the queen to Parker in Cecil's hand, PRO, S.P. 12/17/37; the queen to Parker, 24 June 1561, Parker to the bishops, 1 July 1561, *Parker Correspondence*, pp. 142–4; Grindal to the bishops, 12 July 1561, PRO, S.P. 12/17/39.
25 PRO, S.P. 12/22/69; Privy Council to Parker, 21 June 1563, *Parker Correspondence*, pp. 178–9; Cox to Cecil, 12 June 1563, BL, MS. Lansd. 6, no. 53, fol. 133.
26 *Parker Correspondence*, pp. 152–3; Grindal to dean of St Paul's, 6 Sept. 1561, PRO, S.P. 12/19/42.
27 *Hayward's Annuals*, pp. 88–9; 'A brieffe rehersall of all the somes of money receavyde towarde the reedyfyenge of the churche of Paules from the laste day of June 1561 unto the last of Aprill 1562 and of the employment of the said money', PRO, S.P. 12/22/69. Some details have been supplied from an account of timber received, 2 July–12 Oct. 1561, PRO, S.P. 12/20/41; and from the documentation of the litigation over dilapidations between Bishop Aylmer of London and Archbishop Sandys of York, PRO, S.P. 12/149/17.
28 PRO, S.P. 12/17/34. From internal evidence it is clear that this commission belongs to 1562 and not to 24 June 1561 as the *Calendar* suggests.
29 *Hayward's Annuals*, pp. 88–9; Dugdale, op. cit., p. 136.
30 PRO, S.P. 70/51/301; PRO, S.P. 12/44/32; *Remains*, pp. 272–3.
31 Grindal to Cecil, 2 May 1564, PRO, S.P. 12/34/1; *Cal. of Patent Rolls, Eliz.*, iii. 1563–66, pp. 122–6.
32 PRO, S.P. 12/44/32.
33 The total was variously reported at £1,144. 18s. 6d., £1,180. 18s. 6d. and £1,184. 18s. 11d. (PRO, S.P. 12/137/54, S.P. 12/149/18, 23.)
34 PRO, S.P. 12/149/17, 18, 23, 24.
35 *Stow's Survey*, ii. 347.
36 *Hayward's Annuals*, p 89; Milman, op. cit., pp. 316–19, 334–43.
37 CLRO, JOR 17, fols 316ᵛ–17.
38 *Stow's Survey*, ii. 347–8.
39 W. P. Haugaard, *Elizabeth and the English Reformation*, Cambridge 1968, passim; J. C. Barry, 'The Convocation of 1563', *History Today*, xiii. 1963, 490–501.
40 ITL, MS. Petyt 538/47, fol. 29.
41 Haugaard, op. cit., esp. p. 345.
42 Strype, *Annals*, I.i. 522–5.
43 *A sermon at the funeral solemnitie of the most high and mighty prince Ferdinandus, the late Emperor*, 1564; in *Remains*, pp. 1–33.
44 GLL, MS. 9531/13, fol. 26ᵛ.
45 *Stow's Memoranda*, pp. 123–5, 144–7; F. P. Wilson, *The Plague in Shakespeare's London*, Oxford 1963 edn, pp. 114, 193; F. F. Foster, *The Politics of Stability: A Portrait of the Rulers in Elizabethan London*, 1977, p. 7, n. 2.
46 CLRO, JOR 18, fol. 153ʳ.
47 Ibid., fols 123ᵛ, 136, 139, 154, 184, 189ᵛ–90; *Stow's Memoranda*, p. 123; *Machyn's Diary*, pp. 310, 396; Wilson, op. cit., p. 63; *Tudor Proclamations*, ii. nos 510, 514, 515, pp. 229–31, 236–40.
48 *Remains*, p. 265.

49 Grindal wrote to Cecil on 3, 12, 17, 30, 31 July, and on 1, 12 and 21 August. All are printed (from MS. Lansd. 6) in *Remains*, pp. 257–61, 272–5. Occasional services for the plague printed in *Remains*, pp. 75–120. Parker's letters to Cecil, 23 July, 1, 6 August, *Parker Correspondence*, pp. 182–3, 185.

50 *Remains*, pp. 257–8, 78, 83, 259, 261; CLRO, JOR 18, fol. 140ᵛ.

51 *Remains*, p. 269; CLRO, JOR 18, fol. 184.

52 *Remains*, pp. 111–20, 265.

53 *Parker Correspondence*, pp. 201–2, 185.

54 *Remains*, pp. 280–2.

9 Puritanism

1 *Visitation Articles and Injunctions of the Period of the Reformation*, iii. ed. W. H. Frere, Alcuin Club Collections, xvi. Oxford 1910, 59–73; W. P. M. Kennedy, *Studies in Tudor History*, 1916, pp. 143–64; W. P. Haugaard, *Elizabeth and the English Reformation*, Cambridge 1968, pp. 163–5, 197–200.

2 *Documentary Annals of the Reformed Church of England*, ed. E. Cardwell, Oxford 1844, i. 323–4.

3 *Parker Correspondence*, pp. 223–7; referred by Parker to Grindal for transmission to the province, 30 Jan. 1565, ibid., pp. 227–30.

4 *Documentary Annals*, i. 321–31.

5 Thomas Earl's notebook, CUL, MS. Mm.1.38, fol. 2ʳ.

6 *Three Fifteenth-Century Chronicles with Historical Memoranda by John Stow*, ed. J. Gairdner, CS n.s. xxvi. 1880, p. 143.

7 See especially R. W. Dixon's urbane account, *History of the Church of England from the Abolition of the Roman Jurisdiction*, vi. Oxford 1902; and a modern published dissertation, J. H. Primus, *The Vestments Controversy*, Kampen 1960.

8 *Parker Correspondence*, p. 284.

9 *Cambridge Modern History*, iii. Cambridge 1907, 341.

10 See pp. 111–17.

11 C. J. Vaughan, master of the Temple from 1869 to 1879.

12 GLL, MS. 9535/1, fols 83ᵛ, 85, 104ᵛ, 108ʳ, 120; P. Collinson, 'John Field and Elizabethan Puritanism', in *Elizabethan Government and Society*, ed. S. T. Bindoff, J. Hurstfield and C. H. Williams, 1961, p. 129. Gough is identified with the son of the printer by *The Diary of Henry Machyn, Citizen and Merchant-Taylor of London from A.D. 1550 to A.D. 1563*, ed. J. G. Nichols, CS xlii. 1848, p. 269.

13 *Remains*, pp. 283–5, 203; GLL, MS. 9531/13, fols 33–4ʳ.

14 *Machyn's Diary*, passim; Bodl., MS. Tanner 50, no. 10, fols 18–93.

15 *Machyn's Diary*, pp. 269, 285.

16 *Stow's Memoranda*, p. 133; Bodl., MS. Tanner 50, No. 10, fols 23, 18.

17 *An answere for the tyme*, 1566, Sig. A iiiiᵛ.

18 *Parker Correspondence*, pp. 239–40.

19 Grindal to William Cole, preacher to the Merchant Adventurers, 17 May 1564, Corpus Christi College Oxford, MS. 297, no. 8, fol. 18 (copy, ibid., MS. 316, no. 12, fol. 67); *Life and Death of Mr William Whittingham*, ed. M.A.E. Green, Camden Miscellany vi. 1870, pp. 15–17.

20 William Alley, Πτωχομυσεῖον. *The poore mans librarie*, Rapsodiae G.A. byshop of Exceter upon the first epistle of S. Peter, 1571 edn, p. 185.

21 Edwin Sandys, *Sermons*, ed. J. Ayre, PS 1841, p. 448.

22 *Remains*, pp. 211, 203.

23 See especially Bernard J. Verkamp, *The Indifferent Mean: Adiaphorism in the English Reformation to 1554*, Studies in the Reformation, i. Athens Ohio and Detroit 1977.

24 William Whitaker, quoted by H. C. Porter, 'The Nose of Wax: Scripture and the Spirit from Erasmus to Milton', *Transactions of the Royal Historical Socy*, 5th ser. xiv. 1964, 162–3.

25 J. S. Coolidge, *The Pauline Renaissance in England: Puritanism and the Bible*, Oxford 1970, pp. 23–54; BL, MS. Add. 32091, fols 201–4; Robert Crowley et al., *A briefe discourse against the outwarde apparell and ministring garmentes of the popishe churche*, 1566; Knox to Sampson, 20 May 1565, BL, MS. Add. 48117, no. 8, fols 154–5ʳ; *Parker Correspondence*, p. 245.

26 See p. 114.

27 Grindal to Archdeacon Pulleyn of Colchester, 5 June 1560; Corpus Christi College Oxford, MS. 319, no. 54, fol. 183 (copy in ibid., MS. 297, no. 7, fol. 17).

28 *Parker Correspondence*, pp. 246, 264.

29 *Remains*, p. 270.

30 LPL, MS. 2019, fols 1–2 is the original of this address, known to Strype from a copy in BL, MS. Lansd. 8, fols 17–18, which bears the names of Sampson and Humphrey only.

31 BL, MS. Add. 48117, no. 8, fols 154–5ʳ.

32 *Parker Correspondence*, pp. 223, 234. The question of who was responsible for the queen's letter is discussed in Dixon, op. cit., vi. 44 and in *Elizabethan Puritan Movement*, pp. 69–70.

33 *Parker Correspondence*, pp. 233–7.

34 H. G. Owen, 'The London Parish Clergy in the Reign of Elizabeth I', unpublished London Ph.D. thesis, 1957, pp. 491–4.

35 It is so dated by Strype (p. 153), but Strype's chronology of these events is confused.

36 BL, MS. Add. 19398, fol. 70. The letter is a holograph. The text in *Remains* (pp. 290–1) is taken from Strype (pp. 153–4) who cites a Parker MS. in Corpus Christi College Cambridge.

37 Thomas Earl's notebook, CUL, MS. Mm.1.38, fol. 2ᵛ; Owen, op. cit., pp. 494–6.

38 *Parker Correspondence*, p. 263.

39 Ibid., pp. 267–9; BL, MS. Lansd. 8, no. 82, fol. 205, no. 86, fol. 213; PRO, S.P. 15/13/40.

40 *Elizabeth Puritan Movement*, p. 148.

41 *Parker Correspondence*, pp. 269–70, 277–9.

42 PRO, S.P. 12/39/76.

43 *Parker Correspondence*, p. 268.

44 Ibid., p. 278.

45 *Elizabethan Puritan Movement*, pp. 75–83; Owen, op cit., pp. 500–14.

46 The 'literary warfare' of 1566 is briefly discussed in *Elizabethan Puritan Movement*, pp. 77–9, and M. M. Knappen, *Tudor Puritanism*, 1965 edn, pp. 198–204; and is analysed in Primus, op cit., pp. 107–48. The pamphlets are listed by Peter Milward, *Religious Controversies of the Elizabethan Age*, Leeds 1977, pp. 25–9.

47 *An answere for the tyme*, BL copy, pressmark 702.a.37, Sig. A iiᵛ, p. 86.

48 Anthony Gilby, *A pleasaunt dialogue betweene a soldiour of Barwicke and an English chaplaine*, (printed) 1581, Sig. D 6ᵛ.

49 *Elizabethan Puritan Movement*, p. 79.

50 See p. 181.
51 *Remains,* pp. 288–9. The possibly significant 'etc.' has been supplied from the original MS., PRO, S.P. 12/39/66.
52 *Remains,* p. 289; *Stow's Memoranda,* p. 140; PRO, S.P. 12/44/20.
53 Albert Peel, *The First Congregational Churches,* Cambridge 1920; C. C. Burrage, *Early English Dissenters,* 2 vols, Cambridge 1912; B. R. White, *The English Separatist Tradition,* Oxford 1971, pp. 20–43.
54 Foxe, viii. passim; White, op. cit., pp. 1–19.
55 *Narratives of the Days of the Reformation,* ed. J. G. Nichols, CS lxxvii. 1859, p. 171; Charles Wriothesly, *Chronicle,* ed. W. D. Hamilton, i. CS n.s. xi. 1875, p. 82; J. F. Davis, 'Heresy and the Reformation in the South-East of England 1520–1559', unpublished Oxford D.Phil. thesis, 1968, p. 303.
56 In a letter to John Knox, printed, Peter Lorimer, *John Knox and the Church of England,* 1875, pp. 298–300.
57 *Remains,* pp. 203–4.
58 Especially that of the late H. G. Owen in his thesis, op. cit., pp. 517–24, and in two published papers: 'A Nursery of Elizabethan Nonconformity, 1567–1572', *J.E.H.,* xvii. 1966, 65–76, and 'The Liberty of the Minories: A Study in Elizabethan Religious Radicalism', *East London Papers,* viii. 1965, 81–97. Much of the evidence is in print, in E. M. Tomlinson, *History of the Minories London,* 1907.
59 *The Seconde Parte of a Register,* ed. A. Peel, Cambridge 1915, i. 64–6.
60 The transcript ('the true report of our examination and conference') was printed in 1593 in the collection of puritan documents known as *A parte of a register;* whence included in *Remains,* pp. 202–16; recently reprinted, H. C. Porter, *Puritanism in Tudor England,* 1970, pp. 80–94.
61 Burrage, op. cit., ii. 9–11; *Stow's Memoranda,* p. 143; White, op. cit., pp. 25–6.
62 *Remains,* pp. 316–19; BL, MS. Lansd. 12, no. 28, fols 65–7; *Writings of Henry Barrow 1587–1590,* ed. L. H. Carlson, Elizabethan Nonconformist Texts iii. 1962, p. 254; *Seconde Parte of a Register,* i. 147–52.
63 *Z.L.,* i. 201–5.
64 *Remains,* pp. 295–6; BL, MS. Add. 48117, no. 8, fols 154–5^r; Lorimer, op. cit., pp. 298–300.
65 *Seconde Parte of a Register,* i. 65.
66 Owen, op. cit., pp. 524–5.
67 *Elizabethan Puritan Movement,* pp. 101–45.
68 Beza, *Epistolae,* 2nd edn Geneva 1575, Epist. 8. I follow the translation made by Field and Wilcox in their edition of the letter in 1572 (see below).
69 *Z.L.,* ii. 153–4.
70 Beza to Grindal, 3 July 1568; *Epistolae,* Epist. 23.
71 *Puritan Manifestoes,* ed. W. H. Frere and C. E. Douglas, 1954 edn, pp. 43–55.
72 Beza to Jean Cousin, 3 August 1572; *Ecclesiae Londino-Batavae Archivum,* ed. J. H. Hessels, ii. Cambridge 1889, 426–7.
73 *The iudgment of a most reverend and learned man* (1581?), Sig. A3.
74 Grindal to Cecil, 27 July 1570, *Remains,* pp. 304–5; Grindal to Cecil, 25 June 1570, PRO, S.P. 12/71/23 (incomplete and misdated transcript in *Remains,* pp. 323–4); Grindal to Parker, 9 Dec. 1573, *Remains,* pp. 347–8.
75 *Elizabethan Puritan Movement,* pp. 120–1.
76 Sampson to Grindal, 9 Nov. 1574; ITL, MS. Petyt 538/47, no. 188, fols 336–7.

77 Bullinger to Beza, 15 March 1567; *Z.L.*, ii. 152.

10 Apostle of the North

This and the chapter which follows are based on the original records of Grindal's archiepiscopate, preserved in the Borthwick Institute of Historical Research of the University of York. One of these sources has been published: *Archbishop Grindal's Visitation, 1575 Comperta et Detecta Book*, ed. W. J. Sheils, Borthwick Texts and Calendars: Records of the Northern Province, 4. Use has been made of the small library of monographs relating more or less directly to the religious history of Elizabethan Yorkshire: Hugh Aveling, *Post-Reformation Catholicism in East Yorkshire, 1558–1790*, East Yorkshire Local History Socy, 1960; *The Catholic Recusants of the West riding of Yorkshire, 1558–1790*, Proceedings of the Leeds Philosophical and Literary Institute, 1963; *Northern Catholics: the Catholic Recusants of the North Riding of Yorkshire, 1558–1790*, 1966; *Catholic Recusancy in the City of York, 1558–1791*, Catholic Record Socy Monographs 2, 1970. J. T. Cliffe, *The Yorkshire Gentry from the Reformation to the Civil War*, 1969. Claire Cross, *The Puritan Earl: the Life of Henry Hastings, Third Earl of Huntingdon, 1536–1595*, 1966. A. G. Dickens, *The Marian Reaction in the Diocese of York, Part II: The Laity*, St Anthony's Hall Publications 12, 1957; 'The First Stage of Romanist Recusancy in Yorkshire, 1560–1590', *Yorkshire Archaeological Journal*, xxxv. 1943, 157–81. R. A. Marchant, *The Puritans and the Church Courts in the Diocese of York, 1560–1642*, 1960; 'Church Courts and Administration in the Diocese of York, 1560–1642', unpublished work on deposit in the Borthwick Institute; *The Church Under the Law: Justice, Administration and Discipline in the Diocese of York, 1560–1640*, Cambridge 1969. J. A. Newton, 'Puritanism in the Diocese of York, Excluding Nottinghamshire, 1603–1640', unpublished London Ph.D. thesis, 1956. J. S. Purvis, *Tudor Parish Documents of the Diocese of York*, 1948. Philip Tyler, *The Ecclesiastical Commission and Catholicism in the North, 1562–1577*, 1960; 'The Administrative Character of the Ecclesiastical Commission for the Province of York', unpublished Oxford B.Litt. thesis, 1960: 'The Ecclesiastical Commission for the Province of York, 1561–1641', unpublished Oxford D.Phil. thesis, 1965.

1 *Parker Correspondence*, pp. 359–60; PRO, S.P. 12/66/42; Grindal to Cecil, 21 April 1570, BL, MS. Lansd. 12, no. 81, fol. 180; Grindal to Cecil, 25 June 1570, PRO, S.P. 12/71/23. In *Remains* the transcript of the last item (pp. 323–4) is misdated and omits the relevant passage.

2 *John Le Neve Fasti Ecclesiae Anglicanae, 1541–1857*, iv. *York Diocese*, comp. J. M. Horn and D. M. Smith, 1975, pp. 1–2; *Cal. of Patent Rolls, Eliz. I*, v. 1569–72, nos 1055, 1056, p. 118.

3 Parker to Grindal (and not, as the Catalogue has it, Grindal to Parker), 8 Sept. 1571; ITL, MS. Petyt 538/47, no. 28, fol. 34.

4 M. E. James, *Change and Continuity in the Tudor North: the Rise of Thomas, First Lord Wharton*, Borthwick Papers 27, 1965. See also Dr James's article 'The Concept of Order and the Northern Rising of 1569', *Past and Present*, no. 60, 1973, and his *Family, Lineage and Civil Society: A Study of Society, Politics and Mentality in the Durham Region, 1500–1640*, Oxford 1974.

5 R. R. Reid, *The King's Council of the North*, 1921, pp. 193–8.

6 Matthew Hutton to Cecil, 13 Nov. 1568; PRO, S.P. 12/48/41.

7 William Camden, *Annals*, 1630 edn, Bk II, p. 24.

8 Grindal to Sir Nicholas Bacon, 5 Oct. 1573; BL, MS. Add. 33271, fol. 40.

9 Aveling, Cliffe, Dickens, Tyler, opera cit.; John Bossy, 'The Character of

Elizabeth Catholicism', *Past and Present*, no. 21, 1962, and his *The English Catholic Community, 1570–1850*, 1975.

10 Will of Thomas Lather, clerk, rector of St Saviour's York, made 8 Feb., proved 24 Oct. 1567; Borthwick, Reg. 30 (Registers of Young and Grindal), fol. 30^r.

11 Grindal to Cecil, 29 August 1570; *Remains*, pp. 325–6.

12 There are other competitors for the title 'Apostle of the North', including the seventeenth-century divine Richard Rothwell. (Samuel Clark, *The Lives of Thirty-Two English Divines*, 1677, p. 70.)

13 John Strype, *The Life and Acts of Matthew Parker*, Oxford 1821, ii. 20–1, iii. 291–3, 319.

14 Grindal to Cecil, 25 June 1570, postscript omitted in transcript in *Remains* (pp. 323–4); PRO, S.P. 12/71/23.

15 M. B. Donald, *Elizabethan Copper: the History of the Mines Royal, 1568–1605*, 1955, pp. 15–35; PRO, S.P. 12/71, 38, 38I, 55, 58, 66, 66I; BL, MS. Lansd. 19, no. 4, fol. 8, no. 62, fol. 140.

16 Z.L., i. 224–5, 258–60; Cliffe, op. cit., p. 169; Gargrave to Cecil, 12 April 1570, PRO, S.P. 15/18/39; *Remains*, pp. 325–6.

17 PRO, S.P. 12/111/14.

18 Borthwick, Reg. 30, fol. 62^v; PRO, S.P. 12/74/32; Borthwick, Inst. AB 2, pt iii, fol. 80^v.

19 Borthwick, Reg. 30, fols 16^v–17^r, 37, 86, 97^v, 157; George Carleton, *Life of Bernard Gilpin*, 1727 edn, pp. 82–9.

20 Marchant, *The Church Under the Law*, esp. pp. 38–60.

21 Ibid., pp. 82–4.

22 BL, MS. Lansd. 982, fol. 34^v. Grindal had warmly commended Shrewsbury to Cecil in a letter of 10 Nov. 1570. (PRO, S.P. 12/74/32.)

11   Delenda and Agenda

1 *Visitation Articles and Injunctions of the Period of the Reformation*, iii. ed. W. H. Frere, Alcuin Club Collections, 1910, 253–93. See also R. L. Arundale, 'Edmund Grindal and the Northern Province', *Church Quarterly Review*, clx. 1959, 182–99.

2 *Notes & Queries*, 13th ser. cliii. 26; Borthwick, Inst. AB 2, pt iii, fol. 146. I owe this reference to Dr W. J. Sheils.

3 Borthwick, Reg. 30, fol 95^v, Inst. AB 2, pt iii, fol. 146; J. S. Purvis, *Tudor Parish Documents of the Diocese of York*, 1948, p. 202.

4 Ibid., pp. 15–34, 146–8; Hugh Aveling, *Northern Catholics: the Catholic Recusants of the North Riding of Yorkshire, 1558–1790*, 1966, pp. 23–4.

5 *Archbishop Grindal's Visitation, 1575 Comperta et Detecta Book*, ed. W. J. Sheils, Borthwick Texts and Calendars: Records of the Northern Province, 4, pp. xi–xii; Purvis, op. cit., pp. 109–25.

6 Borthwick, V. 1571–2/CB, fol. 1; *Visitation Articles and Injunctions*, iii. 345–54, ii. 310–12; A. G. Dickens, *Robert Holgate, Archbishop of York and President of the King's Council in the North*, St Anthony's Hall Publications 8, 1955; *A History of York Minster*, ed. G. E. Aylmer and R. Cant, Oxford 1977, pp. 206–10, 218.

7 Borthwick, V. 1571–2/CB: Grindal to Leicester, 16 July 1571, BL, MS. Add. 32091, fol. 242; George Carleton, *Life of Bernard Gilpin*, 1727 edn, pp. 38, 84. For a detailed account of procedures at diocesan and provincial visitations, see R. A. Marchant, *The Church Under the Law: Justice, Adminis-*

tration and Discipline in the Diocese of York, 1560–1640, Cambridge 1969, ch. 4.

8 Borthwick, V. 1571–2/CB, fols 121ᵛ–2, 217, 220ᵛ–1ʳ.

9 Ibid., fols 122ʳ, 138ʳ.

10 Dr Philip Tyler is the historian of the York Ecclesiastical Commission. See the introduction to the notes for ch. 10, and his article 'The Significance of the Ecclesiastical Commission at York' in *Northern History,* ii. 1967, 27–44; also his Introduction to the 1968 reissue of R. G. Usher, *The Rise and Fall of the High Commission.* Four act books of the Commission span the years of Grindal's presidency: Borthwick, HC.AB.5–8. On Nottinghamshire, see R. A. Marchant, 'The Jurisdiction of the Archdeacon of Nottingham, 1565–1800', unpublished essay in 'Church Courts and Administration in the Diocese of York, 1560–1642', on deposit in the Borthwick Institute, and *The Church Under the Law,* pp. 122–8, 147–203.

11 Tyler, D.Phil. thesis, Appendix 7. Gaps occur in the act books between 19 March and 30 April 1571 and 7 April and 14 October 1574.

12 PRO, S.P. 15/21/84, 86.

13 Borthwick, HC.AB.5, fols 234ᵛ, 237ᵛ–8ʳ, HC.AB.6, fols 3ʳ, 7, 8ʳ, 31ʳ, HC.AB.7, fol. 41, HC.AB.9, fol. 20.

14 Ibid., HC.AB.9, fol. 20; Harold C. Gardiner, *Mysteries' End: an Investigation of the Last Days of the Medieval Religious Stage,* New Haven 1967, pp. 72–83.

15 Borthwick, HC.AB.6, fols 33ʳ, 48ʳ, 96ᵛ.

16 I am grateful to Dr Sheils for this suggestion.

17 Borthwick, HC.AB.6, fols 48ʳ, 54ᵛ–6.

18 Aveling, *Northern Catholics,* p. 22; *Archbishop Grindal's Visitation, 1575,* pp. 17, 26, 43, 44, 56, 59, 60, 72, 81–3, 88, with Dr Sheils's gloss on the Scarborough evidence, pp. x–xi; Borthwick, V. 1571–2/CB, fol. 163ʳ.

19 Neville Williams, *Elizabeth Queen of England,* 1967, p. 170.

20 BL, MS. Add. 32091, fol. 242.

21 Tyler, D.Phil. thesis, pp. 377–8; Borthwick, Inst. AB 2, 3, HC.AB.6, fols 63ᵛ–4ᵛ, 65ᵛ, 81 seq., 107ᵛ, 109ᵛ, 121ᵛ; Grindal to Mildmay, 6 April 1573, PRO, S.P. 46/29, fol. 235.

22 Purvis, op. cit., pp. 109–21.

23 P. Collinson, 'Lectures by Combination: Structures and Characteristics of Church Life in Seventeenth-Century England', *B.I.H.R.,* xlviii. 1975, 182–213; R. A. Marchant, *The Puritans and the Church Courts in the Diocese of York, 1560–1642,* 1960, pp. 132–5; Claire Cross, *The Puritan Earl: the Life of Henry Hastings, Third Earl of Huntingdon, 1536–1595,* 1966, pp. 259–60; J. A. Newton, 'Puritanism in the Diocese of York, Excluding Nottinghamshire, 1603–1640', unpublished London Ph.D. thesis, 1956, passim.

24 Borthwick, Reg. 30; Inst. AB 2, 3.

25 *A History of York Minster,* pp. 209, 436, 499, 208.

26 Borthwick, Inst. AB 2, pt iii, fol. 113ᵛ, Inst. AB 3, fol. 9.

27 Ibid., Inst. AB 2, pt iii, fol. 126ʳ, Inst. AB 3, fols 4ᵛ, 6, 8ᵛ, 10ʳ, 21ᵛ, 23ᵛ–4ʳ, 46ᵛ–7ʳ, 81.

28 *Remains,* pp. 345–6; *A.P.C.,* viii. 170. On the limited powers of bishops to refuse ordination and institution on grounds of insufficiency, see M. R. O'Day, 'Clerical Patronage and Recruitment in the Elizabethan and Jacobean Periods, with Special Reference to the Diocese of Coventry and Lichfield', unpublished London Ph.D. thesis, 1972, and her 'The Law of Patronage in Early Modern England', *J.E.H.,* xxvi. 1975, 247–60.

29 Borthwick, Chanc. AB.9, fol. 212, HC.CP.1567/8. I owe these references to

Dr W. J. Sheils. Cf. G. C. F. Forster, 'Hull in the 16th and 17th Centuries', in *Victoria History of the County of York East Riding*, ed. K. J. Allison, i. *The City of Kingston upon Hull*, Oxford 1969, 95–6.

30 *Remains*, p. 354.
31 See pp. 146–51.
32 Marchant, *The Church Under the Law*, pp. 147–57.
33 *Narratives of the Days of the Reformation*, ed. J. G. Nichols, CS lxxvii. 1859, p. 50.
34 Cross, op. cit., pp. 247–69; Marchant, *Puritans and the Church Courts*, p. 213. See also J. T. Cliffe, *The Yorkshire Gentry from the Reformation to the Civil War*, 1969, pp. 270–1 for further examples of collaboration among the puritan gentry to promote religion.
35 Grindal to Parker, 9 Dec. 1573; ITL, MS. Petyt 538/47, no. 21, fol. 27. In the text as given in *Remains* (pp. 347–8) the reference to 'novelties' is followed by this sentence: 'I have written to them to reform them without delay, or else I will.' There is a tear in the MS. and the reading 'I will' is dubious.
36 This is clear from the biographical lists of puritan clergy appended to Marchant's *Puritans and the Church Courts*.
37 *Remains*, pp. 380–1.
38 Borthwick, HC.AB.6, fol. 51^v, HC.AB.8, fol. 4^r, HC.AB.6, fol. 13^r; Tyler, *The Ecclesiastical Commission and Catholicism*, pp. 97–8; Tyler, D.Phil. thesis, pp. 235–42.
39 *D.N.B.*, art. Grindal.
40 Tyler, D.Phil. thesis, pp. 235–61.
41 J. E. Neale, *Elizabeth I and her Parliaments, 1559–1581*, 1953, pp. 192–3, 212–16, 304, 349, 386–92; F. X. Walker, 'The Implementation of the Elizabethan Statutes against Recusants, 1581–1603', unpublished London Ph.D. thesis, 1961, pp. 33–43; Tyler, D.Phil. thesis, pp. 265–89.
42 Grindal to Burghley, 10 Dec. 1575; BL, MS. Lansd. 20, no. 69, fol. 168.

12   Grindal's Hundred Days

1 *Puritan Manifestoes*, ed. W. H. Frere and C. E. Douglas, 1954 edn, pp. 30–1.
2 *Parker Correspondence*, pp. 478, 418–19, 454, 472.
3 Ibid., p. 461. See A. F. Scott Pearson, *Thomas Cartwright and Elizabethan Puritanism 1535–1603*, Cambridge 1925, pp. 125–9, and *Elizabethan Puritan Movement*, pp. 154–5.
4 *Parker Correspondence*, pp. 472, 478, 446, 473.
5 This letter is neither signed, nor addressed, nor dated. Yet it is written in Parker's hand and it is among Burghley's papers, BL, MS. Lansd. 15, no. 34, fol. 66. Parker appears to apologize for this outburst in a letter to Burghley, endorsed 6 Oct. 1572; ibid., no. 43, fol. 84.
6 *Parker Correspondence*, p. 479.
7 Ibid., pp. 474, 419.
8 Ibid., p. 425.
9 *Short-Title Catalogue* revised no. 1929a. See *Elizabethan Puritan Movement*, pp. 146, 153.
10 *Parker Correspondence*, pp. 473, 476, 477–8.
11 Gonville and Caius College Cambridge, MS. 30/53, fol. 42^v. The letter is dated 23 May (1575).
12 Huntingdon to Burghley, 24 June 1575; BL, MS. Lansd. 20, no. 50, fol. 130.
13 Nowell to Burghley, 16 May 1575; PRO, S.P. 12/103/49.

14 *Remains*, p. 402.
15 Burghley to Walsingham, 15 May 1575; PRO, S.P. 12/103/48.
16 Huntingdon had heard that Grindal was 'in election for Canterbury' by 24 June.
17 Burghley to Grindal (holograph), 25 Nov. 1575; ITL, MS. Petyt 538/47, no. 267, fol. 502.
18 Grindal to Burghley, 10 Dec. 1575; BL, MS. Lansd. 20, no. 69, fol. 168.
19 BL, MS. Lansd. 20, no. 50, fol. 130.
20 John Harington, *A briefe viewe of the state of the church of England* (1608), 1653, p. 7.
21 *Parker Correspondence*, p. 478.
22 ITL, MS. Petyt 538/47, no. 267, fol 502.
23 Blank in the MS.
24 PRO, S.P. 59/19, fol. 248ᵛ. The item is numbered '983' from its old location in S.P. 70/141 (see *Cal. of State Papers, Foreign, 1575–7*, pp. 468–9), from where it was transferred to State Papers, Scotland and the Borders.
25 CALC, MS. Y.11.3, Chapter Acts, fol. 93; Accounts 41, Chapter Accounts for 1576.
26 Strype, p. 287.
27 LPL, Grindal's register, i. fol. 8; CALC, MS. Z.5.1, fols 111ᵛ–15ᵛ.
28 Ibid., MS. Y.11.3, fol. 93ᵛ.
29 *Parker Correspondence*, p. 360.
30 CALC, Accounts 41, accounts for 1576.
31 LPL, Grindal's register, i. fols 78–83ʳ.
32 CALC, City of Canterbury Archives, AC 2, Minutes of Burmote 1542–1578, entry of 9 Sept. 1578, fol. 338ʳ.
33 Strype, p. 312.
34 J. E. Neale, *Elizabeth I and her Parliaments, 1559–1581*, 1953, p. 349.
35 Ibid., pp. 349, 382–92; F. X. Walker, 'The Implementation of the Elizabethan Statutes against Recusants, 1581–1603', unpublished London Ph.D. thesis, 1961, pp. 36–118.
36 Neale, op. cit., p. 350.
37 Ibid., pp. 349–52; *Elizabethan Puritan Movement*, pp. 161–3.
38 Drafts in PRO, S.P. 12/107/61, 65, 66. Included in lists of bills in this Parliament, ibid., 77, 78. And see Simonds D'Ewes, *Journals of all the Parliaments of Queen Elizabeth*, 1682, p. 262.
39 Neale, op. cit., p. 352.
40 See Thomas Norton's remarks at the end of the session: *Archaeologia*, xxxvi. 109–15; and Robert Beale to Sir Christopher Hatton, 25 Nov. 1589: BL, MS. Add. 48039, fols 63–70.
41 *Synodalia*, ed. E. Cardwell, i. Oxford 1842, 132–8.
42 *Elizabethan Puritan Movement*, p. 162.
43 ITL, MS. Petyt 538/54, fols 247 seq.
44 *Elizabethan Puritan Movement*, p. 163.
45 *Puritan Manifestoes*, pp. 32–3; John Whitgift, *Works*, ed. J. Ayre, iii. PS 1853, 12.
46 PRO, S.P. 12/107/41.
47 PRO, S.P. 15/24/72.
48 Parker to Cecil, 1 April 1570, *Parker Correspondence*, pp. 361–3; John Strype, *Life of Whitgift*, Oxford 1822, iii. 133–4; John Strype, *The Life and Acts of Matthew Parker*, Oxford 1821, ii. 15–17.
49 Strype, p. 300.

50 BL, MS. Lansd. 23, no. 61, fol. 127.

51 See pp. 30–1.

52 A.P.C., xi. *1578–1580*, 16–20. Two MS. copies of the orders, PRO, S.P. 12/129/25, 26, date from the 1578 ratification and are headed 'A memorandum of the 30 of January remaining in the Council to be perused for the understanding of the Lords' meaning concerning these articles'; and one article is dated '13 January 1578'. The Privy Council dealt with the matter on 15 Jan. 1578.

53 ITL, MS. Petyt 538/54, fols 265–71, 282ʳ, 284; partly printed, Strype, pp. 302–9.

54 Ibid., p. 307.

55 ITL, MS. Petyt 538/54, fol. 269ᵛ.

56 Christopher Kitching, 'The Prerogative Court of Canterbury from Warham to Whitgift', in *Continuity and Change: Personnel and Administration of the Church in England 1500–1642*, ed. R. O'Day and F. Heal, Leicester 1976, pp. 207–8.

57 ITL, MS. Petyt 538/54, fols 7–11, 16–18, 21–2, 23–5, 64–7. The last of these papers is endorsed by Grindal '3° Maij 1576' (not 23 May as in Strype, p. 309).

58 *The plea of the innocent*, 1602, pp. 9–10, 216–17.

59 PRO, S.P. 15/25/119.

60 *A Brief Discourse of the Troubles Begun at Frankfort*, ed. J. Petheram, 1846, pp. 191–4. L. J. Trinterud discusses the problem in *Elizabethan Puritanism*, Library of Protestant Thought, New York 1971, pp. 202–8.

61 *Elizabethan Puritan Movement*, pp. 165, 365.

13 A Scruple of Conscience

1 Grindal to Burghley, 10 June 1576, BL, MS. Lansd. 23, no. 4, fol. 7; Sir Nicholas Bacon's speech to Grindal in Council, BL, MS. Harl. 5176, fol. 95; *Elizabethan Puritan Movement*, pp. 193–4.

2 Ibid., pp. 168–76; P. Collinson, 'Lectures by Combination: Structures and Characteristics of Church Life in Seventeenth-Century England', *B.I.H.R.*, xlviii. 1975, 182–213.

3 LPL, MS. 2003, fol. 5.

4 Ibid., fol. 29.

5 *The Letter Book of John Parkhurst, Bishop of Norwich, Compiled During the Years 1571–5*, ed. R. A. Houlbrooke, Norfolk Record Socy xliii. 1974 and 1975, 231–3, 235–6, 241–7.

6 Sandys to the Council, 13 July 1574, enclosing the postscript of a letter to Sandys from Parker, received the same day, LPL, MS. 2003, fols 27, 22. Stanford E. Lehmberg in his edition of this MS. (see n. 13 below) misdates the letter 1576, with the misleading implication that it was Grindal who had passed on the queen's order to Sandys in the postscript.

7 BL, MS. Add. 21565, fol. 26.

8 LPL, MS. 2003, fol. 29.

9 *Elizabethan Puritan Movement*, passim; W. J. Sheils, 'The Puritans in Church and Politics in the Diocese of Peterborough 1570–1610', unpublished London Ph.D. thesis, 1974.

10 *Letters of Thomas Wood*, pp. xvi–xix, 18, 15.

11 The only record of what passed between the queen and the archbishop in this interview (apart from what Grindal himself discloses in his letter to the

queen) is contained in an account of Grindal's troubles evidently composed by Sir Walter Mildmay. (Northamptonshire Record Office, F.(M).P.70.c.).

12 *Elizabethan Puritan Movement*, pp. 168–76; Collinson, 'Lectures by Combination', 195.

13 Most of the letters, including reports to Sandys from the archdeacons of London, Essex and St Albans, and from the schoolmaster of St Albans, included in Sandys's return, are in LPL, MS. 2003. An incomplete and imperfect edition of this material has been published by Stanford E. Lehmberg in 'Archbishop Grindal and the Prophesyings', *The Historical Magazine of the Protestant Episcopal Church*, xxxiv. 87–145. There are eighteenth-century copies of most of the letters, together with the copy of a letter from Bishop Cheyney of Gloucester which is not otherwise extant, in BL, MS. Add. 29546, fols 36–57; and extracts from the correspondence, adding information from four further letters no longer extant, in BL, MS. Add. 21565, fol. 26, and in LPL, MS. 2003, fols 35–6.

14 Ibid., fol. 7.

15 Bentham of Coventry and Lichfield, Berkeley of Bath and Wells, Bradbridge of Exeter, Cheyney of Gloucester, Cooper of Lincoln, Curteys of Chichester, Piers of Rochester and Sandys of London.

16 Bradbridge wrote on 9 July, Curteys on 15 July, Bentham on 16 July and Cooper on 27 July; LPL, MS. 2003, fols 8, 4, 5, 29–30.

17 BL, MS. Add. 21565, fol. 26.

18 Northamptonshire Record Office, F. (M).P.70.b.

19 Ibid.

20 LPL, MS. 2014, fols 72–80, MS. 2007, fols 126–44, MS. 2872.

21 Ibid., MS. 2007, fol. 134ᵛ.

22 *Remains*, pp. 373–4 (from BL, MS. Cotton, Cleopatra F. II, p. 261).

23 Northamptonshire Record Office, F.(M).P.70.c.

24 See pp. 219–20.

25 Several MS. copies of this celebrated document are extant: in BL, MS. Lansd. 23, MSS. Add. 22587, 33271, MS. Harl. 1877; in Bodl., MS. Tanner 79, and Queen's College Oxford, MS. 292; in LPL, MS. 595; in the Hastings MSS. (*H.M.C. Report, Hastings MSS.*, i. 433); in the Morrice MSS. in Dr Williams's Library (*The Seconde Parte of a Register*, ed. A. Peel, Cambridge 1915, i. 135). The Lansdowne copy (23, no. 12, fols 24–9ʳ), printed in *Remains* (pp. 376–90) with only minor errors, in the hand of a secretary or scribe, headed in a hand different from that of the letter 'To her Majesty 20 December 1576', and endorsed in Burghley's hand '20 December 1576 Epistola Edmundi Cantuar Arch. ad D. Reginam'. A very similar copy is in the Northamptonshire Record Office, F.(M).P.54. The letter is variously dated (1598 in Queen's College Oxford MS. 292!), but most authors take the date of 20 December from the Lansdowne copy. The true date of 8 December is inferred from Grindal's letter to Burghley of 16 December, MS. Lansd. 23, no. 9, fol. 18.

26 J. E. Neale, *Elizabeth I and her Parliaments, 1584–1601*, 1957, p. 70.

27 Northamptonshire Record Office, F.(M).P.70.c.

28 W. H. Frere, *The English Church in the Reigns of Elizabeth and James I*, 1904, p. 192.

29 *Early Latin Theology*, ed. S. L. Greenslade, Library of Christian Classics, v. 1956, 229–30.

30 Ibid., 178–81.

31 *Omnia quotquot extant divi Ambrosii episcopi Mediolanensis opera cum per Des.*

Erasmum Roterodamum, tum per alios eruditos viros, accurata diversorum codicum collatione, nunc de novo emendata, Basle 1538, 5 tom. in 2 vv.

32 See pp. 96.

33 *Ambrosii opera,* tom. 1, Sig. AA3, tom. 3, pp. 129, 136, 145, 154, 156.

34 Ibid., p. 128. The letter (*Remains,* p. 376) contains a direct quotation from the epistle: 'Scribo manu mea, quod sola legas.'

35 BL, MS. Lansd. 23, no. 12, fols 24–9ʳ. But see pp. 246–7.

36 *Ambrosii opera,* tom. 3, p. 134.

37 Ibid., p. 145; P. de Labriolle, tr. H. Wilson, *The Life and Times of St Ambrose,* 1928, pp. 40–1.

38 *A History of the Church ... by Theodoret,* Bohn's Ecclesiastical Library, 1854, Bk v ch. 18, pp. 219–20. Grindal may have known the passage from the 1549 Basle edition of *Ecclesiasticae historiae autores.*

39 John Jewel, *An Apology of the Church of England,* ed. J. E. Booty, Folger Documents of Tudor and Stuart Civilization, Ithaca 1963, pp. 116–17.

40 Foxe, i. 290, 303, 296, 293.

41 *Ambrosii opera,* tom. 3, p. 147.

42 J. H. Hexter, *More's Utopia: the Biography of an Idea,* Princeton 1952.

43 *Pasquil the playne.* See Stanford E. Lehmberg, *Sir Thomas Elyot, Tudor Humanist,* Austin Texas 1961, pp. 116–20.

44 *Cal. of State Papers, Foreign, 1579–80,* pp. 99–100.

45 *Remains,* p. 391.

46 Leicester's proposal is referred to in Grindal's letter to Burghley of 17 December; ibid., pp. 391–2.

47 James Spedding, *Life and Letters of Francis Bacon,* i. 1861, 88. For other references see my 'The Puritan Classical Movement in the Reign of Elizabeth I', unpublished London Ph.D. thesis, 1957, pp. 261–5.

48 *Remains,* p. 391.

49 BL, MS. Lansd. 23, no. 12, fol. 29ᵛ.

50 Northamptonshire Record Office, F.(M).P.54.

51 LPL, Grindal's register, i. fols 18ᵛ, 23ᵛ, 28ᵛ.

52 Ibid., fols 92–6.

53 Ibid., fol. 98 (printed, *Remains,* pp. 183–4).

54 BL, MS. Harl. 6992, no. 34, fol. 69.

55 Burghley to Grindal (holograph), 23 Feb. 1576(/7); LPL, MS. 2003, fol. 39.

56 BL, MS. Lansd. 25, no. 44, fol. 92.

57 Ibid., fol. 93.

58 Ibid., fols 94–5. A fair copy of this final version is in BL, MS. Cotton, Cleopatra F. 2, fol. 289, whence printed by Strype (pp. 574–6) and in *Remains* (pp. 467–9). Whitgift's copy is in LPL, MS. 2003, fols 40–1.

59 BL, MS. Add. 32092, fol. 22.

60 This is inferred from Sir Nicholas Bacon's speech to Grindal in Council on a later occasion. (BL, MS. Harl. 5176, fol. 95.)

61 LPL, Grindal's register, ii. fol. 406.

62 Grindal to the Council, 11 Nov. 1577 (sic), LPL, MS. 2003, fols 37–8; the Council to Grindal, 7 Nov. 1577, ibid., Grindal's register, i. fol. 157ᵛ. The original patent of appointment of Drury and Hussey is in LPL, MS. C.M. XII, no. 52.

63 LPL, Grindal's register, i. fols 167, 159ᵛ, 239ᵛ, 244ᵛ.

64 Walsingham to Burghley (holograph), 31 May 1577; PRO, S.P. 12/113/17.

65 Ibid.; Burghley to Walsingham (18th-century [?] copy), 31 May 1577, BL, MS. Add. 5935, fol. 68.

66 Grindal to an unnamed correspondent, 13 July 1577; LPL, MS. 2004, fol. 1. Lehmberg, who printed the letter in 'Archbishop Grindal and the Prophesyings', 143-4, assumed that Burghley must have been the recipient since he was Grindal's 'principal advocate at court'. But Burghley was not and could not have been Grindal's advocate, publicly. In February he had advised the archbishop to continue to use Leicester as his 'intercessor'. (See p. 248.) Somewhat later Sir Christopher Hatton was to step into this role. (See pp. 263-4.)

14 Policy and Intrigue

1 William Camden, *History of the most renowned and victorious princess Elizabeth*, 4th edn 1688, pp. 287-8.
2 See, for example, Sir John Hayward's account: *Annals of the First Four Years of the Reign of Queen Elizabeth*, ed. J. Bruce, CS, 1840, p. 89.
3 *A briefe viewe of the state of the church of England* (1608), 1653, pp. 5-7.
4 Fuller, iv. 455, v. 58-9.
5 Peter Heylyn, *Aerius redivivus: or the history of the presbyterians*, 1672, pp. 247-8.
6 John Harington, *A Tract on the Succession to the Crown* (1602), Roxburghe Club, 1880, p. 44. I owe this reference to my colleague Dr P. R. Roberts.
7 *The copie of a leter wryten by a Master of Arte of Cambridge*, 1584, pp. 26-7, 29, 89.
8 Strype, pp. 334-6.
9 Dr Julio to the earl of Leicester, 4 Dec. 1576; BL, MS. Cotton, Titus B.VII, fol. 36. I owe this reference to Mr D. C. Peck, late of Ohio State University.
10 Burghley to Walsingham, 31 May 1577; BL, MS. Add. 5935, fol 68.
11 Leicester to Burghley, 12 Nov. 1579; BL, MS. Harl. 6992, no. 57, fols 114-15.
12 H. R. Trevor-Roper, *Queen Elizabeth's First Historian: William Camden and the Beginnings of English 'Civil History'*, 1971.
13 *Letters of Thomas Wood*, passim.
14 Bishop Barnes of Durham to Burghley, 11 Feb. 1577(/8); BL, MS. Lansd. 25, no. 78, fols 161-2.
15 Leicester wrote to Burghley on 25 Jan. 1578 from Buxton: 'My lord, having so convenient a messenger as Mr Dr Julio ... '(BL, MS. Harl. 6992, no. 51, fol. 102.)
16 *Cal. of State Papers, Venetian, 1558-1580*, p. 545.
17 Sir Harris Nicolas, *Life and Times of Sir Christopher Hatton*, 1847, p. 24; E. St. J. Brooks, *Sir Christopher Hatton*, 1946, pp. 94, 98.
18 *H.M.C. Report, Hastings MSS.*, i. 433.
19 *Elizabethan Puritan Movement*, pp. 193-4, 201, 259, 312-14.
20 See pp. 263-4.
21 I have discussed the political context of Grindal's troubles more extensively in my essay 'The Downfall of Archbishop Grindal and its Place in Elizabethan Political and Ecclesiastical History', in *The English Commonwealth 1547-1660*, ed. P. Clark, N. R. N. Tyacke and A. G. R. Smith, Leicester 1979.
22 Charles Wilson, *Queen Elizabeth and the Revolt of the Netherlands*, 1970, p. 43.
23 Knollys to Wilson, 9 Jan. 1577(/8); BL, MS. Harl. 6992, no. 44, fol. 89.
24 Killigrew to Davison, 3 April 1578; PRO, S.P. 15/25/79.

25 *Remains*, p. 389.
26 Cheke to Davison, 8 August 1577; PRO, S.P. 15/25/30.
27 Killigrew to Davison, 3 April 1578; PRO, S.P. 83/2/43.
28 Cheke to Davison, 19 Sept. 1577; PRO, S.P. 15/25/35.
29 Grindal to the Privy Council, 24 Oct. 1577; PRO, S.P. 12/117/9.
30 Grindal to Matthew Hutton, 2 Dec. 1577; *Remains*, pp. 394-5.
31 'The occasion whereupon the displeasure grew from the queen's Majesty to the archbishop of Canterbury'; Northamptonshire Record Office, Fitzwilliam of Milton Papers, F.(M).P.70.c. F.(M).P.70a is an account of what transpired in the Star Chamber on 30 Nov. 1577 and F.(M).P.70.b is a skeleton memorandum in Mildmay's hand dated 22 Jan. 1577(/8), 'Touching the archbishop of Canterbury in the matter of the exercises'. This material is discussed by Stanford E. Lehmberg in *Sir Walter Mildmay and Tudor Government*, Austin Texas 1964, pp. 148-53, but without reference to the meeting at Bacon's house which is the most interesting part of the story.
32 Strype, pp. 348-50.
33 Copies in BL, MS. Cotton, Cleopatra F. II, fol. 273 (whence printed by Strype, pp. 350-2), endorsed '29 No[vember] 1577. The request of the archbishop of Canterbury to my lords of the Privy Council'; and in BL, MS. Lansd. 25, no. 79, fols 163-4, endorsed: 'The humble submission of Edmund archbishop of Canterbury to the lords of her Majesty's Privy Council in the Star Chamber. Touching the exercise of prophesying. Sent by Sir Walter Mildmay.' A nearly illegible date follows which has been (mistakenly) read as 3 March 1577(/8). Both copies bear Grindal's signature.
34 Northamptonshire Record Office, F.(M).P.70.a.
35 Copies in BL, MS. Harl. 398, fol. 12ʳ, and Folger Shakespeare Library, MS. V.a.197, fol. 19.
36 Northamptonshire Record Office, F.(M).P.70.a.
37 Copies in BL, MS. Harl. 5176, fol. 95 (whence printed, *Remains*, pp. 471-3), MS. Harl. 36, no. 55, fol. 391-2 (renumbered 298-9), Huntington Library, MS. EL 2579, fols 59-60ʳ.
38 Killigrew to Davison, 29 Jan. 1578; PRO, S.P. 15/25/71. The letter has been damaged by damp and uncertainty persists about the reading of the words italicized, after prolonged scrutiny under ultraviolet light.
39 Northamptonshire Record Office, F.(M).P.70.b.
40 Sir Thomas Wilson to Burghley, 23 Jan. 1578; PRO, S.P. 12/122/15.
41 Ibid.
42 Killigrew to Davison, 22 Feb. 1578; PRO, S.P. 15/25/74.
43 PRO, S.P. 15/25/35.
44 Cox to the queen, 8 June 1577, 8 Jan, 1578; Gonville and Caius College Cambridge, MS. 30/53, fols 50ᵛ, 42ᵛ.
45 Cox to Aylmer (?), March 1577(/8); ibid., fol. 53.
46 Grindal to Hatton, 2 May 1578; BL, MS. Add. 15891, fol. 33ᵛ (fol. 30 old numbering), whence printed, Nicolas, op. cit., pp. 52-3.
47 Huntingdon to Hutton, 20 May 1578; *The Correspondence of Dr Matthew Hutton*, ed. J. Raines, Surtees Socy, xvii. 1843, 59-60.
48 Ibid.
49 Grindal to Hutton, 28 April 1577; ibid., 56-7.
50 In a letter of 24 March 1576 (BL, MS. Lansd. 24, no. 17, fol. 36) he called Burghley his 'singular good lord and patron', testified that 'your lordship was mine only preferrer to Carlisle' and rendered 'most entire thanks to your Honour for your goodness towards me in commending me to her Highness in way of my preferment to Durham'.

51 Barnes to Burghley, 11 Feb. 1577(/8); BL, MS. Lansd. 25, no. 78, fols 161–2.

15   Our English Eli

1 Walsingham to Burghley, 27 May 1580, PRO, S.P. 12/138/26; Leicester to Burghley, 12 Nov. 1579, BL, MS. Harl. 6992, no. 57, fols 114–15.
2 Grindal to Hatton, 15 Nov. 1578; BL, MS. Add. 15891, fol. 33ᵛ (fol. 30 old numbering), whence printed, Sir Harris Nicolas, *Life and Times of Sir Christopher Hatton*, 1847, pp. 98–9.
3 Grindal to Hutton, 18 Feb. 1579; *Remains*, p. 395.
4 Grindal to Privy Council (autograph), 30 March 1580; BL, MS. Cotton, Vespasian F XII, fol. 192.
5 Northamptonshire Record Office, F.(M).P.70.a.
6 BL, MS. Add. 32092, fol. 22.
7 LPL, Grindal's register, i. fols 139–40. The original commission is in LPL, MS. C.M. II, no. 79. All but one of the subsequent documents connected with this visitation were issued in the name of Dr Aubrey. (Register, fols 141–3.)
8 Ibid., fol. 244ᵛ.
9 Strype, p. 403, and generally, Bk II, ch. 13.
10 Ibid., p. 382. For Aylmer's activities during Grindal's sequestration, see John Strype, *Life of Aylmer*, Oxford 1821, esp. pp. 60–4; and H. G. Owen, 'The London Parish Clergy in the Reign of Elizabeth I', unpublished London Ph.D. thesis, 1957, pp. 540–52.
11 David Wilkins ed., *Concilia*, 1737, iv. 292.
12 Aylmer to the earl of Sussex, 27 Jan. 1577(/8); BL, MS. Harl. 6992, no. 46, fol. 92.
13 *Elizabethan Puritan Movement*, pp. 205–7.
14 See pp. 227–8; and *Elizabethan Puritan Movement*, pp. 162–3.
15 Strype, pp. 385–9, 589–91.
16 ITL, MS. Petyt 538/38, nos 28, 88, 98, fols 69–70, 119–200, 219–20.
17 Ibid., no. 72, fols 165–6; Strype, pp. 387–9.
18 LPL, Grindal's register, i. fols 48, 49, 53, 54, 58ᵛ, 59ᵛ, 64ᵛ, 66ʳ, 70ᵛ, 71ᵛ, 77.
19 Ibid., fol. 234ᵛ.
20 PRO, S.P. 12/117/9, 14; *A.P.C.*, x. 87–8; LPL, Grindal's register, i. fols 158ʳ, 205–6ʳ, 236–7ʳ, 258ᵛ–9ʳ.
21 Ibid., fol. 191. For the significance of this order and the circumstances surrounding it, see *Elizabethan Puritan Movement*, p. 205.
22 LPL, Grindal's register, i. fols 198ᵛ–9ʳ.
23 Ibid., fol. 245.
24 Ibid., fols 164ʳ, 171, 176, 193, 206, 234–5ʳ.
25 Ibid., fols 274ᵛ–5ᵛ; Strype, pp. 412–20; *Remains*, pp. 429–35. In PRO, S.P. 12/161/21 there is a paper book containing 'The particulars of the contribution of the diocese of Canterbury towards the relief of Geneva 1583'. Grindal's personal share was £66. 13s. 4d. out of a total clerical contribution of £196. 7s. 4d. The laity contributed £470. 16s. 5d.
26 Walsingham to Grindal, 18, 29 March 1583, Grindal, Aylmer, Piers and Young to Walsingham, with accompanying arguments and articles, 4 April 1583; BL, MS. Add. 32092, fols 26–33.
27 Ibid., fols 13, 15–16, 18–20, 21.
28 See p. 37.

29 Strype, pp. 371–7.

30 LPL, Grindal's register, ii. fols 591–2ᵛ, 596–7. Grindal's original order, dated 22 April 1580, is translated from the register and printed by Strype, pp. 370–1.

31 LPL, Grindal's register, ii. fol. 598.

32 In *The Correspondence of Dr Matthew Hutton*, ed. J. Raines, Surtees Socy, xvii. 1843, 63–70; R. A. Marchant, *The Church Under the Law: Justice, Administration and Discipline in the Diocese of York, 1560–1640*, Cambridge 1969, p. 42 n.; I. J. Churchill, *Canterbury Administration*, 1933, i. 608–9.

33 Copies in Bodl., MS. Tanner 280, fol. 330ᵛ, ITL, MS. Petyt 538/54, fol. 278.

34 Bodl., MS. Top Oxon. c.5, pp. 1–7.

35 Ibid., pp. 45–7. Another copy is in BL, MS. Sloane 1710, fols 106ᵛ–7ʳ. The text printed in Wilkins, op. cit., iv. 295 is taken from Fuller, I.ix.120.

36 Bodl., MS. e. Museo. 55, no. 1, fol. 3; printed, E. Cardwell, *Documentary Annals of the Reformed Church of England*, Oxford 1844, i. 441–6.

37 G. L. Blackman in his Cambridge Ph.D. thesis on Bishop Cox ('The Career and Influence of Bishop Richard Cox, 1547–1581', 1953, p. 196) has suggested on the basis of comparison with Coxian material in Gonville and Caius College that Cox composed this letter.

38 *Remains*, p. 395; Grindal to Leicester, 15 August 1581, PRO, S.P. 12/150/5; BL, MS. Cotton, Vespasian F. XII, fol. 192; Grindal to Walsingham, 7 July 1582, PRO, S.P. 12/154/61; *Remains*, p. 397.

39 Fuller, v. 58.

40 *The three volumes of chronicles*, 1587, p. 1354.

41 *The shepheardes calender*, 1579, fol. 29. On the political context of these passages, see J. J. Higgenson, *Spencer's 'Shepheardes Calendar' in Relation to Contemporary Affairs*, New York, 1912; Edwin Greenlaw, 'The Shepheardes Calender', *Publications of the Modern Language Association of America*, xxvi. 1911, 419–51; Paul E. McLane, *Spenser's Shepheardes Calender: A Study in Elizabethan Allegory*, Notre Dame 1961, esp. pp. 140–57.

42 Mentioned in Grindal's will; *Remains*, p. 459.

43 Ibid., p. 397.

44 The letters are dated 30 Jan., 9 Feb., 27 Feb., 12 April; BL, MSS. Lansd. 37, nos 17, 18, 23, fols 36, 38, 50, Lansd. 38, no. 69, fol. 172; *Remains*, pp. 397–400, 401–3.

45 Blackman, op. cit., pp. 363–72.

46 *Elizabethan Puritan Movement*, esp. pp. 270–2.

47 BL, MS. Lansd. 39, no. 14, fol. 28ᵛ.

48 PRO, S.P. 12/160/31.

49 Faunt to Bacon, 6 May, 6 August 1583; LPL, MS 647, nos 72, 74, fols 150–2, 157ᵛ.

50 Walsingham to Egerton, 25 March 1583; Huntington Library, MS. Ellesmere 29, item 1984. I owe this reference to the kindness of Professor Leland H. Carlson.

51 George Paule, *Life of Whitgift*, 1699 edn, pp. 34–6.

52 *Remains*, p. 397.

53 Ibid., pp. 458–63.

54 John Strype, *Life and Acts of Matthew Parker*, Oxford 1821, ii. 432–4, iii. 340–2.

55 'Things prepared at the funeral of Edmund Grindal archbishop of Canterbury who died on Saturday 6 July 1583', PRO, S.P. 14/89/6 (originally located in S.P. 12/161, between 30 and 31); 'The order of the proceeding at

the funeral of Edmund Grindal archbishop of Canterbury, solemnized at Croydon the first of August 1583', Bodl., MS. Ashmolean 817, fol. 25.

56 Strype, pp. 430–1; M. H. Bloxam, *On the Monumental Effigies in Croydon Church*, n.p. (1856).

57 BL, MS. Add. 39802, fols 33, 35, 36.

58 Strype, pp. 420–2, 427–8; William Jackson, 'Archbishop Grindal and his Grammar School of St Bees' (an account written for the tercentenary in 1888), in *Papers and Pedigrees Mainly Relating to Cumberland*, ii. Cumberland and Westmorland Antiquarian and Archaeological Socy, Extra Ser. vi. 1892, 186–255; A. Attwater, *Pembroke College Cambridge: A Short History*, Camridge 1930, pp. 51–2.

59 For references to these books, see pp. 36, 56, 82, 243–4.

60 See p. 29.

61 *Life of Parker*, ii. 438.

62 *Remains*, p. 395.

Epilogue

1 Richard Baxter, Preface to *Gildas salvianus: the reformed pastor*, 1656. I owe this reference to Dr W. M. Lamont of the University of Sussex.

2 W. M. Lamont, *Godly Rule: Politics and Religion, 1603–60*, 1969; P. Collinson, 'Magistracy and Ministry: A Suffolk Miniature', in *Reformation Conformity and Dissent: Essays in Honour of Geoffrey Nuttall*, ed. R. B. Knox, 1977, pp. 70–91.

3 George Paule, *Life of Whitgift*, 1699 edn, p. 82.

4 Roger B. Manning, *Religion and Society in Elizabethan Sussex*, Leicester 1969, pp. 91–125.

5 Extensive documentation in PRO, S.P. 12/126, S.P. 15/25. See A. H. Smith, *County and Court: Government and Politics in Norfolk, 1558–1603*, Oxford 1974, pp. 210–25. Bishop Freke's struggle with the puritan gentry of West Suffolk is described in detail in my unpublished London Ph.D. thesis 'The Puritan Classical Movement in the reign of Elizabeth I', 1957, pp. 881–929, which is followed by J. S. Cockburn, *A History of English Assizes*, Cambridge 1972, pp. 199–206.

6 Documentation in PRO, S.P. 12/158/1, 22, 22 II.

7 Privy Council memorandum to the archbishop of Canterbury, 'concerning the bishop of Hereford', June 1583; BL, MS. Egerton 3048, fols 207ᵛ–8. Cf. F. O. White, *Lives of the Elizabethan Bishops*, 1898, pp. 13–19.

8 Compare the account in White, op. cit., pp. 97–108, and *D.N.B.*, art. Sandys, with the unpublished theses by I. P. Ellis, 'Edwin Sandys and the Settlement of Religion in England, 1558–88', B.Litt., Oxford 1962, and Susan Storer, 'The Life and Times of Edwin Sandys, Archbishop of York', M.Phil., London 1973. Letters from Sandys to Burghley, 4 April, 28 Dec. 1579; BL, MS. Lansd. 28, nos 68, 80, fols 152, 175.

9 Aylmer to Burghley, 26 May 1579; BL, MS. Lansd. 28, no. 72, fol. 159. For the Council enquiry into the wastage of timber, see pp. 306–8.

10 Nicholas Faunt to Anthony Bacon, 6 May, 6 August 1583; LPL, MS. 647, nos 72, 74, fols 150–2, 157ᵛ. For the great dilapidations suit between Sandys and Alymer and also involving Grindal, see pp. 302–6.

11 Bodl., MS. Tanner 280, fol. 330ᵛ.

12 Dr Williams's Library, MS. Morrice L, no. V, pp. 8–11.

13 Rosemary O'Day, 'The Reformation of the Ministry, 1558–1642', in *Con-*

tinuity and Change: Personnel and Administration of the Church in England 1500–1642, ed. R. O'Day and F. Heal, Leicester 1976, pp. 55–75; anticipating a monograph to be published by Dr O'Day on the professionalization of the post-Reformation clergy.

14 Josias Nicholls, *The plea of the innocent*, 1602, pp. 9–10.

15 John Field to Edmund Chapman, 'the 19 of this 11th month' 1583; *The Presbyterian Movement in the Reign of Queen Elizabeth as Illustrated by the Minute Book of the Dedham Classis 1582–1589*, ed R. G. Usher, CS 3rd ser. viii. 1905, 96.

16 *Elizabethan Puritan Movement*, Part 4, 'Moderate Courses', passim. Cf. much of the argument and evidence contained in the unpublished Ph.D. thesis by Peter Lake, 'Laurence Chaderton and the Cambridge Moderate Puritan Tradition, 1570–1604', Cambridge 1978.

17 *Elizabethan Puritan Movement*, Part 5 '1584', passim.

18 R. G. Usher, *The Reconstruction of the English Church*, 2 vols, 1910; S. B. Babbage, *Puritanism and Richard Bancroft*, 1962.

19 Lake, op. cit., passim.

20 Ibid., pp. 234–61, modifying H. C. Porter, *Reformation and Reaction in Tudor Cambridge*, Cambridge 1958, pp. 344–90.

21 N. R. N. Tyacke, 'Puritanism, Arminianism and Counter-Revolution', in *The Origins of the English Civil War*, ed. Conrad Russell, 1973, p. 126.

22 C. H. and K. George, *The Protestant Mind of the English Reformation, 1570–1640*, Princeton 1961, passim; Tyacke, op. cit., p. 120.

23 Northamptonshire Record Office, F.(M).P.70.c.

24 Parker to Cecil, 6 Nov. 1559, Parker to Lady Ann Bacon, 6 Feb. 1568; *Parker Correspondence*, pp. 105, 315.

25 See p. 18.

26 Clarendon, *History of the Great Rebellion*, ed. W. D. Macray, Oxford 1888, i. 118.

27 Tyacke, op. cit., pp. 119–43.

28 Thomas Wilson's transcript of Archbishop Tobie Matthew's Diary, Minster Library York. Cf. R. A. Marchant, *The Puritans and the Church Courts in the Diocese of York 1560–1642*, 1960.

29 Tyacke, op. cit., pp. 126–7.

30 Arthur Lake, *Sermons with some religious and divine meditations ... whereunto is prefixed by way of a preface a short view of the life and vertues of the author*, 1629. I am indebted to Dr N. R. N. Tyacke for alerting me to the importance of Bishop Lake.

31 H. R. Trevor-Roper, 'James I and his Bishops', *Historical Essays*, 1957, pp. 130–45.

32 Verbal communication by Dr Conrad Russell of Bedford College, University of London, anticipating published work to come.

33 The evidence for what follows will be found in my article 'Lectures by Combination: Structures and Characteristics of Church Life in Seventeenth-Century England', *B.I.H.R.*, xlviii. 1975, 182–213.

34 Bishop Bradbridge of Exeter had reported to Grindal in 1576 that the prophesyings were popular because 'the several gifts that men have in the utterance doth more delight the auditory and pierceth deeplier the senses than the speech of one mouth at one time', while Bishop Cooper of Lincoln spoke of 'the fantastical affection that many have to such conferences, more than to preaching'. (LPL, MS. 2003, fols 8, 30.)

35 *The Registrum Vagum of Anthony Harison*, i. ed. T. F. Barton, Norfolk Record Socy xxxii. 1963, 97.

36 Ibid., 100.
37 Bodl., MS. Tanner 68, fol. 2.
38 See the opinions of John Milton and William Prynne, cited above, p. 17.
39 Richard Baxter, *The English nonconformity*, 1689, p. 101. I owe this reference to the Revd Dr G. F. Nuttall.
40 *D.N.B.*, art. Morton.
41 Conrad Russell, *The Crisis of Parliaments: English History 1509–1660*, The Short Oxford History of the Modern World, 1971, p. 263.

Appendix   Getting and Spending: Grindal's Stewardship

1 John Aylmer to Lord Robert Dudley, 12 August 1559; BL, MS. 32091, fol. 172.
2 PRO, S.P. 12/112/45.
3 Grindal to Cecil, 19 Nov. 1567; PRO, S.P. 12/44/43.
4 Grindal to Cecil, 21 April 1570; BL, MS. Lansd. 12, no. 81, fol. 180.
5 The phrase has come into common use, with a particular application to the period between the Reformation and the Revolution, since Dr Christopher Hill published his *Economic Problems of the Church from Whitgift to the Long Parliament*, Oxford 1956. See more recent essays by Dr Felicity Heal in *Continuity and Change: Personnel and Administration of the Church in England 1500–1642*, ed. R. O'Day and F. Heal, Leicester 1976, and *Church and Society in England from Henry VIII to James I*, 1977; and a forthcoming collection of essays on the economic problems of the Church presided over by the same editorial team. See also Gina Alexander, 'Victim or Spendthrift? The Bishop of London and his Income in the Sixteenth Century', in *Wealth and Power in Tudor England: Essays Presented to S.T. Bindoff*, ed. E. W. Ives, R. J. Knecht and J. J. Scarisbrick, 1978, pp. 128–45.
6 PRO, S.P. 12/4/39; BL, MS. Lansd. 23, no. 60, fols 125–6; PRO, S.P. 12/149/17, 18.
7 Alexander, op. cit., p. 133.
8 Claire Cross, 'The Economic Problems of the See of York: Decline and Recovery in the Sixteenth Century', in *Land, Church and People: Essays Presented to Professor H. P. R. Finberg*, ed. Joan Thirsk, Agricultural History Review Supplement, Reading 1970, 64–83; *Remains*, p. 354.
9 PRO, S.P. 12/4/38, 39.
10 BL, MSS. Lansd. 21, no. 20, fol. 40, Lansd. 23, no. 60, fols 125–6.
11 BL, MS. Lansd. 39, no. 14, fol. 28ᵛ.
12 PRO, S.P. 15/24/72.
13 Minster Library York, MS. Wb, fols 162ᵛ–281. I owe this information to Dr W. J. Sheils of the Borthwick Institute, University of York.
14 Ibid., fols 217ᵛ–18.
15 The charge is cited, without reference, by William Pierce in *An Historical Introduction to the Marprelate Tracts*, 1908, p. 66, and is repeated, almost word for word, by Christopher Hill in *Economic Problems of the Church*, p. 19. It provides the basis for Mrs Alexander's statement that 'Grindal's reputation at York was of a man greedy for the welfare of his family.' I have not traced Pierce's source. Sandys was accurate in reporting dean and chapter evidence for four score leases made in Grindal's time, but inaccurate in the implication that all these leases favoured Grindal's kinsman and servants, and guilty of

wild exaggeration in suggesting that there were forty more such leases of which there appears to be no record.

16 Cross, op. cit., 80.
17 *Archbishop Grindal's Visitation, 1575 Comperta et Detecta Book*, ed. W. J. Sheils, Borthwick Texts and Calendars: Records of the Northern Province 4, p. vii.
18 Mrs Alexander has remarked to me in a letter: 'I am sure you are right that Grindal was less of a nepotist than his contemporaries. At the same time I believe that he was as anxious as any of them to improve his immediate cash income rather than even to attempt to rethink the more fundamental problems of the temporalities.'
19 'Answer to objections for my restitution', PRO, S.P. 12/107/41.
20 Minster Library York, MS. Wb, fol. 254; information on Grindal's London leases communicated by Mrs Alexander.
21 Information from Grindal's will, *Remains*, pp. 458–63; summary of educational bequests printed by Strype, pp. 427–8.
22 Fuller, v. 59.
23 Heal, 'Clerical Tax Collection under the Tudors', *Continuity and Change*, ed. O'Day and Heal, pp. 97–122.
24 John Darrell (Horne's son-in-law) to Burghley, 12 June 1579; PRO, S.P. 12/131/23. Valuations of Winchester in PRO, S.P. 12/4/39 and BL, MS. Lansd. 23, no. 60, fols 125–6.
25 Susan Storer, 'The Life and Times of Edwin Sandys, Archbishop of York', unpublished London M.Phil. thesis, 1973, pp. 259–60.
26 PRO, S.P. 12/137/54, 149/19.
27 Sampson to Grindal, 9 Nov. 1576; ITL, MS. Petyt 538/47, no. 188, fols 336–7.
28 *The Diary of Henry Machyn, Citizen and Merchant-Taylor of London from A.D. 1550 to A.D. 1563*, ed. J. G. Nichols, CS xlii. 1848, pp. 287–8.
29 See pp. 133, 141.
30 See p. 177.
31 PRO, S.P. 12/149/19.
32 Quoted, Alexander, op. cit., p. 128.
33 Ibid., p. 132.
34 Bishop Freke of Rochester to the earl of Leicester, 12 Jan. 1573; BL, MS. Add. 32091, fol. 264.
35 Grindal to Parker, 4 March 1575; ITL, MS. Petyt 538/47, no. 18, fol. 21.
36 PRO, S.P. 15/24/72.
37 Heal, 'Clerical Tax Collection under the Tudors', pp. 113, n. 52 p. 266.
38 PRO, S.P. 12/137/54, S.P. 15/24/72, 73.
39 Heal, 'Clerical Tax Collection under the Tudors', pp. 114–22.
40 Grindal to Winchester, 7 Jan. 1563(/4?); PRO, S.P. 46/27, fol. 191.
41 See pp. 154–61.
42 Papers in PRO, S.P. 12/112, 130, 131, 137, 149.
43 Phyllis Hembry, 'Episcopal Palaces, 1535 to 1660', in *Wealth and Power in Tudor England: Essays Presented to S. T. Bindoff*, ed. E. W. Ives, R. J. Knecht and J. J. Scarisbrick, 1978, pp. 146–66.
44 PRO, S.P. 12/137/39.
45 PRO, S.P. 12/149/25.
46 PRO, S.P. 12/131/22.
47 Sandys to Walsingham, 20 April 1579, PRO, S.P. 12/130/39; Sandys to Walsingham, 3 June 1579, S.P. 12/131/21; S.P. 12/112/45.I; S.P. 12/130/39.

48 PRO, S.P. 12/137/35.

49 PRO, S.P. 12/131/14.

50 PRO, S.P. 12/137/54; S.P. 12/149/19; S.P. 12/149/25.

51 PRO, S.P. 12/137/54.

52 PRO, S.P. 12/149/19; S.P. 12/130/39; S.P. 12/131/21; S.P. 12/149/17, 18, 23. On the neglect of St Paul's see above, pp. 160–1.

53 John Harington, *A briefe viewe of the state of the church of England* (1608), 1653, pp. 199–201.

54 Grindal to Cecil, 10 Nov. 1570, PRO, S.P. 12/74/32; *Cal. of Patent Rolls, Eliz. I*, v. 1569–72, no. 2106, p. 262.

55 PRO, S.P. 12/137/39; S.P. 12/172/23.I. However on 3 June 1579 Sandys alleged that he had received no dilapidations from Grindal at either London or York. (S.P. 12/131/21.)

56 Grindal to Burghley, 9 Feb. 1583; *Remains*, pp. 399–400.

57 John Scott to Walsingham, 12 July 1584, PRO, S.P. 12/172/23; 'Certain reasons that move the executors of Archbishop Grindal to think that they are not so deeply to be charged for dilapidations as is required by my lord of Canterbury his Grace that now is, by a view for him made', ibid., 23.I.

58 Andrew Foster, 'The Function of a Bishop: the Career of Richard Neile, 1562–1640', in *Continuity and Change*, ed. O'Day and Heal, p. 48.

59 *Narratives of the Days of the Reformation*, ed. J. G. Nichols, CS lxxvii. 1859, pp. 267–8.

60 PRO, S.P. 12/112/45.I.

61 *Oh read over D. John Bridges for it is a worthy worke: Or an epitome*, 1588, p. 21.

62 PRO, S.P. 12/111/24.

63 In PRO, S.P. 12/136 and 137.

64 PRO, S.P. 12/136/45, 33.

65 PRO, S.P. 12/137/9, 10, 11, 12, 73; Strype, *Annals*, II.ii. 693–5.

66 Aylmer to Burghley, 26 May 1579; BL, MS. Lansd. 28, no. 72, fol. 159.

67 PRO, S.P. 12/137/73, 136/71.

INDEX

Madame first of all I my[...]
[...]ou is not our [...] Creature to
ma[...] [...] [...] beinge [...]
the more [...] hath [...] [...] [...]
told [...] her for, muche lesse d[...]
my most bounden dewtie with all [...]
most humble faithfull [...] [...]
knowledge [...] [...] [...] / [...]
[...], perlesse in the cause of [...]
office [...] burden of consc[...]
[...] they so [...] [...] I try
[...] I [...] [...] dessemblinge or
[...] [...] ma[...] so many [...]
both you might fall into [...] to
[...]amnation [...] [...] prophe[...]
[...] [...] [...] [...]res, and [...]
[...] [...] by [...] [...]
[...] [...], or [...] [...] bloode
al our handes /   H. b[...]